❧ TRANSATLANTIC DIALOGUE ❧

*Selected American Correspondence
of Edmund Gosse*

Edmund William Gosse
March 1899

TRANSATLANTIC DIALOGUE

*Selected American Correspondence
of Edmund Gosse*

Edited, with an Introduction, by
PAUL F. MATTHEISEN
and
MICHAEL MILLGATE

UNIVERSITY OF TEXAS PRESS, AUSTIN

Library of Congress Catalog Card No. 65–16471
Copyright © 1965 by Paul F. Mattheisen and Michael Millgate
All Rights Reserved

*Published with the assistance of a grant
from the Ford Foundation
under its program for the support of publications
in the humanities and social sciences*

ISBN 978-0-292-74137-9

*Acknowledgments of permissions to reproduce
copyrighted material begin on facing page.*

First paperback printing, 2012

ACKNOWLEDGMENTS

The editors thank the following for permission to print letters and other unpublished materials by the authors indicated:

Miss Eleanor L. Aldrich (Thomas Bailey Aldrich); Mr. Horace H. F. Jayne (Horace Howard Furness); Miss Rosamond Gilder (Richard Watson Gilder); Miss Jennifer Gosse (Sir Edmund Gosse); Professor W. W. Howells (William Dean Howells); Mr. B. R. James (Henry James); Mr. Milton Dees (Edmund Clarence Stedman); Mr. Armitage Watkins, for the Edith Wharton Estate (Edith Wharton); Mrs. Walter Stokes (Owen Wister).

The editors thank the following for permission to make use of materials in their possession:

Miss Rosamond Gilder; Mrs. Philip Guedalla; Mr. Oliver Lodge; Mr. Norman Armour; Mr. Charles E. Feinberg; the British Museum; the Brotherton Collection, Leeds University Library; Columbia University Library; the Alderman Library, University of Virginia; Pennsylvania State University Library; Rutgers University Library; the New York Public Library; the Houghton Library, Harvard University; Cambridge University Library; Princeton University Library; the Library of Congress; Yale University Library; Duke University Library; the Miriam Lutcher Stark Library, The University of Texas; University of Kentucky Library; the Henry E. Huntington Library; the Horace Howard Furness Memorial Library, University of Pennsylvania.

The editors thank the following for permission to reprint materials previously published:

Poetry; New York *Herald Tribune*; *Sunday Times* (London); *Notes and Queries*; *Journal of the Rutgers University Library*; Houghton Mifflin Company. Letters 200 and 207 are reprinted with the permission of Paul R. Reynolds, Inc., and of Charles Scribner's Sons from *The Letters of Henry James,* edited by Percy Lubbock, Vol. II, pp. 480–481, 492–493; copyright 1920 Charles Scribner's Sons; renewal copyright 1948 William James and

Margaret James Porter. An excerpt from a letter from Edmund Gosse to Hamo Thornycroft, 20 December 1884, and Letters 1, 30, 70, 85, 90, 103, 113, 115, 116, 120, 121, 136, 152, 175, 201 (for names and dates see Checklist in the Appendices of this volume) are reprinted from *The Life and Letters of Sir Edmund Gosse,* by Sir Evan Charteris, with the permission of Harper & Row, Publishers. Seventeen letters are reprinted from *The Life and Letters of Sir Edmund Gosse,* by Sir Evan Charteris, with the permission of William Heinemann, Ltd. (British Commonwealth excluding Canada).

PREFACE

Despite the recent intensification of research into many aspects of British and American literature and society in the final decades of the nineteenth century and the early years of the twentieth, there has as yet been little detailed study of the literary and cultural interchange between the two sides of the Atlantic, and no serious attempt to reconsider accepted generalizations about its character and extent. Although the editors of the present volume have not ventured to offer any such radical reappraisal, they have sought, by focusing on the career and friendships of one central figure, to exemplify one important aspect of the Anglo-American relationship at an especially significant and sensitive period.

The number and variety of Edmund Gosse's friendships with American men of letters, and the fortunate survival of an extensive body of his correspondence, made him an obvious choice as the central figure. The final form of the volume has been determined by its purpose. Instead of separating out each particular correspondence (between Gosse and Holmes, say, or between Gosse and Stedman), it seemed preferable to retain some suggestion of the total situation by arranging the letters, whether by Gosse or his correspondents, in a single chronological sequence. Since the letters have been rigorously selected according to their relevance to the theme of transatlantic relationships, this policy may occasionally have created an exaggerated effect of unusual epistolary activity or of complete silence; at the same time, the chief impression produced—that Gosse's interest in the United States and in his American reputation was at its height during the 1880's—is unquestionably accurate.

In the Introduction, and in the annotations throughout the volume, the editors have drawn upon additional letters and upon other types of material, published and unpublished (including the diary kept by Gosse during his immensely successful visit to the United States in the winter of 1884–1885), in order to fill out the picture of Gosse's career and of the transatlantic friendships and business arrangements in which he participated. It is to be

xi

hoped that this background material, as well as the letters themselves, will not only illuminate the international theme but also contribute something to biographical and even to critical study of the authors concerned, particularly of Gosse himself and his great friend William Dean Howells.

This book has itself been the product of a prolonged transatlantic co-operation between the two editors, and there are many people both in Britain and in the United States to whom they owe joint or individual debts of gratitude. Their most consistent and most patient common benefactor has been Mr. David L. Masson, of the Brotherton Collection, Leeds University Library, without whose advice and untiring assistance the book could never have been completed. Among others, both in and out of the academic world, who have been helpful far beyond the demands either of duty or of mere politeness have been Mr. Norman Armour, Mr. John Betjeman, Professor Leon Edel, Mr. Charles E. Feinberg, Mr. Colin Franklin, Professor William Gibson, Mrs. Philip Guedalla, Mr. A. H. Hall (of the Guildhall Library, London), Mrs. Frank Holden, Professor W. W. Howells, Mr. H. H. F. Jayne, Mr. Martin Secker, Mr. Donald A. Sinclair (of the Rutgers University Library), and Professor Herbert Smith. Professor George Arms gave his expert advice on the text of the Howells letters; Miss Rosamond Gilder went to great trouble in solving difficulties presented by her father's correspondence; Mr. Rupert Hart-Davis has answered most patiently numerous inquiries about the Beerbohm cartoons; Professors Clara and Rudolf Kirk, who have long been interested in the friendship between Gosse and Howells, gave helpful information and advice.

Dr. Mattheisen is deeply grateful to Sir Edmund's daughter, Miss Sylvia Gosse, and to his granddaughter, Miss Jennifer Gosse, for their cordial aid and support, and especially to the late Dr. Philip Gosse, whose friendship was an honor, and whose help, hospitality, and encouragement can never be sufficiently acknowledged. He is also greatly indebted to Professor Arthur C. Young, of Rutgers University, whose advice and encouragement were indispensable, and to Miss Janet E. Brown, of the Harpur College Library, for her generous and scholarly assistance. He wishes also to add a word of thanks to his former colleague Professor Frederick W. Locke, of the University of Rochester, and to Professor Bernard Levy, of Harpur College. Two grants to Dr. Mattheisen from the Research Foundation of the State University of New York were of great help in supporting the book financially.

Dr. Millgate wishes to acknowledge a personal debt to Mr. Feinberg, and especially to Professor Arms. He is also extremely grateful to Professor Douglas Grant, Professor A. Norman Jeffares, Mr. Douglas Jefferson, and Mr. B. S. Page, all of Leeds University, for constant encouragement and advice. Miss Audrey Stead and Mrs. Margaret Woodward both performed extraordinary typing labors with great efficiency and cheerfulness, and Mr. Allen C. Koretsky, of York University, Toronto, generously took time from his own research to check sources that would otherwise have been out of reach. Dr. Millgate's final, and most important, acknowledgments are to his wife, for her great patience during the long gestation of this volume, and to Professor Bert James Loewenberg, for his friendship, his advice, and the inspiration of his scholarly and personal integrity.

CONTENTS

Preface xi

Introduction 3

The Text of the Letters 59

Appendices
  A. Checklist of Letters 301
  B. "Algernon in London" 307

Index 315

ILLUSTRATIONS

Edmund William Gosse   *Frontispiece*

(Following page 144)

Mural from Rapallo (Max Beerbohm cartoon)

Gosse in his study

Gosse with the young Misses Tennant

Gosse in Spain

Lord Northcliffe and Edmund Gosse (Max Beerbohm cartoon)

Edmund Gosse (Max Beerbohm cartoon)

William Dean Howells

Richard Watson Gilder

Edmund Clarence Stedman

Horace Howard Furness

Oliver Wendell Holmes

ও TRANSATLANTIC DIALOGUE ও

Selected American Correspondence
of Edmund Gosse

INTRODUCTION

Edmund Gosse (1849–1928)

Perhaps the most remarkable fact of Edmund Gosse's career is that he achieved eminence in a field for which nothing in his early life had prepared him. His father, Philip Henry Gosse, was a distinguished naturalist, but he was also a religious fanatic who permitted his son to read no fiction and very little other literature and who declined to prepare him for a university education. When he was seventeen Edmund Gosse took a post as a clerk in the British Museum Library; nine years later he became a translator at the Board of Trade, a position he held until he was fifty-five; from then until his retirement at the age of sixty-five he was Librarian to the House of Lords. There is no doubt that he got a good deal of his reading and writing done during office hours—"I have all sorts [of books] here," he wrote to Robert Louis Stevenson in 1884, "grave and gay, divine and pornographical, elegant and balderdash"[1]—but it remains true that his literary activities had to be conducted in his spare time and that he had to begin by making up for a background that was deficient even in the standard literature of childhood. It is all the more remarkable, therefore, that in 1870, at the age of twenty-one, he published his first book of verse; that by 1882 he was respected as one of England's outstanding literary critics and biographers; that in 1884 he was elected to succeed Leslie Stephen as Clark Lecturer at Trinity College, Cambridge; and that in the winter of 1884–1885, during a lecture tour in the eastern United States, he enjoyed a success more brilliant than that of any visiting Englishman since Thackeray. During his lifetime there were undoubtedly better critics and better biographers, but none of them achieved so consistent a success or so perennial a popularity.

Some notable instances of failure marred the uniformity of Gosse's success. There were times, for instance, when his ambition seduced him into enterprises for which his scholarship had not adequately prepared him. And when

---

[1] Evan Charteris, *The Life and Letters of Sir Edmund Gosse* (London: Heinemann, 1931), p. 164. In annotating the Introduction, the editors' policy has been to identify only those names which do not reappear in the text of the letters; other identifications can be located by consulting the Index. All quotations are identified, but detailed information is not given for letters later printed in full. For a list of abbreviations used to indicate the provenance of letters, see p. 58.

3

he relied too greatly, as he sometimes did, on the accuracy of his memory and of his amanuenses, he committed factual blunders which are credible only when it is remembered that much of his early work was pioneer scholarship. For these errors Gosse was made to pay heavily, perhaps too heavily. The celebrated attack made upon him by John Churton Collins in 1886 not only haunted him for the rest of his life but also gave his critics a permanent weapon by which they could unjustly condemn some of his best work. To the end of his life a reviewer had only to remark that "Gosse has never been noted for his accuracy," and the ghost of John Churton Collins would rise to substantiate the accusation—despite the fact that the inaccuracies which provoked the Collins attack were redeemed a short time later by a biography of Congreve the scholarship of which was not superseded for more than fifty years. Indeed, the tradition of Gosse's scholarly disability persists to the present day, when he is remembered as the author of the autobiographical *Father and Son*, as the biographer of Donne and Swinburne, and, with a certain aura of notoriety, as a close friend of T. J. Wise. It cannot be said that Gosse was a great scholar or critic, but he undoubtedly deserves more recognition than has generally been accorded him since his death for his pioneer work in the fields of Scandinavian studies and of Jacobean and Restoration literature; he was also an engaging literary essayist, and, because of his sensitivity to contemporary movements and his skill in delineating the personalities of his many friends, the study of his career still offers one of the best introductions to the literary scene at the end of the last century and the beginning of this.

The sudden and enduring eclipse of Gosse's reputation immediately after his death makes his immense popularity during his lifetime seem all the more remarkable. He rose quickly to a position of eminence and remained there for the rest of his life; his reputation, despite occasional setbacks, steadily increased, and in fact he achieved his greatest prestige and popularity during his last years. In the latter part of his career new movements of literary and critical thought began to outrun the mild innovations which had helped to make Gosse's early reputation, and he came to be regarded, especially in America, as something of a British institution, an "establishment" figure laying down the "official" line. The characterization was not entirely accurate: the character sketches of his friends and the faintly malicious reviews, especially those which Gosse contributed regularly to the London *Sunday Times* from 1920 onwards, gave him, in England at least, something of a reputation as a critical gadfly. But the role of "institution" was the very one which Gosse had set out to achieve almost from the beginning of his career. In his professional as well as in his personal life he had, it seems, a psychological compulsion to know as many literary figures as possible and, in the case of those still living, to be popular among them. As early as 1879 his friend Robert Louis Stevenson had advised him, "See as many people as you can and make a book of them before you die."[2] Gosse hardly needed such advice except to encourage a natural propensity; in the period between 1870 and 1928 it would be hard to name an important literary figure in England, or even in America and on the Continent, with whom Gosse was not personally acquainted. He also had an astonishing number of friends in nonliterary fields, and if it were possible to discover all that was discussed and accomplished at those famous dinners and Sunday afternoon parties at Gosse's home, when scholars, publishers, editors, writers, artists, travelers, politicians, and members of the aristocracy were brought together, it might well be found that Gosse's influence behind the scenes was even greater than his influence as an author and critic, where he seems less often to have influenced current opinion than to have reflected it.

In his criticism Gosse tended always to be catholic and representative, an authority on the whole of literature rather than an expert in only a single area. His principal aim was the evaluation of literature; literary analysis was for him merely a preparatory act enabling him to make the judgments whose propriety was reinforced by the wide range of his reading and, often, by his personal knowledge of the writers concerned. Towards the end of his life the reviewers began to remark that Gosse seemed to have read everything in the literatures of England, America, continental Europe, and Scandinavia; it is certainly true that his ecumenical taste and enormous reading enabled him to say something about almost every important literary figure, to revive interest in neglected writers of the past, and even to introduce to the English-speaking world some of the important Scandinavian and French writers who later influenced authors in England and America.

Perhaps Gosse's greatest handicap at the outset of his career, the greatest disservice rendered him by his strict religious upbringing, was his lack of a broad cultural background and of a university education. He was extremely ambitious and impatient of success in the literary world; yet he was clearly ill-equipped to undertake full-scale critical work on major literary figures or in those areas of English literature which had already been extensively explored by scholars. His solution to this difficulty—a solution which came naturally to his genuinely and energetically inquisitive mind—was to search for fields of study in which little serious work had so far been done and in which the minor figures could be treated in a fairly discursive and personal way. Gosse found two such fields and for a time made them peculiarly his own. His work in Scandinavian literature, which first bore fruit in his *Studies in the Literature of Northern Europe* (1879), was so new at the time that it underwent no close scrutiny, while the sheer abundance of fresh factual material made it unnecessary for him to undertake any exhaustive study. Simi-

[2] Sidney Colvin, ed., *The Letters of Robert Louis Stevenson* (London: Methuen, 1901), I, 131.

larly he developed an interest in the lesser-known writers of the seventeenth century in England; this was another area in which little substantial scholarship had been carried out, and Gosse was able to establish a considerable reputation on the basis of a minimal amount of original research. It seems possible that his interest in American literature, which also dated from a very early stage in his career, may have had a somewhat similar origin; an additional advantage of this interest, of course, was that it opened the way to a whole new range of literary friendships.

Gosse and America: The Early Period

The same group of people who had first stimulated Gosse's interest in the Jacobean period seems to have been responsible also for his early interest in the work of Walt Whitman and other American writers. This was the mainly Pre-Raphaelite group which centered upon Ford Madox Brown's house in Fitzroy Square and included Dante Gabriel Rossetti, James McNeill Whistler, and Algernon Swinburne. Gosse's introduction to this circle came in 1870; his first meeting with Swinburne—apart from the unhappy encounter in the British Museum which Sir Evan Charteris records in his *Life and Letters of Sir Edmund Gosse*[3]—was in 1871, and the relationship swiftly developed, on Gosse's side, to a point little short of hero worship. Swinburne's own enthusiasm for Whitman at this time is well-known, and the letter of eager discipleship which Gosse wrote to Whitman in December 1873 may well have been, in large measure, a direct reflection of Swinburne's own admiration for *Leaves of Grass*. At this time Gosse thought of himself primarily as a poet, and his letter to Whitman is that of a young poet addressing an older, intensely revered, master of the art; there is no reason to think that the letter had any ulterior motive, apart, perhaps, from Gosse's natural excitement at the thought of entering into correspondence with a man whose work he so much admired.

By late 1875, however, when he began his correspondence with Edmund Clarence Stedman, the American banker, poet, and critic, Gosse had become extremely interested in the possibility of establishing a literary reputation in the United States; as he wrote in his first letter to Stedman: ". . . the hope of recognition in America has always seemed one of the highest objects of ambition."[4] Stedman took it upon himself to see that Gosse's work was properly reviewed in American periodicals: ". . . in one way and another I hope to see that you are appreciated 'over here',"[5] he wrote in March 1876

[3] Charteris, *Life and Letters of Gosse*, p. 20.
[4] Gosse to Stedman, 21 December, 1875, in Laura Stedman and Gerald M. Gould, *Life and Letters of Edmund Clarence Stedman* (New York: Moffat, Yard, 1910), II, 16.
[5] Stedman to Gosse, 19 March 1876, in Stedman and Gould, *Life and Letters of Stedman*, II, 17.

—and Gosse in return did what he could to further Stedman's own ambitions for recognition in England, urging Kegan Paul to bring out an English edition of Stedman's poems and himself taking a hand in the reviewing of Stedman's books. When, late in 1879, he gave Stedman's poems an enthusiastic review in the *Academy*, describing his friend as the "most distinguished poet born in the United States since 1820,"[6] Stedman wrote back to thank him for doing "an open-handed, *plucky*, and most generous thing." "Nothing," he added, "could be of greater service to me *at home* and abroad."[7] Gosse's own interest in establishing an American reputation seems clearly to suggest that he also believed that transatlantic recognition would enhance his standing at home.

The first review of Gosse's work to appear in America seems to have been the rather lukewarm notice of his play *King Erik* and his volume of poems, *On Viol and Flute*, which was published in *Scribner's Monthly* in September 1876. The reviewer described the play as "decidedly readable without being at all great" and said that in both books Gosse made "a pleasing impression," but he castigated the dedication to Browning in *King Erik* as "pretentious in its humility."[8] These early works of Gosse's can have made little impression on the American reading public, for in the July 1879 issue of *Scribner's* the reviewer of Gosse's *Studies in the Literature of Northern Europe* thought it necessary to give a short summary of Gosse's achievements, characterizing him as "a poet of the Rossetti-Swinburne school, a student of Icelandic and Danish and the author of 'On Viol and Flute' and 'King Erik'."[9] In October 1879, again in *Scribner's*, there was a rather slighting mention of Gosse's play *The Unknown Lover*,[10] but in March 1880 this was more than made up for by the extremely generous welcome which the *Scribner's* reviewer gave to his *New Poems*.[11] Gosse was indebted initially to Stedman for this interest shown in him by *Scribner's*, and it was through Stedman that in January 1880 he first met the managing editor of the magazine, Richard Watson Gilder.

In late 1881 Gilder took over the full editorship of the magazine, under its new title of *Century Illustrated Monthly Magazine*, and Gosse was appointed to be its London agent. The appointment must have been less a tribute to his literary reputation at that time—although he was already becoming well-known in England—than to his energy and ambition, his breadth of interest in literature and the arts, and, of course, his establishment of American contacts, and his general friendliness towards America

[6] See Letter 10, n. 1.
[7] See Letter 10.
[8] See Letter 5, n. 5.
[9] *Scribner's Monthy*, XVIII (July 1879), 470.
[10] *Ibid.*, (October 1879), 939–940.
[11] *Ibid.*, XIX (March 1880), 790–791.

and Americans. His usefulness to the *Century* derived largely from his extensive knowledge of the English and, to a lesser degree the European, literary and artistic worlds. He had established himself as a young poet to be taken note of, he had also shown that he could be an effective critic, and, as always, he was assiduous in the cultivation of friendships. He now had a wide acquaintance among literary men; through his brother-in-law Alma-Tadema, the artist, and his close friend Hamo Thornycroft, the sculptor, he moved in artistic circles; his father's eminence as a biologist, and his own youthful background,[12] also enabled him to maintain many scientific friendships. But the *Century*, though it sold widely in England, was aimed primarily at an American audience, and here Gosse had an advantage over other Englishmen who might have been asked to act for the magazine, not only because he had a good knowledge of American writing and American affairs, but because he seems to have found American men of letters particularly easy to get on with. During the early 1880's he constantly added to his list of American friends, and these soon included, in addition to Stedman, Gilder, and Roswell Smith, the chief proprietor of the *Century*, such figures as Thomas Bailey Aldrich, John Hay, William Dean Howells, Henry James, Emma Lazarus, Brander Matthews, Louise Chandler Moulton, and James R. Osgood, as well as Lawrence Barrett, the actor, and a whole group of expatriate American artists, including Edwin Austin Abbey, Frank Millet, Alfred Parsons, and John Singer Sargent. But the greatest expansion of Gosse's American acquaintance came, of course, with his visit to the United States in the winter of 1884–1885.

In a letter to Gilder of March 1881 Gosse wrote, "How kind of you to remember my vague proposal to lecture in America!"[13] Apparently he and Gilder had discussed the possibility while Gilder was in England in 1880, and it is clear that long before he actually went to America Gosse had such a visit in mind. In undertaking a lecture tour in America he would be following in the distinguished footsteps of Thackeray and Dickens—and, as it turned out, Matthew Arnold was also to precede him across the Atlantic. Such a visit might also be expected to perform much the same function as the trips which he had made to Scandinavia a few years earlier, that of providing him with a fresh source of material, a new, relatively untapped area in which he could develop a special competency. In the summer of 1882 Gilder suggested Gosse as a possible candidate for a professorship of literature at Johns Hopkins University, and in 1884 he seems to have been largely instrumental in inspiring the offer of the vacant professorship of English Literature at Yale, an offer which Gosse turned down, ostensibly on the grounds that the post was inadequately paid but largely, no doubt, because

[12] See Charteris, *Life and Letters of Gosse*, pp. 4–8.
[13] Gosse to Gilder, 24 March 1881 (a.l.s.,GP)

he was reluctant to give up England. It was William Dean Howells, how-ever, whom Gosse had met in 1882 and with whom he had immediately established a close friendship, who was mainly responsible for the brief and, as it was to prove, unique visit which Gosse and his wife made to the United States in the winter of 1884–1885. Gilder and Stedman both played some part in the negotiations, but Howells's letters to Gosse during the latter part of 1883 and the first half of 1884 show clearly with what patience and energy he worked to secure for Gosse the invitations to give the Lowell Insti-tute Lectures at Boston and to repeat the same lectures at Johns Hopkins University and elsewhere.

Meanwhile Gosse's appointment in May 1884 to succeed Leslie Stephen as Clark Lecturer in English Literature at Trinity College, Cambridge, had brought him at the age of thirty-four to the crest of his great wave of early success in England, and he was clearly in no mood for long-term transatlantic adventures which would remove him from that exciting milieu of literary and social notables in which he had so recently succeeded in establishing himself. Yet the prospect of a brief visit to America still had obvious advan-tages for him, especially as he was beginning to be well-known there. His *Gray* in the English Men of Letters series was extremely well received by the London reviewers and this approval was reflected in the American notices, though most of them were brief and even perfunctory. In 1883 appeared an American edition, extensively revised, of Gosse's first book of poems, *On Viol and Flute*; the New York *Times* found the verse lacking in vigor, but George Parsons Lathrop, writing anonymously in the *Atlantic Monthly,* was lavish in his praise:

We are struck . . . with a quality of subtile insight very much like that of Emerson. There can be no doubt that Mr. Gosse possesses an exceedingly keen vision and is rigidly true to it in his rhythmic record of what he sees. . . . His fertility is remarkable, and what is more remarkable still is that he almost without exception satisfies by the fullness, the sweetness, the naturalness, and the polished grace of his exposition.

Lathrop, who was also reviewing Browning's *Jocoseria,* concluded by de-scribing Browning as a massive oak and Gosse as "the English violet grow-ing in a hollow at the foot of the oak. Everyone knows that to ascertain the relative value of the oak and the violet, aesthetically, is out of the question, and that we cannot dispense with either."[14]

The American Visit

The general outline of Gosse's visit to the United States in the winter of 1884–1885 is clear from the account given by Charteris in his *Life and*

[14] *Atlantic Monthly*, LI (June 1883), 844; for the New York *Times* review, see Letter 39, n. 6.

Letters of Sir Edmund Gosse, but it is perhaps insufficiently realized just how successful the visit was. In spite of the general rise of his reputation, Gosse's name cannot have been especially well known in the United States at the beginning of 1884, when he accepted the invitation to give the series of winter lectures at the Lowell Institute in Boston, but his friends in America were assiduous on his behalf and had created a considerable "Gosse boom" even before his arrival; once the lecture series itself was under way, once Gosse had begun to appear at receptions and dinners, his fame and popularity were quickly and firmly established. Gosse's lionization is the more remarkable in that this was a period of great American national pride, of a self-conscious national attempt to establish America's artistic and cultural superiority over Britain, and of extreme sensitivity in all matters appertaining to Anglo-American relations. Oscar Wilde's tour of 1882 had been something of a fiasco; even Matthew Arnold's visit of 1883 had aroused resentments; but Gosse was everywhere successful, largely, it appears, because he did not belittle his American audiences or talk down to them in any way.

Among the materials drawn upon for the following account of Gosse's visit is the unpublished manuscript diary—now in the Huntington Library —which Gosse kept while he was in the United States. The diary is in no sense a complete account of the visit and often consists of little more than long lists of those present at the many social functions given in Gosse's honor. To avoid tedious repetition, only a few of these lists have been quoted, but what is clear even from these samples, and what the diary as a whole overwhelmingly proves, is that while he was in America Gosse met not only the leading American authors, artists, editors, and publishers but also a great many of the most distinguished social and political figures. Many of these people he met more than once, exchanging visits with them and talking with them in private as well as on the more formal occasions. All this is striking evidence of Gosse's immediate success, and it was the number, variety, and eminence of his American acquaintances which gave him his special position in the Anglo-American cultural situation, at this period and throughout his life; it was this, too, which made him peculiarly useful as an English representative for the *Century* and, later, for other American magazines and publishing houses.

Gosse and his wife arrived in New York on the *S.S. Germanic* at three o'clock in the afternoon of Saturday, 29 November 1884, and at that point Gosse's diary begins. We learn from the diary that on his first day in the United States he met a considerable number of distinguished Americans, including his friends Roswell Smith, Gilder, and Emma Lazarus, and was interviewed by reporters from the New York *Times* and New York *Herald*. Gosse and his wife stayed at the Hotel Dam, not, as the Boston *Gazette*

10

seems to have reported,[15] with the Gilders. Gosse later told an interviewer from the *Pall Mall Gazette*: "The first night I landed in New York, sea-sick and weary, I naturally wished to retire early. I had opened my bedroom door to put out my boots. An interviewer was there on my door mat. He declined to move until he got the information he required. The door mat was hard. I took pity on him."[16]

The morning after his arrival Gosse was taken by Gilder to visit the studio of Augustus St. Gaudens, one of the two Americans he had told Gilder he was most anxious to meet.[17] The visit is enthusiastically described in a letter which Gosse wrote to his intimate friend Hamo Thornycroft, two days later.[18] By that time Gosse and his wife were in Boston, the guests of Howells and his wife at 302 Beacon Street. Their reception in New York and Boston, he told Thornycroft, has been "something I never dreamed of,"[19] and in his diary for 1 December, the night of his arrival in Boston, he noted of his forthcoming lectures: "All the tickets taken in 25 minutes."[20] The tickets were free, it is true, according to the custom of the Lowell Lectures, but a later report in the Boston *Gazette* suggests that they were in unusual demand:

Last Saturday at 10 o'clock was the time appointed for people to get their seats to hear the far-famed Londoner, the place being the Cadet armory building on Columbus avenue. That morning it rained not only cats and dogs but guns, and lazy folks who had not a small boy at command were loth to go out into the wet, and perhaps stand an hour in a cold armory waiting for their turn. Nevertheless, your correspondent, fearing a ticket would not be forthcoming from any other source, braved the storm, to find about fifty persons, half of them women of the same mind, were already standing in line dripping, umbrellas and all. By 9.30 the line extended round the hall. . . . Several ladies had brought books to read, some found a camp chair to roost on, others entertained themselves by watching the people come in and fall into line, a line that grew longer and longer until it doubled, and at length trebled round the great hall. By and by a bold boy dragged a ladder out from somewhere and ran to the clock on the wall and put the hands forward, at which piece of presumption a shout rang out from the other little boys who had been sent by their families

[15] See Clara and Rudolf Kirk, "Letters to an 'Enchanted Guest': W. D. Howells to Edmund Gosse," *Journal of the Rutgers University Library*, XXII (June 1959), 12. The whole article (pp. 1–25) is interesting for its observations on the relationship between Howells and Gosse.

[16] As quoted in the *Critic*, ns III (14 March 1885), 129.

[17] A.l.s., Gosse to Gilder, 22 June 1884 (HU).

[18] Charteris, *Life and Letters of Gosse*, pp. 166–167.

[19] *Ibid.*, p. 166.

[20] This quotation is from Gosse's manuscript diary of the American tour, now deposited in the Henry E. Huntington Library; all the unannotated quotations in this section are from the diary.

to get tickets. All things must come to an end, and so did this weary waiting, and at 10 o'clock precisely the double-quick march began, each individual receiving his ticket as he passed the door leading to the street. The distribution was over in twenty minutes.[21]

At the first lecture, on Tuesday, 2 December, Gosse records, all 850 seats were filled and 150 people turned away. He especially notes the presence of Dr. Oliver Wendell Holmes ("Chuckling. Bright eye. Little boyish figure.") on whom he had called earlier in the day, thus fulfilling the second of the ambitions he had confided to Gilder; indeed, Dr. Holmes came to all of Gosse's lectures and the two met nearly every day during the next two and a half weeks. Apart from a two-day visit to New York—leaving by a night train on Friday, 12 December, and returning to Boston in the late evening of Sunday, 14 December—Gosse and his wife spent this time in Boston in a whirl of lectures, sight-seeing, receptions, dinners, and visits made and received. The remaining lectures, held on 5, 9, 12, 16, and 19 December, continued to be well attended and well received: the *Gazette* reporter had thought that the first of them "contained nothing new"[22] but accounts of the lectures in other newspapers seem to have been overwhelmingly favorable. On 6 December Gosse went to visit Whittier at Oak Knoll, but the diary has only the brief notes which Gosse later expanded for his essay, "A Visit to Whittier," which was reprinted in *Portraits and Sketches* (1912). The same day he went on to Salem, where he saw the Custom House and the house with seven gables and met an "Old man who knew Hathorne." Gosse also records a visit to Wellesley College on Friday, 12 December, in company with Howells and James R. Osgood, the publisher;[23] he did not lecture but met various members of the faculty, of whom he especially mentions "Miss Lucile Hill (the gymnast)," later the subject of a humorous reference in a letter from Howells.

On 15 December Gosse and his wife were the guests of President Charles William Eliot of Harvard and Gosse lectured to the Harvard students in Sanders Hall; the diary entry reads: "Audience of upwards of 600. Extempore lecture on Gray. Thunderous applause. Students stayed to be presented." In the audience was Miss Elizabeth Peabody, sister-in-law of Hawthorne, whom Gosse had met earlier in the day and who seems to have impressed him both in her own person and as a link with the great days of Transcendentalism: "Miss E. P. 83, Long silky white curls, soft pink complexion, enflamed eyes, long trails of grey beard. Talked about Hawthorne, Emerson

[21] "Edmund W. Gosse: How Boston Goes to Lectures," Boston *Gazette*, 13 December 1884; taken from a clipping in the Rutgers University Library.

[22] *Ibid.*

[23] The report in the *Wellesley Courant*, 19 December 1884, mentions only Gosse and Howells (information supplied by Miss Hannah D. French, Wellesley College Library).

and M. Fuller. Came over from Jamaica Plain on purpose to hear me." The following day President Eliot took his English visitors to Lexington; on 19 December Gosse and Howells went to Concord, and at Emerson's grave they were told, by someone whom Gosse does not identify: "Mr. E. hain't got his stone up yet; he's been dead long enough, but he was very particular about his stone and his son hain't found the right sort yet."

The receptions, the calls, the invitations to "breakfast" and dinner during this period were too numerous to be listed in detail here. The first, and biggest, of all these occasions, and the one which Owen Wister was to recall when writing to Gosse more than thirty years later, was the reception given by Mr. and Mrs. Howells on Thursday, 4 December. This was an important social occasion at which, as the New York *Daily Tribune* put it, a "large number of the best known people of Boston and Cambridge were present."[24] Among those whom Gosse listed in his diary were Edwin Booth, Edward Everett Hale, Thomas Sergeant Perry, Francis Parkman, Horace E. Scudder, Colonel T. W. Higginson, Henry Cabot Lodge,[25] and Thomas Bailey Aldrich and his wife. That evening, at the Museum Theatre, the Gosses saw Booth as Shylock in *The Merchant of Venice.* One other social occasion from this period which seems to demand special mention is the reception given by the Roswell Smiths, for which Gosse and his wife made their brief trip to New York. The names recorded by Gosse on this occasion included those of the *Century* editorial staff and of many leading figures in the New York literary and social worlds, among them Frank R. Stockton,[26] Joseph L. Harper, the publisher, Brander Matthews, Henry Holt, and Andrew Carnegie.

One of the high points of Gosse's social activities in Boston seems to have been his attendance with Howells at a dinner given in his honor by the Tavern Club at Frederic Porter Vinton's studio on 11 December. Earlier that day Gosse, feeling "very poorly," had stayed in bed until half-past twelve, and his host had diverted him by reading from the incomplete manuscript of *The Rise of Silas Lapham,* which was then appearing in serial form. Howells had also read to him on Friday, 5 December, and Gosse's entry for the day may serve as an example of his activities and encounters on one of the quieter days of his Boston visit:

[24] Quoted in Clara and Rudolf Kirk, " 'Enchanted Guest'," Rutgers Library *Journal*, XXII (June 1959), 13.

[25] Parkman: Francis Parkman (1823–1893), the historian. Scudder: Horace Elisha Scudder (1838–1902), editor and writer. Lodge: Henry Cabot Lodge (1850–1924), statesman and author. A letter to Gosse from Lodge, dated 21 December 1884, regretting that a second meeting had not been possible, is in the Brotherton Collection, University of Leeds.

[26] Eight letters to Gosse from Frank R. Stockton (1834–1902), author of humorous novels and short stories, are in the Brotherton Collection: the first dates from May 1884, the last from July 1895.

Friday Dec. 5. Dr. Holmes calls at 10. Howells reads MS. of "Silas Lapham." E. E. Hale calls at 12, I visit Dr. Holmes and borrow his new "Emerson." After lunch C. E. Norton calls, Francis Parkan [sic], Bigelow, etc. Howells and I go up to office of the "Atlantic Monthly." Scudder and Garrison.[27] Walk back. Talk on the passion of love. Lecture. Dr. Holmes.

The entry begins and ends with Dr. Holmes, and Dr. Holmes seems indeed to have been always present. Faithful to the last, he came to the sixth lecture on Friday, 19 December—in an audience which Gosse estimates at eight hundred strong—and Gosse's final errand before leaving for New York the next day was to call on him, Gosse noting as "pathetic" his farewell remark, "Come again, before all the old men are dead."

After the bewildering activity and lionization of his stay in Boston it was perhaps not surprising that Gosse should write home in exultant mood to his friend Hamo Thornycroft, to whom he customarily wrote more frankly and more emotionally than to anyone else:

You will laugh to hear that we have been introduced to more than 600 people already. I try to remember their names and faces, and by dint of tremendous effort should perhaps recollect more or less vaguely 150 of them. Nellie gives up trying to remember any but the most celebrated and the most agreeable.

We have enjoyed—but I must not be reported to have said it—the greatest social success that any Englishman of letters has enjoyed since Thackeray lectured in Boston. Old Dr. Wendell Holmes, who has been the intellectual king of Boston all his life, told me that we must not suppose that all English lecturers were greeted as we have been. He said that he had never known a stranger make such a conquest as I have made. He wrote me, "we are all a little in love with you."[28]

Gosse wrote this letter on 20 December, in the train traveling south. In New York the Gosses stayed with Lawrence Barrett, the actor, and his wife, although Barrett himself, whom Gosse had met in London earlier that year, was away from home during most of their visit. During the Christmas period, which seems to have been comparatively quiet, Gosse called on St. Gaudens, John La Farge, and several others. After Christmas there was a fresh series of parties and receptions and among many now familiar names a number of new ones appear in the diary, notably those of Edward Eggleston, George Washington Cable, and E. L. Godkin.[29] Gosse also spent some

---

[27] Bigelow: John Bigelow (1817–1911), American writer and diplomat, author of biographies and historical works. Garrison: presumably Wendell Phillips Garrison (1840–1907), son of William Lloyd Garrison; he was the literary editor of the New York *Nation*.

[28] Charteris, *Life and Letters of Gosse*, pp. 168–169. Cf. Letter 81.

[29] Eggleston: Edward Eggleston (1837–1902), American author, best known for his novel *The Hoosier Schoolmaster* (1871). Cable: George Washington Cable

time with Stedman, seeing him in his twin guises of banker—during a visit to Wall Street and the stock exchange—and poet—at a joint meeting of the Authors' Club and the Tile Club on New Year's Eve.

On Friday, 2 January, 1885, Gosse went alone to Philadelphia, where he stayed at the Continental Hotel. That night at the Chestnut Street Opera House he saw Lawrence Barrett play Lord Tresham in Browning's *A Blot on the 'Scutcheon*; the performance, Gosse wrote to Browning that night, was "a decided success,"[30] despite the failure of the lighting towards the end of the last act. In his diary, significantly enough, Gosse says nothing of the play but writes at length of General Sherman, with whom he had shared a box. Sherman's presence, rather than Browning's play, had clearly constituted for Gosse the chief excitement of the evening; he describes his distinguished companion as "Bluff, cheerful, the same to all, guessed my age to a fraction, sat well in front, ovation, would take no notice, twinkled his eyes and snuffled, then martial music, rose and bowed." In the letter to Browning Gosse said that it had been like sharing a box "with Alexander the Great, and not a whit less romantic. The old tiger, now reduced to the most agreeable purring cat, sat well forward listening to your poetry, and turning back every now and then to explain the action to me in a very loud whisper."[31] After the performance Barrett gave a dinner in Gosse's honor at the Union League Club; among those present were General Sherman and the other members of the theatre party, including George H. Boker, the playwright. Gosse described Boker as "handsome, heavy, not a talker, gruff," and the Philadelphia *Daily News* the following day noted that the presence of Boker "dispelled the rumors of a misunderstanding between the actor and the author of 'Francesca da Rimini'."[32] Sherman apparently went on talking until a quarter to two in the morning, as Gosse records: "Did not burn Columbia, but has heard so much about it that 'next time he will clear the darned place off the face of the airth'. Real history of burning of Atlanta. Could not afford to leave troops there. Called The Tycoon. Snowy whiskers, very little growth, hair short soft mousey curls. Invited me to come and see him at St. Louis."

The following day, 3 January 1885, Gosse crossed the river by ferry to call on Walt Whitman at Camden. His diary notes of the meeting were later

---

(1844–1925), novelist, short-story writer, and historian, best known for his novel *Old Creole Days* (1879). Godkin: Edwin Lawrence Godkin (1831–1902), founded the *Nation* in 1865 and was editor of the New York *Evening Post* from 1883 to 1899.

[30] Charteris, *Life and Letters of Gosse*, p. 170.

[31] *Ibid.*, pp. 170–171.

[32] Philadelphia *Daily News*, 3 January 1885 (from a clipping in the Rutgers University Library). Barrett had been the first to produce Boker's *Francesca da Rimini* in 1855 and was especially associated with the part of Lanciotto; Gosse was to see him in this role at the Star Theatre, New York, on 17 January 1885 (diary).

worked up into the essay, "Walt Whitman," collected in *Critical Kit-Kats* (1896), but they seem sufficiently interesting to be printed here:

Sat. Jan. 3. By the ferry over to Camden. Walt Whitman's modest little house. (W. Whitman) on the plate. Hobbled half way down stairs. Uncarpeted room with bright outlook on to the street. Stove which he constantly attended to. Long white hair, open shirt, broad white hat lying around. Genial manner. "My friend." Spoke of Swinburne and Tennyson. Most kind. Head from behind like Darwin. Bought a book. He read me a new poem, intoning it, not very distinctly. Miss Smith and her friend, Boston enthusiasts; came in.[33] Whitman consulting us about a preface and a portrait. He talked of his "barbaric yawp" smilingly. Great sense of "the calm within, the light around, and that content, etc." The boys, lovely days when he was young, and about with "the boys" in the sun. Bathes now, and lies in the sun, in a N. J. brooklet in summer. Love of the sun. Portrait of ⟨Harlan⟩.[34] Likes to walk about in Philadelphia.

Writing to Howells a few days later, on 7 January, Gosse declared that he had had "a really enchanting visit to Camden to the dear old man. . . . I am going to begin admiring Walt all over again, his person is so attractive."[35] In the same letter he spoke of Horace Howard Furness, the Shakespearean scholar whom he had met the same day, as "one of the most lovely souls I ever met"; in his diary he simply notes that Furness was "extremely deaf" and that after dinner they went on together to a meeting of the Fortnightly Club.

On Monday, 5 January, Gosse met his wife at the Philadelphia railway station and they traveled together to Baltimore, where they had reserved rooms at the Mount Vernon Hotel. Gosse gave the first of his "From Shakespeare to Pope" lectures at the Peabody Institute on the afternoon of his arrival, the second and third on Wednesday and Friday afternoons, and one of his additional evening lectures on Thursday. His free time during this week was spent fairly quietly in Baltimore, which he seems to have preferred of all the American cities he visited,[36] but after the lecture on Friday, 9 January, he left with his wife for a few days in Washington. Here he met Henry Adams, George Bancroft, and General Sheridan and had a long talk "on politics" with James Blaine;[37] he did not write down any details of his

[33] Cf. Logan Pearsall Smith, *Unforgotten Years* (Boston: Little, Brown, 1939), pp. 103–104.

[34] Unidentified. In his account of the visit in *Critical Kit-Kats* (London: Heinemann, 1896), p. 105, Gosse says that the only portrait he saw was a photograph of a friend of Whitman's, a handsome young man from Canada. Cf. Edwin Haviland Miller, ed., *Collected Writings of Walt Whitman. The Correspondence, Volume III: 1876–1885* (New York: New York University Press, 1964), 189 n.

[35] For Gosse's later attitudes towards Whitman, see below, pp. 28–30.

[36] See, for example, his letter to Thornycroft of 14 January 1885, in Charteris, *Life and Letters of Gosse*, p. 175.

[37] Blaine had just been defeated by Cleveland in the 1884 presidential election. In

conversation with Blaine but he did record some fragments of what Bancroft had said:

His talk with Goethe in 1819. G. insisted that Byron had imitated Faust. In 1848 he was at Stoke Pogis and saw a Shakespeare amended by Gray. Spoke warmly of Moltke. Said the philosophical range of Ranke's last vol.[38] was as wide as ever, but the style showed signs of languor. He praised Parkman's style "it is like amber."

On Sunday, 11 January Gosse and his wife went to the White House: "At 2.30 President Arthur came. Very melancholy, talked about contingencies, 'what a tragedy' under Garfield's[39] picture, very gentleman-like, showed us the White House himself."

The Gosses returned to Baltimore the next day, in time for his lecture, and the following morning, 13 January, Gosse went on again to New York to give one of the "parlor" lectures which Henry Holt, the publisher, and his sister had undertaken to arrange for him.[40] This first lecture was given in Holt's own house and the occasion was reported next day in one of the New York newspapers:

In order to keep this engagement Mr. Gosse had to travel nearly four hundred miles, as he lectured in Baltimore on Monday night, and is due there again to-day. However, as he stood between the two large parlors filled with an audience chiefly composed of ladies, he exhibited no signs of fatigue, and his clear, musical voice aided by the neat but forcible delivery was heard in every corner of the rooms. From the first word to the last Mr. Gosse was listened to with breathless attention, in a silence broken only by the ripple of applause as his last words were uttered and the manuscript closed.[41]

After the lecture Gosse returned to Baltimore overnight and lectured there not only on the next day but on each of the two days following—although at the evening lecture on Thursday, 15 January, he seems to have given over much of the time to a reading of his own poems. Presumably he kept up the quality of his performance, however, for it was on the fifteenth that he

---

an interview published just before he left America, Gosse said that Blaine had impressed him as "the most versatile and magnetic" man he had ever known: *Critic*, ns III (24 January 1885), p. 38.

[38] Leopold Von Ranke (1795–1886), the German historian, was currently publishing the successive volumes of his *Weltgeschichte*.

[39] James Abram Garfield (1831–1881), twentieth President of the United States, had been assassinated by Charles J. Guiteau. The Vice-President, Chester Alan Arthur (1830–1886), succeeded to the Presidency and served out the unexpired portion of Garfield's term of office: when Gosse met him, Arthur was within a few weeks of retirement.

[40] The places, dates and titles of the lectures were given in the *Critic*, ns III (17 January 1885), 35.

[41] "Mr. Gosse in New-York," New York *Daily Tribune*, 14 January 1885, p. 3.

recorded in his diary President Gilman's offer of a post at Johns Hopkins University.

Early on the morning of Saturday, 17 January, the Gosses returned to New York, where Gosse gave another parlor lecture at Mrs. Vicenzo Botta's.[42] On the Sunday afternoon there was a music-party at St. Gauden's, at which H. H. Richardson,[43] the architect, was present, and in the evening a reception at R. H. Stoddard's. On Tuesday, 20 January, after a further parlor lecture, Gosse traveled overnight by train to Aurora, New York, and Wells College, where he lectured the following day. Next morning, 22 January, he went with President White, who had been at his lecture the previous evening, to visit Cornell University, where he met Moses Coit Tyler[44] but did not lecture. He returned to New York and gave another of the parlor lectures ("very successful") the following afternoon. He also lectured at Yale on Saturday, 24 January: "Very crowded and enthusiastic audience; about 700 persons, 100 stood all the time."

Gosse's social life in America remained splendid and distinguished to the last. His last full day in the country was Monday, 26 January, and that morning he went to the Hotel Brunswick to attend the breakfast given in his honor by Laurence Hutton. A copy of the menu in the possession of Mr. Charles E. Feinberg of Detroit bears the autographs of a large number of the leading literary figures of the day, among them Stedman, Stockton, Gilder, Booth, Stoddard, Matthews, Bunner, George Parsons Lathrop, Robert Underwood Johnson, Roswell Smith, G. C. Eggleston, H. H. Boyesen,[45] James R. Osgood, and Henry Holt. That afternoon Gosse gave the last of his parlor lectures, and in the evening he and his wife saw the first night of Barrett's Cassius, in Shakespeare's *Julius Caesar,* one of the parts with which

[42] For Mrs. Anne Charlotte Lynch Botta (1815–1891), author and celebrated hostess of her day, see Stedman and Gould, *Life and Letters of Stedman*, II, 353, and Robert Underwood Johnson, *Remembered Yesterdays* (London: Allen & Unwin, 1923), p. 90.

[43] In the interview published in *Critic* on 24 January 1885 (see above, n. 37), Gosse singled out Richardson (p. 38) for special praise as "the most national artist" America had produced. He also expressed admiration of the American tendency to "combine the arts. . . . I have been delighted to see men like John Lafarge, Augustus St. Gaudens and Stanford White—painter, sculptor and architect—working together. That seems to me to be the right thing" (*ibid.*). Some of Gosse's remarks on American architecture in this interview, and in particular his strictures on Philadelphia's new City Hall, aroused considerable controversy: see, for example, *Critic*, ns III (7 February 1885), 67–68, and ns III (28 February 1885), 106.

[44] Moses Coit Tyler (1835–1900), author of *The Literary History of the American Revolution* (1897).

[45] George Cary Eggleston (1839–1911), journalist and novelist; his experiences as a country schoolmaster in Indiana provided his brother, Edward, with the materials for his novel *The Hoosier Schoolmaster.* Hjalmar Hjorth Boyesen (1848–1895), born in Norway, gained a reputation in the United States both as university teacher and as realistic novelist.

Barrett's name was most closely associated. The following morning Gosse went to the *Century* office to say goodbye, and in the afternoon he and his wife boarded the *S.S. Arizona*. The extent to which Gosse had been impressed by the United States can be nicely gauged from two passages in an interview which appeared in the *Critic* on 24 January 1885, just three days before his departure:

Mr. Gosse was inclined to confess that he had enjoyed opportunities unusual for an Englishman, from the fact of his being introduced into society by his previous knowledge of Americans. Everybody, he said, has seemed eager to be kind. 'I have seen a good deal in a short time. I had come well acquainted with current American literature. My mind was just like touchwood, ready to be fired. I have scarcely seen one of my own countrymen since I have been here. I have been asking questions all day long, and eager to see all I could of life in your Eastern cities. It is hard to understand America, but perhaps the first step towards understanding is sympathy. . . .

'I am surprised and delighted by the welcome I have had in this country. It has far outstripped my deserts or expectations. I came to America intending to enjoy myself, but I have done so to an extent absolutely beyond my hopes. I think I must come back, some day, but not for years to come. I have been pressed to settle in this country, but I cannot give up London and Cambridge. I would sooner live in poverty in London than like a prince anywhere else. I cannot explain it, but we children of London have a sort of passion for it.'[46]

Gosse's Later Reputation in the United States

In the weeks immediately following his departure from the United States a small but striking testimony to Gosse's success was the space, and the praise, devoted in the review pages of several American journals to his four-volume edition of the *Works of Thomas Gray*. The edition was warmly welcomed in *Harper's Monthly*, now under Howells's editorship, in the *Atlantic Monthly*, in the *Critic*, and especially in the New York *Times*.[47] Some of the American reviewers, however, and notably those in the *Nation* and the *Literary World*,[48] were more astute than any of the English critics had been in perceiving a number of errors and inadequacies in Gosse's editing. The reviewer in the *Literary World* was at pains to find excuses for Gosse's mistakes, but the fact seems simply to have been that the rapidity of his success had induced in Gosse a carelessness born of overconfidence. He was soon to pay heavily for this fault.

[46] *Critic*, ns III (24 January 1885), 37–38.
[47] *Harper's Monthly*, LXX (May 1885), 972–973; *Atlantic Monthly*, LV (April 1885), 566–568; *Critic*, ns III (14 February 1885), 74–75; New York *Times*, 22 February 1885, p. 4.
[48] *Nation*, XL (5 March 1885), 204–206; *Literary World*, XVI (7 March 1885), 75.

From Shakespeare to Pope, the volume which Gosse compiled from the lectures he first gave at the Lowell Institute, was published in 1885. The reviewers on both sides of the Atlantic were generally respectful, though those which appeared in America tended to show a greater awareness of the fact that the book had started life as a series of lectures. The New York *Times* reviewer, in observing that Gosse had succeeded with his audience despite an unfortunate choice of subject, threw some interesting light on contemporary American predilections and prejudices:

The epoch between Shakespeare and Pope is indeed American in the sense that English-speaking North America was then a part of Great Britain, but the literary consciousness of the colonies was so slender, and the gulf made by the Revolution and immigration from the rest of Europe is so wide and profound, that it needs an effort of imagination for most Americans to feel any true proprietorship in that section of British literature. Considering these things, and the further fact that careful and delicately discriminate criticism of literary men of any past age is not too popular with audiences, it must be said that Mr. Gosse has done his task in the happiest spirit and with an energy quite unexpected. Part of his success was undoubtedly due to his delivery, which was free from the mannerisms and positive defects of utterance that marred the lectures of several distinguished Britons who lately came across the Atlantic.[49]

In October 1886, however, less than a year after the biting English attacks on Gosse's volume of verse *Firdausi in Exile and Other Poems,* which had also appeared late in 1885, came the savage and sustained attack on *From Shakespeare to Pope,* launched anonymously by John Churton Collins, an able scholar and a former close friend of Gosse, in the *Quarterly Review.*[50] Gosse published in the *Athenaeum*[51] a partial answer to Collins's well-documented charges of inaccuracy and misinterpretation, other correspondents joined in, and a first-class literary row developed.

The history of this celebrated affair, which did Gosse such lasting harm, is outlined in Charteris's *Life and Letters of Sir Edmund Gosse;*[52] at the time it was effectively and rather sardonically summarized for American readers in a series of "London Letters" published in the *Critic.* In the issue of 20 November 1886, the *Critic*'s correspondent wrote:

The Gosse-Collins affair is, so far, the scandal of the year. People—literary people—talk of nothing else. It has generated such rumors as are not to be stated; it has split the town into camps; and by many it is opined that it will cause the death of two men—the assailant and the assailed: the one for his animosity and the suspicion of *mala fides* which is discovered in his work; the

[49] New York *Times,* 6 December 1885, p. 5.

[50] [John Churton Collins], "English Literature at the Universities," *Quarterly Review,* CLXIII (October 1886), 289–329.

[51] *Athenaeum,* 23 October 1886, pp. 534–535.

[52] Charteris, *Life and Letters of Gosse,* pp. 193–202.

other for the ingenuous poverty of his defense against so brilliant, so determined, so irresistible an attack. As matters stand, the victory is to some extent with Mr. Gosse.[53]

These letters gave an interpretation that was, on the whole, favorable to Gosse, and certainly his American friends seem to have had no hesitation in assuring him of their support. Several of them, including James, Howells, Stedman, Furness, and Thomas Sergeant Perry, sent warm letters of encouragement, and one American reviewer of Gosse's *Raleigh* made a particular point of praising Gosse for just those qualities of accuracy and impartiality in which Collins had found him wanting.[54]

By the early 1890's Gosse had undoubtedly won back much of his English reputation as a serious critic and scholar; his American reputation had never been seriously impaired. In 1891 he published *Gossip in a Library*, a book which had been suggested to him by John Eliot Bowen, editor of the New York *Independent*, the journal in which half of the essays had previously appeared. *Gossip in a Library* was a slight work, a collection of miscellaneous essays, most of them on little-known literary figures, and it is characteristic of the Anglo-American cultural situation at that period that the American reviewers tended to mention such things as Gosse's praise of American bibliophiles and his reference to the critical acumen of the American critics in perceiving the merits of Meredith before he was famous in England. The reviewers in the English *Saturday Review*, showing even greater national bias, had commented of the essays first published in America that "it might have been better to clear away some of the marks of this . . . origin so to make the appeal of the book oecumenical and not provincial";[55] a contrary opinion was voiced a month later by the reviewer in the American *Nation*, who made it clear that he thought the book an insult to American intelligence, though it might satisfy the English:

The pieces are the merest gossamer of bibliography, allusion, and comment, and their subjects usually lack novelty. . . . [They] afford the author opportunity to say a baker's dozen of very obvious remarks on each topic before he skims away to his next bastard title. How often need we remind our London cousins that these, like the Abbey, are ours too? *Nec tam aversus*—do our cousins fancy that we haven't primers of our own? We have quite enough just as flashy as this; for the dilettante is a native product, though not fully protected, it seems, from foreign competition.[56]

Gosse, in this matter, was clearly the victim of national prejudice on both sides, but in England and in America *Gossip in a Library* was highly praised

[53] *Critic*, VI (20 November 1886), 251.
[54] *Ibid.*, (13 November 1886), 233.
[55] *Saturday Review*, LXXIII (9 January 1892), 46.
[56] *Nation*, LIV (18 February 1892), 132.

by those reviewers who were not concerned to make patriotic points, and the book undoubtedly increased Gosse's popularity, though less as a profound critic than as a slightly "antiquarian" scholar and a lively conversationalist on out-of-the-way literary matters.

Gosse's next book, the slim romance called *The Secret of Narcisse* (1892), attracted little attention and did nothing either to harm or enhance his standing. In view of the transatlantic argument about romance and realism in which Gosse had for some time been involved, it is a little ironic that the book seems to have been better received in America than in England: the New York *Times*, in fact, called it "a little masterpiece."[57] As we shall see, the debate between the realists and the romanticists was touched upon at many points in Gosse's *Questions at Issue*, published in 1893; if most American reviewers paid little attention to the various arguments on this and other Anglo-American controversies which Gosse advanced, that was presumably because the book was a collection of essays previously published in magazines, and reactions to each essay had been fully ventilated at the time of its first appearance. The reviews of the book on both sides of the Atlantic were generally complimentary, as, in the following years, were those of Gosse's final book of new verse, *In Russet and Silver* (1894), and of his critical studies *Jacobean Poets* (1894), *Critical Kit-Kats* (1896), and the *Short History of Modern English Literature* (1898). The American and English receptions of his *Life and Letters of John Donne* (1899) were also closely parallel, for in both countries the general chorus of praise was interrupted by fierce attacks not so much on Gosse's errors of fact, which had been Churton Collins's main target, but on his maladroit attempts to interpret Donne's early poems and to use them as evidence in reconstructing his early life. A similar pattern can be discerned in the reviews of the Gosse and Garnett four-volume *English Literature: An Illustrated Record* (1903–1904) and of Gosse's *French Profiles* (1905). The American reception of Gosse's *Sir Thomas Browne* (1905) was perceptibly less enthusiastic than that in the English press, however, a reaction which may perhaps be construed as an early sign of the new developments in literary criticism which were at that time proceeding more swiftly in America than in England and which were to make Gosse's work seem increasingly old-fashioned to the younger American critics.

It was only Gosse's criticism which was falling into disfavor. When his autobiographical masterpiece, *Father and Son*, appeared in 1907, the American reviewers, less disturbed than their English counterparts about the propriety of a son's criticizing his father in public, went more directly to the real virtues of the book. Similarly, the American reception of the remarkably

[57] New York *Times*, 1 January 1893, p. 19. For the romance-and-realism controversey, see below, pp. 42–43.

successful *Two Visits to Denmark* (1911) was quite as encomiastic as the one it received in England. When Gosse's *Ibsen* was published in 1907, however, the American reviewers were strongly critical of the work in detail and especially of what seemed to them Gosse's essential lack of sympathy with the author he had done so much to introduce to an English-speaking audience. A note of irritation also appeared in some of the American criticisms of *Portraits and Sketches* (1912), a collection of portrait-studies of recent and contemporary writers. The New York *Times* reviewer, for instance, in acknowledging the "pictorial" value of the book, could not forbear to question Gosse's critical ability or to register an American amusement at his recent British honor: "Whatever your private estimate of Edmund Gosse—nowadays he writes 'C.B.' after his name—as a critic, it is not reasonably to be denied that his impressions of the eminent men he has known have a pictorial quality that gives them peculiar interest and real value."[58] The *Nation* reviewer was also rather unsympathetic, denying Gosse accuracy in his scholarship or philosophy in his criticism,[59] but this lack of appreciation is scarcely surprising in view of the fact that the *Nation* was at this time under the editorship of Paul Elmer More, who employed many reviewers, Upton Sinclair among them, to whom *Portraits and Sketches* must have seemed the merest trivia of criticism.

In the following year the *Nation*'s review of Gosse's *Collected Essays* was generally favorable, but it cast an amused and somewhat scornful glance at his reputed social aspirations:

But Mr. Gosse was to become librarian of the House of Lords, acquiring thereby, as we have heard one of his cynical friends declare, association with the two things he most coveted, rare books and titles—not book titles. At least there is no harm in repeating a bit of innocent gossip, of the kind that might go into one of Mr. Gosse's own anecdotal essays.[60]

It is true that similar observations on Gosse's character and career had been made earlier in English periodicals, but in America they seem to have become increasingly frequent, achieving their most violent form in the writings of Ezra Pound and the Freudian critic Ludwig Lewisohn, both of whom used their reviews of Gosse's work to strike a blow in a much larger critical battle, attacking through Gosse the whole attitude to literature and life which he seemed to them to represent.

In 1918 Ezra Pound reviewed Gosse's *Life of Swinburne* in the avant-garde periodical *Poetry*. The moments in Swinburne's life which Gosse, because of the "embargoes" laid upon him, had been forced to suppress were, to Pound, just those occasions when Swinburne was most truly him-

---

[58] *Ibid.*, 19 January 1913, Book Review Section, p. 23.
[59] *Nation*, XCVI (27 March 1913), 312–313.
[60] *Ibid.*, XCIX (1 October 1914), 407–409.

self, compensating for being born into a world of Gosses—and Pound's impatience is reflected in the language of the review:

> Gosse's *Life of Swinburne* is merely the attempt of a silly and pompous old man to present a man of genius, an attempt necessarily foredoomed to failure and not worth the attention of even the most cursive reviewer. Gosse has written one excellent book: *Father and Son,* prompted according to gossip by his wife's fear that Mr. George Moore, having been rashly allowed access to Mr. Gosse's diaries, proposed to steal the material. Mr. Gosse has also held divers positions of trust under the British government, in one of which, at least, he has fulfilled his functions with great credit and fairness. Apart from that he resembles many literary figures of about his age and generation, who coming after the more or less drunken and more or less obstreperous real Victorians, acquired only the cant and fustiness. . . . We do not however wish a Swinburne coated with veneer of British officialdom and decked out for a psalm-singing audience.
>
> Gosse in the safety of his annual pension of £666, 16 shillings, 8 pence, has little to fear from the slings of fortune or from the criticisms of younger men. If he preferred to present Swinburne as an epileptic rather than as an intemperate drinker, we can only attribute this to his taste, a taste for kowtowing.[61]

To Lewisohn, as he made clear in his review of *Some Diversions of a Man of Letters* (1919), Gosse appeared simply as both symbol and spokesman of a kind of writing which represented the exact antithesis of "life";[62] Lewisohn's later review of *Aspects and Impressions* (1922) began accordingly with an attack on Gosse's personal character and reputation, as well as on his style and scholarship:

> In days that now seem remote Mr. Gosse made his reputation with books that every schoolboy knows. Throughout these volumes—especially his agreeable account of English literature in the eighteenth century—he cultivated a limpid though rather Alexandrian grace of style and a learning so prodigious in mass and inaccurate in detail that his name was always greeted among scholars with something between an obeisance and a grin. In that period he was a poet, too, and composed many pleasant verses in the measures of old France and the manner and style of Theocritus. But by and by he became librarian of the House of Lords, a member of knightly orders, and the friend and companion— to use the expression of his favorite century—of the Great. His prose became flatter and more solemn; he still tries to be urbane and succeeds in being only official; at his most characteristic and terrible moments today he no longer knows who is talking—himself or the British Empire. The identification of the two in his own mind is complete.[63]

[61] *Poetry*, XI (March 1918), 322–324.
[62] *Nation*, CXI (22 May 1920), 691–692.
[63] *Bookman* [New York], LV (July 1922), 526–527.

Gosse, of course, had his staunch defenders among the American reviewers, notably Richard Le Gallienne in the New York *Times*[64] and E. F. Edgett in that conservative bastion, the Boston *Transcript*. Edgett's review of *Aspects and Impressions* identified by name some of the leaders of the opposition: "It is altogether likely that these essays will fail to please the modern school of literary pencillers who scorn scholarship and who fancy that verbal smartness and triviality is the only method of criticism. But they were not written to encourage the Menckens and the Nathans, and they are all the better and more lasting for that reason."[65] These defenders of Gosse, however, were generally less impressive than his opponents, and even the critics who were not especially hostile now tended to identify Gosse with Victorianism and to treat him in a slightly patronizing manner. Stuart P. Sherman, for example, the young New Humanist, reviewed *Aspects and Impressions* in the *Weekly Review* and spoke of Gosse as a critic of "quiet charm" who was "rooted in the best tradition and nourished by habitual contact with men who unfeignedly value in literature a certain vital decorum, the unfailing mark of works worthy of permanent remembrance." Yet even Sherman saw Gosse as the representative of something like an English literary officialdom: "Taste, tact, and temper designated Mr. Gosse from his youth as the man to call upon when a poet laureate died or when the hundredth anniversary of a classic fell to be celebrated or when a new citizen was to be admitted to good and regular standing in the Republic of letters."[66] A similar characterization of Gosse was given in the *Dial* by Robert Morss Lovett, who called him the "Major Pendennis" of literature, "a literary man-of-the-world, unbewildered and unprejudiced. . . . He is correct in dress and manner, discreet in speech; he says the right thing to everyone, and nearly always of every one."[67] Like Sherman, Lovett appreciated the gentlemanly and sociable qualities of Gosse's criticism, but both of them saw clearly that the ground had moved out from under him and his generation.

It is important to note, however, that even some of the more radical critics of the day found good words to say for Gosse. Randolph Bourne, reviewing *Three French Moralists* for the *Dial* in 1918, found much to criticize in the book, but he also found much that was "right and beautifully persuasive."[68] Almost ten years later, early in 1928, the American reviews of Gosse's last book, *Leaves and Fruit,* a collection of reviews from the London *Sunday Times,* provided ample evidence of the high esteem in which Gosse was held even in the last year of his life and even by critics who could be expected to

[64] For his review of *Aspects and Impressions*, see New York *Times*, 30 July 1922, p. 20.

[65] Boston *Transcript*, 3 May 1922, p. 6.

[66] *Weekly Review*, II (8 May 1920), 487.

[67] *Dial*, LXVIII (June 1920), 777–778.

[68] *Ibid.*, LXV (19 October 1918), 309–310.

have little sympathy either with his judgments or with his methods. In the New York *Independent*, for example, Ernest Boyd praised Gosse as "always urbane and judicial."[69] In a lengthy review in the New York *Herald Tribune*, Van Wyck Brooks wrote:

Sir Edmund Gosse is on the verge of eighty, but there is nothing in "Leaves and Fruit", his new collection of essays, to suggest any diminution of the catholicity of mind, the alertness of intelligence, the sureness of taste that make him the most generally satisfactory of living critics. Indeed, he has gained rather than lost with the advance of years.

Gosse, said Brooks, "is never better than when he finds something to praise in those whom others slight or condemn." Alternatively, "he can depreciate with equal convincingness where others praise." Brooks concluded that Gosse "is as ever equally attractive in the spheres of personal portraiture and literary criticism, and 'Leaves and Fruit' in general worthily maintains the quality of a body of work which covers now virtually half a century."[70]

Such a verdict from so distinguished a critic is important both for what it says and for what it leaves out. Brooks levels no charge of superficiality against Gosse but praises him for his sharpness of intellect and catholicity of taste. Especially interesting is the comment that Gosse was at his best when disagreeing with others; he had always been a champion of the underdog and a revivifier of dead reputations, but as reviewer for the *Sunday Times* he had also established himself as a dissenter from many contemporary literary fashions. Yet Brooks's praise of Gosse seems somewhat exaggerated, and some of the necessary qualifications were made by Edmund Wilson, representing a more radical element in American criticism. In his review in the *New Republic* Wilson took it for granted that Gosse was capable of understanding modern literature and recognized Gosse's sensitive perception and intelligent awareness of new movements. What he also recognized, however, was that Gosse's extreme propriety of judgment seemed dangerously close to an "instinct for respectability," and he was primarily concerned in the review to define the reasons why Gosse could not properly be called the greatest critic of the twentieth century. Wilson perhaps made too much of the "irrelevant fears and inhibitions" which he believed to have always hampered Gosse's criticism, but his central argument was extremely astute:

We come to the conclusion that, if we are reluctant to grant Gosse a high place in literature, it is simply because that does not seem to be precisely the kind of high place at which he himself has aimed. . . . He has aimed all his life, perhaps, at becoming not so much a first-rate writer as a distinguished institution.[71]

[69] *Independent*, CXIX (24 December 1927), 635.
[70] New York *Herald Tribune*, 8 January 1928, p. 7.
[71] *New Republic*, LIV (22 February 1928), p. 21.

It is not surprising that Gosse's manner and matter should have been unsympathetic to some of the younger American critics of the early twentieth century. Throughout his life Gosse's poetry and much of his prose continued to be deeply affected by those Pre-Raphaelite influences to which he had been exposed as a young man, and he never moved far from the position that art is a sufficient end in itself. Literature was for Gosse a way of life, a life not of withdrawal and solitary contemplation but, on the contrary, of society and brilliant conversation—the life, in short, of a distinguished, respected, and popular man of letters. If in the later years of his life Gosse took on the character of a British institution, that was in large measure an inevitable result of his remarkably full and successful career, of his having been so long in the public eye; yet there is no doubt that Edmund Wilson was right and that Gosse had a deep determination, perhaps instilled in him by his religious upbringing, to be not so much a literary critic as a literary authority and, what was more, an authority who would command the personal respect of the highest society in the land. That American critics of the caliber of Bourne, Brooks, Sherman, and Wilson should have written about Gosse so energetically and at such length at this late point in his career is in itself a sufficient reminder that the eclipse of Gosse's reputation since his death should not be allowed to obscure the popular and influential position he held during his lifetime, nor the extent to which he realized his early ambitions.

Gosse's American Friendships

Following his return from America, and well on into the first decades of the new century, Gosse maintained and even extended his circle of American friends. Many of the people he had met during his American visit came to call on him when they were in London: Frank Stockton and his wife in 1892, for example, Horace Scudder in 1897, Henry Cabot Lodge in 1899. H. H. Furness, the Shakespeare scholar, wrote Gosse many of his whimsical letters during these years and, on much rarer occasions, he put in an appearance in person. Oliver Wendell Holmes, as we shall see, was entertained by the Gosses in 1886, and they later entertained his son, the jurist, on various occasions in 1901, 1903, and 1907. Old friendships were kept up—with the artists Abbey, Millet, Parsons, and Sargent, for example—and new ones developed: with Joseph and Elizabeth Pennell, with George Allison Armour, with Henry Harland, with the charming Wolcott Balestier and his sisters (one of whom was to marry Rudyard Kipling), and, after the turn of the century, with Hamlin Garland and Edith Wharton and with still younger American writers, such as Stark Young.

More than anything else, it is the sheer range and variety of his American friendships which establishes Gosse as such an interesting figure in the history of Anglo-American literary relations and makes his a distinctive voice in the transatlantic dialogue. Gosse had, too, an extremely wide knowledge of American literature, although in this he was by no means unique: other contemporary English writers and men of letters, such as Swinburne, Robert Louis Stevenson, and John Addington Symonds, were quite as aware as Gosse of the importance of the new literature across the Atlantic and, generally speaking, they found it a good deal more exciting and sympathetic than did Gosse himself. But none of them, even though Stevenson actually lived in America for a time, could match Gosse's list of American friends, and by looking more closely at a few of these friendships we may perhaps throw a little light not only on the men themselves but on the Anglo-American literary situation during the late nineteenth and early twentieth centuries.

The first letter in this selection is the one which Gosse wrote to Walt Whitman in December 1873. It is written in tones of admiration and discipleship, and although it is a highly self-conscious, youthful production we have already suggested that there seems no reason to doubt the sincerity of its commitment. Professor William White, however, in an article in *Victorian Studies*,[72] has had some severe comments to make on the discrepancies between this letter and the somewhat patronizing attitude towards Whitman which Gosse seems to adopt in the account of his 1885 visit to Whitman which is collected in *Critical Kit-Kats*. This severity appears not to be entirely justified. As White himself notes, the attitude which Gosse assumes at the beginning of the essay in *Critical Kit-Kats* is largely a literary strategy, a device for making more dramatic his eventual surrender to the charm of Whitman's person and personality, while of the 1873 letter it is important to remember that Gosse wrote it when he was only twenty-four, still a clerk in the British Museum, and at the very beginning of his literary career. Gosse has himself left a suggestive account of his literary outlook and environment at this period in an essay of 1919, "The Whitman Centenary," which Professor White does not make use of in his article. The account of Gosse's visit to Whitman is well known, as is his description of Whitman's verse in the same essay as "poetry in suspension"; the Centenary essay, however, is in some ways more remarkable and deserves quotation at length. Recalling that Whitman had found his earliest and warmest support in England rather than in America, Gosse writes:

There had been a time when the vogue of Walt Whitman was very active in a small but resolute band of pre-Raphaelites. Looking back on those years, it is easy to understand what it was that attracted these Englishmen to the 'barbaric yawp' of the Long Island carpenter. They were simple, passionate people themselves, and filled with ardent curiosity. They lived intensely in a sharply out-

72 William White, "Sir Edmund Gosse on Walt Whitman," *Victorian Studies*, I (December 1957), 180–182.

lined circle of their own, and cared nothing about social opinion outside it. They were, in the aesthetic sphere, peaceful revolutionaries, as Whitman was in his other sphere of resistance to futility. When the American wrote poetry about 'the white and red pork in the pork store, the tea-table, the home-made sweetmeats,' the British public might laugh, but such themes would not seem ridiculous to admirers of Coventry Patmore, and the early Millais.

So long, therefore, as admiration of *Leaves of Grass* was a flame confined to one esoteric group of young men in London, it burned brightly enough. But there came a fatal day when the world took up the fashion of reading Walt Whitman, and straightaway his influence declined. Looking back to that time, we may perceive that it was never the attacks upon his 'style', not the shrieks of an outraged Mrs. Grundy which reduced his power, but the popular tendency to apologize for him. What lowered the prestige of Whitman was the timidity of his friends when they took to excusing the libertinage of *Enfans d'Adam,* and *Calamus,* by pointing to later proofs of his civic and literary virtue. How gallant were the numbers of *Drum Taps,* they said; how touching the elegy on Lincoln, how estimable the poet's activity in the hospitals!

But, if we will clear our minds of cant, these appendices to his work, charming in themselves, were so much barley water mixed with the strong wine of his message. If it be worth while to study Walt Whitman at all, it is not in the anodyne edges of his nature that we must begin, but at his uncompromising centre. 'I loaf and invite my soul', he sings, and we must not shrink, if we wish to penetrate that soul, from the coarse and bracing perfume of its illustration. The one thing we must never do is to persuade ourselves that Whitman was, 'after all', respectable. He was not; he rolled on the carpet of the world like a grown-up naked baby. But what is decency? It is a vague and fugitive quality, affected not merely by tradition but by geography, and "those who piddle and patter here in collars and tailed coats" must hardly be permitted to define it for the ages.[73]

Critics of Gosse have made much of his "somewhat feline disposition";[74] reviewers in the early years of the twentieth century often accused him of writing as though he were the official voice of English literature; readers of Gosse's letters to his American friends must often be made aware of his lack of sympathy with many aspects of American life and American literature. Yet "The Whitman Centenary" reveals the inadequacy of all these assumptions. The tone here is positive, even passionate, and the attitude towards Whitman reminds us of how profoundly Gosse had been influenced by the beliefs and personalities of Swinburne, Rossetti, and the Pre-Raphaelite group, the figures who made up the first literary environment he encountered as a young man. Gosse seems to be indirectly reaffirming that essentially amoral attitude to art and life which he adopted under the in-

[73] Gosse, "The Whitman Centenary," *Living Age,* CCCII (July 1919), 42–43.

[74] See, for example, White, "Gosse on Whitman," *Victorian Studies,* I (December 1957), 180, where the phrase is quoted from William Rose Benét, *Reader's Encyclopedia* (New York, 1948), p. 448.

fluence of his early literary friendships and in reaction against the excessive morality of his father. And it is clear from the essay that Gosse, for whatever reasons, had an understanding of Whitman, and a sympathy with him, which in 1919 was still unusual, in America or anywhere else. If Gosse's first eager enthusiasm for Whitman became considerably tempered with the passing of the years, with increased maturity and experience, he nonetheless retained throughout his life an admiration for certain aspects of Whitman's work, and in his old age he testified warmly to that admiration and to the eagerness of his early discipleship.[75]

Some ten years after he made his first approach to Whitman, Gosse sought in somewhat similar fashion the acquaintance of Oliver Wendell Holmes, whom he regarded as the most distinguished American man of letters of the day. Once again the sequel was to be a happy one. In 1884 Gosse, in company with many other English and American authors, was asked for a contribution to the special number of the *Critic* which was to be issued in celebration of Dr. Holmes's seventy-fifth birthday. Gosse sent the *Critic* "An Epistle to Dr. Oliver Wendell Holmes on his seventy-fifth Birthday," and this was duly published, with the other complimentary pieces, on 30 August. Gosse also had the poem privately printed in an edition of forty copies, one of which he sent to Dr. Holmes. Up to this time Gosse seems not to have had any correspondence with Holmes, but the latter now wrote, on 7 September 1884, a generous if somewhat formal letter of thanks. In a letter to Gilder of June that year Gosse had mentioned that Holmes was one of the two people in America whom he most wanted to meet,[76] and in his reply to Holmes, dated 18 September 1884, he announced that while he was in Boston the following winter he would take the opportunity of calling on Holmes in person.

When Gosse actually met Holmes for the first time, in December 1884, the latter, at seventy-five, had been retired for two years from the Parkman Professorship of Anatomy and Physiology at Harvard University, a post he had held since 1847, two years before Gosse was born. Gosse, of course, was fully conscious of Holmes's importance as the acknowledged leader of literature and his respectful attitude may have helped to recommend him to the older man. Gosse, however, was a young man of considerable personal charm and conversational brilliance, and it was these qualities which Holmes, himself famous for his conversation, seems to have found attractive. Holmes attended without fail every one of the Lowell Lectures; he allowed Gosse to read the proofs of his biography of Emerson and Gosse was thus able to

[75] For Whitman's early influence on Symonds, Gosse, Stevenson, and others, see Phyllis Grosskurth, *John Addington Symonds: A Biography* (London: Longmans, 1964), pp. 119–121, 149, 209.

[76] A.l.s., Gosse to Gilder, 22 June 1884 (HU).

publish the earliest review of the book; when Gosse gave Holmes a volume of his poems Holmes wrote to thank him and concluded, "We are all a little in love with you"—the phrase which the delighted Gosse repeated in his letter to Hamo Thornycroft a week later.[77]

Gosse's letter of 19 August 1885, sending good wishes for Holmes's seventy-sixth birthday, seems to suggest that the two men had not corresponded since Gosse's return to England, but it recalls in warmly affectionate terms various incidents of their hours of intimacy the previous winter. In succeeding months letters and books were exchanged and in December Gosse wrote thanking Holmes for his praise of Gosse's *Firdausi in Exile and Other Poems,* a volume which had been unfavorably received by some of the English reviewers. The following year Holmes, accompanied by his daughter, Mrs. Turner Sargent, came to England and received three honorary degrees—Cambridge gave him a Litt.D., Oxford a D.C.L., and Edinburgh an LL.D. The visit, his biographer wrote, "was in reality a triumphal tour; he was overwhelmed with attentions, so that it was only by extreme care that he extricated himself alive from the hospitalities of his British friends."[78] Gosse entertained him twice, once in London, on 1 June 1886, and again at Trinity College, Cambridge, where Gosse was Clark Lecturer, on 12 and 13 June. In his book *Our Hundred Days in Europe,* the account of his 1886 visit, Holmes recorded of the reception at the Gosses': "It was pleasant to meet artists and scholars,—the kind of company to which we are much used in our aesthetic city [Boston]. I found our host as agreeable at home as he was in Boston, where he became a favorite, both as a lecturer and a visitor."[79]

In September 1888 it was to Holmes of all his American friends that Gosse first wrote, in almost exultant mood, to share his discovery that his mother had been an American and that his great-great-grandmother, Lucy Hancock, was the aunt of Governor Hancock, one of the signers of the Declaration of Independence. Although this letter strikes, in its enthusiasm, an intimate note, the formal tone of other letters in the later years of their correspondence makes it clear that the relationship between them remained essentially that of the young aspirant and the celebrated old master, a relationship characterized on the one side by respectful attention and on the other by indulgent encouragement. Undoubtedly, however, there was affection on both sides and the friendship was one in which each had something of value to offer the other: Gosse felt honored by his intimacy with a man of Holmes's eminence, but Holmes may also have been flattered by the eager-

[77] See above, p. 14.

[78] John T. Morse, *Life and Letters of Oliver Wendell Holmes* (London: Sampson, Low, Marston, 1896), II, 65. But see Letter 121.

[79] Oliver Wendell Holmes, *Our Hundred Days in Europe* (Boston and New York: Houghton Mifflin, 1888), p. 80.

ness with which he was pursued by this charming and brilliant young representative of the English literary world.

Gosse's relationship with Richard Watson Gilder was of quite a different order. The two men were almost exact contemporaries, and they were not greatly dissimilar in talent. They first met, through the good offices of E. C. Stedman, in the winter of 1879–1880; the first meeting seems to have been on Sunday, 4 January 1880, and a month later, on 11 February, Gosse wrote enthusiastically to Stedman: "What good, dear people the Gilders are! Their acquaintance has been a real joy to us." In November 1881, as we have seen, *Scribner's* became the *Century Illustrated Monthly Magazine,* with Gilder as editor, and it was apparently at this moment that Gosse's appointment as London agent for the magazine became officially effective, although the arrangements for the appointment had been made some time previously and Gosse had already undertaken a number of commissions on behalf of the magazine. From this time onwards the letters passing between Gosse and Gilder are mostly full of business matters, and, mainly for this reason, only a small proportion of them have been included in the present selection.

During these years the *Century* sold widely in England and by 1900 its circulation was larger than that of any comparable British periodical.[80] From the beginning, the English edition was printed in London, but its contents were identical with those of the American edition, and Gilder as editor seems to have made no concessions whatsoever to British tastes and interests, or even to British sensitivities. Refusal to pirate English works and inability to pay competitive prices to English authors for new work had driven the magazine, while still *Scribner's Monthly,* to rely almost entirely on native American contributions. By 1880 it had become the settled policy of the magazine to publish American authors in preference to all others.[81] During the first years of its new career as the *Century,* when Roswell Smith had become virtually sole sowner and Gilder had assumed for the first time full editorial control, the magazine went through an expansive period when the policy favoring American authors seems to have been allowed to slip slightly into abeyance. Gosse's appointment was itself one sign of this, and for several years he was kept busy passing on his own and other people's ideas for individual articles or for whole series, writing his own numerous contributions, reading manuscripts submitted to him by other English authors, and trying to find authors for articles which the New York office wanted to commission. For these services Gosse received the substantial salary of £200 a year.

A good deal of the business correspondence was carried on between Gosse on the one hand and Gilder's subordinates, especially Robert Underwood

[80] See Herbert F. Smith, "The Editorial Influence of Richard Watson Gilder, 1870–1909" (unpublished Ph.D. dissertation, Rutgers University, 1961), p. 153.
[81] *Ibid.,* pp. 154–155.

Johnson, on the other; but Gosse often wrote to Gilder himself. A certain sharpness crept into the correspondence from time to time, as when Gosse felt that one of his own articles was being held over too long, that his advice was being foolishly ignored, or that some payment to him was over-due—or when Gilder, for his part, felt it necessary to take a firm line in laying down editorial policy. The turning point in Gosse's business relation-ship with the *Century* seems to have come during the winter of 1886–1887. Gilder and Gosse had clearly been at odds over the Civil War series which the magazine had been running; the series, in which appeared the memoirs of leading participants in the American Civil War, had been excessively long, and, to Gosse's mind, it was of peculiarly American interest. On 30 June 1885, exasperated at Gosse's criticisms, Gilder had expostulated: "Is there nothing interesting to you but art and literature?" In view of what we have already seen of Gosse's excitement at meeting Generals Sherman and Sheri-dan, it seems possible that Gilder may have misunderstood the source of Gosse's objections to the Civil War series. Perhaps the misunderstanding was deliberate, in the interests of avoiding a direct confrontation with Gosse over the much more fundamental issue of the extent to which the interests of the *Century*'s British readership were to be considered.

Such a confrontation, however, was not to be long delayed. Gosse was to learn, to his cost, that Gilder, for whatever reasons, intended to use his position in a quite deliberate way to encourage American writing of all kinds—journalism and belles-lettres quite as much as fiction and poetry. In November 1886 Gosse's mild suggestion that the *Century* might consider publishing a monthly literary letter from England was answered on Gilder's part by a passionate declaration of American rights to preferential treatment in American magazines. Gosse must have entered a strong protest against the rigidity of this view, for on 7 March 1887 Gilder wrote him a vigorous restatement of the *Century*'s position. Underlying the Civil War series, he declared, was "the purpose of helping to nationalize this gigantic country. . . . It is impregnating the mind of the entire nation, lately in civil conflict, as nothing else could have done in so brief a time, with the idea of nation-ality." He explained the sense in which the magazine did in fact follow the advice, "get the best," which Gosse had given him: granted that Tolstoy was the greatest novelist of the day, the *Century* nevertheless preferred to pub-lish George Washington Cable, because he was American; what they did do, however, was to send an American to interview Tolstoy and write an article about him. Gilder continued:

We do try to get the best, . . . but when you suggest a department of English Open Letters and when, through Mr. Unwin's wide literary acquaintance all sorts of mss. pour in upon us, in order to avoid misunderstanding we simply reassert the old idea of The Century and we hope in doing so you will not think us narrow, boycotting, or provincial. Is not the genuine provincialism the neglect of whatever may be admirable in the provinces for something which may be no better in the metropolis?[82]

From an American point of view, as Herbert Smith rightly points out,[83] Gilder deserved, and continues to deserve, considerable credit for his steadfast support of American writers. On the other hand, Gosse's natural impatience at this policy and at Gilder's justification of it is not hard to conceive. It must have become clear to both men that a magazine operating on such principles had no real need for a permanent English representative. From this time onwards Gosse's official association with the *Century* progressively declined. In 1888 his salary was cut from £200 to £100, and after 1893 it ceased altogether. In the late 1880's he sought the opportunity of remunerative employment with other American magazines, and in 1889 he accepted the post of London representative for S. S. McClure's Associated Literary Press, an appointment which seems to have lasted only four years. At the turn of the century he earned for a short while a substantial salary from the Appleton company, primarily for his work as general editor of their *Short Histories of the Literatures of the World*. Gosse did manage to find alternative sources of income as his work for the *Century* declined, but there is no doubt that he was for a time financially inconvenienced by this development. It is also clear that he was personally distressed by the policy which Gilder had so unequivocally laid down, and in exploring Gosse's relationship with Howells we shall see that in some of his most effective essays he spoke in strong terms of the evil effects which followed the introduction of narrowly patriotic criteria into the evaluation of literature.

There seems to have been no serious interruption of the friendship between Gosse and Gilder, despite the breakdown of Gosse's business connection with the *Century* and the constant irritations inevitably involved in conducting business by letter across the Atlantic. Early proof of Gilder's admiration for Gosse appears in his letter of 6 July 1882 to President Gilman of Johns Hopkins, where he suggests that Gosse and Dobson might be possible candidates for the Caroline Donovan Professorship of Literature at the University,[84] while in 1884 he not only assisted in the arrangements for Gosse's American visit but wrote to Professor Henry A. Beers recommending Gosse for the vacant professorship in English Literature at Yale.[85] Gilder and Gosse saw a good deal of each other during the two months which Gosse spent in America, and their friendship was renewed during the visits Gilder subsequently made to Europe. The "Book of Gosse," [86] for example, records

---

[82] Quoted in *ibid.*, pp. 377–378.
[83] *Ibid.*, p. 377.
[84] *Ibid.*, p. 320.
[85] Gilder to Beers, 8 April 1884, quoted in *ibid.*, p. 166.
[86] This is the phrase Gosse himself used in referring to the book in which he re-

34

a number of visits by the Gilders in 1895 and 1900, and on 15 September, 1900, after Gilder had left, Gosse wrote:

It was so delightful, dear Gilder, to see you again, and to see you so happy and so gay. You are one of those few in whom the passage of years tarnishes nothing of the brightness of friendship. You are always the same, always affectionate and keen and loyal. As one gets on in life one values more and more those who defy as you do the passage of the years.[87]

Gilder and Gosse were not to meet again, but the correspondence continued with undiminished cordiality, delicately balancing business and friendship, until just before Gilder's death in 1909. It seems possible to wonder, indeed, whether it was the admixture of business and the corresponding lack of real intimacy, of emotional involvement, which made it possible to sustain the cordiality over so many years. Gosse clearly felt that Gilder was misguided on many matters and it may very often have been only his sense of being in some measure an employee of Gilder and the *Century* which restrained his pen. On the other hand, Gilder, with his wide interests in such matters as social and political reform, undoubtedly found Gosse rather limited in outlook, too exclusively literary in his tastes. This was not, in fact, the most intimate of Gosse's American friendships, but it would appear to have been the most sustained, the most frequent, transatlantic correspondence in which he engaged.

A closer friendship, though of lesser historical importance, was that between Gosse and George Allison Armour—"American citizen, bibliophile, and patron of letters," as Charteris describes him[88]—who lived first in Chicago and, from 1895, at Princeton. Armour was one of the Americans who subscribed towards the erection of a memorial to Thomas Gray at Pembroke College, Cambridge, in 1885, and two of his letters to Gosse, who organized the scheme, still survive from this period.[89] The personal friendship between Gosse and Armour seems to have begun slightly later, however, at the end of 1886. On Gosse's side the correspondence was energetic and sometimes voluminous, although a great many of his letters were filled almost entirely with accounts of family excursions and holidays. Occasionally, as in a letter to Mrs. Armour of 11 September 1887, he treated of such topics in doggerel verse.[90] The friendship extended to all the members of both families, and

---

corded the names of the guests at his celebrated Sunday parties, from 17 November 1875 to 28 November 1920. The book contains the names of virtually every English celebrity, and many foreign ones, of Gosse's day. For an interesting study of it, see Arthur Waugh, "The Book of Gosse," *Fortnightly Review,* CXXXII (September 1932), 284–302.

[87] A.l.s., Gosse to Gilder, 15 September 1900 (GP).

[88] Charteris, *Life and Letters of Gosse,* p. 203.

[89] In bound collection, "Gray Memorial" (BC).

[90] Charteris, *Life and Letters of Gosse,* pp. 212–214.

Armour's youngest son, Edmund, was named after Gosse, who became his godfather. It was to celebrate Edmund's christening that Gosse wrote a delightful letter beginning: "To the youngest of the Armours."[91] Unfortunately, Armour himself was a much less eager correspondent than Gosse, and it is some indication of his shortcomings in this respect that Gosse was able to write on 5 April 1889: "But ah! how long it is since I have had the least little scrap of a letter from you. Your Correspondence for 1889 would not be enough to tie up a jam-pot with or to set light to a fire. Three initials on a diminutive atom of cardboard, do you call that correspondence?"[92] It is clear from Gosse's letters, however, that Armour was continually sending books and other presents across the Atlantic, and Charteris, in alluding to Armour's "strong distaste for correspondence," adds that "he had a more magnificent method of reply by arriving in person at unexpected seasons."[93]

Armour lived until 1935, and his friendship with Gosse was ended only by the latter's death in 1928, but in Gosse's later years there were few other of his old American friends with whom he could still correspond; Stedman had died in 1908, Gilder in 1909, Furness in 1912, James in 1916, and Howells in 1920. After the end of the First World War Gosse's total American correspondence seems to have become a mere fraction of what it had been in its richest period, during the 1880's, and the present selection ends with an autobiographical letter which Gosse wrote to the American critic Lewis Chase in 1917. Other late letters have survived, including some to or from such figures as Edith Wharton, Owen Wister, Edwin Arlington Robinson,[94] Hamlin Garland, and Stark Young, but none is of major importance, and rather than allow the last ten years of Gosse's life to be represented only by a few letters of little interest, it seemed preferable to leave those years completely unrepresented. Nonetheless, Gosse did continue to form friendships among the successive waves of younger Americans who came to Europe, often armed with letters of introduction from friends of an older generation. In the 1890's, for example, Gosse was on affectionate terms with Stedman's godson, Henry Harland, who began his literary career, under the pseudonym of Sidney Luska, as the author of stories about immigrant Jews in New York, but who subsequently came to Europe and, by a remarkable transformation, to the editorship of the *Yellow Book*. Early in the new century Gosse met Edith Wharton, and in 1911 a common admiration and

[91] A.l.s., Gosse to Armour, 12 September 1899 (PU).

[92] A.l.s. (PU).

[93] Charteris, *Life and Letters of Gosse*, p. 203.

[94] In the Brotherton Collection there is only one letter from Robinson to Gosse, dated 1 November 1923. Robinson had sent Gosse a copy of his first book (*The Torrent and the Night Before*) twenty-seven years earlier, but the two did not meet until 1923. In the letter, Robinson expresses both gratitude and surprise that Gosse liked *Roman Bartholow*: "I like to believe," he continued, "that the thing isn't wholly bad, knowing of course that many will insist that such a thing shouldn't be done in verses."

affection for Henry James brought them into more active correspondence and cooperation. A little later came the correspondence with Lewis Chase, and later still the friendships with Hamlin Garland and Stark Young. Neither Garland nor Young is represented in the present selection of letters, but both have left records of their acquaintance with Gosse. Garland visited Gosse in 1922, 1923, and 1924 and found that, despite his interest in American literature and art, he was almost entirely ignorant of recent trends in drama, in criticism, or in painting; at the same time, Garland admitted that Gosse was one of the few English writers or artists who did not retire into his shell but went out of his way to be helpful.[95] Young, in an article contributed to the *New Republic* just after Gosse's death, spoke warmly of the older man's kindness to him and quoted a letter which Gosse had written him only three years previously, in 1925:

It has given me quite an emotion to receive a personal greeting from you after so many years of silence—a book and a kind inscription. I have never forgotten you in the least, and I have followed you in some measure, reading of your movements and achievements, but I did not suppose that you remembered me after so many years, which must have had far more incidents in them for you than for me. I sit here, as I sat then, when you came to me from Texas, and I suppose that you have been wandering greatly, an American Ulysses, with many adventures. I have grown very old—that is all that I have done, outwardly.[96]

There remain the closest and most important of all Gosse's friendships with American men of letters, those with Henry James and with William Dean Howells. The relationship between Gosse and Howells will be separately discussed in the next section; that between Gosse and James stands a little apart from the central theme of the present selection. Their correspondence can scarcely be described as transatlantic, and James, in his relations with Gosse, was for all essential purposes a fellow member of the London literary world. Gosse must always have remained fully aware of the fact that James was an American, and this awareness become more explicit whenever occasion arose for the familiar linking of James's name with that of William Dean Howells. But for the most part their letters deal with personal matters, with social arrangements, with exchanges of notes on places visited or people encountered, and with literary gossip about mutual friends, especially Robert Louis Stevenson, and the current London scene. As with so many of James's friendships, it is in any case impossible to reconstruct the full range and quality of the relationship between Gosse and James because so few of the

[95] See Hamlin Garland, *My Friendly Contemporaries* (New York: Macmillan, 1932), pp. 504–505, and *Afternoon Neighbors* (New York: Macmillan, 1934), pp. 32–34, 183–184; also, an a.l.s., undated, Garland to Gosse (RU).

[96] Stark Young, "Sir Edmund Gosse," *New Republic,* LV (6 June 1928), 72; see also a.l.s., Young to Gosse, 23 July 1913 (BC).

former's letters seem to have survived the latter's famous backyard bonfire of his papers. Many letters from James to Gosse have fortunately survived; some of the most interesting among these were published by Percy Lubbock, others will appear in Leon Edel's forthcoming edition of James's correspondence. All that has been done here is to print a few letters on either side of the Gosse-James correspondence, not in any hope of being able to give an adequate representation of the relationship between the two men but rather as a bare reminder of its existence and of its importance.

Gosse and Howells

Fortunately the materials have survived for a remarkably complete reconstruction of Gosse's relationship with William Dean Howells, perhaps the most intimate of his American friendships and certainly the one which throws most light on the contemporary condition of Anglo-American literary relations. Gosse first met Howells when the latter came to Europe on account of his own and his elder daughter's health in the summer of 1882. At this time Gosse, not quite thirty-three years of age, was already remarkably successful as a poet and as a critic. His reputation, however, could not compare with that of Howells who, at forty-five, was an established literary figure on both sides of the Atlantic, had just completed ten years as editor of the *Atlantic Monthly*, and had already published a number of travel books and plays and several important novels, including the much discussed *A Modern Instance,* then being serialized in the *Century.* It was natural, therefore, that Gosse should make the first advance and that in doing so he should invoke the name of Richard Watson Gilder and mention his own recent appointment as English representative of the *Century.*

Howells found Gosse's letter waiting for him when he arrived in London and replied at once in friendly terms. Gosse promptly sent Howells and his wife an invitation for the following Sunday, 6 August, adding, perhaps a little disingenuously, "Our friend Henry James tells me that you dislike, as I heartily do, Society with a capital S." The visit, which is recorded in the Book of Gosse, was apparently a great success, for on 8 August Howells wrote accepting a further invitation for Sunday, 20 August.[97] Just over two weeks later Howells wrote in extremely affectionate terms, joking about the possibilities of his being adopted as a member of the Gosse household; Gosse replied no less affectionately, using for the first time the term "giggling" which was so often to occur in their subsequent correspondence, and concluding with a joke about Howells's democratic outlook. The same letter contains warm and discriminating praise of *A Modern Instance,* "altogether the greatest work of fiction that America has given us since the death of

[97] See Letter 25, n. 1.

Hawthorne,"[98] Howells's "angel-visit," wrote Gosse on 12 October, had left him "permanently richer," and there can be no doubt of the depth and sincerity of the intimacy which the two men had so quickly and so readily established—an intimacy fostered, no doubt, by Gosse's excitement in the friendship of an older and more famous man and by the exhilaration of Howells's own mood as he rested from the onerous duties of editorship, saw his own and his daughter's health rapidly improve, and enjoyed for the first time the pleasures of international celebrity.

Howells at that time [wrote Gosse after his friend's death almost forty years later] was, what he always remained, affable, gentle, and exquisitely responsive; but he possessed what those who have known him only in later years may not be so ready to recognize—an aëry playfulness, a sort of roguishness which faded from him in years of anxiety and grief. The success of his bouquet of little novels made him something of a lion in London that autumn, and he enjoyed his literary fame with the most unaffected pleasure.[99]

Gosse and Howells were not always to see eye to eye, however, or even fully to appreciate each other's attitudes towards literature and life. While Howells was in Switzerland and Italy during the winter of 1882–1883 two misunderstandings arose, one private, the other more public, neither deeply or permanently harmful to the friendship so recently but so auspiciously begun. Howells was at this time writing his novel *A Woman's Reason,* in which the hero, a naval officer, is sent to Hong Kong and later marooned on a desert island; he had already sought advice from a naval officer, and on 12 October 1882 Gosse offered to supply some background material on Hong Kong in the shape of some government "blue-books," recently published, which presented "quite a Zolaesque study of life in the low quarters of the town." Howells, replying from Villeneuve on 26 October, asked Gosse to send the blue-books, not so much for present use but rather as a matter of general interest: ". . . the trade of novel writing is so corrupting that before I have done with it, I am sure that I shall invent some young man who will at least *wish* to visit all the worst places in Hong Kong." The phrasing here, suggesting an interest in the "Zolaesque" material for its own sake, perhaps casts a certain doubt on the account which Gosse gave of the affair after Howells's death; it seems quite likely that Howells was shocked and that he showed his displeasure, or at least his embarrassment, by failing to acknowledge receipt of the blue-books, but Gosse may have exaggerated a little in saying that Howells was so "horrified and disturbed"

[98] Letters 27 and 28.
[99] Gosse, "The Passing of William Dean Howells," *Living Age,* CCCVI (10 July 1920), 98–99 (reprinted from the London *Sunday Times*).

that he "burned" them and "put away all thought of writing about Hong Kong."[100]

The other episode was not so much a misunderstanding as a straightforward difference of opinion. In the November 1882 issue of the *Century* Howells published his article "Henry James, Jr.," in which he made, in the course of his argument and not as his main point, the first of those attacks on British writing which were to diminish his popularity in England and to make him a mildly notorious figure there during the 1880's and early 1890's. Howells, like James himself, had been greatly impressed by the work of the new continental novelists, and it was largely with their example in mind that he declared in "Henry James, Jr.":

> The art of fiction has, in fact, become a finer art in our day than it was with Dickens and Thackeray. We could not suffer the confidential attitude of the latter now, nor the mannerism of the former, any more than we could endure the prolixity of Richardson or the coarseness of Fielding. These great men are of the past—they and their methods and interests. . . . The new school . . . studies human nature much more in its wonted aspects, and finds its ethical and dramatic examples in the operation of lighter but not really less vital motives. The moving accident is certainly not its trade; and it prefers to avoid all manner of dire catastrophes. It is largely influenced by French fiction in form; but it is the realism of Daudet rather than the realism of Zola that prevails with it.[101]

The essay aroused much protest from English readers and critics, who seized almost exclusively on the apparent slight to Dickens and Thackeray,[102] and it is clear that Gosse was generally in sympathy with their views. As recently appointed English representative for the *Century* Gosse seems to have been somewhat alarmed by the controversy over both Howells's article and the rather hostile article on England by Charles Dudley Warner which had appeared in the same issue,[103] and he was apparently responsible for the statement in the *Athenaeum* to the effect that Howells would shortly explain at

---

[100] *Ibid.*, p. 99.

[101] Howells, "Henry James, Jr.," *Century, XXV* (November 1882), 28.

[102] See Mildred Howells, ed., *Life in Letters of William Dean Howells* (Garden City, New York: Doubleday, Doran, 1928), I, 326–328; W. D. Howells, *Criticism and Fiction and Other Essays,* ed. Clara and Rudolf Kirk (New York: New York University Press, 1959), pp. 93–97; Olov W. Fryckstedt, *In Quest of America: A Study of Howells' Early Development as a Novelist* (Cambridge, Massachusetts: Harvard University Press, 1958), pp. 255–260; E. H. Cady, *The Road to Realism: The Early Years (1837–1885) of William Dean Howells* (Syracuse, New York: Syracuse University Press, 1956), pp. 218–222.

[103] Charles Dudley Warner, "England," *Century, XXV* (November 1882), 134–141.

greater length his views on Dickens and Thackeray.[104] In his letters to Howells himself, his first response to the essay was critical but rather light-hearted. In the "Doggerel by a candid friend" which he appended to his letter of 8 November, he acutely, if a little unfairly, drew attention to the fact that Howells's own practice as a novelist was in line with that of the "new school" which he praised as a critic; but in his next letter, on 14 November, Gosse apologized for its "flippant" predecessor and went on to discuss seriously the views which Howells had expressed and the criticisms which he had provoked. He very sensibly suggested that both Howells and his English critics, including himself, tended to argue from a standpoint of national partiality, and that, if this prejudice could be removed, they would probably find themselves in general agreement, at least about Dickens.

Gosse was undoubtedly right about the existence of prejudice and sensitivity on both sides. In a letter of 13 March 1883 to Thomas Sergeant Perry, Howells commented on the hypersensitivity of the British. All that is required to make the British lion roar, he wrote, is "to have insinuated that all English novels are not perfection. One of my London friends actually asked me if I didn't hate Thackeray and Dickens because they were English!"[105] The previous autumn he told another American friend that he had found Gosse "truly grieved at what I had said of England in *The Fearful Responsibility,* and I was brought to book for it by several others."[106] On the other hand, it seems clear that at this time and for many years to come Howells was so impatient with England, with English society—despite the warmth of his reception in 1882—and even with English writing that it seems fair to call him an Anglophobe. The references in *A Fearful Responsibility* —references, for example, to those "generous and amiable Englishmen" who "never take advantage of anyone they believe stronger than themselves, or fail in consideration for those they imagine their superiors"[107]—were certainly not gracious, and it was less than a year before he came to England

[104] *Athenaeum,* 25 November 1882, p. 700. The passage, in the "Literary Gossip" column, contains several quotations from Howells's letter to Gosse of 16 November 1882, but whereas Howells had said that he would write about Dickens and Thackeray "if the time and chance ever come together," the *Athenaeum* report speaks of his being "determined" to express himself "on the earliest opportunity." Cf. Cady, *The Road to Realism,* p. 129, and Howells's letter to Charles Dudley Warner, 4 March 1883: "I don't know how you ever got the notion that I was going to hurry to 'explain' what I said, unless it was from that extraordinary and unauthorized statement in the *Athenaeum.* I wrote Gosse that when I got time I should like to say my say of D. & T.; but I am far too lazy and too busy to see the hour of doing it" (Mildred Howells, *Life in Letters of Howells,* I, 336).

[105] Mildred Howells, *Life in Letters of Howells,* I, 338.

[106] Howells to Charles Fairchild, 23 October 1882, as quoted in Fryckstedt, *In Quest of America,* p. 258 n.

[107] Howells, *A Fearful Responsibility* (Boston: Osgood, 1881), p. 100.

that Howells wrote to Colonel T. W. Higginson: "What a great thing it is not to be an Englishman! It's a sort of patent of nobility."[108] More than twenty years later, on 11 January 1903, Howells wrote to the Southern poet Madison Cawein commenting on Gosse's introduction to the English edition of Cawein's poems: "I did not find Gosse's introduction warm enough, but it is much for an Englisman to be even tepid toward a man of another nation."[109] Howells may have had ample justification for his irritation with England, with the English literary world, and, indeed, with Gosse himself, but it is not hard to see why his English friends were sometimes distressed at his views.

The differences between Gosse and Howells are worth looking at in a little more detail because they touch at so many points on some of the central transatlantic literary and cultural controversies of the time, and because they are not to be explained simply in terms of national prejudice or of literary taste or of political principle, but only in terms of a combination of these elements. In the great nineteenth-century debate over realism and romance Howells, as the "Henry James, Jr." article suggests, was the leading American champion of realism, while Gosse aligned himself firmly with the supporters of romance; his one substantial adventure into fiction, *The Secret of Narcisse,* was explicitly subtitled "a Romance." In the essay "The Limits of Realism in Fiction," included in the *Questions at Issue* volume of 1893, Gosse did acknowledge the distinction of some of the writers of the realist school, but it was with apparent satisfaction that he looked forward to a reaction against the school:

All points to a reaction in France; and in Russia, too, if what we hear is true, the next step will be one toward the mystical and the introspective. In America it would be rash for a foreigner to say what signs of change are evident. The time has hardly come when we look to America for the symptoms of literary initiative. But it is my conviction that the limits of realism have been reached; that no great writer who has not already adapted [sic] the experimental system will do so; and that we ought now to be on the outlook to welcome (and, of course, to persecute) a school of novelists with a totally new aim, part of whose formula must unquestionably be a concession to the human instinct for mystery and beauty.[110]

The phraseology here is revealing of Gosse's fundamental artistic predilections; the phrase about "mystery and beauty" seems especially reminiscent of the Pre-Raphaelitism to which he had been attracted as a young man, and even at the end of his life, in the essay on Howells published in *Silhouettes* (1925), Gosse was still expressing precisely the same criticism of realism

[108] Howells to Higginson, 14 August 1881, as quoted in Fryckstedt, *In Quest of America,* p. 257 n.
[109] Mildred Howells, *Life in Letters of Howells,* II, 165.
[110] Gosse, *Questions at Issue* (London: Heinemann, 1893), p. 154.

and of its defenders. Howells, said Gosse in that late essay, "sacrificed every-thing to a theory of realism," surrendering "the fine instincts of an artist in favour of an obstinate, and, as it may seem to us, provincial, concentration on the outside of the American cup and platter."[111] As a critic—and Gosse called him " a very bad critic, one of the worst"—Howells had said many wise things, especially in *Criticism and Fiction,* but in later years "he became more and more the slave of his prejudices. He excused Hawthorne for his romance because he was an American, but he was pitiless to Scott and Thack-eray, and indeed to all English novelists."[112]

In thus shifting the ground of his attack from realism to nationalism Gosse revealed what seems to have been the fundamental source of his irri-tation with Howell's critical writings, and we may recall at this point his disagreement with Gilder on a similar question. The strength of Gosse's op-position to Howells's nationalistic tendencies appears even more strongly when he comes to sum up what he saw as Howells's "critical heresies":

He indulged in a cluster of heresies, such as that it is snobbery to pretend to admire any literature except that of our own day; that American poetry is sufficient for all purposes, and that therefore no manly citizen needs visit "the mausoleum of the British poets"; that romance in any form is puerile and even immoral; that sex ought never to be emphasised; and that the American writer not only should satisfy, but does satisfy, every requirement of the American reader. Accordingly, if somebody from St. Louis writes "a real, downright American" book, even though it is a crude affair, that book must be praised to excess and preferred to the best product of an effete Europe.[113]

The reputation of Howells as novelist and as critic stands higher today than it did in 1925, when Gosse was writing, and it may seem obvious from our present perspective that Gosse was here displaying a serious misunder-standing of Howells's aims and achievements and an equally serious failure to appreciate the generosity of his response to a wide range of continental novelists and to a few English writers, notably Hardy. In fact, although Gosse did somewhat misrepresent Howells's position, he was not without justification for his criticisms of Howells's adherence to a principle of liter-ary nationalism. Howells was deeply and consciously involved throughout his life, and especially during his editorships of the *Atlantic* and *Harper's* in the 1870's and 1880's, in the struggle to establish in the United States a native literature and literary tradition which should be firmly independent, and clearly seen to be independent, of the literature of Great Britain. The whole development of a school of American realists, a development in which

[111] Gosse, *Silhouettes* (London: Heinemann, 1925), pp. 195, 199; the essay first appeared in the London *Sunday Times.*
[112] *Ibid.,* pp. 195, 196.
[113] *Ibid.,* p. 195.

Howells played the leading role, was intimately bound up with this concern for an autonomous American literature.

Gosse encountered the problem of American literary nationalism on a number of other occasions. When his essay "Has America Produced a Poet?" first appeared in the *Forum* in 1888, as a review of Stedman's *Anthology of American Poetry*, it aroused a good deal of controversy. Gosse's argument, politely but firmly enforced, was that there was as yet no American poet of comparable stature to the "twelve worthies" among the great English poets of the past;[114] when the editor of the *Critic* invited a number of American poets to answer Gosse's charges, some of them demonstrated considerable patriotic indignation, advancing ludicrous claims for some of their native predecessors, and almost all of them felt that Gosse had not done justice to Emerson.[115] Gosse may have been saddened by the controversy, but he can hardly have been surprised. In the opening paragraph of the essay, which was subsequently collected in *Questions at Issue* (1893), Gosse recognizes that the title of the essay might itself be regarded as unduly provocative, but he declares that the choice had not been his but his American editor's; moreover, at the end of his introductory remarks, which include some highly complimentary allusions to Stedman's distinction as a critic, Gosse goes on to make one of his most eloquent statements against the "patriotic fallacy" in literature:

> One word more in starting. If we admit into our criticism any patriotic or political prejudice, we may as well cease to wrangle on the threshold of our discussion. I cannot think that American current criticism is quite free from this taint of prejudice. In this, if I am right, Americans sin no more nor less than the rest of us English, and French; but in America, I confess, the error seems to me to be occasionally more serious than in Europe. . . . Patriotism is a meaningless term in literary criticism. To prefer what has been written in our own city, or state, or country, for that reason alone, is simply to drop the balance and to relinquish all claims to form a judgment. The true and reasonable lover of literature refuses to be constrained by any meaner or homelier bond than that of good writing. His brain and his taste persist in being independent of his heart, like those of the German soldier who fought through the campaign before Paris, and who was shot at last with an Alfred de Musset, thumbed and scored, in his pocket.[116]

It is a sensible and moderately stated point of view, and one which Gosse with his wide knowledge of literature other than of his own country, could propound with particular authority.

[114] Gosse, "Has America Produced a Poet?" *Forum*, VI (October 1888), 176–186.
[115] *Critic*, X (24 November 1888), 251–253; (1 December), 277–278; (15 December), 304.
[116] Gosse, *Questions at Issue*, pp. 74–75.

However, this was not the view which prevailed. In the late nineteenth century, Anglo-American literary relations were as close as they had ever been, and were conducted on a more equal footing than in the past; yet the general climate was one of extreme tension. Personal and national pride was all too easily hurt, offense all too readily taken, and a mild critical observation might become the focal point of a fierce international controversy. It was natural that the Americans, self-consciously aware of their former junior and even colonial status, should be the more apt to take fire at the first hint of attack. English writers could be equally touchy, but they had less cause to be anxious about their cultural respectability; they were not unaware, however, of the extreme sensitivity of American literary men in their attitudes towards England, and they often deplored this sensitivity, in terms similar to those used by Gosse, as reinforcing that very stigma of provinciality which the Americans were so anxious to remove. Ironically enough, the wide circulation in Great Britain of such excellent American magazines as the *Century,* the *Atlantic,* and *Harper's* provided increased opportunity and scope for such incidents, although in the longer view their popularity undoubtedly contributed to a much wider knowledge, appreciation, and acceptance of American writing by the British reading public.

The search for a native American literature and tradition was not new in the 1880's—it had not been new even at the time of Emerson's "American Scholar" address—and there had already been many instances of mutual transatlantic recrimination on literary as on other issues. Seen in this context, Howells's surprise over the controversy provoked by his *Century* article on James may appear to have been a little disingenuous. In attacking Dickens and Thackeray, with whatever respectful qualifications, he was taking up a slightly unorthodox critical position, and his arguments, coming from an American source, could not fail to strike, intentionally or otherwise, a nationalistic note. Closely involved in the issue of nationality, however, was a further question that related less to simple patriotism than to actual political and social differences between Britain and the United States at that period. In his letter to Howells of 14 November 1882, Gosse had attempted to define what he saw as the basic area of disagreement between Howells and himself:

I think I shall always do battle with you on your favourite literary standpoint, that the intellectual product of a democracy must be finer than that of a monarchy. I am sure the inmost reason of your dislike to Dickens and Thackeray is that they flourished in a corrupt and pestilent royalty. But I really think the muses care very little about the divine right of the masses, and are likely for a long time yet to feel more at home among the old civilizations than in the new. This, I suppose, is just the one theme on which we shall always be content to differ.

Howells in his reply rejected Gosse's suggestion as to the reason for his dislike of Dickens and Thackeray, but various references in later letters make it plain that this political question did remain a fundamental point of difference between the two friends, though one which was rarely allowed to come to the surface except in a humorous context.

The area of their disagreement is, in any case, sufficiently defined in their critical writings. In *Questions at Issue* Gosse expressed his apprehension—provoked by the controversy over his essay "Has America Produced a Poet?" —over what might happen to literary taste in a democracy:

One danger which I have long foreseen from the spread of the democratic sentiment, is that of the traditions of literary taste, the canons of literature, being reversed with success by a popular vote. Up to the present time, in all parts of the world, the masses of uneducated or semi-educated persons, who form the vast majority of readers, though they cannot and do not appreciate the classics of their race, have been content to acknowledge their traditional supremacy. Of late there have seemed to me to be certain signs, especially in America, of a revolt of the mob against our literary masters. In the less distinguished American newspapers which reach me, I am sometimes startled by the boldness with which a great name, like Wordsworth's or Dryden's, will be treated with indignity. If literature is to be judged by a *plébiscite* and if the *plebs* recognises its power, it will certainly by degrees cease to support reputations which give it no pleasure and which it cannot comprehend. The revolution against taste, once begun, will land us in irreparable chaos. It is, therefore, high time that those who recognize that there is no help for us in literature outside the ancient laws and precepts of our profession, should vigorously support the fame of those fountains of inspiration, the impeccable masters of English.[117]

Similar arguments appear in Gosse's essay "The Influence of Democracy on Literature," another of the papers reprinted in *Questions at Issue*. Here Gosse seems to have been deliberately taking issue with some of the views which Howells had been propagating since 1886 in the "Editor's Study" department of *Harper's*, and which were brought together in 1891 in the volume entitled *Criticism and Fiction*.[118] Howells himself was not mentioned in Gosse's essay until the very last pages, when Gosse, in what might be considered a partial defense of his friend's work, took it upon himself to explain Howells's great popularity in America, "except in a certain Europeanized clique," and his unpopularity in England, where many people felt an "instinctive dislike of him, amounting to a blind hereditary prejudice." It was necessary to understand, Gosse wrote, that Howells, a "great novelist," was "absolutely inspired by the democratic spirit," and that his attitude to England was one not of "rebellion" but of indifference:

117 *Ibid.*, pp. 110–111.
118 See Howells, *Criticism and Fiction*, ed. Clara and Rudolf Kirk.

He is superficially irritated at European pretensions, but essentially, and when he becomes absorbed in his work as a creative artist, he ignores everything but that vast level of middle-class of American society out of which he sprang, which he faithfully represents, and which adores him. To English readers, the novels of Mr. Howells must always be something of a puzzle, even if they partly like them, and as a rule they hate them. But to the average educated American who has not been to Europe, these novels appear the most deeply experienced and ripely sympathetic product of modern literature.[119]

In this passage Gosse's prejudices have merged with his critical acumen to produce an extremely shrewd "placing" comment, one which gives Howells his due of sympathy and even admiration, which recognizes that his Anglophobia is merely a by-product of his nationalism, but which closes on a note of severely delimiting irony.

Gosse's criticism of Howells in "The Influence of Democracy on Literature" makes nonsense of any suggestion that he spoke out only in the two articles written after his friend's death. What emerges much more strongly from the two later essays is the warmth of Gosse's friendship and affection for this most intimate of his transatlantic correspondents. Both the late essays are highly critical of Howells's work, but Gosse wrote of him, in "W. D. Howells," the piece reprinted in *Silhouettes* (1925), that he was "the soul of generosity and sweetness, tremblingly alive, like an excited child, ardently devoted to literature as he understood it, wholly without guile."[120] We have already quoted from "The Passing of William Dean Howells" part of the charming and moving description of Howells as he appeared during his first visit to London in the summer of 1882; the passage continues:

I remember his saying about himself that reality always seemed to him 'more irridescent and beautiful' than anticipation, and doubtless this came from his peculiarly sensitive and apprehensive nature. Hence, in that season of 1882— having dreaded London, and feared its unseen inhabitants—we seemed to him to be a sort of angels moving in a golden glory because we were, as who could help being, enthusiastic and responsive. He was a Queen of Sheba to Lowell's Solomon. In process of time, perhaps, the beauty faded; but nothing could tarnish it in 1882, and the shine of it made him a happy man.[121]

"In process of time, perhaps, the beauty faded": this might be the phrase to apply to almost all of Gosse's American friendships. From 1890 onwards Gosse and Howells seem to have corresponded only very intermittently. In 1894 Howells was in Europe with his daughter Mildred; he passed through London early in June without seeing Gosse, and although he had intended to return to London after a visit to Paris he was prevented from

[119] Gosse, *Questions at Issue*, pp. 65–66.
[120] Gosse, *Silhouettes*, p. 199.
[121] Gosse, "The Passing of Howells" *Living Age*, CCCVI (10 July 1920), 99.

doing so by the fatal illness of his father, which summoned him directly back to the United States. Three years later Howells seems to have spent two days in London while on another visit to Europe but to have seen only Henry James—"continuously and exclusively," as he says.[122] Howells did see Gosse, however, when he came to England in 1904, again with his daughter, to receive an honorary degree at Oxford, and he visited Gosse's home on 17 and 24 April that year.[123] In 1910 Gosse wrote expressing his sympathy on the death of Mrs. Howells, and in his reply Howells addressed him as "dear friend of happy days." That summer Howells and his daughter were again in London. He and Gosse seem to have seen a good deal of each other. They exchanged notes on the academies of arts and letters which were being established in their respective countries and, as in the past, they exchanged books, Gosse expressing slightly critical appreciation of *Questionable Shapes* (1903) and Howells declaring himself full of admiration for Gosse's autobiographical *Father and Son* (1907).[124]

In 1911 both men were deeply involved in the attempt to secure for Henry James the Nobel Prize for Literature. The scheme seems to have occurred independently to Gosse and to Edith Wharton late in 1910 and to have been set on foot following Mrs. Wharton's approach to Gosse, through Gaillard Lapsley, in February 1911. Howells did his best to bring American pressure to bear on the Nobel Committee, Gosse did the same in England, and Edith Wharton and Kipling also took an active part in the campaign. Their efforts were unavailing, however, and the prize for that year went to the Belgian poet and playwright Maurice Maeterlinck. Late that summer Howells was back in London and shortly after his arrival he wrote to Gosse, who had been Librarian of the House of Lords since 1904, with a sly allusion to recent political events: "Could you look in some day on your way to or from the ruins of the House of Lords? It ought to be spelled Lloyds, I suppose, now." It was a typical Howells remark, even to its "democratic" bias, and Gosse, who took his office very seriously, may not have found it entirely to his taste. In any case, he was away from London at the time and he and Howells did not meet. Nor, it seems, did they ever meet again.

Gosse, it is clear, came closer to Howells, at least for a brief period from 1882 to about 1886, than he ever came to any other American, even to Armour or James. But despite the deep emotional sympathy which they established during those early years, when Gosse was still a young man and Howells was enjoying his first great success, their friendship seems never to have been a genuine meeting of minds. They had both won their success in the face of very considerable early difficulties; they shared certain admirations and friendships, notably for Henry James; but as a result of profound

[122] Mildred Howells, *Life in Letters of Howells*, II, 83.
[123] *Ibid.*, II, 199; also, the Book of Gosse.
[124] See Letters 183, 181, 182.

differences of taste, temperament, and nationality, the common love of literature which had originally brought them together tended more and more to drive them apart. The renewal of their friendship in 1904 and subsequent years seems to have followed a mellowing of Howells's attitudes towards England and the English; it is certainly clear that there was no significant modification of their differences over questions of political and esthetic principles.

Conclusion: The Intermittent Dialogue

In the obituary notice which he contributed to the *New Republic*, Stark Young spoke of his friendship with Gosse as "a record of kindness such as cannot be common, of an old grace and style almost gone out of the world, and of a warmth of feeling that I can feel yet, so charming, gentle, and impish and penetrating." Young recalled that when he first went to London in 1911 he had a letter of introduction to Gosse from Madison Cawein, and that Gosse invited him to call at the House of Lords:

I remember being handed in, past ropes and tourists, by attendants and officials and coming into the presence of a rather small man, with clear features and a wonderful fairness about the skin and hair and eyes. He spoke quickly, little streams of patter, with a kind of eagerness, and little spurts of self-assertion that came from shyness and a high-strung organism. I must have stayed an outrageous while, and I remember that I thought quite simply, country style, that he was a sweet man, like my father or some cousin. I made, evidently, a happy response on one of his favorite little matters for pride—I learned later from his "Father and Son" what a talent for geography he boasted—his exact knowledge of all my little home villages, rivers and states brought me to wonder and compliments, which in turn brought on more American geography from him. At any rate, there was a dinner soon afterward, one Sunday, with Sir Alfred East, the painter, and two or three other people who were Americans or knew America, and I learned from Mrs. Gosse somewhat more about the library call. She was so glad, Mrs. Gosse said, that Edmund liked me. He asked people first to the library instead of to his house, to see what they would be like; and she quite dreaded his state after seeing them. There was one young man with a letter—really Edmund came home in a rage, it was difficult.[125]

Young saw Gosse again during a visit to London in 1919, and in his article he records some of Gosse's after-dinner conversation:

He talked about America, not without prejudice, and with some of the traditional ironic humor that seemed a trifle out of date; and of America in the War; he had been on a committee for propaganda, he said, and the Americans had swallowed the propaganda hook beyond one's wildest hopes. He spoke of Henry James' enthusiasm, how once he and, I think he said, Mr. Balfour, had seen Henry James coming toward them with extended hands—"Whatever hap-

[125] Young, "Sir Edmund Gosse," *New Republic*, LV (6 June 1928), 71.

pens," Henry James had said, "remember I'm doubly as English as you are," which Mr. Gosse thought poorly of, nobody wanted Mr. James to be doubly English. He gave an account of a visit to his library of the wife of an American poet he knew by correspondence, she had been an "ebullient person, too terrible." He gave a wicked account of a great English statesman's story of how he tried to escape being honored by a certain American university, whose president pursued him to his very room in the hotel and pinned a degree on him; which I promised never to tell.[126]

It is understandable that Gosse's humor, so dependent upon "traditional" British prejudices, should have struck his young American companion as "a trifle out of date." There is nothing very surprising, however, about Gosse's lack of sympathy with many American customs, attitudes, and assumptions. His lack of a formal education seems to have made him all the more jealous of the dignity of that English literary world in which he himself made so large a figure, and it is clear from his reactions to Howells's "attack" on Dickens and Thackeray, and from almost everything he wrote on American literature, that he shared in some degree that distrust and dislike of American culture which was customary among educated Englishmen in the late nineteenth century. Gosse was also committed to a more narrowly esthetic conception of life and art than any of his American friends, and Gilder's remark about his being interested only in art and literature may point to a fundamental difference in outlook of which others among Gosse's American friends may well have been aware. In his later years Gosse's alienation from American manners and American thought seems to have increased: Hamlin Garland thought him lamentably out of touch, and his letters show how little he was capable of comprehending American attitudes towards Britain at moments of crisis such as the Boer War and how fundamentally out of sympathy he became with the democratic character of American society. As the years passed, Gosse apparently experienced a progressive disenchantment with America and even with Americans—except with those like James who were thoroughly Anglicized—and this development is perhaps to be linked with the process by which Gosse took on the character of a British national institution. We have seen, however, that the conception of Gosse as a pillar of respectability and literary orthodoxy is not wholly adequate, and although he was too deeply rooted in British attitudes and traditions to be always in sympathy with the American writing of his day, there is no doubt that he endeavored to maintain a strict sense of critical proportion.

But what is much more remarkable than Gosse's antagonism towards particular aspects of American life is the facility with which he established his numerous American friendships, and the intimacy and affection, implying a considerable surrender of reserve on both sides, which marked his rela-

[126] *Ibid.*

tionships with people as diverse as Stedman, Gilder, Furness, Harland, Howells, and James. Some of the friendships were not especially close and a few of them seem to have been deliberately initiated by Gosse purely in accordance with his desire or need to know famous people and to be known to them. Yet the course of Gosse's relationship with Oliver Wendell Holmes may serve to remind us that even acquaintances of this kind sometimes ripened into genuine affection, and it says much for Gosse that although his American friendships may sometimes have fallen into disrepair, not one of them seems to have ended in anger or disappointment. During his visit of 1884–1885 Gosse seems to have been greatly impressed both by the Americans he met and by the country itself. In the interview he gave to the *Pall Mall Gazette* on his return from the United States early in 1885 Gosse spoke of America as "the most interesting country in the world." The American, he declared, "is much more cultivated than the average Englishman. He reads books more"; the Englishman crossing the Atlantic should start with an understanding that "democracy is the real thing in America."[127] The diary Gosse kept while he was in the United States reveals an interest in American scenes and personalities—Concord, Salem, General Sherman, Whitman, and Whittier—for their own sakes; it reveals too that he did not take his success for granted but was greatly flattered by it, just as he was flattered by hobnobbing with Civil War generals and distinguished American men of letters.

"We are expecting the Gosses at our home early in December, and have plans for making them like this country," wrote Howells to James a few months before Gosse's visit in 1884, "which ought to succeed at least so long as they are in it."[128] Gosse did like America; he also liked, with a deep and abiding affection, a few particular American friends; and he occupies, for these and other reasons, an extremely interesting position in the history of Anglo-American literary relationships. From the time of the 1884–1885 visit onwards Gosse's name was well known in the United States, and the American literary world continued throughout his long career to take full, if not always flattering, notice of his work. His many American friendships gave him a particularly central role to play, and the friendships were themselves the symptom of an interest in America and American literature which was uncommon though by no means unique among English men of letters. Gosse's critical observations on American writers are shrewd and still worth consulting, and he had, from the first, an awareness—unusual for his own day—of the possibilities, in the struggle for literary reputation, of calling in the New World to redress the balance of the Old. If his relationship with

[127] From the *Pall Mall Gazette,* as quoted in *Critic,* ns III (14 March 1885), 129–130.

[128] Howells to James, 22 August 1884, in Mildred Howells, *Life in Letters of Howells,* I, 367–368.

America and with Americans was not uniformly happy, the blame was by no means entirely on his side. Gosse was often unduly sensitive about his work and his position, and he could be difficult and even "feline" in both his public and his personal life. But his views on romance and realism and on the effects of democracy on literature are not without substance and it is easy to understand his irritation with what must have seemed to him the puerility and self-betraying provinciality of American literary nationalism, especially as it affected Gilder's editorial policy and distorted the genius of Howells.

EDITORIAL PROCEDURES

The letters included in this volume have been chosen by the editors from a much larger body of correspondence available to them in libraries and private collections both in England and in the United States. A great deal of this correspondence, as might have been expected from a period before the telephone came into everyday use, consisted of brief notes intended simply to convey greetings or to make appointments and other social arrangements; such communications could readily be discarded. In choosing among more substantial items, the principal criteria of selection have been the intrinsic interest of a letter and its bearing upon the central theme of Anglo-American literary relationships. In accordance with the first criterion, a great many of the letters which passed between Gosse and the editorial staff of the *Century* have been omitted; these letters are of considerable interest to anyone concerned with the history and conduct of the *Century*, but it seemed sufficent for this particular volume to include a selection which would be adequately representative of Gosse's work for the *Century* without subjecting the reader to a mass of minor detail. Application of the second criterion has resulted in the omission of most of Gosse's letters to George Allison Armour: the friendship between the two men was intimate and long-lived, but Armour, although a devoted bibliophile, was not himself a man of letters—he seems, indeed, to have been a very reluctant correspondent—and Gosse's letters to him seldom introduce topics of general interest.

The same principles have operated, though for varying reasons, in selecting letters from the other correspondences in which Gosse engaged. One correspondence which has been printed almost in its entirety, however, is that between Gosse and Howells. This was the deepest and most enduring of Gosse's friendships with American men of letters and the correspondence is undoubtedly the most revealing of transatlantic literary relationships. Since it is happily a correspondence in which most letters on both sides appear to have survived, it has served to provide a continuing thread throughout most of the book. Although the relationship between Gosse and James was comparable in duration and intimacy to that between Gosse and Howells, their correspondence has not been so comprehensively preserved, and for the reasons given on pages 37–38 above, only a few of James's letters are included, chiefly those which deal with his adoption of English citizenship and others for which Gosse's replies are available.

The editors have aimed to present an accurate text with as few editorial intrusions as possible. Addresses are placed in a single line, with no distinction made between embossed and handwritten addresses. Dates are regularized in form, but signatures are retained as the correspondents wrote them; in both cases, final periods have been omitted, but periods are always given to initials in the signatures. The positioning of commas and periods in relation to quotation marks has been regularized in accordance with the customary practice of the individual writer. When dates and places of writing have had to be supplied by the editors, they are placed within the square brackets which are customary for such editorial insertions. Names of addressees which appear formally either before the salutation or after the signature have been omitted, as have the "continuity" words which appear at the bottom of each page of Furness's letters. Last-minute remarks which appear above the salutation have been treated as postscripts, and dates at the end of letters have been moved up to the top.

In the texts of the letters themselves, cancellations of words and mere slips of the pen have been ignored, and words written above the line or in the margins have been inserted in the line without notice. Spelling and punctuation have been retained as written, but missing periods, commas, or quotation marks have been added silently, except where the authors' omissions seemed particularly significant; serious errors of spelling and punctuation have been noted by the customary "[sic]." Words and phrases which the editors could not decipher with absolute confidence are placed within angle brackets, thus: ⟨ ⟩. Dashes and long spaces have sometimes been interpreted as indicating new paragraphs (a device used frequently by Howells); except for these and for dashes between existing paragraphs, all marks have been retained as bearing some rhetorical intention. All abbreviations of common words, such as "wld." and "yrs.," have been silently expanded, both in complimentary closes and elsewhere; abbreviations of proper names and titles of books and journals have been expanded on their first appearance within each letter, but are thereafter left as written. Abbreviations are not expanded, even on their first appearance, when the full name or title has occurred earlier in the letter, nor have any alterations been made to clear and customary abbreviations such as "U.S.A." or "& Co."

Short biographies or identifications of names are given in footnotes on their first appearance only, and can be found by noting "Identified" under the name in the Index. Eminent people are usually identified briefly or not at all. Full publication details are given for any book mentioned in the text, for books written by one of the correspondents, and for books quoted as sources of further information; in other cases, only the date of publication is normally given. Footnotes have been supplied chiefly for purposes of identification and clarification, but the editors have sometimes sought to fill out the context of a letter or of a particularly interesting allusion with quotations from unpublished letters, diaries, reviews, and similar materials.

LETTERS

The following abbreviations and short titles are used to indicate the provenance of letters in the Gosse correspondence which are quoted or referred to in the footnotes. A complete checklist of letters printed in the text appears in Appendix A.

BC—Brotherton Collection, University of Leeds
BM—British Museum
Cambridge—Cambridge University Library
CU—Columbia University Library
Duke—Duke University Library
GL—Gilder Letterbooks, New York Public Library; these contain carbons of Gilder's letters to Gosse.
GP—Gilder Papers, in possession of Miss Rosamond Gilder
HU—Harvard University, Houghton Library
LC—Library of Congress
NYP—New York Public Library
PU—Princeton University Library
RU—Rutgers University Library
UP—University of Pennsylvania, Horace Howard Furness Memorial Library
YU—Yale University Library

a.l.s.—autograph letter signed

ॐ 1. *Gosse to Whitman*[1] ॐ

The Library, / British Museum. / London.

12 December 1873

Dear Sir

When my friend, Mr. Linton[2] was here last, I asked him, during one of our conversations about you, whether I might venture to send you the book I was then writing,[3] as soon as it came out. If he had not encouraged me to do so, I should hardly have liked to trouble you with it, and yet there is no one living by whom I am more desirous to be known than by you. The "Leaves of Grass" have become a part of my every-day thought and experi-

[1] Walt Whitman (1819–1892). For his biography, see Gay Wilson Allen, *The Solitary Singer* (New York: Macmillan, 1955). Whitman seems not to have replied to Gosse's letter. There is, however, a postcard from Whitman to Gosse, dated 19 May [1876], in the University of Virginia Library: "I have this day forwarded to you by mail . . . *my new edition, Two Volumes* (separate parcels)." See Miller, ed., Walt Whitman, *The Correspondence,* III, 48 and n. These two books, both signed "E. W. Gosse from the author," are listed in *The Library of Edmund Gosse,* compiled by E. H. M. Cox (London: Dulau, 1924), p. 289. Also listed are a signed photograph of Whitman and a copy of the 1855 edition of *Leaves of Grass*; this last entry is annotated: "This was the earliest copy to reach England. It was sent to the Earl of Carlyle, but Lady Carlyle, on reading it, was so shocked that she made him sell it" (p. 289). For the exchange of letters between Gosse and Whitman in December 1884 immediately preceding Gosse's visit to Camden, see White, "Gosse on Whitman," *Victorian Studies,* I (December 1957), 180–182. For Gosse's account of the visit itself see Introduction, pp. 15–16.

[2] William James Linton (1812–1897), wood-engraver and author, held advanced republican views and devoted much of his life to their propagation. He migrated from England to the United States in 1867 and set up a printing press at Appledore, near New Haven, Connecticut. In his autobiography, *Memories* (London: Lawrence and Bullen, 1895), pp. 227–228, Linton recalls that he was in England in 1872–1873 and at several other periods between 1867 and 1890, mainly to collect material for his books on wood-engraving; he speaks briefly of Whitman—"a true poet who could not write poetry" (p. 217)—and has an affectionate reference to Austin Dobson (see Letter 2, n. 2) though none to Gosse.

[3] Gosse, *On Viol and Flute* (London: Henry S. King, 1873).

ence. I have considered myself as "the new person drawn toward" you; I have taken your warning, I have weighed all the doubts and the dangers, and the result is that I draw only closer and closer to you.

As I write this I consider how little it can matter to you in America, how you are regarded by a young man in England of whom you have never heard. And yet I cannot believe that you, the poet of comrades, will refuse the sympathy I lay at your feet. In any case I can but thank you for all that I have learned from you, all the beauty you have taught me to see in the common life of healthy men and women, and all the pleasure there is in the mere humanity of other people. The sense of all this was in me, but it was you, and you alone, who really gave it power to express itself. Often when I have been alone in the company of one or other of my dearest friends, in the very deliciousness of the sense of nearness and sympathy, it has seemed to me that you were somewhere invisibly with us.

Accept the homage and love, and forgive the importunity of your sincere disciple

Edmund W. Gosse

❧ 2. *Stedman*[1] *to Gosse* ❧

The Century Club / East 15th. St. New York City

29 November 1875

My dear Sir:

Our common friend, Mr. Dobson[2]—that sweetest modern Horace—has been so thoughtful as to send me a copy of your poems, *On Viol and Flute,* and thus has caused me to feel a great amount of pleasure, and no slight regret: pleasure in the acquaintance which I make with a genuine and most artistic poet, and regret that I had not formed that acquantance in time to do both you and my volume justice by including a notice of your poetry in the *Victorian Poets*.[3] The truth is that I did not conceive the idea of adding,

[1] Edmund Clarence Stedman (1833–1908), a prominent New York stockbroker, was at this time establishing himself both as a poet and as an influential critic. For his biography see Stedman and Gould, *Life and Letters of Stedman.*

[2] [Henry] Austin Dobson (1840–1921), poet, biographer, and essayist, worked at the Board of Trade in London from 1856 to 1901 and was Gosse's close friend and colleague. Stedman would have read his *Vignettes in Rhyme* (London: Henry S. King, 1873). See Stedman's letter to Dobson, 29 November 1875, in Stedman and Gould, *Life and Letters of Stedman*, II, 14.

[3] Stedman, *Victorian Poets* (Boston: Osgood; London: Chatto and Windus, 1876).

to the longer essays in that book, my chapters upon the miscellaneous and younger singers, until within a few months of its publication—and nothing but a good general knowledge of this branch of my subject enabled me to attempt it in the time and space given me. Unfortunately your exquisite volume was not within my reach. I think no other of equal importance is omitted from my survey.

But it is not too late for me to say how much I am charmed with both the execution and the promise of your poetry. While thoroughly charged with the richness of melody and color that distinguish what I call the Neo-Romantic School, I find more restraint and strength of repose in your verse than in that of many of your comrades, and I am sure—both by the work itself and by instinct—that you can do anything which you attempt in the future. I not only observe the finish of your sonnets and strictly romantic studies, but the natural and modern *feeling* of such poems as "Sunshine before Sunrise" and "Lying in the Grass". Your Pre-Raphaelite friends too often, with all their delicious quality, forget that there is a live world around us, and that great things may be found or happen even now.

But I am writing at too great length, my object being merely to make an explanation (which is your *due*) of the absence of your name from a recent book. I discovered Dobson for myself, and wrote of him as I did, before hearing directly from him. How bright, how healthy, how tender and sweet! And I now am under a new obligation to him for giving me the chance to read you, and to sign myself,

Very sincerely yours
Edmund C. Stedman

3. *Stedman to Gosse*

Century Club / 109 East 15th. Street / New York,

12 June 1876

My dear Mr. Gosse:

I have too long delayed my reply to your altogether hearty and winning letter of April 3rd. (—poets, after all, I find to be the men who *have* hearts) but have delayed for the best of purposes. My intention was to send you the June number of *Scribner,* with the review of your "King Erik"[1] etc. promised for that issue by the writer to whom Mr. Gilder,[2] at my request, con-

[1] Gosse, *King Erik: A Tragedy* (London: Chatto & Windus, 1876).
[2] Richard Watson Gilder; see Letter 11, n. 1.

signed your drama. That review, however, has been deferred a month, owing to my own officiousness in your behalf. The fact is that, with the intention of enabling the critic to say something of your former writings, your poetic progress, etc., I also handed in your "On Viol and Flute". The reviewer, instead of referring to the early poems, in a notice of "King Erik", wrote a separate notice of the former and handed it in. This will be used, but in the same number with a review of "King Erik"—which, I am told, is now ready. As soon as these notices appear I shall forward them to you.

Certainly a poet, who at your age has produced two such books, and proved both his lyrical and dramatic gifts (for your tragedy is indeed a noble drama, full of true fire and beauty), has no reason ever to feel depressed. I have observed the reception given to your new book, and the general verdict upon it, and congratulate you with all my heart. You seem to *me* young enough, for I am 42 (*eheu fugaces!*) and have been handicapped with all sorts of vexations during half the creative period of a poet's life. You, indeed, have the world all before you, "where to choose",[3] and my instinct makes generous predictions for your career. A man who is doing just the work that he most enjoys, and whose bent is in sympathy with the rising school, is doubly fortunate. All the trouble in life arises from a man's being out of his special niche—or, as Mr. Lincoln used to say, in his homely fashion, from "a round peg's getting into a square hole". What I said about pecuniary trouble meant just this: I came from what is termed a good family, and, owing to a guardian's mismanagement and my early marriage, found myself at 21 with a poet's tastes and "impracticability", with the habits of a gentleman, with a wife, and with no money to support any of these dangerous luxuries. From that time till my thirtieth year I was wholly occupied in keeping the wolf from my poor-and-proud door, and half-crazy because I had no time nor extra-strength for writing poetry and prose. Was a journalist, earning my bread from week to week. I then vowed I *would* learn how more stupid men made a living, burned my ships behind me, and went into Wall St. From that time I *have* had some means, and a portion of every year for literature, and, in fact, have made all my little reputation here as a poet and critic *since* I left Bohemia and a strictly literary life. But a year or two since I broke down again in health, with a consequent recurrence of "want of pence". It is rather hard, you know, to serve God and Mammon at once. Just now I am busy, with returning health, as a stock-broker, in recruiting my means, and furious because my brain will no longer serve me on 'Change by day and in my study at night. My head is brim-full of "Gold" and "Erie"—my heart, of the etherial [sic] Muse.

You are fond of out-door life? So am I. I have kept myself poor, for

---

[3] *Paradise Lost*, XII, 646.

years, because I *would* have my summers for trouting and hunting, but have also kept up my youth and courage in this way. I know the forests, lakes, and streams, of my magnificent native land, from Maine to Florida; and should you ever come here I will introduce you to the delights of fly-fishing and camping in native woodlands—*unpreserved.* N.B. There's nothing like an aboriginal stream.

With great diffidence I send you, through Scribner, Welford & Co., (London) my collective edition of poems.[4] For I have as yet done nothing which I wish or have vowed to do—they are the things I have stolen a chance to do—although many of my lyrics have been widely welcomed and found a home among my countrymen here. The book, ranging over years, is quite uneven. *Pray skip the opening poem altogether.*[5] It was a boyish, local satire, and is only reprinted because it is so irrevocably afloat as a part of popular American verse that my publishers would not permit me to omit it from this "popular edition". Of course I am ashamed of it: it was a mere *jeu d'esprit* that appeared in a satirical paper, upon a local theme. In like manner treat mercifully most of the Early Poems. I have ventured to mark, in the "Contents", a few which you may just glance at—nothing more. The truth is that I am not willing to be judged by these poems in England, and may yet make up a small volume for Chatto. Should I have a photograph taken soon, I'll remember to send you one: meantime the poor wood-cut in the book will do for the nonce. But do send me one of yourself, for my private "illustrated" edition of the *Vict[orian] Poets.* Your own confidences have beguiled me into all this foolish babble about myself. Forgive it. One should "recruit his friendships" as the years advance, and all this proves that I am

Faithfully yours

Edmund C. Stedman

I took pleasure in showing Mr. Gilder your allusions to his book.[6] You will find my verse less psychological—rather "open-airish" and Yankeefied.

I am sure you will need no second reading to convince you that this irreverent parody[7] is one of the cleverest things (of the sort—a poor sort) ever done in English. Note how all the little mannerisms, or great, of *Atalanta,* are preserved, and how the whole drama is "condensed" in 250

---

[4] Stedman's *The Poetical Works of Edmund Clarence Stedman* (Boston: Osgood, 1873).

[5] The poem, "The Diamond Wedding," a satire on a ridiculously sumptuous wedding, was first printed in the New York *Daily Tribune,* 18 October 1859; see Stedman and Gould, *Life and Letters of Stedman,* I, 183–196.

[6] The letter containing these allusions appears not to have survived.

[7] See Appendix B. The last two paragraphs of this postscript appear on a separate sheet and may have accompanied the parody under separate cover.

lines. The title alone is a stroke of genius! I want you to show it to that most delightful of poets and wits, Dobson, who will relish it with you—as much as any of us *can* relish a sacrilegious travesty upon pure and lofty art. I don't dare to send it to Swinburne: he might receive it in Ercles' vein, and yet it is very excellent fooling.

Of course the text (as to the Arts Club, etc.) is some ancient and worthless gossip, or, maybe, a sheer invention, but that doesn't matter. Would you believe that this was done by an anonymous down-East Yankee, who never has printed anything else, but sent this to a country newspaper. Such is the fact.

❧ 4. *Gosse to Stedman* ❧

1 Whitehall / London S.W.

6 August 1876

My dear Stedman

I was left a considerable time in expectation of your volume[1] after the arrival of your amiable letter. At last, however, it came to hand, and I am able very heartily to thank you for it. It is a serious undertaking in these busy days to read with due care a volume of 342 pages of varied and earnest poetry, so I have delayed a month, giving an hour here and an hour there to the pleasant study. I have enjoyed greatly learning to know you as a poet. That your book would be scholarly, grave and genuine I knew instinctively, but it is much more than this. It reveals to me a poetic individuality very true, brilliant and many-sided. I am amazed that these lyrics have not found their way to us in popular collections and anthologies. The people who undertake to make the American poets known in England seem to be very tasteless; such collections as I know are very fatuous and terrible, dealing largely in ladies of the most blatant type of poetaster. But to return to yourself. (But, by the way, who is your "Estelle"?[2] We used to know a terrible and fearful lady who called herself Estelle, and who was an American poetess, "the Sappho of the South", a Mrs. Lewis.)[3] On the

---

[1] See previous letter, n. 4.

[2] Stedman, "Estelle," *Poetical Works,* pp. 158–160.

[3] Mrs. Estelle (or Sarah) Anna Lewis (1824–1880), a Baltimore poet and friend of Edgar Allan Poe. She published several volumes of verse and her tragedy, *Sappho: A Tragedy* (1875), which passed through a number of editions, was translated into Greek and performed in Athens. "Stella," rather than "Estelle," was the name Mrs.

whole it is the full and delicate romance of "The Blameless Prince"[4] that one naturally thinks of first in considering your works. This is your widest and strongest flight, and full, it seems to me, of strength and charm. "Alice of Monmouth" is antipathetic to *me,* but not on that account to be blamed. Simply it lies beyond what I take pleasure in. "Bohemia", "Pan in Wall Street", "Fuit Ilium" and the whole class of pensively fantastic pieces are my delight; you deal with these themes with an exquisite delicacy and precision. The studies of nature strike me throughout as extremely fine. "Old Brown at Harper's Ferry" is the best ballad that I have ever seen from America, absolutely the best. In such songs as "Toujours Amour" you are eminently successful. I am sure you must be quite tired of having my little patchy criticism. I wish you would bring out a selection of your poems here in London. I think you would find that, in spite of the general hatred of the Muse, you would force your way to attention.

Your last letter gave me much to think about, and drew me very warmly to you. I think I enter distinctly into the difficulties you feel and have felt. These must end, I persuade myself to believe, before any of your power or enthusiasm has ceased: there are certain things a man has to say and if he does not say them soon he says them late, if only the inspiring enthusiasm does not burn out. I wish you would tell me what work you have in hand. I hear something of your translating from the Greek:[5] I imagine it must be from the Idyllists, for the bias of your genius lies wholly towards Sicily. I can imagine you would translate Bion and Moschus most admirably, Theocritus I already know your mastery over.[6]

We have had much verse and little poetry this summer. Browning's "Pacchiarotto" contains a scandalously violent attack against a poor little nonentity called Alfred Austin, a miserable pseudo-Byron quite unworthy of Browning's attention.[7] There has been nothing else, as far as I remember. Swinburne has several volumes nearly ready. By the way thank you very

---

Lewis assumed for literary purposes. See Hervey Allen, *Israfel: The Life and Times of Edgar Allan Poe* (New York: Farrar & Rinehart, 1934), p. 560, also pp. 541, 642–643.

[4] The poems mentioned in this paragraph are all included in Stedman, *Poetical Works.*

[5] Stedman's next volume of poems, *Hawthorne and Other Poems* (Boston: Osgood, 1877), contained translations of the "Death of Agamemnon" from both Homer and Aeschylus, pp. 103–120, and 123–134.

[6] Stedman's *The Blameless Prince, and Other Poems* (Boston: Fields, Osgood, 1869) includes two translations from Theocritus: "The Reapers" (pp. 181–185) and "Hylas" (pp. 186–192).

[7] Robert Browning, *Pacchiarotto and How He Worked in Distemper; With Other Poems* (London: Smith, Elder, 1876); Alfred Austin (1835–1913) was later Poet Laureate, from 1896 until his death.

much for the truly admirable parody of "Atalanta".[8] I had already seen [it], for it appeared without acknowledgment in a little London sheet called the "Hornet". The incident about the hats is quite true. It occurred about 1867 at the Arts Club, and Swinburne was thereupon ejected. But there were touches that showed the parody was not written by a Londoner. For instance, Rossetti and Morris are recluses; they never even enter, much less belong to a club. Swinburne does not smoke at all. But such trifles do not militate against the parody being first-class.

I hope soon to hear from you. I am very anxious to see myself in "Scribner"![9] Thank you most warmly for all.

Yours very sincerely

Edmund W. Gosse

[8] See Letter 3, n. 7, and Appendix B.
[9] See Letter 5, n. 5.

✑ 5. *Gosse to Stedman* ✑

29, Delamere Terrace, / Westbourne Square. [London] W.

28 April 1879

My dear Mr. Stedman

I feel sure you must have thought me very remiss in not writing to you before.[1] Your name has constantly been on my lips, and I have vowed many times to sit down and write you a serious letter, but something has always prevented. Why do you not come to London? I promise you the warmest welcome, and you will be surprised to find how many friends you have here. Take nobody's report of us, but come and see for yourself.

The crown of my ingratitude to you is that I never thanked you for your noble monody on Hawthorne.[2] I much enjoyed it: a true symphony of serious and glowing memorial music. Though I have not written to you, I have several times written of you, in an incidental way. I trace you often in the "Atlantic Monthly",[3] and in the "Masque of Poets" I detected you.

[1] Gosse wrote to Stedman on 31 January 1877 (a.l.s., CU) thanking him for the review in *Scribner's* (see n. 5 below), which he had not at that time seen; there is a gap in the surviving correspondence from then until the present letter.

[2] Stedman, "Hawthorne. Poem read before the Society of the Phi Beta Kappa, Harvard University, Cambridge, June 28, 1877." Printed in *Hawthorne, and Other Poems*, p. 11.

[3] Stedman published four poems in the *Atlantic Monthly* during 1878, the most recent at the time of this letter being "Song," *Atlantic Monthly*, XLII (July 1878), 106, and "The Death of Bryant," XLII (December 1878), 747–749.

I was courteously asked to contribute to the latter.[4] But I declined on the ground that such anonymous collections have no aim but to excite curiosity, not a worthy aim for poetry. Do you not think there is some truth in this? I do not think any but quite the minor "choir" can have had much pleasure from the book.

Pray write and tell me what you are doing. Your last letter accompanied the review in "Scribner" and consoled me for the very dispiriting and disquieting review.[5] I dont think anything ever upset me, in all my literary career, as that review; because it was the verdict of a dispassionate outsider who pronounced that I had no force, no future, no promise of better things. This is the one paralysing criticism: mere blame of the severest and coarsest kind merely nerves one into opposition, but the result of this would have been that I should have stopped writing altogether had I had the power to do so. However, I have not, and I have sent you since then two books, my drama or dramalette, called "The Unknown Lover",[6] and a prose book of "Northern Studies".[7] I hope you received them both, and that one of these days you will write and tell me so. If you do not do so soon, another book will be on the way out to you. I am in the act of copying for the press a volume of "Dorian Poems", written between 1874–1879, which will appear early in the autumn,[8] and to which I pin my rosiest hopes.

Your countrywoman, Mrs. Moulton, was over here for a long time,[9] and

[4] It was Louise Chandler Moulton (see n. 9 below) who had invited Gosse to write a poem for *A Masque of Poets* (Boston: Roberts Brothers, 1878). This volume, edited anonymously by George Parsons Lathrop, was one of a number which appeared under the general title of the "No Name Series." The book is especially notable for containing, on p. 174, Emily Dickinson's poem "Success," the only one of her poems to appear between the covers of a book during her lifetime.

[5] There seems to have been no review of Gosse's works in *Scribner's* other than the one of *On Viol and Flute* and *King Erik* in Vol. XII (September 1876), 758–759 (see Letter 3), the tone of which suggests that it is the one to which Gosse is referring. The final paragraph is as follows: "But the whole [of *King Erik*] is very cleverly managed, and is decidedly readable without being at all great. As in his earlier book of poems, Mr. Gosse makes a pleasing impression, and leaves one with the desire to see something further from his pen. Another work may answer the question which naturally arises, as to whether his smoothness and evenness mean that the limit of his powers is already reached, or that there is a possibility of even better work in the future. There is a dedication to Robert Browning, prefixed to "King Erik," which seems rather out of place. It might be called pretentious in its humility. "King Erik" cannot fail to recall Swinburne's "Chastelard," although we find nothing but an influence of the stronger creation."

[6] Gosse, *The Unknown Lover* (London: Chatto and Windus, 1878).

[7] Gosse, *Studies in the Literature of Northern Europe* (London: Kegan Paul, 1879); the title *Northern Studies* was given to this work when it was reissued, slightly enlarged, in 1890.

[8] A reference to his *New Poems* (London: Kegan Paul, 1879).

[9] Mrs. Louise Chandler Moulton (1835–1908) was born in Connecticut, married a

we had the pleasure of seeing her several times at our house. Unfortunately she became associated with some people that we do not know, and we lost the pleasure of seeing her. Her little volume of Poems[10] had a distinct success. Some of them seemed to me exquisitely touching and sincere.

Aldrich[11] also has been here. But what a grand gentleman he is! You should have warned us: he seemed to find everything on a dreadfully small scale. We get on better with Henry James, Jr., who is absolutely charming, and who is quite the rage this season.[12] My wife and I were specially asked to Leland's[13] the other night to meet Bret Harte,[14] but he was ill and did not come. I think that is all the news I have to give you about your countrymen.

Dobson greets you warmly. You will be sorry to hear that Swinburne has been very dangerously ill, and that his condition still gives his friends great anxiety. Be so kind as not to publish this: it is not generally known here. Browning, who is almost my next-door neighbour, is as hale and genial as possible: he publishes a new volume of poems ("Dramatic Idyls")[15] today. There is no news: there never is. We are too busy to have any news.

Remember me with affection as I do you; and come soon to London.

Yours very sincerely

Edmund W. Gosse

Boston publisher, William U. Moulton, and wrote verse, fiction, travel sketches, and literary criticism. She came to Europe in 1876 and from then onwards her custom was to spend the summer and autumn of each year in London and the remainder in Boston.

[10] Louise Chandler Moulton, *Swallow Flights* (London: Macmillan, 1878).

[11] Thomas Bailey Aldrich (1836–1907) had already established his reputation as a poet and novelist and he was soon (1881) to become editor of the *Atlantic Monthly* in succession to Howells.

[12] For James's social success in England see Leon Edel, *Henry James: The Conquest of London, 1870–1883* (London: Hart-Davis, 1962), *passim*.

[13] Charles Godfrey Leland (1824–1903) was born in Philadelphia but spent much of his life in Europe. He was best known for his humorous dialect poems, collected in 1871 under the general title of *Hans Breitmann's Ballads,* and for his serious studies of folklore. See Mrs. Elizabeth R. Pennell, *Charles Godfrey Leland: A Biography* (Boston and New York: Houghton Mifflin, 1906).

[14] [Francis] Bret Harte (1836–1902) came to Europe following the decline of his American popularity as a writer of humorous and sentimental novels, stories, and poems, most of them about California. He was American consul in Glasgow from 1880 to 1885, and for the rest of his life he lived in London.

[15] Robert Browning, *Dramatic Idyls* [First Series] (London: Smith, Elder, 1879).

❧ 6. Stedman to Gosse ❧

80 Broadway, New York,

5 May 1879

My dear Gosse,

Your beautiful and in every way remarkable volume[1] has been a great treat to me, during a relapse which *compelled* me to stay at home and behave myself. I thus had time to read it at leisure, and have been thoroughly charmed by it—besides learning so much that I never knew before of the field which you've here *made your own.* No one but a poet could have written it—the prose style is perfect—the clear vehicle of your thought— and clear and beautiful thought, in fact, *makes its own co-adequate style.* And the translations are exquisite. Some of the papers I saw as they first appeared—but had not understood how rich and valuable a book the collection would make.

I hope that you, my friend, with your youth and equipment, may be able to do what I have so often been prevented from doing—that you may go on, without long breaks and hindrances, in your literary plans, and make secure the place you are winning. If you can write your History of Icelandic Literature,[2] it will be a fine achievement. For myself, of late I've only been able to lay out the plans of works which, thus written in my head, the hand has no leisure nor strength to complete.

However, my fortunes have mended lately, though the fight has turned my hair prematurely gray and almost broken me down.

I *hope,* ere long, to visit England at last, for a short time. Not to bother you, or anyone else—I wish to keep very quiet, and regain my health, and see the green fields and historic places which every Yankee except myself has seen. Yet my mother and sisters lived abroad for 20 years!—in Italy, where my step-father was U.S. Minister,[3] and elsewhere. I "married a wife and could not go".—Possibly now, I may induce Chatto, or some one, to bring out a collection of my poems—expressly selected and arranged "for the English market"[4]—what a phrase!

Am trying to close up my affairs and unable to do any writing. Taylor's death has brought much grief and labor upon me, though I've declined to

---

[1] Gosse, *Studies in the Literature of Northern Europe:* see Letter 5, n. 7.

[2] Gosse seems never to have written this book.

[3] Stedman's father, Major Edmund Burke Stedman, died in 1835; in 1841 his mother married William Burnet Kinney (1799–1880), proprietor and editor of the Newark *Daily Advertiser,* who in 1850 became United States *chargé d'affaires* at Turin.

[4] The collection was published later in 1879 by Kegan Paul; see subsequent correspondence, especially Letters 7 and 10.

write his biography.[5]—However, I have made a serious onslaught upon *Scribner* in relation to a *proper* review of your important work,[6] as you will see by the enclosed slips from Johnson, the office-editor.[7]—The "Studies" are attracting attention here, and many newspaper "literary items", such as *these,* are going the rounds. Pray give my love to Dobson, and believe me, with many thanks,

Sincerely yours,

Edmund C. Stedman

[5] Bayard Taylor (1825–1878), poet, novelist, travel writer, and translator of Goethe. The *Life and Letters of Bayard Taylor* (Boston: Houghton Mifflin, 1884) was the work of Taylor's wife, Marie Hansen-Taylor, and of H. E. Scudder.
[6] The review of *Studies in the Literature of Northern Europe* appeared in July: *Scribner's Monthly,* XVIII (July 1879), 470–471.
[7] Robert Underwood Johnson (1853–1937) worked for *Scribner's Monthly* and its successor, the *Century,* from 1873 to 1919, succeeding Richard Watson Gilder as editor of the *Century* in 1909. His autobiography, *Remembered Yesterdays,* is a valuable record of the period.

❧ 7. *Gosse to Stedman* ❧

29, Delamere Terrace, / Westbourne Square. [London] W.

17 July 1879

Dear Stedman

I saw Kegan Paul this morning and had a long talk with him about your poems.[1] He would not, of course, say anything definite, but my impression was that he is very strongly inclined to entertain the idea of publishing. You may be sure I did my best to clinch that idea.

Yours always truly

Edmund W. Gosse

[1] See Letter 6, n. 4, and Letter 10, n. 1.

❧ 8. *Gosse to Stedman* ❧

29, Delamere Terrace, / Westbourne Square. [London] W.

12 September 1879

My dear Stedman

You are not to answer this letter—on pain of excommunication from the table of Apollo—but I cannot let you go without briefly telling you what a joy it has been to me to see you.[1] It is always a delicate thing to meet in the flesh a friend whom one has learned to value through his letters; sometimes one feels that the letters were the best part of the friendship—but with you it has been the opposite, I like you better even than I thought I should. I wish we had seen more of one another; this brief flash is nothing. We should have spent a week together in our shirt-sleeves on the river, or on a walking-tour; this great London is a marvellously tight-fitting mask for the spirit, but it is a mask after all. I hope you may find all well in your home, that you may go back better pleased than ever with America and yet preserving some sunny memories of England. I do not suppose I shall ever come to New York: each year makes it harder for me to move: you must come again to us, or else I fear I shall never see you again.

But in every case God bless you, and keep in affectionate remembrance

Yours very sincerely

Edmund W. Gosse

[1] Stedman and his wife spent the summer of 1879 in England. They sailed from America on June 5 and their names are recorded in the Book of Gosse on July 6. Many years later Stedman recalled his moment of arrival in England: "There is no sensation like that of an American's *first* footfall upon England's soil. I have still, somewhere, the grass and pebbles I picked up the moment I took my first step from the quay at Queenstown" (Stedman and Gould, *Life and Letters of Stedman*, II, 23).

❧ 9. *Stedman to Gosse* ❧

19 Sackville St. / London.

20 September 1879

Air: Good-bye, Sweetheart!

My dear Boy,

Nothing could give such "Sweet sorrow" to parting as your affectionate note—which I must acknowledge, despite your prohibition. We *shall* see each other again; I feel it in my bones—as well as in my heart; and I strongly expect yet to welcome you in New York. If the Fates be not adverse, and this season they have deigned to show me much kindness, we shall ere long have a home of our own again. And if our Lares and Penates *should* be thus established you will find a home of your own therein, and a constant pressure for a visit. And so will Dobson.

Whether or no, you cannot henceforth feel without a close friend in New York,—and every day is now bringing the two shores into closer neighborhood.

As for me, as Polyphemus said of Galatea, I liked you at first sight and have done so more and more since that day—and it is a good thing to know from you that my fancy was and is reciprocated.

But this note is to again remind you that I want your photograph, and some little data of your birth, dates of works, etc. By and by they will be of use to me—and, I hope, to you.

Mrs. Stedman joins with me in kind remembrances to Mrs. Gosse. Once more, as we leave, believe me grateful for all your hearty attentions, and always

Sincerely yours,

Edmund C. Stedman

P.S. I have just received a letter from my friend Capt. Mason, of the Cleveland *Leader*,[1] who says he has sent you the "Sweet Singer of Michigan".[2]

---

[1] Frank Holcomb Mason (1840–1916) gained his captaincy in the Civil War and then became, in turn, reporter, editorial writer, and managing editor of the Cleveland *Leader* until 1880; he later served as United States consul and consul general in a number of posts, including Berlin and Paris.

[2] Mrs. Julia A. Moore (1847–1920) was known as "The Sweet Singer of Michigan." Her first book of magnificently bad poems was *The Sentimental Song Book* (1876); the book referred to here is presumably *The Sweet Singer of Michigan* (1878).

❧ 10. *Stedman to Gosse* ❧

71 West 54th. St. New York

Christmas, 1879

My dear and good Friend,

You have done an open-handed, *plucky*, and most generous thing, in your notable review of my book, in the *Academy*.[1] 'Tis one of those things for which it is impossible to thank you sufficiently, for which it will be hard to show adequately my practical appreciation. Nothing could be of greater service to me, *at home* and abroad. I feel indeed how much I owe to you for so timely and outspoken a notice, bearing your signature,—and I never have dared to think so well of myself as now, reading this most sympathetic article from your critical and scholarly hand. It arrived just in time to give

---

[1] Gosse's signed review of Stedman's *Lyrics and Idylls, with other Poems* (London: Kegan Paul, 1879) in the *Academy*, XVI (6 December 1879), 403–404; he described Stedman as "the most distinguished poet born in the United States since 1820" (p. 404).

me a merrier Xmas in our new home; and now I must study in some way to repay you for being so very kind to my virtues—and so tender with my faults. And I well know that actions speak louder than these poorly-written thanks. My wife joins with me in affectionate acknowledgements, and it would speak ill for human-nature if I were not

Faithfully yours,

E. C. Stedman

✿ 11. *Gosse to Gilder*[1] ✿

29, Delamere Terrace, / Westbourne Square. [London] W.

29 December 1879

My dear Sir

A few days ago I learned from my friend Mr. Stedman that you were in London, and I have now discovered your address. I trust you will excuse my saying that it would give my wife and myself particular pleasure if you would favour us with a visit. We are working people, and usually see our friends on Sunday. Will you and Mrs. Gilder come here next Sunday afternoon and take a cup of tea with us about 5.30, arriving here, I hope, considerably earlier that we may have a long talk.[2]

[1] Richard Watson Gilder (1844–1909), American poet and editor, was at this time managing editor of *Scribner's Monthly*. For his life and career see Rosamond Gilder, ed., *Letters of Richard Watson Gilder* (Boston and New York: Houghton Mifflin, 1916) and Herbert F. Smith, "The Editorial Influence of Richard Watson Gilder, 1870–1909" (dissertation, Rutgers). This seems to have been the first letter to pass between Gosse and Gilder, although in 1876 Gosse apparently sent Gilder a message of admiration by way of Stedman (see Letter 3). Smith quotes (p. 159) a letter from Gilder to Stedman of 3 May 1876 in which Gilder confessed that what little of Gosse's work he had read he had not particularly liked, but added: "I think he must be a good fellow, and if you write him, thank him for his kind message." Smith suggests (p. 159 n.) that Gilder may have been the author of the unsigned and rather unfavourable review of Gosse's *On Viol and Flute* and *King Erik* which appeared in *Scribner's Monthly* in September 1876, but Stedman, writing to Gosse on 12 June 1876, speaks of "the writer to whom Mr. Gilder, at my request, consigned your drama" (Letter 3).

[2] The Gilders apparently came to tea on Sunday, 4 January 1880; the occasion is not recorded in the Book of Gosse, but there are no entries whatsoever in the Book between 6 July 1879 and 21 March 1880 and Gosse has noted "Some omissions" here. In a letter home dated 9 January 1880 Gilder wrote: "I have lunched with Gosse and Austin Dobson and tea'd with Gosse, where we met Miss Robinson the young poetess, and Mrs. Alma Tadema" (Rosamond Gilder, *Letters of R. W. Gilder,* p. 97). For Miss Robinson, see Letter 15, n. 6. On 6 February 1880 Gosse invited the Gilders

In the commonwealth of letters some ceremony may perhaps be dispensed with, so I trust you will forgive this blunt invitation. My wife hopes before Sunday to come and call on Mrs. Gilder.

I think I must have been almost the first person in England to procure and enjoy your "New Day", which emboldens me to say "years have flown since I knew thee first".[3]

Believe me, my dear Sir,
Yours very faithfully

Edmund W. Gosse

---

for the following Sunday, promising a meeting with Swinburne; the letter is endorsed by Gilder, "But Swinburne didn't come" (a.l.s., GP).

[3] R. W. Gilder, *The New Day, A Poem in Songs and Sonnets* (New York: Scribner's, 1876). The quotation is the first line of "Song," Poem VII of Part IV, p. 91.

❧ 12. *Gosse to Stedman* ❧

29, Delamere Terrace, / Westbourne Square. [London] W.

11 February 1880

My dear Stedman

What a good, kind, true friend you are! I sum up in this—for the moment —all the thanks I owe you for your kindness.

Your poems have attracted great notice over here. I hear them talked of on all sides: the critics seemed rather afraid of them at first, but now they are taking kindly to them. There is so much jealousy between the "Athenaeum" and the "Academy" that when I saw there was no review in the former, I was afraid I had done you injury by my desire to sound the right note, early, in the latter.[1] I have known the "Athenaeum" decline to notice a book at all because the "Academy" had the start. So, feeling that I was guilty in the matter, I went last week to the editor of the "Athenaeum"[2] about it. He promised me that you should have a review that should satisfy me by its length and importance. He said nothing about the tone of it, but that is sure to be all right, I think.[3]

In a little while you will receive a sort of brief autobiography, a confi-

[1] See Letter 10, n. 1.

[2] Norman MacColl (1843–1904) was a distinguished Spanish scholar and editor of the *Athenaeum* from 1871 to 1900.

[3] An anonymous review of Stedman's *Lyrics and Idylls* appeared in the *Athenaeum*, 14 February 1880, pp. 210–211. The reviewer—apparently Philip Bourke Marston (see Letter 14)—said that Stedman had not been sufficiently selective and that he should confine himself to poems in the lighter vein and to "themes of tender regret and aspiration."

dential sort of chat about myself to you, not for you to print, but to select from, such facts as you care to make known. I should like you to understand how much I have had to fight against, and through how much pain and sorrow I have reached the happiness I now enjoy.

What good, dear people the Gilders are! Their acquaintance has been a real joy to us.

Farewell, dear Poet. Dobson and I constantly talk of you with affection and regret. I wish you would send me a photograph of yourself.

Remember us to Mrs. Stedman and believe me

Your affectionate Friend

Edmund W. Gosse

❧ 13. *Gosse to Stedman*[1] ❧

[London ?]

8 March 1880

My dear Stedman

I come back from lecturing at Birmingham and from a visit to Buckinghamshire, to find your charming notice in Scribner's.[2] Thank you very much: it is most kindly and critically written and will be very useful to me.

You were not very well satisfied, I fear, with the review of yourself in the "Athenaeum". I was by no means pleased with it: there is a great deal too much of that half-hearted and chilly criticism here nowadays. Nobody seems to have the courage to say "this is very good" or "this is very bad", "I love" or "I hate".

Your correspondence with Dobson as printed in Scribner[3] has pleased us all very much. A[ustin] D[obson] is all the qui vive to receive his Poems from the U.S. and I expect your preface[4] will give us much to talk about.

---

[1] The text of this letter has been based on the version printed by R. Baird Shuman, "A New Edmund Gosse Letter," *Notes and Queries*, CCIV (January 1959), 33; the version has been authenticated by the Librarian of the Pennington School, where the letter is now located.

[2] Stedman's review of Gosse's *New Poems* (London: Kegan Paul, 1879) appeared in *Scribner's Monthly*, XIX (March 1880), 790–791.

[3] An exchange of poetic epistles between Austin Dobson and Stedman was published in the "Bric-à-Brac" section of *Scribner's Monthly*, XIX (March 1880), 800. This exchange opens with an epistle from Dobson to Stedman on the latter's going to France.

[4] Stedman wrote the Introduction (pp. v–xiii) to the American edition of Dobson's *Vignettes in Rhyme, and other Verses* (New York: Henry Holt, 1880).

D. tells me you have finished your study of Edgar Poe.[5] I shall look forward to it with the greatest interest. Without doubt it will be the first time that adequate justice has been done to this great master of melodies.

Swinburne has asked me down to his house next week to hear a new volume of Poems[6] he is preparing for the press. Have you seen his Shakespeare?[7] It has had a very kind reception from the press here, and has overwhelmed the camp of the pedants with confusion.

I hope you are not overworking yourself. I am getting very tired and impatient for the holiday. My very kind regards to Mrs. Stedman, in which my wife joins.

Your friend

Edmund W. Gosse

[5] Stedman, "Edgar Allan Poe," *Scribner's Monthly*, XX (May 1880), 107–124.
[6] Presumably Swinburne's *Songs of the Springtides* (London: Chatto & Windus, 1880).
[7] Swinburne, *A Study of Shakespeare* (London: Chatto & Windus, 1880).

༄ 14. *Stedman to Gosse* ༄

71 West 54th. Street / New York,

16 March 1880

My dearest Gosse,

Let me at once inform you of the safe arrival, a few days ago, of the welcome and deeply interesting notes which you so kindly have prepared for my reading and discretionary use. They are of the most touching value to one, who, like myself, admires your poetic genius and has learned to love you as a man. And they are of curious worth as a study of the birth and breeding of a born-poet. They have brought tears to my eyes, for they singularly recall much of my own isolated youth in Puritan New England. I understand you fully: the lesson of it all is that the flower *will* make its way to the light, though planted in a sombre and unfertile nook. Nothing, save death, can hinder it. It "cannot else".

Before now I should have replied to your former letter, containing the picture by Tadema,[1] were it not that I've been driven half wild by over-work

[1] Lawrence [or Laurens] Alma-Tadema (1836–1912), the artist, was born in Holland but came to England in 1870, becoming a naturalized British subject in 1873. He was elected to the Royal Academy in 1879 and knighted in 1899. His second wife, Laura Epps, whom he married in 1871, was the sister of Gosse's wife, Nellie Epps (see Charteris, *Life and Letters of Gosse*, pp. 66–67). The portrait Stedman mentions was used as an illustration to his article on the London poets, p. 876 (see n. 2 below). Dobson's portrait, which Stedman also mentions in this letter, is on the same page.

—especially by my elaborate article on Poe, 40 pages boiled down to 19, happily finished at 2 o'clock A.M. last Saturday, and now permitting me to take up the dropped ends of my correspondence! Knowing that you understand my loyalty to a friend like yourself, I have not worried lest you might feel neglected. The likeness by your famous bro.-in-law is an excellent one for engraving—and that is what I need it for; it also is very characteristic; but for *home-use* I wish I could have you front-face, radiant with welcome, looking at me so kindly-wise and wisely-kind, over the top of your desk in the Whitehall office! That, I find, is the picture of you which oftenest comes to my own remembrance. Dobson has not yet sent me *his.* When I get that, and one or two others, I mean to prepare a sketchy article, illustrated with these portraits, (no attempt at fine-writing—probably anonymous) for *Harper's Magazine*[2]—the most widely sold of all our monthlies. Readers hereabout will be greatly interested in such a group of *portraitured* poets. By this you have read my notice of the "New Poems", in *Scribner.*[3] I tried to say as much as I could in the space allotted me. We are very glad you now know the Gilders personally, Mr. Gilder was broken-down by arduous work, as "managing ed." of *Scribner,* and the owners[4]—whose liberality is always affectionate and unstinted—sent him to Europe for a year. He is a noble, enthusiastic fellow, and I am gratified to learn from friends that London life is bringing him up again. Both he and Mrs. Gilder lead quite an ideal art-and-song life. Dobson's vol. comes out this week, and will be handsomely received. Have not yet seen a copy. His work has elements that appeal at once to the general public, aside from its artistic merits. I cannot sufficiently thank you for your continued services. The *Athenaeum* review, by Mr. Marston,[5] pleased me, because it is really judicial, and discussed the qualities of my best poems—as you did in the *Academy.*[6] The *Sat[urda]y Review* notice[7] seemed too much devoted to petty details, though perfectly fair. All in all my verse has been treated according to its deserts in England, and I have not the slightest ground for complaint. My only regret is that I can't get time to write new poems, and better. We have done all we could to make Mr. Trench[8] enjoy himself, in our homes, at the

[2] The article eventually appeared in May 1882: "Some London Poets," *Harper's Monthly,* LXIV (May 1882), 874–892.

[3] See Letter 13, n. 1.

[4] The owners of *Scribner's Monthly* at this time were Charles Scribner, Dr. J. G. Holland (the editor), and Roswell Smith. See Letter 18, n. 1.

[5] Probably Philip Bourke Marston (1850–1887), son of John Westland Marston, the dramatist; he became almost completely blind as the result of an accident in early childhood. He published three volumes of poetry during his lifetime, and is said to have gained a greater reputation in America than in England; his principal champion on both sides of the Atlantic was Mrs. Moulton (see Letter 5, n. 9).

[6] See Letter 10, n. 1.

[7] *Saturday Review,* XLIX (24 January 1880), 125–126.

[8] Alfred Chevenix Trench, son of Richard Chevenix Trench, Archbishop of Dub-

Clubs, and everywhere, and I think he likes America. Ask him all about it. By and by you will see it all, I trust, for yourself, *in propria persona,* and with *me* as your "guide, philosopher, and friend". Good-bye for to-night, and believe me always most affectionately yours

Edmund C. Stedman

lin, joined C. Kegan Paul in 1878 to form the publishing firm of Kegan Paul, Trench. Although generally a successful publisher, Trench was responsible for rejecting Robert Louis Stevenson's *Treasure Island.* See F. A. Mumby, *The House of Routledge, 1834–1934* (London: Routledge, 1934), pp. 185, 192–193.

❧ 15. *Gosse to Gilder* ❧

29, Delamere Terrace, / Westbourne Square. [London] W.

18 October 1880

My dear Gilder

I have been writing a number of business letters, and all with a steel pen. Now I take up a quill to write to you—the sympathetic instrument befitting the sympathetic man. We were heartily glad to get news of you at last. Your letter came leisurely wandering after us, and found us at Besançon, where we were having a very nice time in the house of some French friends, quite forgetting the Britain that bred us and the Middlesex that gave us suck, in the delights of garlic and frogs and snails. My wife was dreadfully knocked up before she went away: she had cultivated a cough that fairly frightened me, but France has completely restored her.

It is very kind of you "all" in America to remember us so pleasantly. We often talk about you and Stedman, the nicest of all lettered Americans that ever lived. I believe we say that because you are the only ones we know, for I observe that Dobson includes Brander Matthews,[1] as a third. Are you interested in Lowell?[2] We have all made his acquaintance, dropped our curtsey and gone our ways, and I see his flowing frnige of whisker in Whitehall nearly every day. But he is not sympathetic to me, and so I'll not deceive yer, as Sairey Gamp says.

I was very much struck with the poems of Mr. De Kay.[3] They have not

[1] [James] Brander Matthews (1852–1929), American author and critic, was becoming well known in London literary and artistic circles, although Gosse apparently had not met him at this time. Matthews's name appears in the Book of Gosse for 10 July 1881 and on several occasions in subsequent years. See also Letter 44, n. 3.

[2] James Russell Lowell, newly appointed United States minister in London. See Letter 72, n. 1, and Letter 95.

[3] Charles De Kay (1848–1935), American poet, the brother of Gilder's wife,

yet been done justice to over here, but that will come in time. He has genuine force and originality. He reminds me—you will see that the analogy is a remote one—of Crabbe. His peculiar type of imagination and Crabbe's are the same. I expect great things from him: he seems to me so much stronger than your Edgar Fawcetts.[4]

Here not much has happened. Swinburne is writing a good deal. A book of sonnets[5] by living poets is coming out which promises to be interesting. Almost everybody is represented. No new poet has arrived since Mary Robinson,[6] whose book has been withdrawn, partly, I am afraid, at my advice. Ward's book[7] has kept us all busy as you see. I have been writing a good deal of verse. I have about half of a new volume ready. My "New Poems"[8] had really a great success, which made me happy.

By this post I am sending a poem to the Editor of Scribner. It is the portrait of a man I found down in Sussex this spring, such a wonderful old person, a sort of rustic Thoreau; the animals all came freely to him.[9] I was very glad that Mr. De Kay admired Thornycroft's work in the "Academy" this year.[10] He was overpowered with eulogies: all the papers agreed that it was by far the best sculpture of the year, and the Duke of Westminster commissioned him to execute his "Artemis" in marble for Eaton Hall. I

Helena; his *Hesperus, and other Poems* was published in New York by Charles Scribner's Sons in 1880.

[4] Edgar Fawcett (1847–1904), American poet, novelist, and playwright; his poems occasionally appeared in *Scribner's*.

[5] Possibly a reference to T. Hall Caine, ed., *Sonnets of Three Centuries: A Selection, including many examples hitherto unpublished* (London: Elliot Stock, 1882), which includes four sonnets by Gosse.

[6] Agnes Mary Frances Robinson (1857–1944), English poet, critic, and historian, later the wife of James Darmesteter, the French orientalist; after Darmesteter's death she married Émile Duclaux, director of the Pasteur Institute. Her first volume of poems, *A Handful of Honeysuckle,* was published in London in 1875; the reference here is apparently to her second book, *The Crowned Hippolytus, Translated . . . with New Poems* (1881).

[7] Thomas Humphry Ward, ed., *The English Poets: Selections, with critical introductions by various writers, and a general introduction by M. Arnold* (5 vols.; London: Macmillan, 1880–1881.) Gosse wrote almost thirty biographical sketches for this collection.

[8] Gosse's *New Poems* had been published by Kegan Paul in 1879 (for their reception see Charteris, *Life and Letters of Gosse,* p. 141); he did not publish another volume of verse in England until *Firdausi in Exile and Other Poems* (London: Kegan Paul, 1885).

[9] Gosse's poem "The Charcoal-Burner" was published anonymously in *Scribner's Magazine,* XXI (January 1881), 421–422, and republished in his *Firdausi in Exile,* 110–113.

[10] William Hamo Thornycroft (1850–1925), the sculptor, was one of Gosse's most intimate friends. He was elected to the Royal Academy—the "Academy" to which Gosse here refers—in 1888 and knighted in 1917; his "Artemis" of 1880 remained one of his most noted works.

want you to keep for me the place in "Scribner's" for an article one of these days on Thornycroft and his work.[11] I think it would interest the Americans. So don't let anybody else do it for you. I would send you a portrait of himself, if you liked, and photographs of his best works. Perhaps it would be best to put it off till about May next year, and so include what he will have at the Academy next year. He is now doing a David playing before Saul, a life-sized figure to be in bronze. Thornycroft was much struck with your friend Mr. St. Gaudens'[12] work at the Grosvenor. It was he who first pointed it out to me. We shall both look out for his things in future.

Dobson has been very ill giving us some cause for anxiety, but he seems all right again now.

Have you seen Lang's Theocritus, with our verses in it?[13] or his charming "Ballades of Blue China"?[14] Lang is very prolific just now. He and Dobson are writing a little book on books in unison.[15]

Brander Matthews' little book on the French theatre[16] has been very largely noticed here, and with great praise. Do you know him?

You do not tell me whether you are writing poetry. I have lent your "Poet and his Master"[17] to several of our literati, who have all found in it pieces that they enjoyed. You should work with more persistence your happy pastoral vein.

The canard about my trying for the Professorship of poetry at Oxford, which has gone the round of the papers, is an absurd invention. The post is not vacant, nor likely to be, and I am not eligible, if it were, not being an M.A. of the university.[18]

---

[11] Gosse never contributed to the *Century* an article devoted to Thornycroft, but Thornycroft's work was discussed in the first of Gosse's two general articles on English sculpture published in 1883 (see Letter 39, n. 3).

[12] Augustus Saint-Gaudens (1848–1907), the Irish-born American sculptor. His statue of Admiral Farragut, exhibited in Paris in 1880 and erected in Madison Square, New York, the following year, was greatly admired and established him as one of the leading artists of his day.

[13] Andrew Lang (1844–1912), poet, scholar, prolific journalist, and man of letters, was a close friend of Gosse. His volume of translations, *Theocritus, Bion and Moschus* (London: Macmillan, 1880), contains two prefatory poems on Theocritus: "Villanelle," by Austin Dobson, and "Theocritus," by Gosse.

[14] Lang, *XXII Ballades in Blue China* (London: Kegan Paul, 1880).

[15] Lang, *The Library* (London: Macmillan, 1881); the final chapter on English illustrated books is by Austin Dobson.

[16] Brander Matthews, *French Dramatists of the 19th Century* (New York: Scribner's, 1881).

[17] Gilder, *The Poet and His Master, and Other Poems* (New York: Scribner's, 1878).

[18] Gosse had no degree from any university. In 1884, however, he was elected to the Clark Lectureship in English Literature at Trinity College, Cambridge (see Letter 66).

Our kindest remembrances to Mrs. Gilder. Although I have not the honour of knowing Mr. Stoddard[19] or Mr. Bunner,[20] may I send them a poetical greeting through you?

Farewell, my dear Gilder, and write soon to me again.

Yours very sincerely

Edmund W. Gosse

[19] Richard Henry Stoddard (1825–1903), poet and influential critic. His wife, Elizabeth Stoddard (1823–1902), was a novelist, and their house was something of a center of literary society in New York. Four of Stoddard's highly facetious letters to Gosse are in the Brotherton Collection; three of them were written while Gosse was in America, the other shortly afterwards. On 1 May 1882 Gosse had occasion to write to Stedman (a.l.s., CU) about "a very offensive paragraph" in the *Critic* (ns II [22 April 1882], 116), in which Stoddard said: "Rossetti is the intellectual sire of Morris, Swinburne, Gosse, Lang—the whole band of living English warblers, of whom the best are merely mocking-birds. . . . It is severe, no doubt, to call all late English verse rubbish, but rubbish it is, and it is shot largely upon us here in America." Gosse met Stoddard in America, however, and seems to have become very friendly with him.

[20] Henry Cuyler Bunner (1855–1896) was editor of *Puck,* the humorous and satirical weekly, from 1878 until the year of his death; he was also known as an urbane poet and writer of fiction. Both Stoddard and Bunner contributed to the *Century* from time to time.

❧ 16. *Gosse to Stedman* ❧

Board of Trade / 1 Whitehall / [London] S.W.

4 January 1881

My dear Stedman

The present of your friend's translation of Aucassin et Nicolette[1] was a pleasant proof to me that you had not quite forgotten me. It is long indeed since I had a letter from you, but I know well how extremely busy you are. I think the translation singularly well done: I had read the story in the strange old French, it really scarcely loses anything in this graceful and pure English.

You did ill not to send me your little book on Poe.[2] I had already got a promise that I should review it, and lo! it never turned up.

[1] A reference to the Modern French version (by Alexandre Bida) of *Aucassin et Nicolette,* with parallel English translation, published in New York by Fords, Howard and Hulbert in 1880. The translator was Augustus R. Macdonough, who had written one of the earliest critical articles on Stedman's work (see Stedman and Gould, *Life and Letters of Stedman,* I, 47–48, 488.

[2] Stedman's essay on Poe in *Scribner's Monthly* was later published in book form: *Edgar Allan Poe* (Boston: Houghton Mifflin; London: Sampson Low, 1881).

You were once so kind as to say that I might always freely ask you a favour. I want to know if you think that Mr. Holt[3] would bring out in New York a selection of my poems similar in form to that of Dobson's? I am extremely anxious to make an appearance before the American public, and the success my last books have had over here, where popularity is so hard to obtain, makes me inclined to think that an American publisher would lose nothing by me. Moreover, if Mr. Holt liked to undertake the thing at once I could give him several pieces which have not yet been included in any book of mine, and which will be published in the new volume I hope to have ready early in 1882.[4] Dobson, who is most kind in urging me to write thus, promises a letter to Mr. Holt, if that is any use, but I should be very glad if it were convenient for you to sound the publisher first. Perhaps someone out in America who likes my things would write a little introduction, like your exquisite little introduction to Dobson.

In the guild of letters we may ask these favours of one another, may we not, my dear Poet?

Happy new year to you and yours

Yours sincerely

Edmund W. Gosse

[3] Henry Holt (1840–1926), the American publisher, brought out a considerably revised edition of Gosse's *On Viol and Flute* in New York in 1883; there was no introduction. For Holt's life and publishing activities see Henry Holt, *Garrulities of an Octogenarian Editor* (Boston and New York: Houghton Mifflin, 1923).

[4] Apart from the revised American edition of *On Viol and Flute,* Gosse's next volume of verse was not published until 1885 (see Letter 104, n. 1).

17. Gosse to Stedman

1 Whitehall / [London] S.W.

18 June 1881

My dear Stedman

If the fount of tears did not lie so deep I could have cried this morning when I got your letter. But I am truly happy to think you have utterly misunderstood my meaning in the main, and if I blush, as I do, it is from embarrassment and not shame.

I did not answer your first long letter because I felt that in some measure I had made a faux pas in my original suggestion, and because I meant to take your wise advice, and wait till my ⟨prose⟩ was more complete.

The short note[1] which has given you so much pain was a sort of jet of bad temper. But there was no intentional egotism in it. Indeed, my dear Stedman, I should get under the bed, and starve myself in that disgusting seclusion, if I found myself capable of such conduct.

I will make a clean breast of the whole matter. I was extremely moved, and in a manner alarmed, at O'Shaughnessy's death.[2] It was the first time that a contemporary colleague, as it were, had died. When his executors opened his papers, they found proofs of his great and loyal affection to me, which moved me inexpressibly. I recollected that though I had always been a staunch admirer of his poetry, I had never been particularly attached to himself. I was overwhelmed with a sort of remorse, and tried to exonerate my fault—if it were a fault—by clamouring for a recognition of his genius. In the midst of this condition, Dobson received a letter from you containing a phrase which set me in a quite unjustifiable anger, and then and there, having secured a portrait some days before, I sent it to you with that nasty little note. Like a child that has done wrong, I told Dobson next day what I had done, and he promptly said "Then I think it was very unkind of you". *You* then became the object of my remorse, and as soon as my "Odes"[3] came out I sent one of the first copies to you, as a little peace-offering. Painful as it has been to me to read your letter, I am very thankful of an opportunity of explaining.

What you tell me about your quiet kindness to me and my work need not have been said, though it deeply touches me to hear of it from you. Will you not believe, my dear Friend, that it was my entire consciousness of this that gave me the power to write that disagreeable note. I said to myself, as well as temper allowed me to reflect, "He knows that I appreciate his constant friendliness to me, so I need not fear to hint to him about others".

I confess that the later pages of your letter gave me a hard task to read. I was quite overwhelmed to think that you could (and not without justification) charge me with such meanness. I am well repaid with exquisite pain for the wound I was so careless in giving you.

And now, for I write in the first whirl of chagrin, accept this rough

[1] On 21 March 1881 Gosse had written the following curt note to Stedman: "From the executors of poor O'Shaughnessy I have obtained this portrait, which was taken about 1872, and which is extremely like him, although a bad photo. I hope therefore that you will now be able to finish your article on the younger poets who welcomed you with so much warmth on your arrival in London, and to whom you owe the greater part of your success on this side of the Atlantic (a.l.s., CU).

[2] Arthur William Edgar O'Shaughnessy (1844–1881), the poet, worked in the British Museum, where Gosse first met him in 1867. O'Shaughnessy died on 30 January 1881, and his volume, *Songs of a Worker* (London: Chatto & Windus, 1881), edited by A. W. N. Deacon, appeared shortly afterwards.

[3] Gosse, ed., *English Odes* (London: Kegan Paul, 1881).

expression of affectionate distress, if I may say so, and believe me when I say that I have met with no fellow-craftsman in my profession in whom I have recognized so unselfish a spirit or so large a heart as yours.

When I am calmer I will write again. In the meantime try to forgive

Your sincere Friend
Edmund W. Gosse

～ 18. Gosse to Gilder ～

[London?]

20 July 1881

Confidential

My dear Gilder

I daresay you will like to have a private account of the Arrival of the Boss,[1] which of course has been an event of great moment to us. I have seen him three times, and we have had a great deal of talk. I like him very much: he seems to me an honest and even enthusiastic man, whom one can trust, although his manner, of course, is reserved. He and Mrs. R[oswell] S[mith] dined with us last night,[2] to meet Dobson, and we took them on to a reception at Mrs. Alma Tadema's.[3] I think they enjoyed themselves very much.

He has given me a great deal more to do than I had before. I am to act for "St. Nicholas"[4] as well as "Scribner's", and to look at all MSS. sent from

[1] Roswell Smith (1829–1892), with Dr. J. G. Holland and Charles Scribner, founded <i>Scribner's Monthly</i> in 1870. In 1881 Smith bought out Charles Scribner, Jr., and on the withdrawal of Dr. Holland the same year became virtually the sole proprietor of the magazine, the name of which was changed, with the November issue, to the <i>Century Illustrated Monthly Magazine</i>. Gilder became editor-in-chief following Dr. Holland's death in October 1881. See J. G. Holland, " 'Scribner's Monthly.'—Historical," <i>Scribner's Monthly</i>, XXII (June 1881), 302–303; also, Frank Luther Mott, <i>A History of American Magazines, 1865–1885</i> (Cambridge, Massachusetts: Harvard University Press, 1957), pp. 467–468.

[2] There is no mention of this occasion in the Book of Gosse, where the only recorded visit of Mr. and Mrs. Roswell Smith is on 10 June 1883.

[3] See Letter 14, n. 1.

[4] <i>St. Nicholas, an Illustrated Magazine for Young Folks</i> was published by Scribner & Company, the company formed to publish <i>Scribner's Monthly</i>, from its founding in 1873 until 1881; it was then taken over by Roswell Smith's new Century Company.

New York or arriving for the Magazines here, at Warne's.[5] I have agreed to do all this, not without some dismay, as to whether I shall be able to manage it all.

As this is quite confidential I may tell you further that he asked me to name the salary that would repay me for all this work. I answered that I would much rather not attempt to do that, and that I should accept whatever he came to consider the value of my services to the magazine. Was it not better to leave it so? He said he should make me a proposal later on.

Now to business. The article from Dean Stanley[6] is the last piece of literary work on which he was engaged. I have sent a note to that effect to the "Athenaeum" and I think you might make capital out of the circumstance.

I hope Rajon[7] will be in time. I lose no opportunity of stirring him up. If it comes to the worst, your engraver ought to be able—at a push—to run it through in three weeks, ought he not?

Goodbye, my dear Friend. Perhaps as this is a private and confidential epistle, I may sign myself for once

Yours affectionately
Edmund W. Gosse

We have greatly enjoyed seeing a good deal of Brander Matthews.

The first editor was Mary Mapes Dodge. See Mott, *American Magazines, 1865–1885*, pp. 500–505.

[5] Frederick Warne & Company, Bedford Street, London, took over the English printing of *St. Nicholas* and the *Century* in 1881.

[6] Arthur Penrhyn Stanley (1815–1881), Dean of Westminster from 1863 until his death (18 July 1881) was a distinguished ecclesiastical historian and a leader of the Broad Church movement. His article, "Frederick W. Robertson," appeared in the *Century*, XXIII (February 1882), 559–562; it was announced in the "Literary Gossip" department of the *Athenaeum*, 23 July 1881, p. 114.

[7] Paul-Adolphe Rajon (1844–1888), the French engraver, was responsible for engraving Frederick W. Burton's portrait of George Eliot, which appeared in *Century*, XXIII (November 1881); this frontispiece was accompanied by an article on George Eliot portraits, pp. 47–48 (see Letter 43, n. 3). Rajon had also prepared W. W. Ouless's portrait of Cardinal Newman for the *Century*.

❧ 19. Gosse to Stedman ❧

29, Delamere Terrace, / Westbourne Square. [London] W.

14 August 1881

My dear Stedman

I was delighted to get your letter. Your article on American poetry in Scribner[1] was a rather solid but very well-thought-out piece of work. I read it with great interest and with admiration of the skill and tact with which you treated difficult points. I was pleased with your courage. Want of courage in the face of American literature seems to me the terrible fault of your critics. For instance, some writer—a very clever writer—in "Scribner" last year[2] talked of the great world-poets that had died in their prime, such as Catullus, Chénier, Lenau, Keats and *Drake*.[3] I'm not sure of the exact names, but they were all of the first class, except *Drake*. The American critics lack the courage to omit Drake when they talk of Keats. Now, I honour you for taking a larger view in these things; but I sigh with wonder when I see such a book as this vast encyclopædia of poetry by Epes Sargent,[4] which has just reached us. Have you seen it? What a hopeless helpless, *injurious* great bulk it is. Now it quite makes one despair to see the concessions to American vanity made in the course of that book. "Keats and Drake", they are quite names of equal value to Epes Sargent. This is why I specially delight in the good sense and critical wholesomeness of your excellent Scribner essay.

But your poem "Cor [sic] Concordia"[5] is of a higher quality. I assure you that I read it with the very rarest pleasure. It is so elevated in tone, of so pure and austere a music, so firm and ringing in movement of thought alike and sound, that I put it very high among your poems, I could easily be persuaded to put it highest of all.

A curious toadstool, a malodorous parasitic growth, has been put forth in our poetic world in the shape of a volume of "Poems" by Mr. Oscar Wilde,[6] the fat young gentleman in the long hair, whose portrait appears in "Punch". His aristocratic friends have clustered round him, and his atrocious book, which has no merit but its impudence, is in its 3rd edition. It is an

[1] Stedman, "Poetry in America: Part I," *Scribner's Monthly*, XXII (August 1881), 540–550.

[2] No such article appears to have been published in *Scribner's Monthly* during 1880.

[3] Joseph Rodman Drake, the American poet, was born in 1795 and died of consumption in 1820; he was the grandfather of Gilder's wife, Helena.

[4] Epes Sargent (1813–1880), Boston author, journalist, and advocate of spiritualism, was responsible for the posthumously published *Harper's Cyclopaedia of British and American Poetry* (New York: Harper and Brothers, 1881).

[5] Stedman, "Corda Concordia," *Atlantic Monthly*, XLVIII (Aug. 1881), 179–183.

[6] Oscar Wilde, *Poems* (London: David Bogue, 1881).

amusing phase of our social life. People at a distance might imagine it was something serious.

Christina Rossetti has a new volume just out,[7] which I have not yet read. Do you know that I think the greatest error in your "Victorian Poets" is the small importance that you give to her, the finest poetess that the English-speaking world has produced, in my opinion. O'Shaughnessy's posthumous volume[8] has been a blow to us all. It is almost totally without merit: it is difficult to find one piece in it good enough to quote. I am afraid that he had outlived his talent.

Have you seen the new enlarged edition of Lang's "Ballades in Blue and White China"?[9] there are some enchanting things in it.

I am sorry my later pieces are not ready to be discussed in your paper in "Harper's", for I believe I have made a considerable spurt lately, particularly in narrative poetry. Perhaps you have, however, seen what of my things have been published in the "Cornhill"[10] and elsewhere. It matters not.

May I ask one thing. In the sketch of my life I wrote for you, I spoke very freely about my father.[11] It was because I felt complete confidence in you: it is not necessary to remind you that he is still alive, and that it would grieve me intensely to see anything said in print that could wound the old gentleman, on whom age has had a most softening influence, and with whom I am now on the most affectionate and filial footing.

We are all separating for the autumn holidays. I greatly need a change: I have been excessively busy this year. My wife desires kindest remembrances to Mrs. Stedman and yourself.

Believe me

Cordially your friend

Edmund W. Gosse

Lang wrote to you, but only put New-York as the address, by accident. Did you get it? Our good Dobson greets you.

---

[7] Christina Rossetti, *A Pageant, and other Poems* (London: Macmillan, 1881).

[8] Arthur O'Shaughnessy, *Songs of a Worker*: see Letter 17, n. 2.

[9] Andrew Lang, *XXII and X, XXXII Ballades in Blue China* (London: Kegan Paul, 1881).

[10] Poems recently published by Gosse included "Palingenesis," *Cornhill Magazine,* XLI (April 1880), 491–493, and "Timositheos," XLIII (April, 1881), 444–445. Stedman's "paper" was the article, "Some London Poets," published in *Harper's Monthly* in May 1882 (see Letter 14, n. 2).

[11] For mention of the sketch see Letters 12 and 14. Gosse's father was Philip Henry Gosse (1810–1888), the distinguished naturalist. Gosse later wrote his biography, *The Life of Philip Henry Gosse, F.R.S.* (London: Kegan Paul, 1890), and gave a powerful autobiographical account of their relationship in *Father and Son: A Study of Two Temperaments* (London: Heinemann, 1907).

ꙮ 20. *Stedman to Gosse* ꙮ

New York / 71 West 54th Street

15 January 188[2][1]

My dear Gosse,

Remembering your remarks in a letter, not long ago, concerning Mr. Oscar Wilde—who now is giving us a *replica* of his May-Fair invasion[2]—I have had my son collect from the newspapers as much as possible of the comment upon him, and the absurd reports and squibs provoked by his apparition.

All these I have had assorted, and now avail myself of Mr. Bowker's[3] kindness to place in your hands.

As Henry the VIIIth. said to Wolsey

> "Read o'er this;
> And after, this: and then to breakfast, with
> What appetite you have".[4]

As "some" 15000 provincial newspapers are making jokes about Wilde, or reporting him, and as Mr. D'Oyly Carte[5] is "managing" him, I suppose he will draw a large audience, at least *once,* in each city; thousands, who never read other poetry, will buy his book from curiosity. He will take back a small fortune to London, and you will think us all idiots.

This is a confidential letter—pray do not quote it—for I am already in a peck of trouble, being roundly abused for not responding with courteous hospitality to the letters of introduction which he brought me from eminent men to whom I am under obligations. The fact is that I got angry over the display made by certain classes of our "society", and could not bring myself to do homage to the knee-buckles and hose of this youthful apostle. A hasty private letter of mine got into print,[6] and I am reaping the whirlwind. So don't increase my troubles, but sympathize kindly with

Yours ever sincerely,

E. C. Stedman

---

[1] Stedman wrote "1881," but the year is clearly 1882.

[2] For Wilde's visit to America see Lloyd Lewis and Henry Justin Smith, *Oscar Wilde Discovers America [1882]* (New York: Harcourt, Brace, 1936), *passim.*

[3] Richard Rogers Bowker (1848–1933) was the English agent for the British edition of *Harper's Magazine* from 1880 to 1882. From 1884 until his death he edited *Publisher's Weekly,* which he had purchased in 1879.

[4] Shakespeare, *Henry VIII,* III, ii, 202–204. The punctuation and the capitalization are Stedman's.

[5] Richard D'Oyly Carte (1844–1901), theatre manager and impresario, best known for his promotion of Gilbert and Sullivan operas, especially at the Savoy Theatre, which he built in 1881.

[6] Stedman wrote in his diary for 5 January 1882: "This Philistine town is making

The Harper article is to be in the *May number*⁷—out in April—so they now say.

---

a fool of itself over Oscar Wilde. Pah!" (Stedman and Gould, *Life and Letters of Stedman,* II, 31). The letter to the editor of the Boston *Transcript,* also quoted in *Life and Letters of Stedman* (II, 32–33), concludes: "I suppose Wilde and [D'Oyly] Carte will cart away $100,000., and London will think us all d—d fools. I have given Mrs. Bigelow, Mrs. Botta, etc., my future opinion of the value of their courtesies to myself. On Sunday evening, Mrs. Croly gave a reception *To Miss* [Louisa M.] *Alcott.* My wife went. I stayed away, fearing Wilde would be there. He *was* there—and next day my name, to my wrath, was among the guests." For an example of the letters of introduction which Wilde took with him to America see M. A. DeWolfe Howe, *New Letters of James Russell Lowell* (New York and London: Harper, 1932), p. 262. Lowell, writing to Oliver Wendell Holmes on 21 December 1881, asking him to "be serviceable to the bearer of this, Mr. Oscar Wilde, the report of whom has doubtless reached you and who is better than his report."

⁷ See Letter 14, n. 2.

❧ 21. *Gosse to Stedman* ❧

29, Delamere Terrace, / Westbourne Square. / [London] W.

3 February 1882

My dear Friend

Good Mr. Bowker has been so obliging as to place in my hands the budget of Wildiana which you have so kindly had gathered for me. A stinking nosegay, but a medicinal one, which will be of very great use in concocting a Brew or Purge which is in preparation for the animal on his return to these shores. Seriously, he has lost more friends in going to America than all his previous vagaries cost him. Your own conduct in the matter has really been admirable. You showed, I think, a noble social courage, which your known hospitality and width of sympathy must have (heated) into a very important snub for Mr. Oscar. You did quite right, and I am sure that all right-minded will be with you. Bowker tells me that all are, in America.¹

I myself have suffered in the cause of Oscar. I refused to allow any contributions of mine to appear in a book of sonnets (Mr. Hall Caine's, in

---

¹ One of the literary figures in America who approved of Stedman's stand and took a similar line himself was Thomas Bailey Aldrich. See Mrs. Thomas Bailey Aldrich, *Crowding Memories* (Boston and New York: Houghton Mifflin [1920]), pp. 246–250, and especially p. 247: "During the stay of Mr. Wilde in Boston, Mr. Aldrich lived in strict seclusion. No invitations to dinners, receptions, or lunches were accepted, on the chance that this prodigious *poseur* might also be a guest."

which you also appear)[2] if Wilde, who had wormed his way into the book, were not ejected. Ejected he was, but I got heaps of abuse, which however is now turning, I find, to something like approbation.

Enough of him. I am glad to hear of your poetical activity, and wish to see these Christmas poems.[3] I find a review on my desk which I send you, to show you that I have lately been thinking of your work. I am curious to know, moreover, how my view of Whittier,[4] who is rather a crux to us English people, will strike you.

You are coming, Trench tells me, to England this summer, and he thinks you come alone. If so, my wife and I unite in begging that you will come straight to this house, and take up your abode with us. We cannot entertain a married pair, but we can make a bachelor very comfortable. Now, this is not talk, it is sober seriousness. We beg that if you come alone, you will make our house your home—a place of liberty, to act in as you will—as long as you are in London.

Reply.

Yours sincerely

Edmund W. Gosse

[2] T. Hall Caine, ed., *Sonnets of Three Centuries* (1882); the volume includes four sonnets by Gosse (see Letter 15, n. 5) and one by Stedman.

[3] Stedman speaks of these poems in a letter to Gosse of 23 December 1881 (BC); one of them was presumably "Guests at Yule," *Critic*, I (17 December 1881), 358.

[4] "Mr. Whittier's Latest Poems," *Pall Mall Gazette*, 30 January 1882, p. 5; in this unsigned review Gosse gives Whittier rather cautious praise and attempts to account for the high value placed on his work in the United States: "He is the most national of all their writers . . . ." When speaking of Whittier's poem "Jubilee Singers," he makes a reference to Stedman's ballad of John Brown as "one of the finest of his national lyrics."

꧁ 22. *Gosse to Gilder* ꧂

7 Whitehall Gardens / [London] S.W.

20 March 1882

My dear Gilder

You make me proud with the beautiful lines you send me in your gift of Emerson. Of course, I shall be delighted to see them printed in the "Century".[1] As to the book itself, I must thank you for a real revelation.

[1] Gilder's poem "To E. W. G. in England," was printed over the initial "G." in the

Emerson does not shine in excerpts, and hitherto I had only met with him in extracts. There is a spiritual fervour, a depth of feeling, a brilliance of instinct, that sometimes fairly takes away one's breath: linked with them, o mirabile dictu! there is a distinct occasional sense of insincerity. The prophet sees more than his worshippers can guess of in his magic mirror, but alas! they expect him to be always at it, and he goes on energising and pythonising when there is nothing to be seen. I suppose all modern prophets must have a pinchbeck heel; that does not prevent the rest of Emerson's body from being pure silver and gold. Some of these things are miraculous—"Wood-notes", "Monadnock", "Threnody", for instance. I know few staves so enchanting, so full of the very body and blood of poetry, as the closing part of "The Harp", with its vision of the lovely boys of the Parthenon frieze—for this I suppose is Emerson's intention. Or are these New England youths, seen down the aisles of memory, as he saw them in some mountain farm-stead in his boyhood? It does not the least matter, the lines are magical.[2]

You who in Eldorado live
Have no better gift to give, I fancy, than this little book.[3]
Thank you much for it.

Lang wishes to withdraw the verses I lately sent you. He thinks them not first-rate, and if he appears in the "Century" at all, would like to appear always at his best.

It is a great comfort to me that you find the Carlyle[4] interesting. I am afraid that the price was large, and that Sampson, Low & Co. were very sharp, in fact told lies. If a venerable gentleman comes to me with an aspect of frankness, and a charming manner, I am afraid it does not occur to me

---

Century, XXIV (July 1882), 396. The copy of Emerson's *Selected Poems* (Boston: Houghton Mifflin, 1882) which Gilder sent to Gosse is in the Brotherton Collection; the version of the poem printed in the *Century* is two lines longer than that inscribed on a fly leaf of the book and is actually closer to the version included in a brief letter from Gilder to Gosse, dated 5 March 1882, which is pasted into the book.

[2] In the copy of the Emerson *Selected Poems* in the Brotherton Collection someone, presumably Gosse, has marked with a pencil the passage in "The Harp" in which the youths are described (beginning "Not long ago, at eventide"), underlining the last three lines:

> Followed with love
> They knew not of,
> With passion cold and shy.

[3] These lines are an adaptation of Gilder's verses inscribed in the book (see n. 1 above).

[4] Three extracts from Carlyle's diaries appeared under the title "Carlyle in Ireland" in the *Century*, XXIV (1882), 17–30, 244–256, 426–441.

that he may be telling downright falsehoods: Mr. Marston[5] said that they had paid very nearly £500 for it themselves!

Your always sincerely

E. W. G.

[5] *Reminiscences of my Irish Journey in 1849* by Thomas Carlyle, with a preface by J. A. Froude, was published in London by Sampson and Low in 1882; the man mentioned here is possibly Edward Marston, publisher, and author of works on angling, copyright laws, and other topics.

꘏ 23. Gosse to Howells[1] ꘏

7 Whitehall Gardens / [London] S.W.

26 July 1882

My dear Sir

My friend Mr. R. W. Gilder, of the "Century" (of which I am the English representative) has encouraged, and indeed urged, me to thrust myself upon you, and take the liberty of an old acquaintance. As one of your first and warmest English admirers perhaps I may claim to be a one-sided acquaintance. I hear that you have already sailed from New York, and I write to beg you to let me know whether there is anything I can do to make your visit to London pleasant. People are beginning to leave town, and it is possible that you may find the houses of some of your friends deserted. My wife and I hope that this may redound to our advantage, and that we may hope to see you as our guest.

The address at the top of this letter is my official one. I am here, and shall be very glad to see you, every week day (but Saturdays when I leave at 1) from 11 to 5.

Pray believe me

My dear Sir

Very faithfully yours

Edmund W. Gosse

[1] This appears to have been the first letter to pass between Gosse and William Dean Howells (1837–1920), who had just retired from the editorship of the *Atlantic Monthly* and was beginning a year-long visit to Europe on account of his own health and, more especially, that of his elder daughter, Winifred. For Howells's biography see Mildred Howells, *Life in Letters of Howells,* and Clara Marburg Kirk and Rudolph Kirk, eds., *William Dean Howells* (rev. ed.; New York: Hill and Wang, 1961), pp. xv–clxvii.

❧ 24. *Howells to Gosse* ❧

18 Pelham Crescent, / South Kensington. [London].

1 August 1882

My dear Sir:

I found your very kind note at the American Exchange to-day,[1] and I have to thank you for the acquaintance you give me. I shall be only too glad to meet you and make it personal. We are very pleasantly lodged here, but our plans for staying in London are yet very uncertain. We only know that we shall stay till the end of next week, after which we may or may not go to Switzerland.

I shall try to find you at your office, and in the meantime my wife and I will be glad to see Mrs. Gosse and yourself.

Very sincerely yours

W. D. Howells

[1] For Howells's arrival in London see his letter to J. R. Osgood, also dated 1 August 1882, in Mildred Howells, *Life in Letters of Howells*, I, 315–316.

❧ 25. *Gosse to Howells* ❧

7 Whitehall Gardens / [London] S.W.

2 August 1882

Dear Mr. Howells

It was a great pleasure to me to get your letter. Sundays are infinitely horrid in London, and next Sunday will be worse than usual because it precedes one of our barbaric public holidays. Will therefore you and Mrs. Howells break the tedium of it by spending the afternoon and evening with us? My wife hopes to call on Mrs. Howells tomorrow or the next day; it will a little depend upon her health, which is not strong just now. If she should be unable to get so far, she will write to Mrs. Howells.

But I write now to try and secure you both for that day (Sunday). If you would come about 4 p.m., and stay as long into the night as you can, it would give us great pleasure.

Our friend Henry James tells me that you dislike, as I heartily do, Society with a capital S. But we shall probably be alone, except that we may have Alma Tadema and his wife with us, and that I am just writing to ask the much-engaged James himself if he will not come.[1]

[1] The visit made by Howells and his wife on Sunday, 6 August 1882, is recorded

You will, I am sure pardon me for trying to carry you by storm into our little home-circle.

My house is
No. 29 Delamere Terrace
Westbourne Square. W.

If your cab-man hesitates, tell him "at the top of Westbourne Terrace, and facing the canal".

Very sincerely yours

Edmund W. Gosse

---

in the Book of Gosse; Alma-Tadema and his wife were present, but Henry James was not. On 8 August 1882 (a.l.s., BM) Howells wrote accepting a further invitation for Sunday, 20 August; speaking also for his wife, he declared: "We don't consent that anybody began to have half so good a time as we did the other day."

ꙮ 26. *Gosse to Stedman* ꙮ

Board of Trade. [London] S.W.

21 August 1882

My dear Stedman

How many things I have to thank you for! First for the acquaintance of your charming friend Col. John Hay,[1] who is a man of high calibre, and bears his honours with a delightful ease. Then for all your kind letters and notes, and for your assiduous friendship in collecting for me the very indulgent and generous notices of my Gray which have appeared in the American press.[2] That in the New York Times[3] pleased me particularly, by its

[1] Stedman had written introducing Hay in a letter to Gosse of 4 July 1882 (a.l.s., BC). At the top of this letter there is a note in Gosse's hand: "Col. Hay called here and saw me 27.7.82." John Hay (1838–1905), author and statesman, served as Assistant Secretary of State under President Hayes from 1879 to 1881; he was later ambassador to Great Britain (1897–1898) and Secretary of State (1898–1905) under President McKinley and Theodore Roosevelt. His most important literary works before 1882 were *Castilian Days* (1871) and *Pike County Ballads* (1871); his novel *The Bread-Winners* was published anonymously in 1884, having first appeared in the *Century* (see Letter 51, n. 4), and in 1890 he and John Nicolay published their ten-volume *Abraham Lincoln: A History*.

[2] Gosse's *Gray* in the English Men of Letters Series was published in 1882 by Macmillan in London and by Harper in New York. For the American reception of the book see Paul F. Mattheisen, "Edmund Gosse: A Literary Record" (unpublished Ph.D. dissertation, Rutgers University, 1958), pp. 78–79.

[3] New York *Times*, 6 August 1882, p. 10. The anonymous reviewer said that Gosse

thoughtful and savant criticism. The little book has enjoyed a great success over here, and I have been much cheered by the reception it has enjoyed.[4] I trust it may lead to a full edition of Gray's Works.[5]

W. D. Howells is over here, and we have seen a great deal of him. To know him is to love him: I think he is one of the most winning personalities I have ever met, so receptive, yet with so much to give, so modest and sweet, with such a fund of genius and strength. He is your best novelist, I think, and have long thought so. He has a charm for me which I do not find in your more professed humourists, at least to so great an extent.

I was very glad to receive from Col. Hay some account of the reason of your sudden return to America,[6] and to learn that it was not caused by any family anxiety. I hope you are flourishing, and preparing some sound literary labour. How do your American poets[7] get on?

We are just starting for a village on the coast of Northumberland, where we shall moon and vegetate for a month. With kindest regards to Mrs. Stedman and your son

Believe me

Always sincerely yours

Edmund W. Gosse

---

had done his job "with great care, industry, and faithfulness. . . . His book has of course the charm which its subject gives to it, but it is charming in far other ways than that; it is well written; it has a great many pages of intelligent and suggestive criticisms . . ."

[4] For the English reception of the book see Mattheisen, "Edmund Gosse," (dissertation, Rutgers), pp. 51–55.

[5] Gosse's edition of Gray's works was published in London by Macmillan in 1884.

[6] In the letter to Gosse of 4 July 1882 (see n. 1 above) Stedman wrote: "It must seem strange, when I *ought* to be, as you know, in Venice, that I am writing you from New York! It is a sore trial to me—the sudden change." In May and June 1882 Stedman, accompanied by his son Arthur and his friend Clarence King, traveled from America to Venice, spending some time in London on the way. The morning after arriving in Venice he received news of "a business loss" which made it necessary for him to return immediately to New York (Stedman and Gould, *Life and Letters of Stedman*, II, 37–38).

[7] See Letter 102, n. 1.

ϟ 27. *Howells to Gosse* ϟ

18 Pelham Crescent, [London]

26 August 1882

My dear Gosse:

I send you the last no. of A M[odern] I[nstance],[1] and you will see that it is not a thing to make a presentation copy of. Let me have it back (to keep my set whole) at your convenience, and when D. Douglas issues the book about September 30[2], I will give you a copy with my name written all over it.

I had such a lovely time last night that I would now like to cut the ties of a husband and father, and come to live with you. Is there not some law or privilege by which you could adopt an elderly foreigner of fading intellect? I would do chores about the house, run of errands, tell Theresa[3] stories, and make myself generally useful. Think of it seriously: I mean business.

Yours ever

W. D. Howells

[1] Howells's novel, *A Modern Instance*, had been appearing serially in the *Century*; the last installment, comprising Chapters xxxvi-xli, appeared in *Century*, XXIV (October 1882), 897–919.

[2] *A Modern Instance* was published in book form in October 1882 (Boston: Osgood, 1882). David Douglas, the Edinburgh publisher, had begun publishing a number of Howells's novels in 1882 and *A Modern Instance* appeared under his imprint that year.

[3] Theresa ("Tessa") the Gosses' eldest child, had been born in 1877; the other two children were Philip (subsequently to become well-known as a naturalist and author), born 1879, and Sylvia (the artist), born 1881.

ϟ 28. *Gosse to Howells* ϟ

Embleton / Chathill / Northumberland

30 August 1882

Dear Howells

You shall be welcomed, oh! how gladly, into the House of the Gigglers. In that home there are no chores to be done, and no errands to be run. It is giggling and making giggle from morning to night.

We are in a place as rude and wild as any, I think, in America. And with one feature which you have not; for we stood today on a height in the spurs of the Cheviots, and could distinguish at one time the ruins of no less than four historic castles; this is the land of border romance, the land of moss-troopers and wild forays; and the landscape lends itself to the feelings, and seems full of the wild fresh simplicity of a ballad.

The end of A Modern Instance is superb. You draw your threads together with extraordinary skill. The old Judge remains the most striking character all through, but all is strong and consistent. The railway journey is admirable: your journeys are always good. Perhaps Ben is made a little needlessly repulsive when he comes back? That is the only thing which jars on me. I think you colour what he would feel a little from the old conventional water-colour paint-box of what people should feel. Marcia going west is at once an epitome of and a commentary on her whole character. A M. I. is altogether the greatest work of fiction that America has given us since the death of Hawthorne. I am quite sure of that.

If it were not selfish I should wish to have you here. What endless talks by the sea, what rambles over the brown sweet-scented moors that would mean. And we would take a boat over to the Fern [sic] Islands, and start a monarchy. You should be King, because you are so very democratic, and I would be your Fool. Or we would capture Dunstaneborough Castle, and live there; it is thoroughly out of repair.

Please thank Miss Winnie[1] for her kind letter. We unite in kindest remembrances to Mrs. Howells. Any scrap of your writing will be welcome to

Yours very cordially

Edmund W. Gosse

[1] Winifred ("Winny"), Howells's eldest child, was born in 1863.

❧ 29. Howells to Gosse ❧

18 Pelham Crescent, [London]

9 September 1882

My dear Gosse:

With the divination of a St-dm-n,[1] I know that ever since I have not answered your letter, you have been saying to yourself, "The supersensitive H[owells] cannot bear the slightest criticism. Here I have been travelling on the praises of his stupid story ever since he came to England, and at the slightest hint of a conventional color-box in his luggage, he goes off in a rage and wont write to me." I own that the thing has that look, and yet it

[1] The point of this reference to Stedman is unclear; Gosse may, however, have told Howells of the misunderstanding reflected in Letter 17.

is only an appearance. The truth is I have been growing very old since you went away, and I am actually writing this with spectacles. This approach of age warns me to be off from London before I am too superannuated to travel; and we all start for Switzerland on the 18th. I shall not see you again, therefore, till next Spring, and that grieves me, for I love you. But we have enjoyed too much here, and I must go somewhere else to be a wiser and more industrious man, or else the Century will not get its novel for next year.[2] I have written but a hundred pages of it in six weeks, and I have had such a good time that I have been unable to do so much even as kill a consumptive girl, or even make a lover homesick enough to start home from China and get wrecked on an atoll in the South Pacific: he is still shamelessly hanging around Hong-Kong, and I have thrown away no end of geography and geology on his atoll. As long as I dine out four times a week, he will not budge; and I am resolved to try what effect a Swiss pension will have on him.

By the way, I wish you had been here to dine with the herd of Yankees whom Osgood[3] managed to scare up one night in London. What do you say to Aldrich, Harte, Story,[4] Clarence King,[5] Charles Dudley Warner,[6] Edwin Booth[7] and W[illiam] D[ean] H[owells] meeting together at the Hotel Continental? We wanted you; and the only other Englishman we had was a Dutchman—Tadema. We had a famous time; and the enemy was represented by Laffan,[8] who has just come over to replace Bowker.

Last Sunday we went down to Stoke Poges, and viewed it in the pleasant light of your Gray. Mrs. Howells has read scarcely anything else since I brought it home; and she has goaded me to desperation with quotations from it; but she was so handy that day with them that I forgave her. It was a

[2] The novel on which Howells was working was *A Woman's Reason* (Boston: Osgood, 1883), in which the hero is shipwrecked on a Pacific atoll; see Henry Nash Smith and William M. Gibson, eds., *Mark Twain-Howells Letters* (Cambridge, Massachusetts: Harvard University Press, 1960), pp. 232, 234, n. 5.

[3] James Ripley Osgood (1826–1892), the Boston publisher, was at this time publishing both Howells and his friend Mark Twain. He went bankrupt in 1885 and later acted as English representative of Harper and Brothers.

[4] William Wetmore Story (1819–1895), American sculptor, essayist and poet—the subject of Henry James's *William Wetmore Story and his Friends* (1903).

[5] Clarence King (1842–1901), American geologist, former director of the United States Geological Survey; his considerable reputation as an author was based especially on his *Mountaineering in the Sierra Nevada* (1872).

[6] Charles Dudley Warner (1829–1900), essayist and novelist, collaborated with Mark Twain in the writing of *The Gilded Age* (1873).

[7] Edwin [Thomas] Booth (1833–1893), the famous American actor. For his London season of 1882 see William Winter, *Life and Art of Edwin Booth* (London: Unwin, 1893).

[8] William Mackay Laffan (1848–1909), Irish-born artist and journalist, succeeded R. R. Bowker as English representative of Harper and Brothers. He later became editor and proprietor of the New York *Sun*.

heavenly day, and never to be forgotten. What a lovely, lovely place that little churchyard is!

A Boston man returned a copy of Shakespeare once with the remark that he did not believe there were ten men in the State of Massachusetts who could have written that book; and for my part I remember few churches in Ohio at once so old and so picturesque as that of Stoke Poges. I admit as much as that.

We are going to be under the wing of Mdlle. E. Colomb,[9] Le Clos, pres Villeneuve, Vaud; but if you have a moment for me, write me in care of Gillig's American Exchange 449 Strand.

Mrs. Howells joins me in cordial regards to both of you.

Yours ever

W. D. Howells

[9] Mlle. Colomb was the proprietress of the *pension* in which Howells and his family stayed; in a letter to his father of 24 September 1882 Howells wrote: "Mademoiselle is the only one in the house who speaks English besides ourselves. She is a jolly old maid of forty" (Mildred Howells, *Life in Letters of Howells*, I, 323).

❧ 30. *Gosse to Howells* ❧

29 Delamere Terrace / London / W.

12 October 1882

Dear Howells

Your angel-visit was so bright and brief that I hardly know whether it really took place. Perhaps I only dreamed of meeting you, and am now startling a distinguished stranger with the audacious familiarity of my address. I wont however even pretend that an event which left me permanently richer never happened at all. But I will warn you, for your instant satisfaction, and that you may not be cursing deep and free, that I dont expect any answer whatever to this letter. It is simply to relieve my own feelings that I do it. It is an epistolary run-away knock; dont trouble to answer the bell. Unless I can get you any books about reefs or coolies, or send you anything you want for your novel, in which case I shall be much offended if you dont write.

We are all talking about you. I see ladies giggling over little books in the train, and then I know they must be reading "The Parlour Car". A quantity of cads have sworn to behave like gentlemen in consequence of meeting "The Lady of the Aroostook", and the question Have you read "A Wedding

Journey" is one of those tiresome things that make one loathe one's fellow-creatures. I really cannot but think that Douglas' edition[1] must be very successful. My wife gave me the whole series on my birthday: they really are charming little books—I mean in their physical aspect.

I have been so busy ever since I came back that I cant find time to write my necessary business notes: which gives the fact of my writing this needless letter to you almost the zest of a vice. I was very glad you went down to Stoke Pogeis [sic] and that you felt the delicious sentiment of the place: it is wonderfully ancient and secluded for a spot so near London. I have just entered into treaty with Macmillans to edit Gray's Works[2] for them in handsome form. It has never been done before.

If you are really writing much about Hong Kong, you had better let me send you some blue-books lately published here, on the atrocious tyrannies of the local police, quite a Zolaesque study of the life in the low quarter of the town. But perhaps your hero is careful not to get into bad company, and keeps his ethics gilt-edged till he is thrown up upon the atoll. I want to read it very much.

With kindest remembrances to Mrs. Howells and Miss Howells

I am, we are,

Yours very sincerely

Edmund W. Gosse and family

[1] Howells's two novels *The Lady of the Aroostook* and *Their Wedding Journey*, and his two farces *A Counterfeit Presentment* and *The Parlour Car* (in one volume) were published by David Douglas, Edinburgh, in 1882.

[2] See Letter 26, n. 5.

◷ 31. *Howells to Gosse* ◷

Villeneuve [Switzerland],

(26) October 1882

My dear Gosse:

It is a proof of my continued youthfulness, I suppose, that I had begun to be afraid something in my letter had offended you; but take it as a proof also of my curious affection: your letter came just in time to save me from writing to ask you what the matter was. The joyful rebound of my spirits at once enabled me to think out the philosophy of my story, and though it is not much of a philosophy, I have it hard and fast. Thank you for all your kind offers in regard to desolate islands: I have started my man away from his atoll in an open boat, and he is to be presently picked up by a whaler. I think you will be amused by my instinctive efforts to *realize* a desolate island, and the hero's recognition of the stale and hackneyed character of the situation. My great helper has been Dana in his Coral Islands.[1] Is the Mr. Gosse whom he quotes possibly your father? When I came upon the name, I felt almost as if you were a partner of my enterprise. I wish you *would* send me those blue-books:[2] my present hero is a well-principled person, but the trade of novel writing is so corrupting that before I have done with it, I am sure that I shall invent some young man who will at least *wish* to visit all the worst places in Hong Kong. And wont you kindly send me the October Century? I can't "seem to" get hold of it. (I don't know why I should continue to heap up all these obligations: it must be just to see how many I *can* carry.)

This country life in Switzerland is immensely interesting, with astonishing flashes of resemblance to that of New England, which must come from the common Calvanism [sic] and Republicanism. There is nothing lacking here but the comfort of serious men (why not *say* Gosse?) to talk the queer things over with. John[3] and I walk about a good deal, and we row a little on the lake; but outside the house I will own it is not exciting. Within it is rather interesting, and if I were a truly unprincipled person, as I sometimes wish I were, instead of this wretched half way affair—I should scoop nearly everybody into my note-book. But I have a conscience: I may want to come back.

I forgive Mrs. Gosse for anticipating my intention in regard to those little books, but I shall certainly not forgive any one else. The only thing left for me to do now is to *write* you a whole new series.

After sending you my letter, I read your Gray, and I was delighted with it. You have done a difficult piece of work with the most charming skill, and with an unfailing delicacy and *precision* of appreciation. I am glad that you are going to edit Gray's works, for now I shall read *them*. All the family send cordial regards to Mrs. Gosse and yourself. Please tell Theresa that Mildred[4] has drawn me a book full of animals in Swiss costumes.

Yours ever

W. D. Howells

[1] James Dwight Dana, *Corals and Coral Islands* (New York: Dodd and Mead, 1872); there are several references in the book to the work of Gosse's father, Philip Henry Gosse.

[2] For the consequences of this request see Introduction, pp. 39–40.

[3] John Mead Howells, Howells's second child and only son, was born in 1868.

[4] Mildred ("Pilla") Howells, born in 1872, was Howells's third and youngest child.

ॐ 32. *Gosse to Howells* ॐ

29, Delamere Terrace, / Westbourne Square. [London] W.

8 November 1882

My dear Howells

We want your portrait and that of Mrs. Howells. We rage for them: and they must have your names written very plainly underneath them in your own handwritings.

You wrote me a most charming letter. And I sent you a perfect library of loathsome brochures. I hope you enjoyed them. I can imagine that they chimed in very prettily upon the idyllic silence of Villeneuve.

Miss Harriet Preston[1] is most charming. We have tried to make her happy, for your sake at first, but latterly for her own sake.

So you have demolished poor old Dickens and Thackeray,[2] have you? Well, I am glad I was born in the good old times when they were thought good enough for week-day reading.

Our most affectionate remembrances to you all. We often talk of you, and always with affection. I am busy writing folios. C'est vrai, books that will appear in folio, with tottering parchment covers.[3] It makes one feel rather overblown, like a Jerusalem artichoke.

Yours sincerely

Edmund W. Gosse

Motto for the American Critic.

———

Ho! the old school! Thackeray, Dickens!
Throw them out to feed the chickens.—
Ho! the new school! James and ——
Lay the flattery on with trowels.

(Doggerel by a candid friend.)

[1] Harriet Waters Preston (1836–1911), author and translator. She published a number of novels and many translations from French and Latin; her special field was Provençal literature, and she was known particularly for her translation in 1872 of Frédèric Mistral's *Mirèio*. Howells's visiting card on which he wrote introducing Miss Preston to Gosse is in the British Museum.

[2] A reference to Howells's controversial article, "Henry James,Jr.," *Century*, XXV (November, 1882), 25–29. See Letter 33 and Introduction, pp. 40–42.

[3] One of these books must be Gosse's *Cecil Lawson: A Memoir* (London: The Fine Art Society, 1883), which Norman Gullick (in Charteris, *Life and Letters of Gosse*, p. 512) records as having been printed in a small-paper edition and in "a large-paper edition, in white parchment boards"; the other was presumably Gosse's *A Critical Essay on the Life and Works of George Tinworth*, also published in London by The Fine Art Society in 1883.

I was just forgetting to thank you for the great pleasure your sympathetic paper in "Longman's"[4] gave us. I read it out to my wife, and every now and then we almost fancied that we heard your voice. I never read anything that made me so much wish to visit America. I will not say I envy you your delicate style, for envy is a silly vice; but it always stirs me up to write my own little level best.

E. W. G.

[4] Howells, "Lexington," *Longman's Magazine,* I (November 1882), 41–61. See also Letter 70 and n. 1.

∾ 33. *Gosse to Howells* ∾

Board of Trade. [London] S.W.

14 November 1882

My dear Howells

I was quite ashamed, when your lovely letter came, to think that it had been crossed by such a flippant one of mine. But I dare say you did not regard my impertinence. The newspapers here have been discussing your arraignment of Dickens and Thackeray very warmly, though in almost every case in a very courteous spirit towards yourself. I think, to speak of the matter quite soberly, that it is our tendency to overrate these writers from national partiality, just as it is your tendency to underrate them for the same reason. If we can remove this prejudice from each of our minds, I think we shall agree about Dickens to a great degree. He is already antiquated, no doubt. With regard to Thackeray, I do think you are in error. His confidential air, surely, is not that quality in him which is not modern. This attitude of an author towards his audience is neither old nor new: it is a personal idiosyncrasy [sic] which is always cropping up in literature. I should like to take a brisk walk with you along the shores of Leman,[1] and really discuss this matter. I think I shall always do battle with you on your favourite literary stand-point, that the intellectual product of a democracy must be finer than that of a monarchy. I am sure the inmost reason of your dislike to Dickens and Thackeray is that they flourished in a corrupt and pestilent royalty. But I really think the muses care very little about the divine right of the masses, and are likely for a long time yet to feel more at home among the old civi-

[1] On 17 October 1882 Howells wrote to Clemens, "We are having a good, dull, wholesome time in this little pension on the shore of Lake Leman, within gunshot of the Castle of Chillon" (Smith and Gibson, eds., *Mark Twain-Howells Letters,* p. 415).

lizations than in the new. This, I suppose, is just the one theme on which we shall always be content to differ.

We are very much obliged to you for introducing Miss Preston to us. We like her extremely: but I wonder that you do, for she is not at all *democratic*!

A parting shot, a very feeble one. You have only to snort twice to send me flying from the field.

Affectionately yours

Edmund W. Gosse

~ 34. *Howells to Gosse* ~

Villeneuve [Switzerland],

16 November 1882

My dear Gosse:

The American Exchange promised to send me the Century, but it has not done so, and I must ask of your charity to send me the November number so that I can see what the deuce I have been saying of Dickens and Thackeray: when I come back to England, in the spring, I will reimburse you for the small expenses I beg you to make for me, and will still hold myself your debtor for your kindness. I can't intelligently take hold of a matter which you say has interested the London newspapers, for I can't remember just what I wrote, though it must have been what I thought. But I always thought myself quite unapproached in my appreciation of the great qualities of Dickens and Thackeray, and I can hardly believe that I have "arraigned" them. I suspect that no Englishman can rate them higher than I do. If I had the grudge to monarchies which you suppose, both those authors must have fed it fat, for I learned nothing but democracy from them. But you really can't think me so pitiful as to judge men's art by their political opinions or conditions: if that were the case what should I have to say of Shakespeare or Cervantes, whom I quite prefer to Milton or Landor? Why should I think Tourguénief the master of his art, and the first of all novelists, within his range?

When I have seen the Century, and my offence in it against the great Shades, T. and D., I hope you will let me talk to you further about them: I fancy we shall not disagree at all. As to the two little Substances, H[owells] and J[ames], the former is now getting his desert in the American press

104

for presuming to have a mind (which he had forgotten) about D. and T., and the latter has had no praise troweled upon him by American critics hitherto, but rather shovels and pitchforks full of blame. But I dare say this "will all come out right in the end." Only if the time and chance ever came together, I should like to say my say about the art of Dickens and Thackeray in full.

We are thinking of setting our frost-bitten noses southward. The snow is getting lower and lower on the mountains, and this afternoon when I walked out into their lordly presence, their breath cut cold across my cheeks, with a real wintry touch. The sight is lovelier and grander than I could describe; but one of the fine things about it [is] the effect of the pines, whether lightly powdered and etherialized by the snow far up the heights, or, farther yet, climbing in long black files along under the cliffs, or grouped in dark masses at the edge of sloping fields of snow. And the chalets, wading in the drifts of the mountain pastures are not bad, either.

But the weather here below is awfully cold and wet. We shall stay, I suppose, for a fortnight, yet, and then go to Florence.

I am glad and grateful that you have been so kind to Miss Preston. She has gone back to feudalism in religion without affecting my regard for her, and may do so in politics on the same terms, if she likes. If she turned out a duchess in disguise I should still be friends with her, as I should with you my dear Gosse, if some apostate Jew some day got you made a peer.

Yours ever

W. D. Howells

❧ 35. Howells to Gosse ❧

Hotel Minerva / Florence,

9 January 188[3][1]

My dear Gosse:

I was glad to see your hand-writing again, for I was at a loss to know what had happened. We have now been here a month, and are beginning to feel a little "wonted," though as yet we have done no sight seeing to speak of. I write all the morning, and in the afternoon I seem to be driving about and leaving cards upon modern Americans instead of conversing with the minds of medieval Florentines. But this is a kind of thing that cannot go on

[1] Howells wrote "1882."

forever, for I shall pretty soon have no more cards: the Americans are inexhaustible.

I fancy that if one had the time for them there are many intellectual recreations in Florence, and people who know them say that the professional and literary classes are extremely well worth knowing. I met the other night Prof. Villari,[2] the author of the life of Savonarola, a most interesting and agreeable man; and to-day I was promised the acquaintance of a learned baker, the friend of two young New Yorkers, who reads Shakespeare while his bread is burning; he has only one ear, which he keeps entirely for English. Of course he cannot invite one to "fill up the other ear," when one tells him some incredible American story, and altogether he bids fair to be a man after my own heart. He has a farm just out of the city, and we were all to have walked to it; but it is raining, and I am afraid that he must go over till another Sunday.

The weather has been as flat and lifeless as possible, and after the spring of the Swiss air, the atmosphere of Florence is curiously flabby.

Yours ever

W. D. Howells

[2] Pasquale Villari (1827–1917), distinguished Italian historian and politician, was professor of the philosophy of history at the Institute of Studii Superiori in Florence. His study of Savonarola was translated into English as *The History of Girolamo Savonarola and of his Times* (1863); a later edition, revised and augmented, was translated as *The Life and Times of Savonarola* (1888).

◌෧ 36. *Gosse to Howells* ෧◌

29, Delamere Terrace, / Westbourne Square. [London] W.
12 January 1883

My dear Friend

You will jeer at my vagueness, but I cannot be quite sure whether I have or have not told you how exquisite we think your present of the Bernese pewter pot. It was too kind of you, much too kind. Thornycroft has promised to engrave your name and mine on the bottom of it, that my children and devouring Time may know how you indulged me. Your letter was very welcome: it was pleasant to get a real address, not that dubious American Exchange, of which I enterain the gravest and the most perfectly unfounded suspicions.

You are languid in Florence: your letter shows it. Also the endless flow of society must have tired you. I myself can't sustain society in the least, I mean that with a big S. James begged me to tell you that he was hurried off at a moment's notice by the news, which of course you soon saw confirmed by death, of his father's illness.[1] He was very anxious you should not think he had been remiss in not writing to you. I hope the voyage in December did not hurt him: he was looking very poorly, and seemed in a panic terror of the cold and the passage. Did you read his "Point of View"?[2] I thought it one of his most caustic and brilliant things.

I thought I desired you to send us your likeness and that of Mrs. Howells? You are very remiss, and inattentive of my commands; but a prompt packet of photographs may lead to pardon. I want you to come back when all the woods are green, and to come down, you and I alone, for a day or two into Dorsetshire, among the sleepy orchards, to visit Hardy.[3] Will you?

Yours very sincerely

Edmund W. Gosse

[1] Henry James left England on 12 December 1882 and reached New York on 21 December, only to find that his father had died three days earlier and been buried that morning (see Edel, *Henry James: The Conquest of London, 1870–1883*, p. 488).

[2] James's story "The Point of View" first appeared in the *Century*, XXV (December 1882), 248–268.

[3] Thomas Hardy (1840–1928), the novelist and poet. See Letter 38 and n. 2 and Letter 44 and n. 3.

ꙮ 37. *Gosse to Stedman* ꙮ

Board of Trade. [London] S.W.

5 March 1883

My dear Stedman

Your kind gift of Hayne's Poems,[1] which I shall value very much for your sake, brings my sins to my remembrance. I have never acknowledged the very fine and spirited ballad of the West Indies[2] which you so kindly sent me, and which I admired exceedingly. It is delightful to think that among all the emotions of your busy and exciting life, you still remain true to the Muses.

[1] *Poems of Paul Hamilton Hayne* (Boston: Lothrop, 1882). Hayne (1830–1886) was born in South Carolina and edited *Russell's Magazine* from 1857 to 1860.

[2] Presumably a reference to Stedman's poem "Lovers in the Tropics: West-Indian Idyl," first published in the *Century*, XXIII (February 1882), 540.

Henry Holt has brought out an American edition of my Poems,[3] of which I asked him to send you one from me. I think it is nicely done; Dobson and Monkhouse[4] were the friends who made the selection. I am afraid there is no chance of its being well received in America, where very few people, except scholars like yourself and Stoddard, will understand what I have been aiming at. I am sorry for Mr. Holt, who has undertaken the enterprise very generously and may I fear lose money by it. Still I am, as you may judge, excessively pleased, personally, to speak directly to American readers in this way.

I am reading your article on Emerson[5] in proof, and very admirable it is, —one of your best essays. And, oddly enough, although all the world has been mouthing out words on this man lately,[6] the real fact about his poetry has been left for you to say, in your leisurely way, when the time came for you to say it. His poetry has always been very little understood.

I hope, in spite of my bad indolent neglect of you, to be pardoned and to hear soon again.

I am always
Yours very sincerely

Edmund W. Gosse

[3] Gosse, *On Viol and Flute* (New York: Holt, 1883).
[4] William Cosmo Monkhouse (1840–1901), English poet, critic, and art historian.
[5] Stedman, "Emerson," *Century*, XXV (April 1883), 872–886.
[6] Emerson had died in April 1882.

ᘒ 38. *Howells to Gosse* ᘒ

Florence,

3 April 1883

My dear Gosse:

"I am very guilty before you," as the people say in the translations of Tourguénief; but I will not also be tedious in apology. If I had written you as often as I wished to write, you would now be in possession of several volumes of my letters, in which I should have committed myself in all sorts of ways.

We are again in Florence after three weeks in the Middle Ages at Siena, and we are finding our own era rather pleasant. Before we went we had called upon every body, and now we have a good conscience in calling on no one. With little odds and ends of sight-seeing, and with a heavy cold apiece, four weeks have gone swiftly enough, and we are thinking even of setting our faces northward. I suppose we shall be a month or six weeks in Venice, where I must put in some hard work on my Tuscan Cities;[1] and then we shall get gack where you can "heave half a brick at me," if you like. Your notion of going down into some woods with me to see Thomas Hardy is something to my own soul's delight, and yet—I may as well be honest, for once—I may possibly have no time in England at all.[2] I am torn between two homesicknesses: the longing for America, and the desire to stay in Italy. So I may hang about here, and then go home with a rush. Of course, London is the great world, and I would like to see more of it; but I can understand the case of Englishmen who are willing to live in Italy, and eke that of Americans. A friend of mine, a Cornell professor has just taken a villa outside of Porta Sta. Croce, for five years, and goes home to morrow to return with bag and baggage. I drove out with him yesterday to see his villa: an absurdly beautiful splendid and historical affair which he gets *furnished* for ⟨$140⟩ year! It is enough to make one forswear one's country. And then Florence is hardly a foreign city, if you seek its English or American life at all; but *as* a foreign city is full of literary advantages, which one hardly realizes without coming here. Why not colonize it? You get Hardy and Tadema and Thornycroft, and some other literary fellows as good as yourself, and I will bring Mark Twain and Aldrich and John Hay, and Osgood shall come over and publish for us.

By the way I heard with regret from Deschamps[3] that Tadema was not well, and that he was coming south for his health. Does that mean he is coming to Italy? I did greatly hope to see him again, before I returned to America, and I wish that it might be in Italy.

---

[1] Howells, *Tuscan Cities* (Boston: Ticknor, 1886), first published in the *Century*, XXIX-XXX (February-October 1885). One of the objects of Howells's visit to Europe was to gather material for the *Century* articles and subsequent book.

[2] Howells and his family did make a brief visit to England in the early summer of 1883. Howells saw Gosse a number of times but appears not to have made the visit to Dorset with him; he did, however, meet Hardy at a dinner given by Gosse on 25 June (see Letter 44, n. 3); see also, Letter 42 and Mildred Howells, *Life in Letters of Howells*, I, 342–347. The Book of Gosse records a visit by Howells and his wife on 1 July 1883; they sailed on 5 July and arrived in Quebec on 13 July (*Life in Letters*, I, 347, 349). Gosse went to see Hardy in Dorchester in late July (Charteris, *Life and Letters of Gosse*, pp. 156–157).

[3] A Mrs. Deschamps is among the very first visitors recorded in the Book of Gosse, in 1875, and "Mr., Mrs. and Miss Deschamps" were present at a party on 26 June 1876. The man in question is conceivably Pierre Charles Ernest Deschamps (b. 1821), the French bibliographer, author of *Essai bibliographique sur M. T. Cicéron* (1863) and *Dictionaire de géographie ancienne et moderne à l'usage du libraire et de l'amateur de livres* (1870).

We have not met the Middlemores,[4] for they have been all the winter in Rome, where the Doctor warned us not to go with Winny. She has had in slight degree a recurrence of her nervous prostration, and he said she was almost sure to take the fever.

I enclose a fotograf of [a] medallion which my brother-in-law, Mead,[5] has made of me. I think it is an extremely good likeness. Mrs. Howells has no fotograf of herself; but if she ever gets one she will remember that you kindly askt for it.

How much we should both like to see you both again! You are London, you are England to us! You and the Tademas. Receive, my Gosse, what they call a stretto di mano, down here, from your vero amico di cuore, and with Mrs. Howells's love to Mrs. Gosse, believe me

Affectionately yours

W. D. Howells

[4] Samuel George Chetwynd Middlemore, author of *The Great Age of Italian Painting* (1889) and translator of Burckhardt's *The Civilization of the Renaissance in Italy* (1878), was a close friend of the Gosses and his visits are recorded in the Book of Gosse on several occasions between 1878 and 1886. He was present with his wife on 6 August 1882, when Howells and his wife were making their first visit to the Gosses; he was also present on the occasion of their next visit, on 20 August 1882.

[5] Larkin Goldsmith Mead (1835–1910) was Mrs. Howells's brother. He was a sculptor and spent much of his life in Italy; his works include statues of Lincoln in Springfield, Illinois, and of Ethan Allen at the Capitol in Washington, D.C. The photograph of Mead's medallion, signed by Howells and dated "Florence, April 3, '83," is in the Brotherton Collection (See illustration in this volume).

❧ 39. *Gosse to Johnson*[1] ❧

[London?]

31 May 1883

My dear Mr. Johnson

You all write me such tempting panegyrics of Mr. Burroughs[2] and his home and his talk, that I feel the time long till I can taste these pleasures. Alas! I fear it will be longer; but how I should like to come and see you all.

The June no. is admired over here exceedingly, it is making a great

[1] For Robert Underwood Johnson, see Letter 6, n. 7.

[2] John Burroughs (1837–1921) was at this time writing many articles for the *Century*. He began as a teacher and journalist, but later he retired to a New York farm, where he devoted himself to writing and to experimentation in fruit culture. Most of his books, poems, and articles deal with nature and the outdoor life.

mark by its illustrations. I must say that the way in which you have illustrated my sculptors[3] is truly magnificent. Thank you ever so much.

Miss Zimmern shall write 5000 words on the Queen of Roumania[4] with as many good anecdotes and tasteful personalities as she can get into the space.

Have you seen Mr. Aldrich's exceedingly delicate and appreciative article on my poems in the Atlantic Monthly?[5] It is uncommonly kind of him.

The way in which the American press generally has taken the book[6] is one of the most gratifying things which have happened to me. Who wrote the charming little note on my "Cecil Lawson" in the "Critic"?[7]

You shall have a photo of Mrs. Alma Tadema's drawing of George Eliot,[8] and do what you like with it: if you will insert somewhere a little note which I will send for the purpose.

Yours very sincerely

Edmund W. Gosse

Laffan has suddenly been recalled, nobody (including himself) can imagine why. He was getting on so very well over here, and made himself particularly liked.

---

[3] Gosse, "Living English Sculptors," *Century*, XXVI (June 1883), 163–185.

[4] Helen Zimmern, "Carmen Silva, Queen of Roumania," *Century*, XXVIII (August 1884), 524–532. Miss Zimmern (1846–1934), author, translator, and art critic, contributed to the *Athenaeum* and *Spectator*, as well as to German, Italian, and American journals. She translated a book by the Queen of Rumania (*Pilgrim Sorrow*, 1884), and wrote biographies of Schopenhauer (1876) and Lessing (1878).

[5] *Atlantic Monthly*, LI (June 1883), 843–845. This is a review of the American edition of *On Viol and Flute*, published by Holt in 1883. See Letters 40 and 48.

[6] For the American reception of *On Viol and Flute* see Mattheisen, "Edmund Gosse," (dissertation, Rutgers), pp. 79–80. The notice in the *Atlantic Monthly* (see Introduction, p. 9) was extremely appreciative, but the New York *Times* reviewer, while finding the selection of poems better than that in the earlier English edition (1873), found no trace of "dramatic fire or original views of men and things" (New York *Times*, 18 February 1883, p. 10).

[7] "Cecil Lawson," *Critic*, III (12 May, 1883), 225.

[8] The drawing was not published in *Century*. See Letter 43, n. 3.

༄ 40. *Gosse to Aldrich*[1] ༄

29 Delamere Terrace. / [London] W. / (or 7 Whitehall Gardens / S.W.)
2 June 1883
My dear Mr. Aldrich

The "Atlantic Monthly" for this month contains one of those rare messages of sympathy and encouragement which make an artist's life worth living.[2] One gets sick of praise and indifferent to blame, but when a man of high intellectual position actually pays one the compliment of trying to see what it just is that one has done, or striven to do, this is one of the finest pleasures of the literary life. You must forgive me if I feel sure that this article was written by yourself, not merely given kindly space to. I detect your hand in its sentences, in its delicate ingenuity of praise, in its charming style. Such words from a poet of your rank confer a brevet of nobility; and from one of your nation display a singular generosity.

I think this is the first time I ever wrote to thank a reviewer; it is perhaps not quite the proper thing to do; but I cannot allow you to remain unconscious of my gratitude for your insight and sympathy.

Believe me
Dear Mr. Aldrich
Yours very sincerely

Edmund W. Gosse

[1] Thomas Bailey Aldrich was at this time editor of the *Atlantic Monthly*. For his biography see Ferris Greenslet, *The Life of Thomas Bailey Aldrich* (Boston and New York: Houghton Mifflin, 1908). There is no mention of Aldrich's name in the Book of Gosse, but he and Gosse had met previously: in a letter dated from Christiania, Norway, on 26 July 1882 (a.l.s., BC) Aldrich thanks Gosse for the gift of a book and looks forward to meeting him and Mrs. Gosse in London early that September.

[2] See Letter 48 and Introduction, p. 9.

༄ 41. *Gosse to Gilder* ༄

[London?]

13 June 1883

My dear Gilder

I do not happen to have received any cheque from the Century Co. for my Sculpture article in this month's number.[1] I am not in the slightest hurry for

[1] See Letter 39, n. 3.

payment, but knowing the promptitude with which it is your habit to pay, I venture to mention it, lest the cheque should have been mislaid.

The Misses Lazarus are simply charming, and I find myself in close sympathy with Emma,[2] who has a mind of remarkable power and delicacy. I wish we could make their visit more amusing for them, but my wife and children are just gone down to Devonshire. We are, however, hoping to give them (the Misses Lazarus) a little reception again at the end of the month,[3] and in the mean time I hope to see something of them.

London is full of Americans. On Sunday we had a little crowd of visitors all the afternoon and evening, and Miss Mary Robinson was the unique and solitary English specimen!

The Roswell Smiths are looking remarkably well. He is proud, as well he may be, of the beautiful and touching tribute you all signed when he left. I do not like being out of it: I should like to sign at the end. I am sure he thoroughly merits all the affection you feel for him. His character comes out the more and the better one knows him.

All the sculptors have expressed their delight at your engravings of them, and the illustrations have been very much commented on in the press.

Howells is here,—melancholy, fantastic, giggling, restless and in all other respects his charming self.

Yours most sincerely

Edmund W. Gosse

I have just sent to press my little *magnum opus,* my 17th. cent. book[4] that has taken 11 years to write.

[2] Emma Lazarus (1849–1887), American poet, had recently published her *Songs of a Semite* (1882), the volume containing her most notable work, "The Dance to Death," a verse drama about the Thuringian Jews in the fourteenth century. In 1883 she was making her first visit to Europe, in company with her sister.

[3] The Misses Lazarus were among those present at the large party given by the Gosses on 1 July (see Letter 45, n.3).

[4] Gosse, *Seventeenth Century Studies* (London: Kegan Paul, 1883).

❧ 42. Howells to Gosse ❧

51 Upper Bedford Place, [London]

15 June 1883

My dear Gosse:

Will it seriously interrupt your devotions if Mrs. Howells and I look in on Sunday afternoon?[1]

[1] If this visit was made, the Book of Gosse does not record it. But see Letter 38, n. 2.

We have spent the whole week in getting a lodging.[2] My next romance is to be "Houseless in London." I have all the facts for it.

Yours ever

W. D. Howells

[2] Finding suitable lodgings seems to have been a perennial problem besetting the Howells family, and the theme often appears in Howells's novels. See, for example, the trouble which Bartley Hubbard and Marcia experience in finding rooms in *A Modern Instance* (1881), and the long search of March and his wife for an apartment in New York which occupies the greater part of Chapters VII to XII of *A Hazard of New Fortunes* (1890). In his later (1909) Preface to the latter novel Howells plainly implies that the episode had been based on his own experiences. See also Letter 50.

❧ 43. *Gosse to Johnson* ❧

Board of Trade. [London] S.W.

16 June 1883

Dear Mr. Johnson

Harper's Weekly may or may not be correct in the rumour that Cross's life of George Eliot is nearly completed.[1] I am quite sure that whether completed or not, it will not see the light for many years, unless pressure is put on Mr. Cross by threatened publication of other documents. To save his wife's character he may be forced to publish, as he has been forced to write his book, against his will. It would be well for you to dismiss from your mind altogether all idea of publishing any part of this book. It is utterly hopeless. There is no point at which you can touch Mr. Cross. He is extremely rich, without literary ambition, disdainful of popularity, actuated by no feeling but that of a sort of unreasoning canine loyalty to his wife's memory. He does not want to address "a George Eliot constituency"; he only wants to be let alone. Public feeling has refused to let him entirely alone, it has obliged him to write this book; but, as he lately told me, the book when finished will be unprinted for years and years, till curiosity has wasted itself and gossip is silent.

As I say, I think it possible that in the face of Miss Blind's[2] and other

[1] *Harper's Weekly*, XXVII (2 June 1883), 339: "The forthcoming *Life of George Eliot*, by her second husband, Mr. Cross, is nearly finished." The reference is to *George Eliot's Life as Related in Her Letters and Journals*, ed. John W. Cross (Edinburgh and London: Blackwood, 1885).

[2] Mathilda Blind, *George Eliot* (Boston: Roberts, 1883), one of the "Famous Women" series. Miss Blind points out some of the autobiographical elements in *The Mill on the Floss*, and discusses George Eliot's "early engagement."

revelations, he may feel forced to publish. But he will never allow it to pass through a magazine, and as for us, he is only beginning to get over a rancourous feeling of dislike to us for having forced his hand in 1881.[3]

Yours sincerely

E. W. Gosse

[3] This refers to the publication of Frederick W. Burton's portrait of George Eliot as the frontispiece for *Century*, XXIII (November 1881), and to Gosse's accompanying article on pp. 47–48. See Letters 18 and 39. Writing to Gilder on 13 June 1881 (a.l.s, GP), Gosse had offered to tell the readers of a portrait "that is being closely hushed up, and of which they have never heard." Apparently Cross wanted no portrait to appear, but preferred to see Burton's portrait published rather than one that was entirely unauthorized. In a letter to Johnson of 12 April 1883 (a.l.s., HU) Gosse wrote: "I think it would be considered an act of deliberate bad faith if we even opened the subject of recurring to the portrait of George Eliot which we discarded in favour of Burton's. Mr. Cross's condemnation of it was unqualified, and we entered into what I understood to be a distinct contract to do our best to destroy and put out of existence that other profile, as far as lay in our power." He then offered Johnson the sketch of Eliot done by Mrs. Alma-Tadema (see Letter 39), but it seems never to have been published in the *Century*; what is presumably the same sketch, dated 1877, is now in the National Portrait Gallery, London (No. 1758).

❧ 44. Howells to Gosse ❧

51 Upper Bedford Place, [London]

26 June 1883

My dear Gosse:

Mr. Brownell[1] called last night while I was immeritoriously banqueting with you immortals, but he left no address. If he is the sort of discouraged and isolated man that I have inferred from talk of yours, I should hate extremely to seem indifferent to his acquaintance; and this is to beg his street and number of you.

What a charming night that was, last night! Du Maurier[2] and Hardy went most to my heart (you and Thornycroft were there already) but I felt that after all I had only shaken hands with Hardy across his threshold.[3]

[1] William Crary Brownell (1851–1928), distinguished American critic, was for many years literary adviser to the publishing firm of Charles Scribner's Sons.

[2] George [Louis Palmella Busson] Du Maurier (1834–1896), the artist and writer, best known for his novel *Trilby* (1894).

[3] For this first meeting between Howells and Hardy, at the dinner given by Gosse at the Savile Club on 25 June 1883, see the extract from Hardy's notebooks quoted in Florence Emily Hardy, *The Early Life of Thomas Hardy, 1840–1891* (London: Mac-

115

What a world of delightful people, and only one little life to go round them all with! There seems to be a mistake somewhere: perhaps it's mine in not making sure of passing a leisurely eternity with you and your friends.

Woolner[4] is a fine old head.

Yours ever

W. D. Howells

---

millan, 1928), pp. 208–209: Howells told of Emerson's forgetting Longfellow's name when delivering his funeral oration, and of Mark Twain's disastrous speech at the Whittier dinner. Brander Matthews was also present and noted the occasion in his diary; he lists several more guests, among them Austin Dobson. The editors are indebted for this and other references to the Brander Matthews diaries to Professor Herbert L. Kleinfield of Temple University; the diaries are now in the Butler Library, Columbia University.

[4] Thomas Woolner (1825–1892), the sculptor, had been one of the original members of the Pre-Raphaelite Brotherhood.

45. *Gosse to Gilder*

[London?]

4 July 1883

My dear Gilder

I am quite in despair, and fear that you will think me very neglectful of your business. It really is not so, but various things have made it difficult for me to write. The rush of American friends—the Howells', the Lazarus', the Brander Matthews', Osgood, L. Hutton,[1] Clarence King, President Gilman[2] —though enchanting to the highest degree, is a little overwhelming. The other day I was receiving a consecutive stream of American friends without a break for seven hours on end.[3] Of course this is an exception, or one would die, but it explains to you why I have seemed unable to write to you. I have

---

[1] Laurence Hutton (1843–1904), the American essayist, editor, and critic, was literary editor of *Harper's Weekly* from 1886 until 1898. He wrote a series of guidebooks and several books on actors, including *Plays and Players* (1875) and *Actors and Actresses of Great Britain and the United States* (with Brander Matthews, 1886).

[2] Daniel Coit Gilman (1831–1908) became president of the University of California in 1872 and subsequently the first president of Johns Hopkins University (1875–1901). Several of Gosse's letters to him are among the Gilman Papers at Johns Hopkins.

[3] The Book of Gosse records the names of several Americans who dined at Gosse's home on 1 July 1883: Edwin Austin Abbey, W. D. Howells, Brander Matthews, Louise Chandler Moulton, Emma and Annie Lazarus, and Laurence Hutton.

tried to make London pleasant to the Miss[es] Lazarus. They have seen everybody and everything, and must be quite glutted with celebrities. They are most charming, that is to say, to be perfectly frank, Emma is; the other is slightly commonplace. But I really think Emma Lazarus one of the most delightful and inspiring women I have ever met. She breathes an atmosphere of moral distinction.

Some experts are now engaged in trying to work out the Beswick problem.[4] Do not be in a hurry, and you shall have the result as soon as possible.

Before Mr. Roswell Smith left, he asked me to discuss with you the desirability of printing some richly illustrated articles which would specially interest our great provincial cities, Liverpool, Manchester, Glasgow, etc. I have been thinking a great deal over this, but I am not inspired with anything very well worth mentioning. I fancy such articles ought to be written by Americans, and should be very vivid and yet technical. The misfortune is that the technical writer seldom is vivid. Then I feel we must not repeat what "Harper" is doing; they have had articles, and jolly vulgar articles too, on some of our provincial cities.[5]

I had much more to say to you, but here comes the card of a gentleman from Milwaukee, so goodbye.

Ever yours sincerely

Edmund W. Gosse

I don't begin my holidays till August 1.

[4] In a letter to Gilder of 1 June 1883 (a.l.s, HU) Gosse wrote: "I am making all possible inquiries regarding Samuel Beswick. Surely you will not even consider a second contribution from such a tainted source? I suppose you wish to come down upon him for the first offence." In another letter to Gilder, dated 5 June 1883 (a.l.s., HU), Gosse reports: "The postal authorities know of no 'Dog and Partridge' at Liverpool, but there is an inn of that name at Manchester. They therefore forwarded my letter to the proprietor of that, who replies that he knows nothing of any Mr. Samuel Beswick, and has no record of his having put up at his house on the 30th of Sept. 1866." The Samuel Beswick in question is presumably the man who wrote *Swedenborg Rite and the Great Masonic Leaders of the Eighteenth Century* (New York: Masonic Publishing Company, 1870).

[5] Between June 1882 and July 1883 *Harper's Weekly* published only three articles on English towns: William E. Rideing, "Quaint Old Yarmouth," LXV (June 1882), 1–19; Alice R. Hobbins, "Some Worthies of Old Norwich," LXV (August 1882), 393–400; William R. Rideing, "A Famous London Suburb," LXVII (July 1883), 165–182. Gosse's suggestion was apparently rejected, although the *Century* did print two articles of this kind: Andrew Lang, "Edinboro Old Town," XXVII (January 1884), 323–340; and Edward Dowden, "Dublin City," XXIX (December 1884), 163–179.

∾ 46. *Gosse to Osgood*[1] ∾

Board of Trade. [London] S.W.

25 July 1883

My dear Mr. Osgood

I have been very much upset by having it suggested to me that Mr. Holt, who is the American publisher of my Poems, will be offended at my not offering him the 17th Cent. book.[2] I confess this would never have entered my head, for here in England we do not think anything of a change of publisher, if it is convenient. Within the last 3 years I have published with Kegan Paul, and then with Macmillan and then with the Fine Art Soc., and now again with Paul while remaining the best of friends with them all.[3] But I learn that this is not the case in America, and what am I to do? Mr. Holt has been very kind and polite, and the last thing in the world that I should wish to do is to seem to treat him with disrespect. I am quite vague as to what should be done, and I write this to tell you what I feel and to ask your advice. If I could have seen you it would have been best, but I leave for Switzerland on Saturday.

Would you kindly write to me here by return of post.

I am very sorry to trouble you with correspondence during your holiday. My very kind regards to Mr. Hutton

Yours very truly

Edmund W. Gosse

[1] James Ripley Osgood: see Letter 29, n. 3.
[2] See Letter 41 and n. 5, also Letter 47 and n. 7.
[3] The books were, respectively, *English Odes* (Kegan Paul, 1881); *Gray* (Macmillan, 1882); *Cecil Lawson: A Memoir* and *A Critical Essay on the Life and Works of George Tinworth* (both Fine Art Society, 1883); and the book here in question, *Seventeenth Century Studies* (Kegan Paul, 1883).

∾ 47. *Gosse to Gilder* ∾

Board of Trade. [London] S.W.

28 July 1883

My dear Gilder

The office has kept my nose to the grindstone this month, and you are very wise to do so, for today I escape you altogether for a month. Tomorrow morning I hope to breakfast at Troyes, where a number of the "Century" has probably been never seen.

I have been very much exercised about the John Bright article.[1] It ought to be very good, and by a good man. Smalley[2] shilly-shallied and finally declined. Then I tried Bryce,[3] but Bryce says that he is so intimate with Bright, meeting him daily and hourly, that it would be impossible for him to sign a candid critical survey of his career. Sir Lyon Playfair[4] won't do either, for the same reason. But what do you say to John Morley?[5] That would be better than any one ever thought of, would it not? When I proposed it to him, however, he declined at once,—impossible, he hadn't the time, never should have. However, I pressed it, and he really is considering it. He is to give me a final answer in a day or two, and my wife will write to you about it. I told him we *must* have the MS. within 2 months; and he is to name his own terms. If he refuses, I must wait for your instructions. It will be impossible, I think, to get it done by any other man in Parliament. I should say some leading provincial liberal would be the man, and I should suggest R. S. Watson, the president of the caucus in Newcastle, himself a quaker and a very good writer, as witness his amusing "Ride to the Sacred City of Wazan."[6] Tell me how you like this idea of a leading *provincial* liberal.

I hope I have cleared up all the other things I had to see to. I have certain letters to answer, which I can do from Switzerland. I have got in a stupid mess about my 17th Cent. book.[7] Osgood came and offered me lovely terms for it (money down) and I accepted like a crab; when conscience began to prick and to nudge with "How about Holt?", until I felt obliged to write and tell Osgood what Conscience said. Whereat Osgood retired with a dreadful promptitude, and left me on the floor between my two

---

[1] John Bright (1811–1889), the British statesman: see Letter 51, n. 1.

[2] George Washburn Smalley (1833–1916), an American journalist working in London; he subsequently became United States correspondent for the London *Times*.

[3] James Bryce, first Viscount Bryce (1838–1922), statesman, jurist, and historian, was at this time Regius professor of Civil Law at Oxford. His classic work, *The American Commonwealth*, was published in 1888, and he later became ambassador to the United States (1907–1913).

[4] Sir Lyon Playfair (1818–1898) was professor of chemistry at Edinburgh University from 1856 to 1869; from 1868 to 1892 he sat as a Member of Parliament. He was active in many areas of social reform, and was created first Baron Playfair in 1892.

[5] John Morley, first Viscount Morley of Blackburn (1838–1923), statesman, historian, and man of letters.

[6] Robert Spence Watson (1837–1911); his *A Visit to Wazan, the Second City of Morocco* was published in 1880 (London: Macmillan). He was involved in many reform movements.

[7] See Letter 46; there was no American edition of *Seventeenth Century Studies* until 1897, when it was brought out by Dodd, Mead.

chairs. But let this be confidential, for I am trying to patch up the matter somehow.

Two days ago I sent off my final sculpture paper.[8] I hope you will be satisfied with it.

Now adieu, with all best wishes.

Yours very sincerely

Edmund W. Gosse

[8] Gosse, "Living English Sculptors, II," *Century*, XXXI (November 1885), 39–50.

❧ 48. *Aldrich to Gosse* ❧

Editorial office of / The Atlantic Monthly, / Boston.

2 August 1883

Dear Mr. Gosse:

I have just returned from a cruise along the New England coast, and find your note and sonnet among the pleasantest welcomes home. It will give me great pleasure to print that charming sonnet in *The Atlantic*.[1]

I am in your debt for a very kind letter that reached me several weeks ago.[2] You speak so handsomely of the review of your poems that it gives a wrench to my honesty to tell you that I did not write it, though I inspired it and had a finger if not a hand in the composition. It was written by one of the men upon whom I call when I want something done better than I can do it myself. Your reviewer was Mr. Geo. P. Lathrop,[3] the son-in-law of Hawthorne.

When you see Dobson will you please give him my warmest remembrances, and believe me yourself to be always

Very faithfully yours,

T. B. Aldrich

We are glad to get Howells back again!

[1] Gosse, "Unheard Music," *Atlantic Monthly*, LIII (January 1884), 130. On 6 July 1883 (a.l.s., HU) Gosse had written to Aldrich: "If you like the enclosed sonnet, and if you think it proper for the taste of the 'Atlantic Monthly', I shall be proud; and if you do not like it, I shall not be indignant."

[2] Letter 40.

[3] George Parsons Lathrop (1851–1898), author and editor, was born in Honolulu and educated in Dresden, where he met Rose Hawthorne, Nathaniel Hawthorne's daughter; they were married in 1871. From 1875 to 1877 he was associate editor of the *Atlantic Monthly*, under Howells; he founded the American Copyright League, and wrote several books, including *A Study of Hawthorne* (1876) and *Spanish Vistas* (1883). For the review, see Introduction, p. 9.

❧ 49. *Stedman to Gosse* ❧

Office of E. C. Stedman & Co. / Bankers & Brokers, / No. 36 Broad
Street, / New York,

27 August 1883

My dear friend,

You will understand with what a feeling of humiliation I enclose to you
this slip from *The Times*[1]—the *general* statements of which are in the main
correct. And yet I am compelled to send it to you—first, because my friends
in London may hear incorrect rumors of the fact that I have lost my little
fortune; secondly, because at any time you or others, whom I long have
wished to lodge under my roof-tree, may come over here and think me
strangely ungrateful and inhospitable. However this thing may turn out, and
even if I succeed in retaining my valuable seat in the Stock Exchange, I must
for a long time be a poor man. I owe nothing in Wall St., and made my
assignment to protect my honest clients against fraudulent outside claims.
But I have felt it right to surrender everything, and when any of you *do*
come over here you will find me, probably, homeless. I have had such a
lovely home—and have so long expected to have you or Dobson, and others
of our comrades, among its guests!

[1] The cutting from the New York *Times* (16 August 1883, p. 1) is still attached
to this letter (BC); it is a report of Stedman's bankruptcy and contains the following
passage: "No member of the Stock Exchange enjoys a more pronounced reputation for
integrity and conservatism than Edmund C. Stedman, the banker poet, and when the
news that he had suspended reached the ears of the business men in Wall-street there
was a general feeling of amazement. When the cause of the suspension became known
a strong tide of sympathy set toward the unfortunate broker, and his own rigid sense
of honor was all that prevented his resuming business at once with funds generously
proffered him by his many friends. Tenders of financial aid aggregating hundreds of
thousands of dollars were made to Mr. Stedman during the day, but he felt bound to
decline them all, inasmuch as the disaster that had befallen his firm had been brought
about by the unwarrantable speculations of his son and partner [Frederick S. Sted-
man], and the extent of the trouble was involved in doubt. The conduct of Mr. Stedman, Sr., excited feelings of admiration among the hard-headed money-makers of
Wall-street, who usually give but little attention to matters of sentiment."

The report goes on to describe Stedman's office: "The offices of E. C. Stedman &
Co. are on the third floor of a building in Broad-street, just below Exchange-place.
They are neatly and comfortably furnished, and the pictures upon the walls bear evi-
dence of the banker-poet's literary tastes. Large portraits of Longfellow and William
Cullen Bryant adorn the large room, and upon the mantel rests a portrait of Edwin
Booth. Over the elder Stedman's desk is a picture of Ralph Waldo Emerson."

For a further account of Stedman's failure see Stedman and Gould, *Life and Letters
of Stedman*, I, 577–581. He retained his seat on the Stock Exchange and was re-
admitted to active membership on 3 January 1884: "As the day following was a
Friday, he would not return to the Board that day as 'One must respect traditions.' But
on Saturday he went on Change for the first time, receiving an ovation, and was
hand-shaken warmly by some five hundred men" (I, 579).

You see now why I feel moved to tell you of the misfortune which has befallen me, and of which the money loss is the least portion!

You can do me a favor by incidentally telling my friends of the situation. One thing in particular—Mr. Swinburne[2] has talked of visiting America ere long, and had written me that he should make my house his home in N[ew] Y[ork]. It would greatly distress me to be misunderstood by you, or him. Should you see him, or Mr. Watts,[3] you might mention these things— mortifying as they are. Not that I shall not be delighted to welcome my friends as heretofore; but I *should* be embarrassed to have my hospitalities be thought churlish.

Sincerely yours,

Edmund C. Stedman

[2] In a letter to Swinburne of 20 March 1882 (see *ibid.*, II, 33–34), Stedman had written: "On our return to New York [after his English visit of 1879] I made some 'ventures', and was successful enough to secure a house of my own: a pretty home, where I absolutely expect, soon or late, to welcome you as a guest whom all here, worth knowing, will delight to welcome and honor. . . ." (p. 33). Apparently Gosse forwarded the present letter to Swinburne; in a letter to Gosse of 8 September 1883 Swinburne says he is returning "the letter and enclosure" and adds: "I am of course very sorry to hear of Mr. Stedman's distress, and touched by his considerate recollection of the fact that I had provisionally accepted his invitation to become a guest under his roof if ever I went to New York. I agree with you that the tone of his letter is very manful and creditable" (*The Swinburne Letters*, ed. Cecil Y. Lang [New Haven: Yale University Press, 1962], V, 36).

[3] Walter Theodore Watts, subsequently Watts-Dunton, (1832–1914), the English critic, poet and novelist, was a close friend of many of the Pre-Raphaelites; Swinburne lived under his care at Putney from 1879 until his death in 1909.

ॐ 50. Howells to Gosse ॐ

4 Louisburg Square, / Boston,

9 September 1883

My dear Gosse:

You must have been thinking all sorts of savage things of me; but I assure you I am not guilty, as this letter from the manager of the Lowell Lectures[1]

[1] The Boston educational foundation known as the Lowell Institute had been established under the will of John Lowell (d. 1836). The director, or, more properly, the trustee of the Institute at this time was Augustus Lowell, the secretary Dr. Benjamin E. Cotting. The reference here is presumably to Lowell. In a letter to Gosse dated 17 June 1884 (a.l.s., BC), Cotting explains that it is the custom for lecturers at the

will partly prove. Three times I went to see him, during his brief visits to town in August, and the third time he made me wait so long, without seeing me, while my heart was getting hot, and my dinner at home getting cold, that I got up to go away, and had a moment with him in an ante-room, where I said that I had perhaps written all that was necessary in the letter I had sent him about you, and that I would not bother him by coming again, but would hope to hear from him. The fact of which he seems conscious will, I think, operate favorably for us, and I shall be able to write you that the Lectures for the winter of '84–'85 have been secured for you.

We were a long time getting into a house, and had a tragical season of hotels and boarding-houses, but now we have a roof over us at last, and if we had you and Mrs. Gosse under it with us, we should be perfectly happy. There are several good fellows over here who would be exceedingly glad to see you; and if we should be able to arrange for your visit a year from now I can promise you a friendly welcome.

I sent you a short note from The Memphremagog House[2] the day after I arrived in Quebec. I wonder if you ever got it? I got your line about Bertini,[3] and was greatly relieved to learn that I had not burdened you with a load of alien adversity. How good you are! How kind you were to us in London. When we think over the mingled sweetness of Mrs. Gosse and yourself, it seems too precious ever to have been poured into such earthen cups as we are.

With the whole family's love

Yours ever

W. D. Howells

Lowell Institute to make their appearance at "the *exact* time appointed" and to begin "at once, without introductory or preliminary remarks (as such are always sure to prejudice the audience against him)."

[2] Memphremagog House was a resort hotel in Newport, Vermont, at the southern tip of Lake Memphremagog. See Mildred Howells, *Life and Letters of Howells*, I, 349.

[3] Clara and Rudolf Kirk (" 'Enchanted Guest,' " Rutgers Library *Journal*, XXII [June 1959], 8 n.) identify him as Domenico Bertini, an Italian musician. In the Book of Gosse entries for 1884 and 1895, he is listed simply as "Mr. Bertini," but on 13 July 1902 he appears as "P. Bertini"; the man in question is possibly Professor Pietro Bertini, author of *Tristi e Lieti Poesie* (1878) and of *Scritti Varii* (1879). In a postcard to Gosse of 26 June 1886), (BC) John Addington Symonds supplied some information about a sixteenth-century Italian poet called Pietro Bertini.

❧ 51. *Gosse to Gilder* ❧

My dear Gilder

Mr. Escott,[1] editor of the Fortnightly Review and author of the "English Citizen", one of the most lively political writers we possess, has consented to do the article on Bright. I think he is quite the best man obtainable, and I have guarded him about with every species of warning, besides giving him Bryce's Beaconsfield[2] as a model. He will supply the MS. early in November.

Our September number has been particularly successful over here with the press. Everybody is discussing with much entertainment the New York Cosmetropolis article.[3] What an admirable story "The Bread Winners"[4] is! Do tell me by whom it is written. H. H. on Burns[5] is very pretty and effective. Bunner's Love-Letters[6] are good. Altogether the whole number seems to me excellent, with exception of Howells, who is writing a really maudlin and weak story[7] for the first time in his life. What trash it is! and unhappily the poor dear creature knows that it is trash. He attributes it to the fact that he wrote it when he was without a home, wandering from one hotel to another.

By the way, don't we want an article on Tourgéneff,[8] that mighty man? Is it going to be written in America, France or England?

Yours always

Edmund W. Gosse

[1] Thomas Hay Sweet Escott, "John Bright," *Century*, XXVIII (July 1884) 439–447. Escott (d. 1924) taught Classical Literature at King's College, London, from 1866 to 1873. He wrote leading articles for the *Standard*, succeeded John Morley as editor of the *Fortnightly Review*, and was a prolific journalist and author. Gosse is probably referring to his book *England: Its People, Polity, and Pursuits* (London: Cassell, Petter, Galpin, 1879).

[2] James Bryce, "Lord Beaconsfield," *Century*, XXIII (March 1882), 729–744.

[3] William C. Conant, "Will New York Be the Final World Metropolis?" *Century*, XXVI (September 1883), 687–696.

[4] Anonymous, "The Bread-Winners," *ibid.*, 737–752—an installment of the novel by John Hay, published anonymously both in the *Century* and as a book (Harper, 1884). The novel's treatment of social and economic conditions stirred up a controversy, and the *Critic*, among other periodicals, published many letters speculating as to the authorship. Various people who were suspected publicly denied authorship, and Hay himself wrote anonymously to say that he was employed in a place where his work would suffer if it were known that he had written a novel.

[5] H. H. [Helen Hunt Jackson], "A Burns Pilgrimage," *ibid.*, 752–761.

[6] H. C. Bunner, "Love in Old Cloathes," *ibid.*, 768–772.

[7] Howells, "A Woman's Reason," [Chapters VIII–XIX], *ibid.*, 659–671.

[8] Alphonse Daudet, "Tourgéneff in Paris," *Century*, XXVII (November 1883), 48–53. Gosse did not know that this article had already been planned; on 19 September 1883 he wrote to Gilder: "Henry James tells me Daudet has written you an article on Tourgéneff and that it is very bad" (a.l.s., HU).

Pennell[9] has suddenly made up his mind to go back to America.

[9] Joseph Pennell (1860–1926), American artist, illustrator, and author, spent much of his life in England. He and his wife, Elizabeth Robins Pennell, were close friends of the Gosses; their names appear many times in the Book of Gosse and a number of letters to them from both Gosse and his wife are now in the Library of Congress.

ꙮ 52. *Howells to Gosse* ꙮ

4 Louisburg Square, / Boston,

9 December 1883

My dear Gosse—

I waited a month or two for the decision of the autocrat of the Lowell Lectures,[1] and then addresst him a modest reminder of our joint existence. The effect was the letter which I enclose. Upon the whole this experience of mine with Mr. Augustus Lowell is the most disagreeable that I have had since I past the age of being justly snubbed for poverty and obscurity. I don't know what he may finally conclude upon, but I can't conceal that I have very little hopes. It is a real grief and disappointment to me, for I had counted very confidently upon having you here, and I am afraid that I must have a very fraudulent appearance to you.

I wonder if you ever got two notes that I sent you to 29 Delamere Terrace? I wrote you directly after I reacht home, and then a month later about the lectures; but I have not had a squeak from you in response, and I can't console myself with the hope that you were abroad, for Brunetta[2] writes me from Verona that you have not shown yourself there.

We are having Matthew Arnold rather intensely. His lectures in Boston at least have been a great success. I only heard that on Emerson,[3] which seemed to me just and good: I never was too fervid an Emersonian, liking my poetry and philosophy best without conundrums. There were 500 people to hear him, who paid $2 apiece for the privilege. I have twice been his commensal, and like him. I don't know whether he quite makes us out; he

[1] For Augustus Lowell, see Letter 50.

[2] Eugenio Brunetta was the young Florentine whom Howells had met in 1862, while he was American consul in Venice. He wrote about him in an article entitled "A Young Venetian Friend," *Harper's Monthly*, CXXXVIII (May 1919), 827–833. For a fuller account, see James L. Woodress, Jr., *Howells in Italy* (Durham, North Carolina: Duke University Press, 1952), pp. 18–19.

[3] Arnold gave his Emerson lecture at Chickering Hall, Boston, on 1 December 1883. For Arnold's visit to the United States, see James Dow McCallum, "The Apostle of Culture Meets America," *New England Quarterly*, II (July 1929), 357–381.

seems at times rather bewildered, and I don't wonder. I found America changed even in the year I was gone; it had grown more American, and I with my crimson opinions was scarcely more than a dull purple in politics and religion. I put it extravagantly, but there is some truth in what I say.

James Bryce is also here, and him I *do* like. Irving[4] I am to meet twice at least; he's just come to Boston.

I'm far into the heart of a new story,[5] the idea of which pleases me greatly. It is that of a man whose youth was broken sharp off in Florence twenty years ago, and who after a busy newspaper life in our West, fancies that he can resume his youth by going back to Italy. There he falls in love with a girl young enough to be his daughter. It is largely a study of the feelings of middle-life in contrast with those of earlier years.

Entre nous—I have just finisht writing a play with Mark Twain[6] from which I hope big money. It seems to me now at least very droll. We have the notion of doing half a dozen, with always the same character for protagonist, whom we wish to make the American mask—like Pantalone for Venice, Stenteretto for Florence, etc.[7]

I met Harriet Preston the other evening, and had a long Gosse-sip with her. She is gone back to England already, and will give you all my news, with all my heart.

Now write and give me yours, individually and collectively!

Mrs. Howells is not very strong this winter, but is overpowering in her regrets for London. She and the children join me in love to Mrs. Gosse and yourself.

Yours ever

W. D. Howells

[4] Sir Henry Irving (1838–1905), the English actor-manager; this was the first of several visits he made to America, taking the whole Lyceum company with him. He was knighted in 1895.

[5] Here, as in Letter 54, Howells seems to be working out the plot of *Indian Summer* (Boston: Ticknor, 1886); he already had the theme of youth and age very clearly in mind but was still seeking the best story through which to treat it. See Smith and Gibson, *Mark Twain-Howells Letters*, p. 536.

[6] "Colonel Sellers as a Scientist" was performed (as *The American Claimant*) in 1887, but not published. See Smith and Gibson, *Mark Twain-Howells Letters*, pp. 446–453, 569, 591–592, etc., and W. J. Meserve, ed., *The Complete Plays of W. D. Howells* (New York: New York University Press, 1960), pp. 205–208.

[7] Cf. Smith and Gibson, *Mark Twain-Howells Letters*, p. 479.

53. *Gosse to Howells*

Board of Trade. [London] S.W.

20 December 1883

My very dear Friend

I am so horribly in your debt for two letters, one book, innumerable kind exertions, and affectionate messages, that when again another letter overwhelmed me this afternoon, I sank and simply wallowed in my shame. How to thank you for all your sincere and loyal friendship, how to express my regret at all the trouble you have taken, well! it can't be done. But as regards the Lowell Lectures, do not mind failure on that score, for I am deeply grateful to you, and I don't suppose, now I come to think of it, that the Government would let me go.

The very same hand that put your last letter into my hands, put there also the Pall Mall Gazette with a little notice which I have ventured to write of your little girl's book.[1] It seems rather absurd that I, who have never taken my pen in hand yet to review you, should review your child. But it is hardly a review, merely a word of greeting, and I send it you instead of further thanking you for the book.

All your news comes in a mass, for I saw Harriet Preston this morning, and we indulged in long Howls over you. (You notice that the art of punning is not confined to Boston.) I am much taken with your notion of a novel of middle life, a sort of Rip Van Winkle.

I brought out my 17th Century book in October, and it has been better received than any previous enterprise of mine.[2] But I got into a regular mess about the American edition,—a dark tale too long to tell you, and I have not sent one copy across the Atlantic. In the spring I hope to have a new volume of poems ready, and shall send them to you.

I have seen a good deal of Henry James, who has been in low spirits. He seems to be (if you are dark purple) sooty black or lurid blue towards the new American crimson. I hope America is not going to sink into the Greater Ireland. We have been grieved over here at your government's weak interference about the murderer O'Donnell.[3]

[1] Mildred Howells, *A Little Girl Among Old Masters*, with introduction and comment by W. D. Howells (Boston: Osgood, 1883). Gosse's review of this book of drawings by Howells's young daughter appeared anonymously in the *Pall Mall Gazette*, 20 December 1883, pp. 4–5. See Letter 54, n. 2.

[2] Gosse's *Seventeenth Century Studies* (London: Kegan Paul, 1883) was well received: for typical reviews, see Edward Dowden's in *Academy*, XXIV (November 1883), 308; *Athenaeum*, 8 December 1883, p. 731; *Saturday Review*, LVI (10 November 1883), 603–604; *Spectator*, LVII (June 1884, Supplement), 766–767. For the "regular mess" over the American edition, see Letters 46 and 47.

[3] Patrick O'Donnell, a member of the Irish Sinn Fein movement, had been hanged for murder on 17 December 1883, despite efforts made in the United States Congress

You will be disgusted to hear that I never saw Lowell.[4] I sent him your letter, and got a polite note back asking me for a date ten days ahead. This I was obliged to decline, for I was just starting for Switzerland, and I have not heard again. I did not get into Italy at all. We stayed by the Lake of Geneva and among the Bernese Alps, and found our way home through Germany.

My wife has been much better in health this winter than for a year previously. She will be very much grieved to hear of Mrs. Howells' indisposition. The Tademas are well: we are going to spend a very quiet Xmas with them.

Burne Jones[5] and Thornycroft ask after you often. I shall be delighted to hear more about your plays. Which is the more theatrical of you two, you or Mark Twain?

My wife would join me, and in fact does join me, in love to Mrs. Howells and yourself, and I am ever

Your very attached Friend

Edmund W. Gosse

Happy New Year to you all.

---

to prevent the execution. For a more detailed account see Clara and Rudolf Kirk, "'Enchanted Guest,'" Rutgers Library *Journal*, XXII (June 1959), 9 n.

[4] James Russell Lowell, Howells had suggested that Gosse should go to see Lowell as part of the campaign to secure for himself an invitation to deliver the Lowell Lectures for 1884–1885; Howells gave Gosse a note of introduction to Lowell and wrote to Lowell himself asking him to "remember" Gosse in connection with the Lectures (Mildred Howells, *Life in Letters of Howells*, I, 347). Lowell sent Gosse a friendly note, dated 26 July 1883 (a.l.s., BC); as Gosse confesses here, he was going on holiday and unable to see Lowell on the day proposed.

[5] Sir Edward Burne-Jones (1833–1898), artist and designer, whom Gosse had first met as one of the circle around Dante Gabriel Rossetti.

❧ 54. *Howells to Gosse* ❧

4 Louisburg Square, / Boston,

2 January 188[4] [1]

My dear Gosse:

Your letter came day before yesterday, and this morning came your notice of Pilla's book in the Pall Mall. In the first place I didn't dream of your writing of it at all, and then for you to write of it in *that* way—it toucht her mother's heart and mine more than I can tell you. The review was copied

[1] Howells wrote "1883."

entire into a Boston paper[2] which I don't see, and all our friends had read it before we had; imagine our astonishment at finding one of the little drawings actually reproduced in your review! We *yelled* with joy when we saw it. And your kind words—*basta*! I am *used* to being treated better than I deserve!—Since you have taken an interest in the little book, it seems due to you to say that if we had not known the child's unspoilableness we should not have ventured upon it. I don't think any one could be less conscious of it than she. At first she was very proud of having made a book —as a book, merely; but she never was in the least "set up" with any one's praise of it, nor vain of her little skill, which we ourselves feel is probably an efflorescence of her childish spirit, with no sort of future before it. If it should come to anything it will not be through any prompting or petting of ours. The book has been quite successful: 2000 were sold here, fifty copies being sent to Trübner's in London. It has earned her $1000 which shall be for her *dot,* or for her schooling if ever she wishes to study art.

I wish you *had* told me about your American edition of the Seventeenth Century poets! Can't you still be served in regard to it? I thought Osgood was to publish it?

You may be sure that I for one American was ashamed of our silly and impertinent interference with justice in O'Donnell's case. I think no man should be hung; but that man was a cruel and pitiless assassin, and rightly suffered under the law. If he had been a man of any other nationality Congress would not have dreamt of interfering; how then can I explain that this Irish forcing of our national action appeared merely grotesque to us? Congress is "Democratic": by seeming to befriend O'Donnell it could capture Irish votes for its party; and by making a Republican president[3] its instrument it could foist any disagreeable consequences upon us.

It is all part of our "jokes"; come over and try to understand it. The joke is not such a bad one in the long run.

I don't despair yet of the Lowell Lectures: when they are secured, I will get Congress to instruct the President to ask the British Government *why* my friend Gosse cannot have three months' leave.

We had a stand-up lunch party this afternoon to entertain Stillman,[4] an

---

[2] "A Tiny Artist," Boston *Daily Advertiser*, 1 January 1884, p. 5 (Gosse's review originally appeared in the *Pall Mall Gazette* [see Letter 53, n. 1]). The review includes a reprint of a drawing from the book, of young women walking in pairs through the streets of Florence. Howells's reference, a few lines further on, to Pilla's "unspoilableness," was occasioned by the following remark in Gosse's review: "It is always pleasant to tread, as Cowley says, 'in the little footsteps of a child,' and if the artist is not hurt by this publicity the rest of us may be thankful for so pretty a jeu d'esprit."

[3] Chester A. Arthur, President from 1881 to 1885.

[4] William James Stillman (1828–1901), American painter and journalist, who spent most of his later life as correspondent for the London *Times* in Greece and Italy. See Letter 171.

old friend of ours who dined us last winter in Florence. It makes the round world seem no thicker than a map to meet at this rate on both sides of it.

Our good and delightful Henschel[5] is going back to London in the spring. Perhaps he will carry with him the libretto of an opera by me, for which he wishes to make the music.

I amuse myself, in my new story,[6] with the figure of a New England hill-country minister who has gone out to Florence, to spend his last days. His Unitarianism had frayed out into a sort of benevolent agnosticism before he left home, and in a furlined coat, over a *scaldino* he shudders at all he left behind in Haddam East Village. He had deliberately proposed to die as far away from the lingering puritanism and winter of his native hills as he can; and he thinks that Savonarola made a great mistake in trying to kill the Carnival.

Mrs. Howells and I are going up into the hills tomorrow, for a little change and a great deal of snow. Before we go we join in love to Mrs. Gosse and you.

Yours ever

W. D. Howells

Love to the Tademas too.

[5] Georg[e] Henschel (1850–1934), the German-born conductor, composer, and singer, became a naturalized British subject in 1890, and was knighted in 1914. From 1881 to 1884 he was the first conductor of the Boston Symphony Orchestra. The opera was *A Sea-Change, or Love's Stowaway*, libretto by W. D. Howells, music by Henschel. According to Meserve (*Plays of Howells*, pp. 269–270), the opera was completed in 1885 but never performed; the owner of the Bijou Theatre died, and because of the enormous staging difficulties his successors were not interested in the work. However, an "orchestra reading" or "rehearsal" took place on 27 January 1885. It was published in *Harper's Weekly*, XXXII (14 July 1888), 505 and (Supplement) 521–524; an augmented version was published by Ticknor (Boston) the same year.

[6] Howells was still working on *Indian Summer*, which first appeared in *Century*, LXXI-LXXII (July 1885 to February 1886), and was published in book form by Ticknor, Boston, 1886. See Letter 52.

꧁ *55. Gosse to Howells* ꧂

29 Delamere Terrace / [London] W.

29 February 1884

My dear, my very dear Howells

I have given myself one day to reflect on your proposal, which arrived together with Mr. Augustus Lowell's invitation. I have not yet seen the authorities of the Board of Trade.[1] I wait further light from you.

[1] According to Gosse's letter to his mother, 9 April 1884 (Charteris, *Life and Letters*

If indeed I could secure all that you so kindly propose,—that is to say £500 on lectures to be delivered within a space of 6 weeks at the outside—I would make a great effort to come. It must really rather depend on my being able to make enough to recuperate me for all my expenses and for expenditure of time. I want you to understand that money is not my object in coming to America. I only want not to lose. I shall have to give up all other work now directly, and work on these lectures and these alone for the rest of the year. £400 or £500 when I get there would just recoup this.[2]

Let me ask you some questions:—

1. Could I get Lowell, Johns Hopkins and Cornell[3] into one set of 6 weeks? I should not mind any fatigue connected with it, if the institutions could contrive it.

2. Would the same course of 6 lectures do for the three institutions? I should bring some single lectures (3 or 4) besides.

Please let me clearly know these particulars. In a day or two I shall probably know whether the thing is impossible, and if not impossible I shall write to thank Mr. Lowell, and to ask for a few weeks' time to think of it.

My wife and I join in loving acceptance, if we do come, of yours and Mrs. Howells' hospitality. It will be a downright wicked shame to burden you with us, but we shall just do it, without a blush. And you know that I am only saying the truth when I say that of all the pleasant sights which would await us in America, that of your face is to me the most wished-for.

Ever affectionately and gratefully

Edmund Gosse

---

of Gosse, pp. 161–162), the Board of Trade granted Gosse leave of absence "with the utmost courtesy and readiness."

[2] Gosse's total income from his American lectures was £490 (see Letter 90, and Letter 60, n. 1).

[3] Gosse did not lecture at Cornell, although he did pay a brief visit to the university (see Introduction, p. 18). For comment on the Lowell and Johns Hopkins lectures, also see Introduction, especially pp. 11–12, 16–18.

ᘒ 56. *Gosse to Howells* ᘒ

Board of Trade. [London] S.W.

4 March 1884

My dear Howells

Not hearing from you by this mail, I have felt that I ought to delay no longer, and I have written to Mr. Augustus Lowell, telling him that I feel his invitation to be a distinguished compliment, and that I should very much like to accept it, and moreover that if I do get away, it will be for nine weeks in all, from the end of November to the beginning of February, giving me the 3 last weeks of December and the 3 first weeks of January in America.

This is about my limit. I might perhaps get an extra week on one side or the other.

I long to come. My wife, too, is now quite eager. I send you a scheme of the course I should give at the Lowell Institute. You are quite at liberty to mention it. It is quite a new chapter of criticism, the history of the passage from Romanticism to Classicism, from Shakespeare to Pope. Besides these I have four or five unconnected lectures, of a literary kind, much more popular, "Hans Christian Andersen", "Rossetti", etc.

Thou art a most dear angel of the bon Dieu[1] to take all this trouble. Bless you.

Your affectionate Friend

Edmund Gosse

[1] For explanation of this expression see letter 69.

❧ 57. *Howells to Gosse* ❧

Boston,

4 March 1884

My dear Gosse:

I wish to make you acquainted with my friend Mr. Laurence Barrett,[1] who goes to London to succeed Miss Andersen[2] [sic] at the Lyceum Theatre. He is perhaps not so pretty as Miss Andersen, but I don't think he is otherwise inferior; I have my decided preoccupations to the contrary, in fact, and I think you will share them when you see him on the stage. He will open with a tragedy from the Spanish which I translated[3] and did my worst to

[1] Lawrence Barrett (1838–1891), the American actor, first appeared in Detroit in 1853 and made his New York debut in 1857; he subsequently became a star actor and manager, frequently playing Shakespearean roles with Edwin Booth. In 1884 he took over the Lyceum Theatre while Irving was in America. See Introduction, pp. 14–15.

[2] Mary Anderson (1859–1940), the American-English actress, was born in Sacramento, California. She began her stage life at the age of sixteen, and had many successful seasons (several in London) before her sudden retirement in 1889.

[3] The "tragedy from the Spanish" is *Yorick's Love*, which Howells translated from the play *Un Drama Nuevo* by Joaquin Estébanez (the pseudonym of Manuel Tamaya y Baus), which took its theme from Hamlet. According to Meserve (*Plays of Howells*,

spoil for him, and he expects to give my comedy of A Counterfeit Present-ment[4] as long as he can afford the loss of money which its representation always involves. So I ask you to love him a little for my sake as well as his own. He will show you what a nice fellow he is in every way, and I leave his deserts as an artist to your perception. They have long ceased to be matters of question here, where his fame is commensurate with them.

Yours ever

W. D. Howells

----

pp. 110–114), Howells had Barrett in mind when he translated it in 1877–1878, and it remained in Barrett's repertory until he died. It was not published until Meserve included it in his book in 1960. See Smith and Gibson, *Mark Twain-Howells Letters*, pp. 868–869.

[4] Howells, *A Counterfeit Presentment* (Boston: Osgood, 1877) was first published serially in the *Atlantic Monthly*, XL (August-October 1877).

❦ 58. *Gilder to Gosse* ❦

[New York]

8 March 1884

My dear Gosse,

I am greatly obliged to you for this most exquisitely made Tinworth book.[1] As it only came today, I havent had time to read it—but only to glance through it. The illustrations are highly interesting. He is at any rate an individualist; I shall read what you say about him with great interest.

I bade Mr. Arnold and family good-bye on the steamer this afternoon. He goes away with a kindly feeling, I am sure. I like him very much. He has committed, perhaps, some awkwardnesses here in his "endeavor to pro-pitiate a people whom he does not respect," but besides the great regard for his literature we have always had, we all like him personally—and his family too. He promises to come back, and he will have a hearty welcome whenever he comes. So will you and Dobson. When are you coming?

Truly thine

R. W. Gilder

[1] Gosse, *A Critical Essay on the Life and Works of George Tinworth*.

↬ 59. *Gosse to Howells* ↫

29, Delamere Terrace, / Westbourne Square. [London] W.

8 March 1884

My dear Howells

I have just been talking to Lang about my proposed set of 6 lectures, and he, while approving the subject, disapproves the title. He thinks that nobody knows who Waller was, and that I ought to call the lectures: "From Shakespeare to Pope: a history of the decline of romantic poetry."[1] The individual lectures would (or might) bear the titles I indicated to you. I leave it to your discretion.

You see I am trespassing vilely on your patience. Our love to you all.

Yours affectionately

Edmund Gosse

[1] Lang's suggestion was adopted, both for the lectures themselves and for the book which they eventually became.

↬ 60. *Howells to Gosse* ↫

Boston,

23 March 1884

My dear Gosse:

You will be thinking me very remiss, but I have not really been so. On the contrary I have been diligently working up a boom for you in the lecture-field. I am sorry to say that the boom is not yet satisfactory. You realize that your Lowell course will give you only $750 or £150.[1] I wrote to the Johns Hopkins people for their $1000 = £200 course; they replied offering you $300 = £60 for six lectures. I have again written Dr. Gilman that he promised you the $1000 at my lodgings in London, and I hope to bring him to reason. Mrs. Fields[2] has applied to the Cornell University for

[1] The cash account in Gosse's pocket diary for 1884 shows that he received £206.3.9. from the Lowell Institute; the account for January 1885 lists £80 from Johns Hopkins, £10 from Yale, £20 from Wells College, and £150 from parlor lectures in New York (see Letter 90).

[2] Mrs. Annie Adams Fields, second wife of James Thomas Fields, the publisher, was an author and a prominent literary hostess. Howells's letter of 15 February 1884 to Mrs. Fields is in Mildred Howells, *Life in Letters of Howells*, I, 360: "I wish something might be done for him at Cornell! The six Lowell Lectures only give him $750, and that would be too little to come so far on."

their $600 course, and I have urged on Mr. Lowell that you ought to have the full course of twelve lectures for $1500. Something will come of it all; and I am rejoiced that you wish to come. I will write you as soon as I hear from the various people. I like your subject, and I think Lang's title, "From Shakespeare to Pope,"[3] excellent. Remember to save yourself work in the Lectures, if they run beyond six (as they must to justify you in coming) by leaving space for copious selections and extracts. The more desultory you can make them, after a first sharp outline, the better.

Mrs. Howells joins me in love to both of you, and hopes of seeing you here, our guests.

Yours ever

W. D. Howells

I've finished my novel[4] and am writing Georg Henschel (Tadema's friend) the libretto for a comic opera.[5]

[3] See Letter 59.
[4] Presumably *Indian Summer*.
[5] See Letter 54, n. 4.

❧ 61. *Gosse to Howells* ❧

29 Delamere Terrace / London W.

5 April 1884

My dear Howells

Your letter, much longed for, has just arrived. "Remiss", indeed! I do not [know] where to look among older and far less busy friends for such persistent and unselfish kindness; nor do I know how you are ever to be rewarded, except by my affection, which you know that you possess already.

Now about business: I cannot undertake the 12 lectures. I could make 6 a really good piece of literature, I think, but I could not suffuse myself over 12 without loss of self-respect, I mean in consideration of the very short time I have for writing them.

Let us then say 6. I should be perfectly satisfied if to the Lowell Institute £150 I could add £150 by delivering the same in *one* other place, and £100 by delivering parlour lectures in New York or elsewhere. I do not think I have the right to wish to do more than this. For less than this I could hardly afford to come, for I suppose—with all consideration of the hospitality which I know we should find lavished on our shamelessness,— we must take £150 as the minimum of our travelling expenses? I should have to pay some one here to do my work for the "Century", and I should be earning nothing all the time that I was writing the Lectures, so that I conceive with a receipt of £400 for lectures, I should return to London just about where I should be without going to America, merely having had a lovely time at no expense.

Do not therefore try to get me more than £400. If the Baltimore people had stuck to their $1000, I would have risked the rest, and have accepted, but $300 is ridiculous. It is less than one gets in our poverty-stricken little England for talking to mechanics at Birmingham.[1]

Then you will not overlook the fact that the whole of the boom must be concentrated into six weeks at the outside? Perhaps seven weeks, at a great effort. This no doubt adds to the difficulty.

Of course, I ought to know soon, in order to prepare. I have already begun to buy books, and think of epigrams. I fancy I may promise that this shall be the best book I have ever written, if I do write it. It would fill a gap in English criticism, and my reading for fifteen years has prepared me to fill it. It would be no rechauffée of other people's notions. I can promise original research, and the time is romantic to a surprising degree.

May I then ask you, if you feel that you have secured me not less than £350, to be squeezed into the space from the second week of December to the third week of January (about Dec. 5 to Jan. 25, say), to be so kind as to write to Mr. R. W. Gilder, of the "Century", and ask him to cable to me the word "boom", and then, without waiting for details, I will demand leave of absence from the Government, and if it is granted begin my 6 lectures.

You need not explain to Gilder what "boom" means. They keep up cipher communication with me. Perhaps I ought to be the first to tell Mr. Roswell Smith, whose kindness to me has been extraordinary, if I do come.

Believe me ever yours affectionately and gratefully

Edmund Gosse

[1] According to Gosse's own accounts for 1883, he received ten guineas for lecturing at the Midland Institute in Birmingham, and this seems to have been his usual fee for many years. A series of six lectures at Birmingham would thus earn him £3 (or $15) more than he was offered for six lectures at Johns Hopkins.

❧ 62. *Gosse to Howells* ❧

29, Delamere Terrace, / Westbourne Square. [London] W.

Easter Sunday [13 April] 1884

Dear Howells

Your beautiful poem[1] was played last night to a crowded audience at the Lyceum. I am staying away in the country, but I came up to town expressly, not to miss the first night. I wish to write you my impression before I see anybody or any newspaper. It left upon my mind, then, the impression of *a great popular success.* The writing told well, the situations were sharply and brightly defined, and Barrett, though painfully nervous, was superb. The play was received very warmly indeed and so was Barrett. He was well supported by Fernandez,[2] and pretty badly by the rest.

It was very exciting to us—my wife and me—to see your tragedy. We thought you were Yorick yourself, in your desire to prove that your magna vis comica does not exclude your tragic vein. You are right, my dear Poet!

Ever affectionately and delightedly yours

Edmund Gosse

[1] *Yorick's Love* (see Letter 57, n. 3).

[2] James Fernandez, a popular actor in England, was born in St. Petersburg, Russia, in 1835.

❧ 63. *Gosse to Stedman* ❧

29, Delamere Terrace, / Westbourne Square. [London] W.

20 April 1884

My dear Stedman

The event which you have long predicted has actually come off,—I have been invited to America and have accepted. The Lowell Institute has asked me to come over in December next, and deliver a course of 6 lectures. I have rather rashly, I am afraid, said Yes. I shall write a book for them, in six chapters, called "From Shakespeare to Pope", a particular history of the evolution of English poetry from the romantic to the classical school,—thus divided:—

1. Poetry at the death of Shakespeare.
2. Waller and Sacharissa.
3. Early adherents to the new school.
4. The attempted reaction.
5. Sir William Davenant and the exiles.
6. Poetry at the birth of Pope.

I am thus particular because, with your literary influence, you might possibly hear of some institutions which would allow me to repeat my series to them. I shall lose money if I only have the Lowell. Now, I don't come to America with the notion of money-making, but I have no fortune of my own, and I have to try to manage it so that I lose nothing by so pleasant a holiday. I should be in the States from the second week in December to the last week in January.

In coming one of my very great pleasures will be the expectation of seeing you. Last year, when you were still rich, I could not have said this to you so frankly, for it would have been to pull at the strings of your too noble and generous hospitality. But now that I know you are poor,[1]—as Homer and as Milton were,—I can without reserve say that one of my very greatest pleasures in coming is the thought of seeing you.

I hope you will not think it very rash and immodest of me to come. I shall give the Boston people of my very best,—I mean to write them the best book that I can, and a genuine addition to the history of criticism. I do not underrate the value of my audience: I know that it is a more intelligent and a more instructed audience than any I could address over here.

The invitation was absolutely unasked. It was even twice refused, until a third asking, in most flattering terms, made refusal seem uncourteous. I hope you do not think it presumptuous in me to have accepted?

I am ever

Your affectionate Friend

Edmund Gosse

[1] For Stedman's reduced circumstances, see Letter 49 and n. 1.

∾ 64. Gilder to Gosse ∾

[New York]

24 April 1884

Confidential

My dear Gosse:

I submit to you in confidence, two letters received by me from Prof. Henry A. Beers,[1] of Yale College. Prof. Beers I think is assistant professor of English Literature at Yale, and one of the best critical writers on the Century. He is also a poet. I have told him that I could not speak for you in

[1] Henry Augustin Beers (1847–1926), professor of English at Yale. His most substantial works were his *History of English Romanticism in the Eighteenth Century* (1889) and *History of English Romanticism in the Nineteenth Century* (1901).

this matter with any authority whatever, or with any certainty of what you would be likely to say.

I do not like to advise you in a matter of such grave importance. Of course you know the reputation of Yale—nothing could be better. Harvard, Yale, and Johns Hopkins are our principal institutions of learning.

As to the salary—$3,500 might not go as far in New Haven as it would in London for I fear living may be dearer in New Haven than it is with you —although of this I am not sure. I doubt if it is cheaper.

I am going to suggest to Prof. Beers that they offer two chairs, if such a thing is possible, one of Literature, and the other of Scandinavian Languages, or something of that sort. Of course you will keep Prof. Beers' suggestion in confidence.

The great question as to whether you would wish to come to America for permanent residence, is one no one can decide for you.

I wish the offer might hold till you had the opportunity of visiting the U.S. I do not know whether that would be possible or not.

Very sincerely yours

R. W. Gilder[2]

[2] Apparently Gilder dictated this letter: it is not in his hand, but he has signed it and inserted a few additional words.

❧ 65. *Howells to Gosse* ❧

Hartford, Conn.

27 April 1884

My dear Gosse:

I am writing you from Mark Twain's, where Mrs. Howells has come down to meet me on my way home from New York. She brought with her your note about Yorick's Love,[1] and I make haste to say, as I have already said here in print that I merely translated that play, and slightly adapted it from the Spanish. This fact Mr. Barrett promised me to make very distinct in all advertisements and play-bills; but he has an incurable superstition that I am the author of all that is good in the piece, and I suppose he has inoculated you with his disease. The author still lives and writes in Madrid under the pseudonym of Joaquin Estebanez; almost the entire dramatic frame, and the whole imagination of the piece is his; I wrote in a few subordinate scenes, and turned the better speeches into blank verse. I abhor

[1] See Letter 62.

139

all manner of theft, and I must refuse as clearly as possible to be taken for the author of Yorick's Love. That honor—and I think it a very great one—is another man's.

At New York I talked with Gilder and R. Smith a great deal about you. They have a mystery and a secret[2] which they will spring upon you. I will merely say, as your friend that in reaching any conclusion about it, you must remember that you can't live in any Eastern town in the United States for less than $5000 a year, as you now live in London.

I am glad you have accepted the Lowell Lectures, and that there is a reasonable hope of having you here next winter. But I must not let you come on uncertainties. They give you only $1000, and you ought to have $2000 at the least. While you are delivering them—three weeks—in Boston, you will be at no expense except "car-fares and washing," but I do not see how anything could be done to increase your income there. Gilder will look up the matter of private lectures in New York; but *don't* come till the figures are clear, or you may incur a great disappointment—which would embitter my existence. I have done all that I know how. The Cornell University declines, as you will see by a letter I will send you from Boston. Gilder may get you something from Yale College; the Johns Hopkins people have not answered my last letter; but Gilder told me you had written him that they had renewed their ⟨original⟩ offer. As soon as something is ascertained, I'll write you again.

Yours ever
W. D. Howells

[2] This was probably the Yale chair mentioned in Letter 64.

∾ *66. Gosse to Howells* ∾

[London?]

7 May 1884

Dear Howells

You will be startled to hear—but not more startled than I was yesterday to be told—that I have just been appointed Professor of English Literature in the University of Cambridge,[1] in the room of Leslie Stephen,[2] who has just resigned.

[1] For Gosse's appointment to the Clark Lectureship in English Literature at Trinity College, Cambridge, see also his letter to Robert Louis Stevenson of the same date (Charteris, *Life and Letters of Gosse*, pp. 162–164).
[2] Sir Leslie Stephen (1832–1904), philosopher and man of letters.

This will, I think, justify you a little,—with your American friends,—in your too generous estimate of me.

The appointment makes no difference in my ability to come to Boston early in December.

I am seeing a good deal of Barrett. What a truly amiable and sympathetic man he is! I thank you for the opportunity of knowing him.

Yours always affectionately

Edmund Gosse

The offer from Cambridge is all the more flattering because I made no sort of appeal for it, not indeed having the vaguest notion that it was open.

❧ 67. *Gosse to Howells* ❧

29, Delamere Terrace, / Westbourne Square. [London] W.

8 May 1884

My dear Howells

I have just received your very kind letter from Mark Twain's. I am becoming a burden to you, although I know you would refuse to allow it. I am,—a horrid burden, and therefore I wish at once to put the whole matter straight.

This unexpected improvement in my condition, the Professorship at Cambridge, puts me out of anxiety about my daily bread.[1] I have now a very nice regular income, for it does not cost so much to live in London as to live in one of your eastern towns.

By your very great kindness—a kindness which I never shall forget—I have secured the Lowell Institute offer of $1000. This will more than cover our immediate expenses, and I will not seek any more. All this year we shall live very quietly, taking no outing, and as everybody must have some sort of holiday, we will make the winter trip to Boston our holiday. Don't you bother yourself to write one more letter, or give the matter one more thought. I shall be thoroughly satisfied and more than satisfied to do nothing in America but deliver the Lowell set,—which will be—let me boast to you —the best things I have ever written. Again I say, and I say it most sincerely, I don't want to come to America to make money, but to see friends and a new sympathetic country.

---

[1] According to the memoranda in Gosse's pocket diaries, he received £292.10.0 from Cambridge in 1885 and again in 1886; in 1887, 1888, and 1889 he received £200 annually.

We are also getting extremely uncomfortable about the crude way in which I accepted your and Mrs. Howells' offer of hospitality. My wife has never been a party to this, and constantly upbraids me for my greediness. It really was timidity that made me so eager; I feel such a terror of a great strange city. But we want to ask you now to just take us in at the first moment of our coming, and then help us to find some quiet lodgings close to you. You will agree to this, will you not? or else we shall be very haughty and refuse to come, for it would be monstrous for us to destroy your peace of heart and hearth all the time we are in Boston.

We were quite deceived about the authorship of "Yorick's Love". We thought that Estebanez was merely a pseudonym of yours, or at least that you had but taken the hint from some foreign source. I hope Barrett may be induced to play the Counterfeit Presentment before he goes.[2]

Yours very sincerely

Edmund Gosse

[2] See Letter 57, and n. 4.

❧ 68. *Howells to Gosse* ❧

4 Louisburg Square, / Boston,

20 May 1884

My dear Gosse:

I rejoice with you, with all my heart, on your appointment which I suppose is about the pleasantest thing that could happen to you. I can imagine you there in that beautiful old town, in some college with a "back" as lovely as one of Watteau's women, and if I could envy you at all, I should envy you that fate. But I can't envy you; I shall only love you the more the luckier you are.

I have been written [sic] your 17th century poets[1] since I came home from New York and enjoying every word: perhaps we can get up a "boom" for the book here on your appointment.

I am very glad that this will not prevent your coming here. Maybe we shall receive you at our own house in the *real* Cambridge, which is, you know, a suburb of Boston.

Tell Tadema that Henschel and I are working together at a comic opera[2]

[1] Gosse, *Seventeenth Century Studies.*
[2] See Letter 54, n. 5.

(the libretto is done) which is to be brought out here this fall, and we hope in London. Henschel's music is lovely.

My wife joins me in love and rejoicing.

Yours ever

W. D. Howells

∾ 69. *Gosse to Howells* ∾

29 Delamere Terrace / [London] W.

6 June 1884

My best of Howells's

We have had a lovely card of yours, and a letter from Mrs. Howells so sweet that we fell into one another's arms and sobbed. But we don't know what baby she means, tell her. No baby at 29 Delamere Terrace since your visit; and Miss Sylvia Laura, in the honours of her 4th. year, declines the name. Good God, I hope it isn't an omen! No more babys wanted in this establishment.

Well! President Gilman has written to me at last a very vague letter, to which I have replied a very decisive one, and have referred him to you. I hope I have not done wrong? I am quite careless about terms; I will go to Baltimore for anything they choose to give me. But he must understand my time and my subject are fixed.

I once helped an eminent French painter to three bananas at once, and he wreathed his arms suddenly about me, and said "O thou dear angel of the good God!" That is just what I say of you.

Ever thine and Mrs. Howells's and the young people's

Affectionate

Edmund Gosse

∾ 70. *Gosse to Howells* ∾

[London ?]

8 July 1884

My dear Howells

I wish to explain to you that only this minute has the Johns Hopkins University completed its arrangements with me. I am to lecture there during

143

the first two weeks in January, which is very convenient, as I am very anxious to get back here before the month of February begins.

I have been wanting to tell you how much I have enjoyed the lovely little book you have sent my wife. It is all new to me, except, of course, your English child, the Lexington.[1] The style all through is so delicate, so pure, so appropriate, that it awakes my envy. No, my sympathetic admiration. I think it wonderful that you, and the few that write well when they have attained your eminence, should be able to do so. A person like myself, still hanging by my eyelids to the outer cliff of fame, is nerved and stimulated to write well, or sink into oblivion amid the titters of exasperated relatives. But you, who might write like a waart-pig (Have you ever seen a waart-pig? —ugh!) if you chose, and would still be certain of praise,—for you to put in those little touches, fairy-bells at the tips of your sentences, tiny wafts of perfumed wit, which only about a dozen of your readers ever perceive, this is very creditable, my dear fellow; it shows that you are an artist down to the tips of your toes. Do you notice that women never can do this? All of them, the best of them, George Sand herself, calls her work her *métier*, never her *art*.

I have got the works of Capt. John Smith, all about Pocahontas, etc. for you, if you care to have them. It is a new reprint, not likely to have reached America, being privately issued.[2] It is very taking reading, nutty and odd. Say on a postcard if you care to have it.

I have heard of you from Aldrich, Pennell and others. You have taken a new house, I hear, at the back of the Bay.[3]

My wife desires her love to Mrs. Howells and I mine to you.

Yours very cordially

Edmund Gosse

[1] The book was Howells's *Three Villages* (Boston: Osgood, 1884). The first essay was entitled "Lexington," and was first published in *Longman's Magazine*, I (November 1882), 41–61. See also Letter 32.

[2] *The Works of Captain John Smith, Governor of Virginia*, ed. Edward Arber. The title page gives the date of publication as 10 June 1884 and the place as Birmingham; it bears the general title "The English Scholar's Library."

[3] This was Howells's new house at 302 Beacon Street, Boston. The phrase in the letter has been annotated in holograph by Howells: "Isn't that a funny translation of Back Bay?"

A Mural from Rapallo

This rare drawing by Max Beerbohm portrays a number of prominent persons of his time, among them literary figures, painters, politicians. Their only connection apparently was that they were all friends of Beerbohm whom he enjoyed caricaturing. The drawing is one of several murals Beerbohm painted on the walls of his villa at Rapallo. After his death they were shaved off the walls with incredible skill by Italian workmen and transferred to canvas. This one, which so far as is known has never before been published, now hangs in the Undergraduate Library and Academic Center, The University of Texas.

Identities are (see numbers in silhouette above): 1) unidentified, 2) Henry Chaplin, 3) J. J. Sargent, 4) G. K. Chesterton, 5) J. E. B. Seely, 6) P. Wilson Steer, 7) Edward Carson, 8) William Nicholson, 9) John Galsworthy, 10) John Masefield, 11) George Bernard Shaw, 12) John Davidson, 13) R. B. Cunninghame Graham, 14) Gordon Craig, 15) Ray Lankester, 16) unidentified, 17) Charles Conder, 18) Lytton Strachey, 19) Edmund Gosse, 20) unidentified, 21) H. H. Asquith. (Identifications supplied by Mr. Rupert Hart-Davis.)

Gosse in his study.

Gosse with the young Misses Tennant,
4 July 1923.

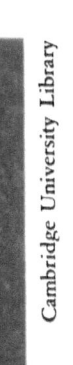

Gosse at about middle age, on a visit to Spain.

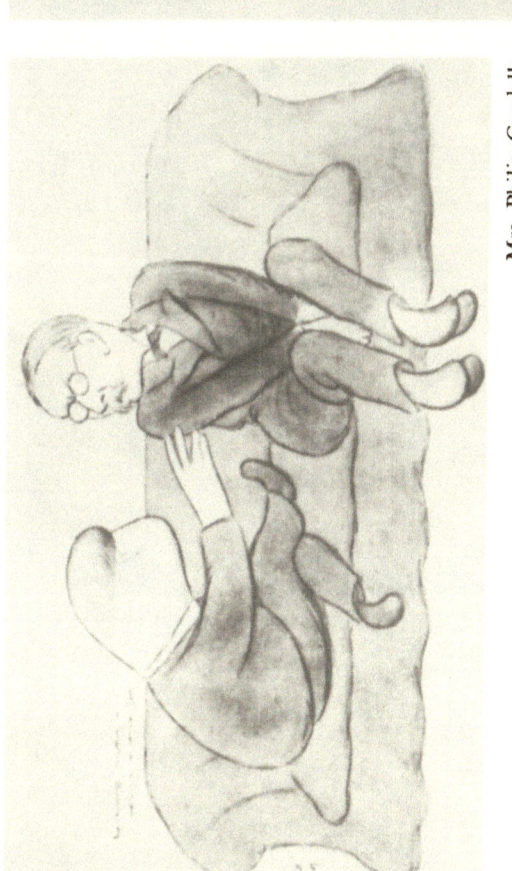

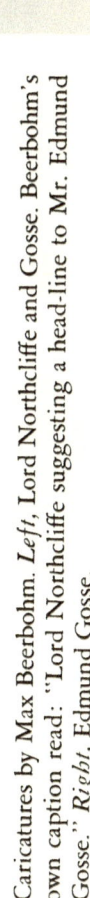

Caricatures by Max Beerbohm. *Left*, Lord Northcliffe and Gosse. Beerbohm's own caption read: "Lord Northcliffe suggesting a head-line to Mr. Edmund Gosse." *Right*, Edmund Gosse.

Brotherton Collection, University of Leeds

William Dean Howells

Miss Rosamond Gilder

Richard Watson Gilder

Edmund Clarence Stedman

Horace H. F. Jayne

Horace Howard Furness

Oliver Wendell Holmes

🙲 71. *Gosse to Stedman* 🙲

7 Whitehall Gardens / [London] S.W.

21 August 1884

My dear Stedman

It is two months since I received your interesting and most kind letter. Since that time I have been excessively occupied, and have put off longer than I should have done the pleasant task of thanking you. I have not had any holiday, however brief, as yet, and expect none until I come to America at the end of November. It takes up all my time to write my lectures for the Lowell Institute. I am most anxious that having been paid the extraordinary honour of being invited to deliver my opinions to such an audience, I should not lay myself open to the charge of being jejune, slovenly or thin. I am in hopes that, if I have any literary men in my audience, they will find my lectures to be *good work*. I believe I have never written so well before, I have certainly never tried before so original and difficult a thesis.

The President of Cornell[1] is no doubt wise in refusing the offer you were so extremely kind as to make to him. But, although Mr. Corson[2] may have been over some of the same ground, I do not think they would find that I repeated what he said. He, I believe, dealt mainly with Dryden, whom I barely touch. At the Johns Hopkins also, Corson has lately preceded me, but there they hailed this as a fortunate accident, which would make my course only the more àpropos.

Today I am sending you—just to show that I am alive—a copy of my new edition of Sir Joshua Reynolds' *Discourses*.[3] You will find a number of odd notes and verses, never hitherto known, which I copied from Blake's handwriting in the British Museum.

I shall also send you in a day or two, a copy of an edition, strictly limited to 40 copies, which I have had printed of an epistle of mine to Dr. Holmes on his 75th. birthday.[4] You, no doubt, received the same appeal as I and Dobson did.[5]

You please me very much by promising me a welcome from the literary

[1] Andrew Dickson White (1832–1918) was co-founder, with Ezra Cornell, of Cornell University, and its first president (1868–1885); he was later United States minister to Russia (1892–1894), and ambassador to Germany (1897–1899).

[2] Hiram Corson (1828–1911), who lectured at Johns Hopkins just prior to Gosse's visit, was professor of literature at Cornell University; he wrote studies of Browning (1886) and Shakespeare (1889), and *The Aims of Literary Study* (1895).

[3] Gosse, ed., *The Discourses of Sir Joshua Reynolds* (London: Kegan Paul, 1884).

[4] Gosse, *An Epistle to Dr. Oliver Wendell Holmes on his Seventy-Fifth Birthday, August 29, 1884* (printed privately).

[5] Gosse's "epistle" appeared in the *Critic*, ns II (30 August 1884), 102; this was a special issue of the *Critic* in celebration of Holmes's seventy-fifth birthday, and Gosse's poem was one of many tributes to Holmes from distinguished contemporaries.

class in America. Of course, I am utterly unknown out of that class. I am very shy of coming, very much afraid that it will seem presumptuous of me to come on such an errand. But I throw myself on American kindess and American indulgence.

Your interesting and genial friend Mrs. Sherwood,[6] for whom we felt at once a real affection, left us after too short a visit, in which, however, I hope she saw much that pleased her. We were particularly glad that you were so good as to introduce her to us.

When will the project, of which you speak so darkly in all your recent letters, be unveiled? I am filled with curiosity.

What you say about my Cambridge chair is very grateful to me. No doubt you are quite right, Newhaven would not have suited me. I cannot think how the news leaked out that I was offered the chair at Yale? It was a profound secret, which I was asked to reveal to no soul, and I did reveal it to no one. I rejected it, with profound thanks, by return of post, of course. Do I gather from a rather strange expression in the letter you wrote the *Tribune*, that I should have been looked upon as an unsuitable man for the post?[7] You say my election would have been "universally condemned". Humility bids me agree to this, but amour-propre wonders why, if I am not thought too bad for Cambridge, I should be "universally condemned" for Yale!

The disadvantage which you possess in being unable to examine the *documents*, will for a long while yet leave America behind England in the department of historical criticism. You lack the opportunity for research.

With kindest regards

Ever yours sincerely

Edmund Gosse

[6] Mrs. Mary Elizabeth Wilson Sherwood (1826–1903), wife of John Sherwood, a New York lawyer, was a well-known literary hostess in New York during the 1870's; she also wrote a number of books and gave readings. Robert Underwood Johnson refers to her as "an estimable lady known from her initials as 'The Tenth Muse' " (Johnson, *Remembered Yesterdays*, p. 91).

[7] See Stedman's reply: Letter 75.

72. *Lowell[1] to Gosse*

Legation of the United States / London

6 September 1884

Dear Mr Gosse,

Many thanks for your kindness in honouring me with No. 2 of your delightful poem.[2] So nearly as human nature (since Adam's fall) will tolerate, I was as much pleased with it as if it had been addressed to myself, and I am sure that my old friend Dr. Holmes will like it as well as I do. You have hit the characteristic features with the point of your etchingneedle. I like also the quaint form you have chosen[3] and so will he.

It is a little cruel of you to make me say all this for I too have commemorated Holmes's last birthday in verse[4]—and not so well.

Faithfully yours

J. R. Lowell

[1] James Russell Lowell (1819–1891) was United States minister in London from 1880 to 1885. The appointment was at first controversial in view of Lowell's earlier anti-British opinions, but it turned out to be remarkably successful. For an account of earlier exchanges between Lowell and Gosse see Letter 15 and Letter 53, n. 4.

[2] See Letter 71, n. 4.

[3] The whole poem was cast in the form of a letter and Gosse had imitated not only Pope's manner and versification but also the spelling and punctuation of the period.

[4] "To Holmes on his seventy-fifth birthday," in *Poetical Works of James Russell Lowell* (London: Macmillan, 1908), pp. 467–468.

73. *Holmes[1] to Gosse*

Beverly Farms, Mass.

7 September 1884

My dear Mr. Gosse,

I have issued a general Manifesto of thanks to the many kind friends who have covered me with flowers and felicitations[2] until I was in danger of being smothered like the heroine of one of Zola's stories.[3] I will send you

[1] For comment on Gosse's friendship with Oliver Wendell Holmes (1809–1894), see Introduction, pp. 30–32.

[2] See Letter 71, n. 5; Holmes's general reply, "To My Birthday Correspondents," appeared in the next issue of the *Critic*, ns II (6 September, 1894), 109.

[3] Presumably an allusion to the death of Albine in Chapter XIV of Zola's novel *La Faute de l'Abbé Mouret*.

a copy of "The Critic", though I trust that you have received one from the Editors before this time.

But I cannot accept such a tribute as yours without a special acknowledgment. You do me great honor in coupling my name with that [of] any of those whom you mention.[4] I should feel very proud if I had not lived through so many years of earthly vanities. I have but very recently had a sorrow which tempers all the pleasurable excitement of my birthday chorus of compliment. No one took more delight in the praise I received than my second son, Edward, who died suddenly a few weeks ago. There is a slight allusion to this loss in my general letter of acknowledgment.

Mr. Frederick Locker[5] once sent me a first edition copy, in folio form, of Pope's Epistle to Dr. Arbuthnot. As I read the carefully studied imprint of your lines, which Jacob Tonson or Bernard Lintot would have sworn to as from his own press, I feel as Arbuthnot felt, I doubt not, when he got that famous Letter from the famous little poet. I shall lay the two poems together, feeling sure that the older "copy of verses" will find the newer one a worthy companion.

If I am not mistaken I have been your debtor before this for kind words, but I am a hopeless bankrupt in thanks for all the favors I have received from friends, known and unknown. I cannot thank all my friends individually, but so exceptional and so pleasing a remembrance from a man of letters whose name has long been familiarly known to me as holding an honored position insists on this expression of my gratitude.

Believe me, dear Mr. Gosse

Faithfully yours,

Oliver Wendell Holmes

[4] Among the names Gosse had invoked in his "Epistle" were those of Dryden, Pope, Gay, Congreve, and Steele.

[5] Frederick Locker-Lampson (1821–1895), the English author known especially for his light verse; in *Books on the Table* (London: Heinemann, 1921), p. 170, Gosse describes him as "the most skilful of all [Holmes's] disciples." He added his wife's name of Lampson to his own in 1885.

∾ 74. *Gosse to Holmes* ∾

29, Delamere Terrace, / Westbourne Square. [London] W.

18 September 1884

Dear Dr. Holmes

You have done me too much honour to respond separately to my copy of verses. I had already seen your general reply, and had taken it to myself.

148

I am, however, exceedingly touched and flattered by your kind personal letter, and I must write to warn you that when I come to Boston this winter to lecture at the Lowell Institute, I shall make no ceremony of calling to present my respects to you.[1] I was intending to ask our common friend Mr. Matthew Arnold for a note of introduction, but your most kind letter bids me think that I shall take no liberty in considering myself as already honoured by your acquaintance, and I shall boldly present myself to you without an usher.

Pray believe me to be

With great regard and respect
Dear Dr. Holmes
Yours faithfully
Edmund Gosse

[1] See Introduction, pp. 12. Gosse had already written to Gilder on 22 June 1884 (a.l.s., HU) to say that he wanted most to meet Holmes and Augustus St. Gaudens.

✧ 75. *Stedman to Gosse* ✧

"Kelp Rock" / New Castle, N[ew] H[ampshire]

18 September 1884

My dear Gosse,

A few lines in reply to your nice letter of Aug. 21st. I am always glad to get one of your letters,—they are more "stimulating" than those from most persons of the Anglo-Saxon breed. There is a good deal of the American about you, as I always have said. Depend on't that the American, besides his natural "drive" and ambition, and despite the *lack* of taste he displays in his vulgar and ignorant classes and sections, has a surer *inborn taste* than the Englishman. I notice that the English have a passion for doing the right thing, and are always on the *search* after the fit and beautiful. But taste is not inborn with them, as with some of the Continental peoples. Hence they are always *groping* and importing, and seeking for leaders and teachers,—and, when they think they have the right thing, all London, all England, goes *en masse* after it. The Yankee needs teaching badly, but it is —even to me, a Yankee—a perpetual marvel how quickly, instinctively, our more refined people seize on ideas and forms of beauty from abroad, and modify, adapt, even improve them. We are natural artists. Even the rustic journeyman-masons, who laid the rubble-walls of this country-house last year, caught the spirit of my suggestions and became Venetian stone-layers in three days—giving me exquisite mosaic walls.—Now, I see in your writings and poetry *taste* everywhere instinctive and predominant, above that of most Englishmen whose ancestors, unlike your father's, have been England-dwellers for centuries,—and whose chief lack, as Arnold says, is "lucidity". (Yankee-wise, *gumption*.)

I am greatly pleased that you are coming over. My regret is that you will come in the middle of what promises to be a savage winter-season. The country is a paradise now—in December it will be cold, yellow or gray, barren and forbidding. The town-*interiors*, of course, will be pleasant,—and for another trip you can select our country-season.—I am writing, now, from our really unique little home on the down-East sea-coast, where I have been for near two months,—and don't I wish you were here with us! We contrived to save "Kelp Rock" in our recent "unpleasantness",[1]—it is on the heart with me, like Mary Tudor's Calais. By the way, I have written a carefully critical paper on Holmes,[2] while down here,—taking occasion to discuss modern tendencies in art and poetry. For various reasons, I *know* this article will interest you,—although Holmes himself affords a far less vital subject than Poe, or Whitman, or Emerson, or Lowell. This reminds me that I have here received your private text of your clever 18th. century poem to the Autocrat—and congratulate you on the manner in which [you] got through with the perfunctory duty imposed on us by *The Critic*.[3] I also have to thank you for your exquisite edition of Reynolds's discourses. We have few books, as yet, in this cottage, but this one alone gives a refined air to our centre-table. Your Preface is perfect, with one little flaw—you have changed the pronoun in your sentence from Sir Thomas Browne.[4] Your other changes, of course, are a justifiable license.

You are quite right in your belief that Corson's work would only pave the way for your own at Cornell. The truth is, I suppose, that White had his engagements completed. I have a lingering notion that he may yet feel he can't get along without your course. As to Yale College, I should be sorry to leave you under a mistake. You certainly have seen no letter of mine in *The Tribune*, or anywhere else, relative to the Yale Chair of Literature, for I never have written any.[5] I think the *Tribune* had a badly mangled item,

[1] See Letter 49.

[2] Stedman, "Oliver Wendell Holmes," *Century*, XXX (February 1885), 502–512.

[3] See Letter 71, n. 5.

[4] There is no direct quotation from Sir Thomas Browne in the Preface to Gosse's edition of *The Discourses of Sir Joshua Reynolds* (London: Kegan Paul, 1884), but Stedman is presumably referring to the sentence on p. vii, beginning: "The inquity of oblivion hath blindly scattered his poppy over the pompous hexameters of the *De Arte Graphica* . . . ." The figure originates in Browne's *Urn Burial*, where it reads: "her poppy."

[5] See Letter 71. See also Stedman and Gould, *Life and Letters of Stedman*, II, 160–161.

abbreviating a very incorrect "alleged" "interview" with me—which an obscure paper printed last Spring. That is probably what you saw. Nor have I ever, in any way, expressed a doubt of your (in fact) unusual competency to fill the place. If any Englishman were to fill it, there is no one—as I have said often—so fit to do so as you or whom *I* would prefer. I did express my doubt of the Chair having been offered you, as members of the Faculty told me it had not been—but that *Prof. Beers* had asked a friend to "sound" you, and see if the idea of going to Yale would suit you, if the offer should be made. I also said that you were too good for the place,—and that any long established and successful author would decline its hack-work and obscure and ill-paid routine. Furthermore, that I am one of the many Yale Alumni who, for reasons too long to explain here, and *purely local to Yale,* am [sic] strongly opposed to inviting *any* foreign author or scholar to take the vacant professorship. Some of the wealthier friends of the College offered last winter to double the endowment of the Chair if I would take it. Though very deeply gratified, I stopped the matter at once. It would put an end to all my literary plans; furthermore, my life itself is pledged to the settlement of debts of honor and the readjustment of my affairs, and I could not and would not accept the *Presidency* of Yale or Harvard! But the idea of my undervaluing, or publicly depreciating, *your* abilities—in view of that paltry professorship—is simply preposterous. You ought to know better!

Historical and critical scholarship, relating to correct texts and "documents", has little to do with the burdens of that Professorship—the correction of Sophomore compositions is the chief work. You are right, of course, and in the main, with respect to the superior advantages, as workers "in the department of historical criticism", possessed by England over America. It is odd, however, that the *best and most important work* in that department, now publishing, is Prof. Childs' great Edition (limited) of the English Ballad Texts; possibly the next best is Furness's Variorum Shakespeare.[6] Beat those two, if you can.

Mr. Robert Buchanan[7] is in New York. My absence has prevented me from seeing him—his cards have been forwarded to me. You have seen, I presume, his talks in the newspapers.

Shall you not bring Mrs. Gosse with you? If so, you will be doubly wel-

[6] Francis James Child (1825–1896), *English and Scottish Popular Ballads,* published in five volumes between 1883 and 1898. For Horace Howard Furness, see Letter 85, n. 3; his New Variorum edition of Shakespeare began appearing in 1871, and the work was continued by his son Horace Howard Furness, Jr. See Stedman's letter to Furness, Stedman and Gould, *Life and Letters of Stedman,* II, 134–135.

[7] Robert Williams Buchanan (1841–1901), the English poet, novelist, and dramatist, now chiefly remembered for his attacks on Swinburne and the Pre-Raphaelites.

come. —Here—I started to write "a few lines", but as it will be my last chance to write *at leisure* for many months, I have suffered my pen to run on. Forgive me. Mrs. Sherwood wrote me from Paris, *very grateful* for your kindness to her.

Ever sincerely yours,

Edmund C. Stedman

❧ 76. *Howells to Gosse* ❧

302 Beacon St., / Boston,

25 September 1884

My dear Gosse:

Pilla was made a very proud and happy little girl by your lovely book, and wants me to write the thanks which she will a little later express to you. We are now all looking forward to your coming. We are in our new house, and we talk habitually of "the Gosses' room," "the Gosses' closet," "the Gosses' wash-stand," etc., and have all but bodily installed you. I have been elected President of a pleasant club of young fellows,[1] some of whom have seen you, and they are going to put up a dinner on you, as soon as you come.

My wife hopes Mrs. Gosse got the map of Boston which she sent her some weeks ago, and joins with me in affectionate regards to both of you.

Ever yours

W. D. Howells

[1] The Tavern Club. "In 1884 Howells was chosen for the first president of the Tavern Club, which had grown from the meetings of some of the younger artists, musicians, writers, and professional men, at the Carrolton Hotel. When they became a club they took rooms in a building at the corner of Park Square, under those of Frederic P. Vinton who had William Hunt's old studio there. At Mrs. Vinton's invitation they held their entertainments in her husband's studio, as their own rooms were small and bare. When the club grew larger they decided to move to a house of their own on Boylston Place" (Mildred Howells, *Life in Letters of Howells,* I, 391). The present address of the Club is at 4 Boylston Place, Boston. The dinner for Gosse was held on 18 December 1884 (Gosse's American diary), and among those whose names Gosse recorded in his diary were: "Vinton, Porter, Gaugengügl [sic], Watson, Munzig, Luce and Osgood." Frederic Porter Vinton, Benjamin Curtis Porter, Ignaz Marcel Gaugengigl, Francis Sedgwick Watson, George Chickering Munzig, John Dandridge Henley Luce, and James Ripley Osgood were all Charter Members of the Club: see M. A. DeWolfe Howe, *Semi-Centennial History of the Tavern Club, 1884–1934* ([Boston]: printed for the Tavern Club, 1934).

❧ 77. *Gosse to Gilder* ❧

Board of Trade. [London] S.W.

26 September 1884

My dear Gilder

I am sure Mr. *Watts*[1] would be delighted to see "Love and Life" engraved in the magazine[2] and so should I. But I am bound to tell you that both figures are entirely naked: I don't think the gentleman has so much as a wisp of calico round his middle—so what would Chaste Connecticut say, not to speak of Virtuous Vermont?

Ever thine

Edmund Gosse

Did you get a book and a wisp of verses from me?

[1] George Frederic Watts (1817–1904), the English painter and sculptor.
[2] It seems not to have appeared in the *Century*.

❧ 78. *Gosse to Howells* ❧

29 Delamere Terrace / [London] W.

8 October 1884

My dear Howells

It was a great delight to me to hear from you again. The last letter I had from you was dated May 20, and I could not imagine by what accident or chance I heard nothing for six whole months. In the mean time I have written you three letters, sent you two books, and a pointed concern; besides what my wife has sent to Mrs. Howells. If you got these things, all right. But there were definite questions in two of my letters which I thought you could answer. It does not the least matter, if you got all these things, but you only happen to mention one of the whole lot, namely, the book I sent to your daughter. You did not tell us you were changing houses, and we wrote to an outlandish address on one of Mrs. Howells' letters, I am afraid our things never reached you. However, all is well that ends well, and we hold you now between our finger and thumb.

All is prepared, and we are longing to come. We sail by the Germanic (White Star Line) on the 20th. of November. They promise to land us at New York on the 30th. My first lecture is on the 3rd. In case we should be wrecked or delayed by icebergs or eaten of polar bears, I am going to send you a set of my lectures printed,[1] so that if anything totally unforeseen prevented my being at the Lowell Institute on the 3rd., somebody might read the lecture for me, and not disappoint the audience.

All you are so very kind as to say about the welcome we shall receive, is most touching to us. Dont we mean to have a lovely time? The "Boston Herald" seems to be an enterprising paper: it has sent a gentleman to interview me already. If you see what he says, you might send it to me.

We were so much obliged to Mrs. Howells for her map, which first revealed to us that you had changed your house. Our love to you all.

Ever Thine

Edmund Gosse

[1] *Six Lectures written to be delivered before the Lowell Institute in December, 1884* (privately printed in an impression of only four copies at the Chiswick Press in London, October 1884). See Norman Gullick's Bibliography in Charteris, *Life and Letters of Gosse*, 512–513.

❧ 79. Gosse to Holmes ❧

302 Beacon St. / Boston[1]

5 December 1884

Dear Dr. Holmes

Successive visits from Mr. E. E. Hale,[2] Mr. C. E. Norton[3] and various other people have so broken up my day that it is only now,—at midnight, —that I have been able to finish reading your truly delightful life of Emerson.[4] Forgive me, therefore, for not returning it, as I promised to do, this

[1] Gosse and his wife arrived in New York on 29 November 1884 and in Boston on 1 December. See Introduction, pp. 10 *et seq.*

[2] Edward Everett Hale (1822–1909), Unitarian minister, writer, and reformer; he edited religious journals, and wrote short stories, of which "The Man Without a Country" is the best known. Two letters written by him to Gosse while the latter was in America are in the Brotherton Collection.

[3] Charles Eliot Norton (1827–1908) was professor of Fine Art at Harvard from 1874 to 1898; he had earlier edited the *North American Review* from 1864 to 1868 jointly with James Russell Lowell. He had an exceptionally wide range of friends, particularly in England, and he edited the letters of many of these, including Carlyle, Emerson, Lowell, and Ruskin.

[4] O. W. Holmes, *Ralph Waldo Emerson*, in the American Men of Letters series (Boston: Houghton Mifflin, 1885).

afternoon. It is full of touches and reflections that only your brain could have conceived.

Thank you for once more supporting me at my lecture tonight. Your face there in the centre of the crowd is as good as a laurel wreath put publicly about my brows.

Believe me, dear Dr. Holmes,

Ever cordially and gratefully yours

Edmund Gosse

P.S. I should come up with the book, but I am starting off to Danvers to pay Mr. Whittier a visit,[5] and you—I know—are going to Wellesley.

[5] John Greenleaf Whittier (1807–1892), the poet. See Gosse, "A Visit to Whittier," *Bookman*, VIII (January 1899), 459–462, subsequently collected in Gosse's *Portraits and Sketches* (London: Heinemann, 1912), pp. 137–147.

෨ 80. *Gosse to Holmes* ෨

302 Beacon St. / Boston / Mass.

12 December 1884

Dear Dr. Holmes

You overwhelm me! I do not know in what terms to thank you for your lovely Christmas gift. I shall go back to England with a rich sheaf of proofs of your kindness.

I want to ask you to accept the American volume of my Selected Poems,[1] but one result of the bewildering Gosse boom which my too-kind friends have got up is, that not a copy of any book with my name on the titlepage is to be bought in Boston. But I am hourly expecting the book from New York, and you will honour me very much if you will accept it.

Yours most faithfully

Edmund Gosse

Will Wednesday suit you?

[1] Gosse, *On Viol and Flute*: see Letter 37, n. 3.

81. *Holmes to Gosse*

296, Beacon Street. [Boston]

13 December 1884

My dear Mr. Gosse,

Mr. Aldrich promises to come on Wednesday (2 o'clock) to meet you at my house.

I have just received the volume of poems[1] you send me. Many thanks. The inscription to me is lovely and the poems I have tasted are like the honey of Hybla.—We are all a little in love with you.

Faithfully yours

Oliver Wendell Holmes

[1] See Letter 80.

82. *Gosse to Moulton*[1]

1 East 28th. St. / New York

20 December 1884

My dear Mrs. Moulton

It seems shabby indeed of us to leave Boston without seeing something more of you, and thanking you better for your cordial hospitality. We intended to be with you yesterday afternoon, both of us, but the weather was really more than we could face. I have felt the extraordinary cold a good deal, and I was obliged to nurse my throat for my duties. Unless, then, we meet in New York, it will have to be in our own house that we tell you by word of mouth how much we appreciate your kind exertions in our behalf.

These three weeks in Boston and Cambridge have seemed like a flattering and incredible dream: the warmth of the welcome, the intelligent friendship extended to us on every side, the bright sympathy and indulgent appreciation,—these have all surpassed my utmost expectations. I knew Boston was intelligent and brilliant, I had to learn that she was so friendly, and I wish you would further oblige me by making known to any who speak of us with kindness our deep and warm recognisance. As to the poets, from Dr. Holmes to Miss Guiney[2] (some of whose things are most remarkable) they have

[1] Mrs. Louise Chandler Moulton was a regular visitor to England and Gosse had known her for several years. See Letter 5, n. 9. Other of Gosse's letters to her are in the Library of Congress; a few of her letters to Gosse are in the Brotherton Collection.
[2] Louise Imogen Guiney (1861–1920), poet and essayist, was born in Boston but

been like dear family friends to me.

Farewell, dear Mrs. Moulton, and believe us both to be, what one of us signs himself,

Yours very sincerely
Edmund Gosse

_____

spent much of her later life in England. She occasionally assisted Gosse in his research (see Charteris, *Life and Letters of Gosse,* pp. 287–288).

✑ 83. *Gosse to Howells* ✑

1 East 28th. St. / New York

20 December 1884

My dear, dear Howells

We have got here safe and sound. What you lightly suggested, however, came true. On the chair immediately opposite mine sat an enthusiastic Harvard freshman, who addressed me as Professor directly I returned from saying farewell to you, and who kept up a running interview with me until I fell asleep in his face. Mrs. L[awrence] B[arrett][1] was waiting for us at the station with her carriage and brought us on at once. Merely a calm feminine welcome awaited us, the dramatic arms have not been as yet extended, nor the Smile smiled. This will come off tomorrow, probably, for he is expected then from some place in P[ennsylvani]a.

Nellie joins me in love to you both—you have given us a feast of good things, and we shall be all our life digesting it into the Blood of affection and the Chyle of literature.

Ever Thine

Edmund Gosse

[1] The Gosses stayed with the Barretts at 1 East Twenty-eighth Street, New York, over Christmas 1884.

✑ 84. *Howells to Gosse* ✑

302 Beacon st. / Boston.

24 December 1884

Dearest Gossy:

The children are busy trimming their Christmas tree, and all our hearts go out in self-satisfied compassion towards you poor things. We have missed

157

you terribly; and like the prisoner who was liberated after many years of confinement, we long for our bondage again. (There is no extra charge for this figure.) Boston still palpitates with you, and the weather has come on with a snow storm which you ought to have seen. But no doubt you prefer basking on the Battery in New York. Three letters to-day and three yesterday came for you and were promptly forwarded. They seemed to be mostly English.

Do be very nice, and tell all about Mrs. Bryant Godwin if you meet her, and what she says of "R. S. connected with the C."[1] Also, any other social adventures that befall you. I wonder if your host[2] will play a simple American citizen's Christmas, or something medieval-baronial. In either case, give him my love, and good wishes, for he is heartily worthy.

The Tavern Club men think the Gosse dinner was the pleasantest they have yet had, and the spotted baby has covered you with glory.[3]

Mrs Howells has been sending you laurels plucked from various boughs, and there are but a few sprigs of parsley left me to glean. But the Perrys[4] were talking you over with me, and they said—he, mostly—"And isn't *Mrs.* Gosse nice, too! I liked *her.*" I saw the good little Doctor[5] on the street, but avoided his eye: I could *not* stand any more praise of Gosse from him.

I've been working like a beaver since you left, and am getting Silas[6] well on to disaster. He is about to be "squeezed" by a railroad, in a trade.

I do wish you could both see the brave old Boston in this snow. It's superb.

---

[1] Mrs. Bryant Godwin, mother of Miss Nora Godwin, a young American whom the Gosses had twice entertained in London shortly before their departure, had written to Mrs. Gosse on 13 December [1884] (a.l.s., BC) to complain that her attempts to get in touch with Mrs. Gosse had been "frustrated by the refusal of Mr. R. Smith (connected with the Century) to give me your address." The joke, of course, was that Roswell Smith owned the *Century.* There is also in the Brotherton Collection a draft, in Gosse's hand, of a conciliatory letter which Mrs. Gosse presumably sent to Mrs. Godwin: "My husband joins me [it concludes] in sincere hope that you will not allow this extraordinary and deplorable misunderstanding to deprive us of the pleasure of seeing you."

[2] Lawrence Barrett (see Letter 83).

[3] See Letter 76 and n. 1. The allusion is presumably to a joke which Gosse told on this occasion.

[4] Thomas Sergeant Perry (1845–1928) and his wife. Perry, a distinguished critic and scholar, especially in the field of modern languages, was a close friend of Howells. He wrote Gosse a letter of encouragement on 10 November 1886 (a.l.s, BC), at the time when Gosse had been attacked by Churton Collins.

[5] Dr. Oliver Wendell Holmes.

[6] At the time of Gosse's visit to America Howells was at work on *The Rise of Silas Lapham*; Gosse records in his diary that while he was studying in Boston Howells sometimes read to him from the manuscript (see Introduction, pp. 13–14).

Mrs. Howells says "Mrs. Proudie's regards to Mr. Pepys."[7] I don't know what it means. Sass, probably.

All the family join me in love to both of you.

Yours ever

W. D. Howells

[7] Apparently a private joke involving allusions to Gosse's activities as a diarist and to the Mrs. Proudie of Trollope's *Barchester Towers*.

ॐ 85. *Gosse to Howells* ॐ

Maryland Club. / Baltimore

7 January 1885

My dear Howells

I have been wanting to write to you for days past. But in this flagrant sort of life it is quite difficult to settle to a quiet pleasure. I had three remarkably showy days at Philadelphia. Imagine the interest of an evening spent with Gen. Sherman,[1] and of hearing from his own lips why he burned Columbia and what he really did at Atlanta. He struck me as an affable kind of tiger, reduced to purring good-nature by peace and praise, but with a tremendous clawsomeness somewhere down under the fur. He was monstrously good-natured to me, and on parting, at 2 in the morning, invited me to come and see him at St. Louis. Then I saw Boker,[2]—a handsome sort of barber's image, I thought,—waxy, self-contented and dumb out of sheer satisfaction with his own silence,—Furness,[3] who is one of the most lovely souls I ever met, perfectly sweet and patient under the burdens of his bereavement and his deafness, full of literature, gay, unaffected, in short a lovely person,—Walt Whitman,[4] with whom I was immensely pleased, I had a really enchanting visit to Camden to the dear old man, with his beautiful head and sweet, smiling, calm, affectionate ways. I am going to begin admiring Walt over again, his person is so attractive. Other people

[1] General William Tecumseh Sherman (1820–1891), the famous Union general in the American Civil War: see Introduction, p. 15.

[2] George Henry Boker (1823–1890), the American poet and playwright, is chiefly remembered for his verse tragedy, *Francesca da Rimini* (1855).

[3] Horace Howard Furness (1833–1912), the Shakespearean scholar: see Introduction, p. 16. Furness's impression of this meeting with Gosse is recorded in a letter to two of his sons, dated 4 January 1885 (see H[orace] H[oward] F[urness] J[ayne], ed., *The Letters of Horace Howard Furness* [Boston and New York: Houghton Mifflin Company, 1922], I, 226–227).

[4] For Gosse's meeting with Whitman see Introduction, pp. 15–16.

were civil at Philadelphia,—Dr. and Mrs. Whister[5] [sic], Gov. Curtin,[6] the Journalists' Club—what memories I shall bear away of this thrice-delightful country,—but Boston was the best of it.

We are going for three days to Washington, then back here, then to lecture (probably) in New York, and then, possibly, to Aurora, Yale and Princeton. How will it be possible to squeeze all this in before we sail on the 27th.?

If you see Dr. Holmes give him my love. I see that today's papers telegraph bits of my review of his "Emerson" in the Pall Mall Gazette.[7]

Our most affectionate remembrances to you all. Thank Mrs. Howells for her letter. Our address for at least a week will be

Mt. Vernon Hotel
Baltimore.

Ever your affectionate Friend

Edmund Gosse

[5] This is presumably Furness's sister, Mrs. Annis Lee Wister (1830–1908), and her husband, Dr. Casper Wister (1817–1888). For Mrs. Wister, see Jayne, *Letters of H. H. Furness*, I, xviii; she was well-known for her translations from the German.

[6] Andrew Gregg Curtin (1817–1894) was Republican governor of Pennsylvania from 1861 to 1867; he later served as minister to Russia and sat in the House of Representatives as a Democrat from 1881 to 1887.

[7] "Dr. O. W. Holmes's Life of Emerson," *Pall Mall Gazette*, 6 January 1885, p. 4. In this unsigned review Gosse describes the book as "the biography of the greatest American man of letters in the past by the greatest American man of letters in the present."

◊ *86. Gosse to Lounsbury*[1] ◊

Mount Vernon Hotel / Baltimore, Ma[ryland]

7 January 1885

My dear Mr. Lounsbury

You and Mr. Beers were so very good in saying that you wished to see me in Yale, that I write to propose a visit. I could deliver a lecture any time

[1] Thomas Raynesford Lounsbury (1838–1915), distinguished American scholar and professor of English language and literature at Yale; his works include *A History of the English Language* (1879), *Studies in Chaucer* (1891), and books on Shakespeare, Browning, Tennyson, and Fenimore Cooper. In 1897 Gosse invited Lounsbury to write a history of American literature in the series of Short Histories of the Literature of the World, which Gosse was then editing for the American publishing house of Appleton: Gosse to Lounsbury, 20 March 1897 (a.l.s., YU). Lounsbury must have refused the offer since the book was eventually written by W. P. Trent (see Letter 164 and n. 2).

on Saturday, the 24th. inst.,[2] coming perhaps on Friday night, if there be a train which would take me to Newhaven after my New York lecture ending at 6. I am afraid Saturday would be my only day, at any hour, however, that you found convenient throughout that day.

I would give the opening lecture of my Lowell course, "Poetry at the Death of Shakespeare". Terms we would not differ about. I am asking 100 dollars for a single lecture from those colleges that write to me. At Harvard I lectured for nothing. Anything between these ranges will satisfy me.[3] Perhaps somebody would put me up at night?

Will you kindly just consider this proposition, and let me know if you think anything can be arranged. I do not want to go back without having glanced at Yale, if possible.

It is rather crude to push myself upon you in this way, but you encouraged me to do so.

With kindest regards to yourself and Prof. Beers

I am
Dear Mr. Lounsbury
Very faithfully yours

Edmund Gosse

We shall be here at least a week longer, at the above address

[2] Gosse did lecture at Yale on 24 January 1885, the date he suggested (see Introduction, p. 18).
[3] Gosse received £10 for the Yale lecture (see Letter 60, n. 1).

☙ 87. *Howells to Gosse* ❧

302 Beacon St. / Boston,

19 January 1885

My dear Gosse:

I see, with great satisfaction, that you are to give some parlor lectures in New York,[1] and that you are to have the stamp of metropolitan approval before you quit these shores. People here still remember you, and I can still make something of you as a topic in the wild round of afternoon teas through which I'm whirled. The talk on all sides has a quality of personal affection for you which I'm sure would please you. There are persons who

[1] The idea of giving "parlor" lectures in New York apparently originated with Henry Holt and his sister, who solicited the aid of Andrew Carnegie; Gosse in turn asked Stedman's help (letter of 2 January 1885 [a.l.s.,CU]—see Introduction, p. 17.

ask me to give you their love, and when they are men, they include Mrs. Gosse. Mr. Frank Bartlett,[2] for instance.

I delight in all your triumphs and joys, and long to hear of your adventures in Baltimore and Washington. Do tell me about them.

By the way President Eliot,[3] whom I met the other night, asked me if I thought you would be willing to come to Cambridge from [sic] a year. All that I could say was that I thought you would like to be askt. And then I told him of your various incomes, that he might not fall under the mark if he meant business. Mrs. Eliot and he were full of your sickening praises. I threw in a little ridicule and detraction.

Did you carry off my poem "No Love Lost"?[4] I can't find it, and I would give you anything *but* that, which is my only copy.

Yours ever

W. D. Howells

[2] Possibly Francis Bartlett, wealthy Boston lawyer and art collector, who was a friend of Holmes and later a member of the Tavern Club. He was for many years a director of the Boston Museum of Fine Arts, to which in 1903 he presented a collection of antiquarian art valued at more than a million dollars. He died in 1913 at the age of seventy-seven.

[3] Charles William Eliot (1834–1926) was president of Harvard University from 1869 to 1909. He instituted a number of reforms, increased the size of the University, revised the system of courses and requirements, and improved the standards of the professional schools.

[4] *No Love Lost* (New York: Putnam, 1869) was about to be reprinted in Howells's *Poems* (Boston: Ticknor, 1886).

❧ 88. *Howells to Gosse* ❧

302 Beacon St. [Boston]

25 January 1885

My dear Gosse:

I am ever so sorry I can't come to the breakfast[1] but it's quite impossible to leave Lapham in his present troubles, and I can only wish you God-speed. As you have publicly taken the Vow of London Poverty in preference to American Affluence,[2] we mayn't hope to see you soon again here; but our hearts—Mrs. Howells's and mine in the same neat package—go with you

[1] For the breakfast, see Introduction, p. 18.

[2] An allusion to the interview with Gosse which was published in the *Critic* on 24 January 1885 (see Introduction, p. 19).

both, and we trust some day to see you over your dry crusts in your simple hut at Delamere Terrace.

Good-by, dear boy! Try not to forget us—we shall always remember you; and when Mrs. Gosse is sobered down by the sea-voyage my wife will write and tell her a thousand things now impossible through a bad cold.

We hear that you were *such* a bother at Baltimore! And oh, was any Professorin at Wells[3] equal to the heaven-kissing Hill[4] at Wellesley? And was she as frankly gymnastic?

Yours ever

W. D. Howells

[3] Gosse lectured at Wells College on 21 January 1885 (American diary).

[4] The humor of this comment can be imagined but, at this date, not fully explained. Miss Lucile Eaton Hill is described in the *Wellesley Bulletin* as a teacher of physical training 1882–1894, director of gymnastics 1884–1894, and director of physical training 1894–1909. The *Wellesley Alumnae Magazine* for August 1925 contains the following comment: "Genius is almost too cold and formal a word to apply to the richness of Miss Hill's nature, but a genius she is in many directions. One of her old pupils apostrophizes her as a sportswoman, artist, educator, fellow-student, and friend. Whatever she is, she is generously" (pp. 317–318). Information kindly supplied by Miss Hannah D. French, Wellesley College Library.

৩ৎ 89. *Gosse to Holmes* ৩ৎ

New York

26 January 1885

My dear Dr. Holmes

The day you were so kind as to lend me the advance copy of your Emerson, I burned the midnight oil and sent off the enclosed feeble little review of it to the Pall Mall Gazette.[1] All the critics, from Mr. Bancroft downwards,[2] have had their say about the book now, and the only claim the review has on your attention is that it was the *earliest*.

I am going back to England tomorrow. America has been wonderfully good to me. I am full of gratitude and happiness and surprise. My eight or nine weeks here have been a long ovation. But I hold to the first loves, and dearest of all is that first anxious night in Huntington Hall, with Dr. Holmes's face in the centre of the desparate [sic] throng!

[1] See Letter 85, n. 7.

[2] George Bancroft, "Holmes's Life of Emerson," *North American Review*, CXL (February 1885), 129–143.

If you have time, think of me with affection, and if it goes so far as the privilege of a note from you, remember that I live at

29 Delamere Terrace
London W.

With kindest remembrances to Mrs. Holmes, pray believe me,

Dear Doctor,

Yours with great affection and respect

Edmund Gosse

ᘓ 90. *Gosse to Howells* ᘓ

29, Delamere Terrace, / Westbourne Square. [London] W.

15 February 1885

My dear Howells

Our inner selves have come together too closely for you to mistake my silence, or I yours, if ever you should be silent, and so I will not pretend to apologise for my forced silence. Since I came back to England I have been ill, tired, bothered and overworked, the proper penalty for having enjoyed myself too much. Now I am getting over the change, and renaturalising myself, and yesterday I sent you a leaf of olive in the form of the first edition of the "Pastor Fido",[1] which is more fit for your library than mine, and which you will please accept with my love.

Last week I dined with Henry James at the Reform Club, to satisfy his craving for gossip, which proved insatiable. You will be perfectly charmed to hear that the very first question he asked, over the soup, was "And how is poor Howells?" But the other part of your prophecy was unfulfilled, for he was eager to know every little tiny thing that had befallen us, and what "poor" everybody said and was doing, and in fact was a most agreeable recipient of all that I was primed with.

There is not much news. Poor Mrs. Lowell has been raving mad for a month past, and dying for a week past.[2] The news last night was that she seemed a little better, which no one can in pity wish her to be. Lowell is very much overstrained, I hear. James has been dismayed to be told, first by Lowell, next by me, and next by a quite independent third witness, that everybody in Boston will take his Miss Birdseye[3] for a portrait of Elizabeth Peabody.

[1] Giovanni Battista Guarini (1538–1612) wrote *Il Pastor Fido* in 1583; it was published late in 1589, bearing the date 1590.

[2] Maria White Lowell, wife of James Russell Lowell, died on 19 February 1885.

[3] Miss Birdseye is a character in Henry James's novel *The Bostonians*. When the

Is there a stir about it? Is the Devil to pay on Jamaica Plains [sic]?[4] You may tell the Ear of Renown that the portrait of Miss Birdseye is intended to be flattering in the extreme, and that she is presently (about May or June) to die in an odour of white roses. Tadema has probably written to tell you that he was charmed with his Cincinatti [sic] pot, and still more with your thought of him.

By the way, I hope you have invested those $2 I left with you in some good thing. I gave them to you to buy photographs of Boston for me, but if you were tempted to put them for your children's sake into some excellent speculation, I can't blame you. But at a less interest than 6% it would be sheer vulgar peculation; your only real excuse is that you are turning off a handsome profit. Lord knows I don't grudge it to you, if it really will put Pilla out of the fear of penury.

A great many friends asked news of you. I find a great deal of admiration excited by your "Silas Lapham",[5] as I knew would be the case. I believe you are going to hear from a certain actor of the name of Beerbohm Tree[6] about the possibility of bringing out your Venetian play here in London. But I cannot give you the particulars. On the other hand I am very anxious to hear what was the result of the rehearsal of your opera.[7] Osgood told me that he was quite sanguine about it.

You took so complete an interest in my American affairs that I think you will let me tell you that the total result of my lectures was far more important than you had suggested it would be in your first and most sanguine idea. Altogether I made £490 in America.[8] The New York drawing-room lectures were very lucrative, they were crowded, and tickets were $5 for the

---

first chapters of the novel appeared in the *Century* for February 1885 it was widely believed that the character was based on Miss Elizabeth Palmer Peabody (1804–1894), venerable survivor of the Transcendental movement and sister-in-law of Nathaniel Hawthorne. See James's letter to William James, 14 February [1885], in Percy Lubbock, ed., *The Letters of Henry James* (New York: Scribner's, 1920), II, 115. Gosse could speak in this matter since he had met Miss Peabody in Boston in 1884 (see Introduction, pp. 12–13).

[4] Miss Peabody's home during her last years was at Jamaica Plain, on the outskirts of Boston.

[5] *The Rise of Silas Lapham* was serialized in the *Century* XXIX–XXX (November 1884–August 1885).

[6] Sir Herbert Beerbohm Tree (1853–1917), the English actor-manager, was Max Beerbohm's half-brother. The "Venetian" play mentioned here is Howells's *A Foregone Conclusion*, a dramatization of his novel. Beerbohm Tree showed an interest in it in 1884, and this letter is evidence that the interest continued. However, negotiations between Tree and Howells broke down, and Tree seems never to have performed it. For a detailed account see Meserve, *Plays of Howells*, pp. 314–315.

[7] Gosse here refers to the "orchestra reading" of *A Sea-Change* given on 27 January 1885, in the Boston Museum. The result of this "rehearsal" was not encouraging. See Meserve, *Plays of Howells*, p. 270, and Letter 54, n. 5.

[8] See Letter 60, n. 1.

course. If I could have stopped another two months, I could have been busy all the time, for invitations kept flowing in upon me to the very last.

Nothing is yet settled about my future. For the present I linger on at the Board of Trade, and if I can only manage to make myself invisible there for a few months more, I think it very possible I may be spared for a year or two. I should like to scrape on until 1887, and then retire altogether from the service.

I constantly think of what you so affectionately confided to me at Concord, and without any curiosity of a vulgar kind, I am solicitous to know as much as you ever feel inclined to tell me of your troubles and anxieties.

With our united love to you all, but with my special love to you especially, I am

My very dear Friend

Yours

Edmund Gosse

✍ 91. *Howells to Gosse* ✍

302 Beacon St. / Boston,

9 March 1885

My dear Gosse:

I don't know which has more touched my heart, your letter or your present. I read Pastor Fido[1] long ago in a dear little copy in vellum, for which my friend Dyer[2] gave me in exchange, very much against my will, his Omar Khayyam, and I had remained inconsolable till your gift came. Think of having that loveliest bit of Unreality in the first edition, a Venetian edition! I am more than grateful—I am forgiving. I almost truly pardon you from this hour for having scalped me on our glove trade. As soon as I set eyes on those seal-skin gloves of yours, I said to myself, "This simple islander does not know the value of seal-skin gloves on the mainland. Come, let me get the better of him." Hardly had you turned your back on Boston when your gloves, for which I had given a beautiful pair of beaver gauntlets and a collar, began to go to pieces on my hands. Then we examined

---

[1] See Letter 90, n. 1.

[2] Louis Dyer (1851–1908), the American classical scholar, graduated from Harvard in 1874, studied at Oxford, and returned to Harvard in 1877, becoming a tutor and professor of Greek. After 1887 he spent most of his life at Oxford, but he delivered the Lowell Lectures in 1889.

them and found by the figures inside that you had given seven and sixpence for them. Was this right, was it kind—to lay for the American in his lair, and do him under his own roof? Come and live among us! You are worthy! You need not take naturalization papers; I will tell them this little story at the polls, and they will let you vote any where! Perhaps I shall send you those fotografs when I have quite digested the glove-trade; I find the Pastor Fido a famous stomachic.

We are just now in an excitement as great as the Gosse boom at its wildest, about Charles Egbert Craddock,[3] the author of the Tennessee mountain stories, who has turned up in Boston, a little *girl-cripple*, not so big as Pilla. She visited Aldrich first, and as soon as he could get his breath, he sat down and wrote me asking me to meet "Craddock" at dinner! He had Holmes and Barrett too, and he simply revelled in our successive gasps. Now, Craddock (Miss M. S.[sic] Murfree) is being lunched, (here yesterday) dined, receptioned and breakfasted from one end of Boston to another. She has a most manful and womanly soul in her poor, twisted little body. Her stories are extraordinary; but I dare say you know them.

I'm afraid poor Barrett is going to lose his daughter—the next oldest, not Milly. She was taken here last week with peritonitis, and there is scarcely a hope of her recovery. It will be terrible for them all. Her mother was in New York, but came on, on Friday.

I am delighted that the American foray turned out so well, money wise. It's too bad you couldn't have had more time. You might as well have carried home three times as much. You ought to write a popular lecture and make the grand lecturing tour.

The Museum people found it too expensive to produce the opera.[4] There is a *chance* that it may be given in New York. My father's affairs in Virginia are going somewhat better;[5] I hope to run down to see him during the spring.

Our teapot was stirred to its depths by the Birdseye sacrilege,[6] but public

---

[3] Charles Egbert Craddock was the pseudonym of Mary Noailles Murfree (1850–1922), American novelist and short-story writer. She became well-known through her short stories in the *Atlantic Monthly* from 1878 onward, but her identity was not known until 1885. She was born in Tennessee, and her best stories are about the Tennessee mountain people.

[4] See Letters 54, n. 5, and 90, n. 7.

[5] See Mildred Howells, *Life in Letters of Howells,* I, 340, where the editor describes William Cooper Howells's attempt to take up farming in Virginia at the age of seventy-six: "He first hired a farm in Goochland County, and in 1884 he bought one at Westham, Henrico County, on the James River near Richmond, where with characteristic optimism he planted a vineyard, peach and pear orchards, and made a carp pond. The farming part of the venture proved a failure, and he retired with his family to Jefferson, Ohio."

[6] See Letter 90, n. 3.

feeling is rapidly reconciling itself. Even a sacrilege does not hold us long. Of course, nobody of any sense supposed James *meant to mean* the venerable Miss P[eabody].

S. Lapham is finished, and I am hammering away at my Italian papers[7] for the Century. "R. Smith, connected with the Century magazine"[8] is in town, and called upon us yesterday. In the dearth of other topics he spoke occasionally of the periodical. Of course he was kind to your memory.

Gosse, I suppose I shall never have as good a time again as I had with you. You just suited my complaint. These laughs at nothing, these senseless giggles, what intellectual pleasure ever equalled them? When shall I see your like again? (Never)!

We "some talk" of taking the Old Manse in Concord for the summer.[9] Hey? All of us join in love to both of you. My wife ardently awaits your wife's report on all your adventures.

Your affectionate

W. D. Howells

[7] Howells, "Panforte di Sienna," *Century*, XXX (August–September 1885), 534–549, 659–673, and "Tuscan Cities," *Century*, XXX (October, 1885), 890–910.

[8] For the background of this expression see Letter 84, n. 1.

[9] This was the house—still standing today—in which both Emerson and Hawthorne had lived; Howells, however, seems not to have proceeded with the idea of renting it.

◐ 92. Furness[1] to Gosse ◑

222 West Washington Square. [Philadelphia]

22 March 1885

You dear good boy, your three charming and delightful books reached me in safest haste, but I resolved before I thanked you that I would read through at least one.

Just as I was finishing the last pages of the Life of Gray,[2] and, with infinite relish, rolling under my tongue some of the tidbits therein, and longing for a gossip with you thereanent, this dear, bright letter, every line of which you must have known would charm me, illumined the gloom of my library.

Maximas gratias tibi ago for each and all. You are very, very good ever to think of me again.

[1] For Furness's life, see Jayne, *Letters of H. H. Furness.* See also introduction, p. 16, and Letter 85, especially n. 3.

[2] Goss, *Gray*, English Men of Letters Series (London: Macmillan, 1882).

You will never know how much good your brief little visit gave me. It half revealed to me that there were some folk in the world who really did care whether or not I worked for them. And for the first time for many a long year, after you went away, I opened by bookcases of my own accord and looked over my notes on 'Othello.'[3] Since then I have actually worked an evening or two every week. It has been agony but I have done it. If ever I buckle to, again in earnest, I shall date the change from your evening's invigorating talk. Awares and unawares I entertained an angel.

There, dear boy, after this confession, nothing remains to us but to exchange locks of hair—and you must speak quick or time will leave none on my head.

Tell Aldis Wright[4] what a sentimental goose I am, and, when you think he has fairly grasped the heighth (Milton) and depth of my sentimentality, give him my love. Our friendship began in gloom, but, like the acquired taste for olives, it is all the stronger and more enduring for it.

Your Life of Gray interested me from the first word to the last. I liked what you say about Mutual Admiration Societies, and I was delighted whenever you snub Mason,[5] especially do I like your discovery of the authorship of the last four lines of his Sonnet on the death of his Wife. I have often said that it was these lines and the first one that constituted the charm and strength of the piece. The first line 'Take, holy earth,' was a genuine inspiration, whose beauty rendered incomprehensible the apostrophe to 'dead Maria'! But it is useless for me to specify what I enjoyed in the book, when I enjoyed it all.

By this same mail I send you a Phototype[6] which I should like to have you insert in the 'Concordance to the Poems.' When the spirit prompts you, dear Gosse, write to me and dont forget that I am

Yours cordially

Horace Howard Furness

[3] Furness's New Variorum edition of *Othello* was published the following year.

[4] [William] Aldis Wright (1831–1914), the English scholar, was at this time Librarian of Trinity College, Cambridge, where Gosse held the Clark Lectureship in English Literature. Wright and Furness were close friends, and a number of Furness's letters to him are included in Jayne, *Letters of H. H. Furness.*

[5] William Mason (1725–1797), the English poet, was Thomas Gray's literary executor; Gosse, in his *Gray* (see n. 2 above), described Mason as lacking in character and imagination (p. 87) and accused him of tampering with texts (p. 214). Gosse also considered Mason to have been a poor poet (p. 127) and claimed that the final four lines of Mason's poem on his wife's death had actually been written by Gray (pp. 176–177).

[6] The "Phototype" was presumably a portrait of Furness's dead wife, Helen Kate Rogers Furness (1837–1883), compiler of *A Concordance of Shakespeare's Poems* (Philadelphia: Lippincott, 1874).

༚ 93. *Gosse to Lowell* ༚

Trinity College, / Cambridge

8 May 1885

Dear Mr. Lowell

The Master of Pembroke wishes me to write to you privately and urge such influence as I may possess to try and persuade you to give us your presence at the unveiling of the monument to Gray, by Lord Houghton,[1] on Tuesday, the 26th. inst. You have received, or will shortly receive, a formal invitation from the College to lunch on that day. I may perhaps be allowed to say that it will be a very great personal gratification to me if you find yourself able to indulge us with your company. We expect some of the nicest people in the world.

May I say how deeply I enjoyed your brilliant and penetrative analysis of the genius of Coleridge?[2] I don't know when I have had such a pleasure.

> Believe me
> Dear Mr. Lowell
> Yours very truly
>
> Edmund Gosse

[1] Richard Monckton Milnes, first Baron Houghton (1809–1885), politician and man of letters, the biographer of Keats.

[2] Gosse refers to Lowell's "Address on unveiling the bust of Coleridge at Westminster Abbey, 7 May, 1885," which was subsequently collected in James Russell Lowell, *Democracy and Other Addresses* (Boston and New York: Houghton Mifflin, 1887), pp. 105–133.

༚ 94. *Lowell to Gosse* ༚

31, Lowndes Square. / [London] S.W.

10 May 1885

Dear Mr. Gosse,

I don't know how it may be with others, but, as for me, I grow Grayer as I grow older. I shall be glad to see Cambridge again before I go back to my native town (her namesake) hardly more dear, and shall be happy to represent America in the Pembroke boat—especially as Houghton is to have the labouring oar. And the occasion draws me strongly.

I shall be happy also in coming as a simple man of letters, for I shall have ceased to be an Excellency (Praise be blest!) before the 26th.

Will you kindly warn me later on of the proper train.

I am glad you found anything to like in my Coleridge pribble prabble. I am less charitable. But perhaps I shall write it out and fill in the *lacunae*.

Faithfully yours

J. R. Lowell

❧ 95. *Gosse to Lowell* ❧

29, Delamere Terrace, / Westbourne Square. [London] W.

27 May 1885

Dear Mr. Lowell

One of my pet undergraduates at Trinity took a full report of the proceedings yesterday, and prints it today in a local paper.[1]

I make the sending of this paper an excuse for saying to you how deeply you touched us all, and in particular me, by your beautiful address to us yesterday.

I have not thrust myself upon your company while you were here as a Minister, and full of public duties, because I knew that you were overwhelmed with visitors of far greater social importance than I. But now that you are no longer a Minister and merely a Poet again, may I tell you how admiringly I have followed all that you have said and done here in England? You have been a great power for good, you have kept the public honour of literature high above the muddy level of life, and I for one shall miss the knowledge that you are here as keenly, almost, as if it had been my good fortune to enjoy your friendship.

If we never meet again, will you let me feel that I have your permission to add to my respect for you something like affection?

Do not answer this note, which I perhaps ought not to send you. But believe me

Yours very sincerely

Edmund Gosse

[1] Gosse had copies of the report in the *Cambridge Review* privately printed in pamphlet form, presumably for circulation to subscribers. Lowell said near the beginning of his speech: "I came here to speak, simply as the representative of several countrymen and countrywomen of mine who have renewed that affirmation which I like always to renew, of the unity of our English race, by giving something more solid than words in commemoration of the poet they loved" (p. 10).

✑ 96. Bancroft[1] to Gosse ✑

Washington D.C. just before going for
the summer to Newport, R.I.

30 May 1885

Dear Mr. Gosse,

Your letter of April was most welcome. I am glad you remember your
days at Washington with pleasure.[2] It is very thoughtful and kind of you to
have spoken of me to the Editor of the Fortnightly Review;[3] when you
chance to meet him aprise him that I am very grateful for the hospitable
reception he offers me. Being in my eighty fifth year, I dare make no
promises; but I wish to write a few sober words on the nature of this increas-
ing power of the people which marks the political character of the last
centuries.

I fear I did not send you a copy of what I have written on the Formation
of our Federal Constitution.[4] By my countrymen it has been received with
exceeding kindness, and as soon as I am settled in Newport, I will send
you a copy of it.

Our new President,[5] you may be sure, is a man of sound judgment and
upright intentions and great firmness of character; the relations of our
country and yours are coming to rest on more solid foundations of friendship, than ever before. The old idea of relationships is passing away: and
the confidence resting on mutual integrity and mutual fair intentions is
taking a deeper foundation in both nations than ever before. We are content
with our territory as it is. If you were to offer us India as a gift, we could not

[1] George Bancroft (1800–1891), American historian and statesman, served in the
Cabinet of President Polk (1845–1846) and as U.S. minister in London (1846–1849)
and Berlin (1867–1874). *A History of the United States*, completed in ten volumes in
1875 (final revision, in six volumes, 1883–1885), represents his major achievement
as an historian.

[2] For Gosse's meeting with Bancroft in Washington on 10 January 1885, see Introduction, p. 17. In a letter to Gosse of 2 March 1885 (a.l.s., BC) Bancroft had written: "Let me say to you how much pleasure we all had in welcoming you to Washington. You in England ought to devise a word to comprehend all the English speaking world. . . . The English tongue which already is the language of one hundred
million, is their bond of union. . . . The spirit of peace prevails with us; and we
hope for lasting good relations with you, so long as the English shall be spoken by
us all."

[3] Thomas Hay Sweet Escott (see Letter 51, n. 1) was editor of the *Fortnightly Review* from 1882 to 1886. Despite Gosse's intervention Bancroft seems not to have
written anything for the magazine.

[4] George Bancroft, *A History of the Formation of the Constitution of the United
States of America* (New York: Appleton, 1882).

[5] Grover Cleveland (1837–1908), had just begun the first of his two terms as
President of the United States (1885–1889; 1893–1897).

accept it. Its ownership would be our ruin. I trust and believe that if Spain were to be willing to cede to us Cuba, we should shrink from the negotiation; and I know not the man among us who longs for the acquisition of Canada. For myself I am persuaded that our country is now as large as one nation can organize and govern. The policy of settling international difficulties by arbitration may grow into some sort of a federation of all civilization; but no desire of territorial aggrandizement dwells in the Americans.

Best and kindest regards from Mrs. B[ancroft] and myself to Mrs. Gosse; I am ever, dear Mr. Gosse, in truth and sincerity yours,

Geo. Bancroft

❧ 97. *Gilder to Gosse* ❧

Marion. Mass[achusetts].

30 [June] 1885

My dear Gosse,

Very many thanks for your kind notes. I am quite myself again—except not quite at my full physical strength—which is, however, coming back rapidly.

Thanks for what you say about a collection. I am to put all my verses into a volume of about 260 pages next fall (Scribner's)[1] but remembering what you once ⟨said⟩ about an English volume,[2] I want to anticipate your renewal of the offer to find me a publisher—by saying that I will not wish to bring out this book in England. I will send my friends copies, for remembrance,—and cannot consent that they or any publisher should bother with a book for which, in England, there is no demand that I cannot supply myself without the assistance of a book seller—namely free copies to my half dozen personal friends. A thousand thanks to you all the same for the suggestion once made, and which, I am thinking, would be renewed if it were not for this.

What you say about the war[3] is duly noted. We know it all. We will do the best we can under the circumstances. The Battles cannot stop till probably *next October a year*. But we will give all the variety we can, and

[1] R. W. Gilder, *Lyrics and Other Poems* (New York: Scribner's, 1885).

[2] In a letter of 1 June 1883 (carbon copy, GL) Gilder declined Gosse's efforts towards an English edition.

[3] The *Century* was at this time publishing a monthly section devoted to accounts of Civil War battles written by well-known participants; the series, entitled "Battles and Leaders of the Civil War," extended from November 1884 to April 1888.

as it happens there will be a good deal about England. We will send you a prospectus when we have fully determined upon it, and will, in fact, make up a special one for England.

What you say about delay of articles is wickedly true. We are trying to reform by not accepting. We cannot place the Harvard article[4] (*honestly*) for 18 months or two years. We must not take; it is of local interest in New England—I suggest the Atlantic for this article—and perhaps Houghton—or some other Boston firm for the book.

Can't you suggest a way of stirring up an interest among military men about our war articles? I know they don't "think highly" of our war—but there was considerable of a ⟨war⟩—after all, and at least the naval part of it revolutionized [a few words indecipherable].

1 July 1885

My dear Gosse,

I take another sheet to scold you on. Is there nothing interesting to you but art and literature? Now let me tell you—I would rather have one article by Grant[5] on a battle won by him, I would rather read it—print it—publish it than twenty articles by Daudet on Mistral.[6] And yet I know all the Provençals—one of the happiest times of my life was the few days spent among them. Daudet is enthusiastic—but not enough for me. Provence, Avignon—they are among the magic words for me.—But Heavens! a great world-changing heroic event—told by the hero of it!—The conquering of the Rebellion meant not only the extinction of human slavery over a vast territory—but it meant the salvation of this great experiment of self-government in the New World. Grant was the leading military figure in that ⟨war⟩—one of the most important that the world has known—Beauregard,[7] Johnston,[8] etc. were among his leading opponents—these men are all telling in a more intimate manner than ever before the story of their deeds.

---

[4] But Gilder did publish it: Ernest Ingersoll, "Harvard's Botanic Gardens and its Botanists," *Century*, XXXII (June 1886), 237–248.

[5] General Ulysses S. Grant, "The Battle of Shiloh," *Century*, XXIX (February 1885), 593–613, and "The Siege of Vicksburg," *Century*, XXX (September 1885), 752–765.

[6] Alphonse Daudet, "Mistral," *Century*, XXX (July 1885), 416–422.

[7] Pierre Gustave Toutant Beauregard (1818–1893) resigned as superintendent of West Point to become a Confederate brigadier general, and directed the firing at Fort Sumter which began the Civil War; he wrote "The Battle of Bull Run," *Century*, XXIX (November 1884), 80–106.

[8] There were two Confederate Generals Johnston. General Albert Sidney Johnston (1803–1862) is represented by an article written by his son William Preston Johnston, entitled "Albert Sidney Johnston and the Shiloh Campaign," *Century*, XXIX (February 1885), 614–628. General Joseph Eggleston Johnston (1807–1891) wrote "Manassas to Seven Pines," *Century*, XXX (May 1885), 99–120.

MacClellan[9] too, Porter[10]—a score of other generals—whoever has some new chapter to add or old one to fill out. The world has never seen such a ⟨thing⟩. Yes bloody, indeed; all wars are, alas, bloody and there is no blood in my sonnet, and in Dobson's song that you like.[11] But is there nothing stirring in blood,—in heroism, in devotion to a political and moral conviction.—Yes, you ought to be proud of a magazine that is conducting to unparaleled [sic] success the largest enterprise yet undertaken by a periodical. Don't let literature and art make dilettantes of us! Suppose that twenty years after Waterloo—its hero, his Generals,—and the Marshalls of the dead Napoleon had written out, in a familiar way, the stories of their campaigns and battles. How bloody it would have been—and how genuine and important a piece of journalism if any magazine could have published that war series! It is not for us to discriminate against ourselves in the relative importance of those and these campaigns. There were brave men in both periods, and I like to hear them tell of the great work.

Selah.

Thine most truly

R. W. Gilder

[9] General George Brinton McClellan (1826–1885), the Union General, wrote "The Peninsular Campaign," *Century*, XXX (May 1885), 136–150.

[10] There were two Generals Porter in the Union army. General Fitz-John Porter (1822–1901), wrote three articles for the *Century*: "The Battle of Gaines's Mill and its Preliminaries," XXX (June 1885), 309–324; "The Last of the Seven Days' Battles," XXX (August 1885), 615–632; "The Offer of a Union Command to General A. S. Johnston," XXIX (February 1885), 634–635. General Horace Porter (1837–1921) wrote "Lincoln and Grant," XXX (October 1885), 939–947.

[11] Gilder's sonnet was "The New Troubadours," *Century*, XXX (July 1885), 422; Dobson's song, "A Fancy from Fontanelle," was printed on the same page.

ஐ 98. *Gosse to Furness* ஐ

29, Delamere Terrace, / Westbourne Square. [London] W.

28 September 1885

Dear Furness

Is it true that you once proposed to buy of Halliwell-Phillips[1] the old priory at Broadway in Worcestershire? So they say at Broadway, and the

[1] James Orchard Halliwell-Phillips (1820–1889), English Shakespearean scholar, antiquarian, and librarian. He added the Phillips, his wife's surname, in 1872. He was Librarian of Jesus College, Cambridge, and wrote, among other works, *Outlines of the Life of Shakespeare* (1848).

legend has increased my pleasure in sitting there, with Millet,[2] Edwin Abbey[3] and John Sargent,[4] who have made a Studio of it.

I owe you my hearty thanks for the gift of your son's very ingenious and curious Composite Portrait of Shakespeare.[5] I mean,—as soon as term begins, —to talk with Aldis Wright and see what he says about it.

Do you ever see Walt Whitman? I should like to know how he is, and whether you ever meet him. If you do, remember me to him.

I had a very beautiful letter from Browning about a letter I had received. He was greatly touched and gratified.

My thoughts often go out to you, and sometimes seem to meet yours half-way. When shall we meet again?

My dear Friend, farewell once more.

I am ever yours sincerely

Edmund Gosse

[2] Francis Davis Millet (1846–1912), an American artist and journalist. As a correspondent he covered the Russo-Turkish war of 1877–1878 and was in the Philippines in 1898. As an artist, he was known especially as a painter of murals. He lived in England for many years, and visited Gosse quite often between 1883 and 1890. For the visits paid by Gosse and James to the group of expatriate American artists at the Cotswold village of Broadway, see Charteris, *Life and Letters of Gosse,* pp. 191–192. Also see Charteris, *John Sargent* (London: Heinemann, 1927), pp. 72–79.

[3] Edwin Austin Abbey (1852–1911), another member of the Broadway group, was an American painter who settled in England after being sent there in 1878 by *Harper's Weekly,* for which he was staff illustrator; he became a member of the Royal Academy in 1898. He is best known for his illustrations of Herrick's poems and Shakespeare's plays, though he was also responsible for murals in the House of Parliament, Boston Public Library, and elsewhere. He knew Gosse well and designed a bookplate for him; several of his letters to Gosse are in the Brotherton Collection.

[4] John Singer Sargent (1856–1925), the artist, was born in Florence of American parents, studied in Paris, and lived most of his later life in London, though he made visits to America and maintained a studio in Boston for several years. In 1897 he was elected to full membership of the Royal Academy, but in 1907 he declined a knighthood on the grounds that he was not an English citizen. A few brief letters from Sargent to Gosse are in the Brotherton Collection.

[5] In the Sotheby Catalogue from the sale of Gosse's library, Part II, p. 85, Lot 698 (fourth day, 6 December 1928), this item is described as "Composite Photography applied to the Portraits of Shakespeare by Walter Rogers Furness, *one of 50 copies printed,* 1885."

ᴥ 99. *Gosse to Roswell Smith*[1] ᴥ

Board of Trade. [London] S.W.

23 October 1885

My dear Mr. Roswell Smith

I have for some time past been revolving a scheme for a book on the Pilgrim places of English literature. I need not recapitulate here the particulars of my scheme, because I have already laid them before Gilder,[2] and I am writing by this mail to ask him to show them to you.

I proposed this scheme, which I had previously talked over with Fraser,[3] to Gilder in a letter to which I have just received an answer.

He is kind enough to say that he thinks the scheme an excellent one, and he even goes so far as to commission me to order the various papers from the most eminent authors. But he says, that, owing to the press on the magazine, they could not appear in the Magazine "for several years". This is absolutely crushing to me; for literature is not, like wine, improved by being kept in a cellar.

So I write today to ask you whether you would not like to take up this idea as a book for next holiday season, or, perhaps, as it might be difficult to get all the work in, for 1887? and not carry it through the magazine at all?

It might be made a lovely book, and I think that if it were written by the very best Englishmen, and illustrated under Fraser's care, it would supply a real demand, and become quite a classic for American pilgrims to English shrines.

Gilder asks me to "edit the scheme myself with Mr. Fraser's concurrence as to the pictures", and that is just what I should like to propose with regard to the book.

It would be necessary, of course, that I should have a certain amount of carte blanche as regards payment to contributors. If you are taken with the idea, you would perhaps touch on that point. To tempt a man like Matthew

---

[1] For Smith, see Johnson, *Remembered Yesterdays*, especially pp. 96–98; also Gosse's poem "Roswell Smith, died April 19, 1892," *Century*, XLIV (June 1892), 309; also Letter 18 and note 1.

[2] In a letter to Gilder of 9 September 1885 (a.l.s., HU) Gosse had set out his scheme for "a series of, say, 12 short articles by distinguished *English* writers" which would describe Stratford-on-Avon and similar places of literary pilgrimage in such a way as to "connect the dead great man with the living village." The articles would be aimed at "cultivated Americans," and he hoped to persuade Matthew Arnold to write the one on Stratford, Hardy the one on Milton at Chalfont St. Giles, and Stevenson the one on Burns at Ayr. The project was not taken up by the *Century*.

[3] William Lewis Fraser (1841–1905), London-born writer and lecturer on art, and art manager of the *Century*.

Arnold it would be needful to pay more than to other contributors; yet I would suggest asking none but such as command, by their position, good terms. I should not like to undertake it at all, unless it could be made a book that everyone would be forced to recognize as the best.

May I ask you to talk to Mr. Gilder and Mr. Fraser on the subject, and to let me hear?

Yours very truly

Edmund Gosse

❧ 100. *Furness to Gosse* ❧

Wallingford P.O. / Delaware County / Pennsylvania

25 October 1885

Thou, busy bee! how you do improve each shining hour, and, best of bees, let me sip the honey.

Here is your charming volume, dear Gosse, just fresh from Dodd, and Mead.[1] How good of you to think of me! I long for the quiet hour when I shall feast on it, and at every delicate morsel think of your happy face.

You ask me if I once really tried to buy Halliwell's old Grange at Pershore or Broadway.[2] I did, indeed, but Halliwell wouldn't let me, fearing lest its charms or proportions were unduly magnified by distance and that when I came to see it, I might repent and think I was overreached. And so the dream faded and I had utterly forgotten it, until your letter recalled it. It is only one of the infinite number of dreams, ah, so heavenly, which my whole past life has become. But that way madness lies.

Dear old Walt Whitman has a tough time of it, I fear; and the worst of it for me, is that I do not see any clear way of helping him. My gorge rises at sending him money outright, and yet he might take it as George Selwyn said Fox would take the sum that his friends were about to raise to pay his debts; you remember some one wondered how Fox would take it. 'Why quarterly to be sure,' said Selwyn. However we did send one good thing to Walt lately.[3] I enclose the circular, which I dare say Lawrence Barrett sent

---

[1] The American edition of Gosse's *From Shakespeare to Pope* was published by Dodd and Mead, 1885.

[2] See Letter 98.

[3] The "good thing" was the gift of a horse and buggy, for which thirty-two of his friends subscribed $10 each. See the account in Gay Wilson Allen, *The Solitary Singer*, 522–523.

you long ago. With that Jove-like head and bearing it is hard to believe that Walt can lack anything terrestrial. But goodbye, goodbye—

Yours affectionately

Horace Howard Furness

❧ 101. *Howells to Gosse* ❧

Woodland Park, / Auburndale, Mass.,

26 October 1885

My dear Gosse:

Nothing could have been kinder or sweeter than that review of yours in the Pall Mall Gazette,[1] and I thank you for it with all my heart. It has been copied here far and wide; and now comes under cover from you the criticism of the Saturday.[2] I do not see how the greediest of authors could ask better things, and if you know the critic will you tell him that it is such a notice as I would have written myself. Truly there were just the things said there that I was aching to have said. Both of these reviews are far friendlier than most things on this side.

I wish I *were* going to London; but I have only come as far as this on the Boston & Albany RR. (Wellesley College, with the heaven-kissing Hill[3] in the gymnasium is but a station or two beyond.) I have let the pretty house on Beacon Street because poor Winny is too poorly[4] to do any society in it, and without that her mother and I have no heart for it. I suppose we shall stay

[1] Gosse's unsigned review of *The Rise of Silas Lapham* appeared in the *Pall Mall Gazette,* 11 September 1885, p. 5. Although normally antagonistic towards realism in fiction (see Introduction, pp. 42–43). Gosse was warm in his praise of this particular novel, which he described as "undoubtedly up to date the high-water mark of Mr. Howells's great and unique photographic genius. It is a marvellously minute and realistic picture of life in Boston . . . and yet (for the consolation of the British public we say it) with a little more of romance and plot than Mr. Howells has deigned to bestow upon his inimitable sketches of real contemporary American society." Gosse then attempted to define what Howells was trying to do in his fiction: "His system is unvarnished naturalism, but naturalism of a healthy, sensible, wholesome kind." He even mildly ridiculed the British public's fondness for improbability and excess in its novels: "The after ages will wonder that we preferred our assassins and our bigamists to the Lady of the Aroostook."

[2] "The Rise of Silas Lapham," *Saturday Review,* LX (17 October 1885), 517–518.

[3] See Letter 88, n. 4.

[4] Winifred Howells never fully recovered her health; she died on 3 March 1889. For her illness and death, see Smith and Gibson, *Mark Twain-Howells Letters,* pp. 603–604.

179

here till March, and then I shall have two months in New York. You'll have heard of my contract with the Harpers,[5] which is incredibly advantageous for me; and I'm to do a department for them each month, about literature. Your lovely book[6] is in my hands, and will be the text of one of the little papers.[7] Merely looking into it gives me a queer homesick longing for last winter. It *was* a pretty time, wasn't it? We must have it again, some day. We are presently to dine Lowell at the Tavern Club,[8] and I wish you were to be there too!

Mrs. Howells joins me in love to Mrs. Gosse and yourself.

Yours ever

W. D. Howells

[5] Howells assumed the editorship of *Harper's Monthly* and published his first "Editor's Study" column in January 1886. For other features of his contract with Harper & Brothers, see Smith and Gibson, *Mark Twain-Howells Letters*, pp. 537–538.

[6] Gosse, *From Shakespeare to Pope*.

[7] See Letter 105, n. 4.

[8] For the Tavern Club, see Letter 76, n. 1.

❧ 102. *Gosse to Stedman* ❧

Board of Trade. [London] S.W.

10 December 1885

My dear Stedman

I ought before now to have thanked you for the gift of your "American Poets",[1] almost every page of which I had already read, and which I am very glad to possess in this handsome form. I did not write before, because I was busy drawing up for you the information you require about recent English poets. I made quite an elaborate table with names and dates of books, and have been so careless as to mislay it. If I do not find it, I must work it all out again. It is not a thing that can be done in a moment.

I have found my notes. I hope you will see your way to make some modifications in "V[ictorian] P[oets]".[2] At the time when you wrote that

[1] Stedman, *Poets of America* (Boston and New York: Houghton Mifflin, 1885). Gosse had read many of the essays as they appeared in the *Century*, the last only four months previously: "The Twilight of the Poets," *Century*, XXX (September 1885), 787–800.

[2] Stedman's *Victorian Poets* was first published in 1875 (see Letter 2, n. 3).

volume Buchanan seemed to be somewhat, and you generously strained a point in his favour. Now he has proved that there was no stuff in him, and it seems quite ludicrous to find 11 pages dedicated to him in a book that spares ¾ of one for Patmore, a few lines for the most admirable of all our female poets, C. G. Rossetti, and ½ a page for Austin Dobson. This is really absurd. You must revise your opinion of Patmore, by the light of his noble volume the "Unknown Eros".[3] If you are to bring your book up to date at all, you must have the courage to cancel as well as add.

I shall most gladly help you; but please do not quote me as doing so.

Yours very sincerely

Edmund Gosse

I don't know what your address is this winter.

[3] Coventry Patmore, *The Unknown Eros and Other Odes* (London: Bell, 1878).

❧ 103. *Gosse to Howells* ❧

29, Delamere Terrace, / Westbourne Square. [London] W.

28 December 1885

My dear Howells

I really thought you were going to allow me to go down to Oblivion on the arm of Obloquy. When one has a friend who writes the very best letters in the world, one is apt to be exacting. How busy you must be at Auburn (loveliest village of the)-dale.[1] I cannot help thinking you will want to get back to Boston again. You must have slipped away like a Boojum, for Dr. Holmes, who writes frequently to me (you see, some of the distinguished *do* write to me—turbans *are* worn, as the lady said in "Cranford"),[2] complains that he does not know what has become of you. I am in a mournful frame of mind, for I have come in for a veritable vendetta of criticism,—the storm has long been brooding,—and my new books this winter have caught it from the crawling things of criticism.[3] It is extraordinary how offensive the small reviewer can be. I have never suffered from him before. He is not sufficiently educated to discuss one's book, and so makes it a peg for insulting one on the score of one's friends, one's politics, one's manners, one's very travels,— for one of the proofs brought to show that I am a poetaster and criticaster is that I have been to America! In several cases I can trace the direct personal

[1] See Letter 101.
[2] An allusion to a humorous incident in Chapter IX of Mrs. Gaskell's *Cranford*.
[3] See, for example, Letter 104 and n. 2.

enmity; in others, I see no reason for attack. I suppose in a sort of negative way, these things show the result of success. But they are nasty, my dear, and they embitter existence. Enough of this.

It is just a year since the dearest of friends and the refreshingest of gigglers made Boston more than a city of palm-trees to us. What a lovely time! But it has made all the rest of life seem rather flat since. With all our love to you all

I am ever

Dearest Howells

Yours affectionately

Edmund Gosse

❧ 104. *Stedman to Gosse* ❧

45 East 30th. St. / New York,
Personal   13 January 1886
My dear Gosse,

I am deeply indebted to you, *imprimis,* for the gift of your lovely "Firdausi" volume[1]—which, in form, I take to be the initial book of a new (publishers') series. With most of the poetry I am familiar—it contains some of your best. I am glad to see my favorite, that splendid ballad of the "Rover", given an early place. The title-poem is a fine, sustained piece of work—very likely too fine, and too well sustained, for the brief, impatient, frolicsome taste of the passing day. This taste you, at least, do not wholly yield to. Often you seem to say *Altiora peto.* Nor do I find anything but pure poetry in your verse. In the end, you probably will come out as well for giving obedience to your own taste as if you should adapt yourself to trivial fashions.

I am not going to refrain from mentioning the fact that I have seen a most contemptible fling at you, in that fragrant journal—the *Pall Mall Gazette.*[2] Our intimacy has been such, in former days, that I should be a very

---

[1] Gosse, *Firdausi in Exile and Other Poems* (London: Kegan Paul, 1885).

[2] "Mr. Gosse as 'The Poet'," an unsigned review of *Firdausi in Exile,* in *Pall Mall Gazette,* 14 December 1885, p. 6. The reviewer does not comment on the poems as such, but makes a rather savage attack on Gosse for his presumption in referring to himself as "the Poet" and in addressing Dobson, in the dedication, as his peer. He continues: "The difference between the two writers is simply this, that Mr. Dobson's manner is his own, while Mr. Gosse's manner is everyone else's. Mr. Dobson has done

timorous comrade if I did not mention it—and say my word to strengthen your conviction that such an attack is a tribute to your record and position. It is the evidence of the spleen with which meaner natures regard unquestionable success, won by courage, brains, work. It will make you friends; it has warmed up my own friendship and that of your other associates here. All the same, it is despicably brutal—especially toward poor Dobson; whom it places in a cruelly embarrassing category, and whose honest soul must be roused to Homeric wrath. And it certainly is surprising, even to Americans, to see the scurrilous license which anonymous criticism is permitted to take in well-printed English columns.

And now my cordial thanks for your painstaking response to my queries anent the last decade of verse in England. I shall hold your advice in due regard. But you must understand that Houghton, M. & Co. do not propose to change the *early plates* of the *Vict. Poets,* except as to statistical corrections. What can be done is to add a *supplementary* chapter, covering the period 1875–1885—the works of elder poets, the new poets, &c. &c. In this I can modify and extend earlier judgments. Pray remember, as to Dobson, that the *"V.P."* came out just in time for me to *take note* of his appearance and quality—and that I rather plume myself on having rightly surmised his future. It was *after its completion* that I first saw your "Viol and Flute".[3] This new chapter is to cover just such cases. Patmore I probably never shall esteem as highly as you do, but I will examine his other work. Buchanan had not only space, but some severe criticism—and certainly deserves no more praise. His Pegasus long since threw him.

Of course Miss Rossetti is at the head of your living female poets. Mrs. Browning, however, was my *main exemplar.* Her career was various, impassioned, complete.

Thanks for your dates, etc. You will be amused to know that near all of the dates affecting *living* poets reached me from the poets themselves. Shall very carefully revise them. I suppose the *Athenaeum* obituaries etc. are correct—or good collateral evidence, at least. I don't believe much in "Men of the Time".[4] Your letters shall be held, as you desired, in confidence.

---

little things incomparably, Mr. Gosse has done greater things tolerably. . . . Mr. Dobson, setting forth to be a verse-writer, becomes a poet, so to speak, in his own despite; Mr. Gosse, setting forth to be a poet, is lost in the modern throng of clever verse-writers. There are many Gosses, but only one Dobson." This, of course, explains Stedman's later reference to the embarrassment of Dobson.

[3] See Letter 2.

[4] *Men of the Time,* containing short biographies of eminent men (later men and women), was first published in London by the firm of Bogue (later Kent) and in New York by Redfield in 1852. A number of revised editions appeared during the remainder of the century, the seventh (1868) and later ones taken over by Routledge. The most recent which Stedman could have used was the eleventh, 1884.

Mrs. Stedman and Arthur[5] join me in love and good wishes. Pray believe me always

Faithfully yours

Edmund C. Stedman

[5] Stedman's son.

105. *Howells to Gosse*

Auburndale,

24 January 1886

My dear Gosse:

It was delightful to get your broken-spirited letter of Dec. 28, and all this sympathetic family joined in the laugh at your calamity. We loved you, and for that reason we rejoiced to see you brought low. Pil was especially so charmed with the notion of your going down to Oblivion on the arm of Obloquy,[1] that she made a picture of you, at once, in the act. Mrs. Proudy[2] was jubilant; and I tried to affect a compassion which I didn't feel. The fact is that ever since I opened my "Study" in Harper's,[3] the small fry of critics swarm upon me; and it was impossible not to be glad another fellow was getting it, too. Here is a paragraph about you for the March number,[4] which I expect to put an end to our friendship, if you take it as wildly awry as the other people do the other things.

But it's fun, having one's open say again, and banging the babes of Romance about. It does my soul lots of good; and how every number makes 'em dance! There hasn't been so much honest truth aired in this country since Columbus's second mate shouted "Land, ho!" and Columbus retorted "What a lie! It's clouds."

I am pulling in from my long fictitious voyage;[5] and when the story is quite done—say March 1st—Mrs. Howells and I expect to go to Washington

[1] See Letter 103.

[2] For the Mrs. Proudie reference, see Letter 84 and n. 7.

[3] Howells began his "Editor's Study" in January 1886.

[4] "Editor's Study," *Harper's Monthly*, LXXII (March 1886), 648–649. Howells praises Gosse's style and approach in *From Shakespeare to Pope, Seventeenth Century Studies*, and *Life of Gray*; he also mentions Gosse's geniality and good humor.

[5] Howells was working on *The Minister's Charge* (Boston: Ticknor, 1887), then about to be serialized in the *Century*.

for a month or two. I've a notion that W. would be a good place for us to live; but I'm not certain, yet.

We have read "Firdausi" aloud, and I am glad of the whole book. I like the shorter and more familiar pieces best because they are more full of you.

All join me in love to Mrs. Gosse and yourself.

Yours ever

W. D. Howells

ꙮ 106. *Gosse to Stedman* ꙮ

29, Delamere Terrace, / Westbourne Square. [London] W.

25 January 1886

My dear Stedman

I am extremely indebted to you for your kind letter. It is true that my course, which had of late been very smooth, has had a rough check this winter. My Poems, before serious criticism could express itself at all, were attacked in the brutal articles of the "Pall Mall Gazette" and of the "World",[1] to the former of which you refer. This seems to have encouraged the many who have no voice of their own, and the book has been received— with the solitary instance of the "Athenaeum"[2]—with scurrility. But such letters as I have had from O[liver] W[endell] H[olmes], from Symonds, from old Trench,[3] and now from you, convert this temporary loss into a

---

[1] For the *Pall Mall Gazette* review see Letter 104, n. 2. A remarkably similar attack appeared in the *World*, 2 December 1885, p. 19; here the anonymous reviewer moved on from a brief discussion of Austin Dobson's *At the Sign of the Lyre* to say of *Firdausi in Exile and Other Poems*: "Mr. Gosse, too, has been stringing rhymes . . . feeble echoes strained to the cracking pitch. . . . In a pretty impudent rhyming dedication to Mr. Dobson he assumes the probability that their names may be confounded together hereafter. Let us hope that Mr. Dobson may never be confounded in that perilous time; certainly posterity, whatever else it may do, will never mistake him for Mr. Gosse."

[2] *Athenaeum*, 23 January 1886, pp. 130–131. For less favorable comments see the review by George Cottrell in the *Academy*, XXVIII (12 December 1885), 386–387, and the anonymous reviews in the *Spectator*, LIX (13 March 1886), 357–358, and the *British Quarterly Review*, LXXXIII (April 1886), 473. The *Athenaeum* review was probably written by Theodore Watts-Dunton, then chief poetry reviewer for that journal. On 23 January 1886, the date the *Athenaeum* review appeared, Gosse wrote to him: "You have honoured me with a most kind, as well as a most accomplished and graceful review of my poems. I am, as ever, much your debtor" (a.l.s., BC).

[3] The letters from Oliver Wendell Holmes and Richard Chevenix Trench, Arch-

gain; and I struggle very hard against the discouragement which means barrenness, the unwillingness to write at all, (since what one writes is disliked)—which results from such attacks, till such good and generous letters dispell it. You are very good and true, as I have so often proved you; and I thank you from my heart for these kind and too indulgent words.

You hit with great acuteness on one chief reason of my unsuccess. I am struggling for the poetry of serious passion and reflection against "the lighter lyre". Dobson is now by far the most popular poet under 60 over here; Lang follows in his footsteps, and to gain a hearing for mystery, tender gravity and empassioned sincerity is now impossible: but a reaction may come.

If your earlier sheets of V[ictorian] P[oets] are not to be reprinted, it makes your task a much simpler one. You will note no doubt, how great has been the reaction in ten years against Swinburne's rhetoric and Rossetti's pictorial richness; these, the strongest elements in 1874, hardly exist except in parody in 1886.

Robert Bridges has published a very remarkable little epic of "Eros and Psyche"[4] this winter; you ought to see that. Bridges is coming well to the front, and will hold a very considerable place when all is said. How excellent Tennyson's "Tiresias" volume is.[5] With Browning utterly run to seed, Arnold and Morris silent, and Swinburne so flatulent and uninteresting, the vitality of our best as well as oldest poet is very remarkable.

Perhaps it may amuse you to know why the P[all] M[all] G[azette] has been abusing me. I was on the staff of the paper (since 1880) until the obscene and forged revelations appeared last autumn,[6] when I, knowing from within how worthless they were as fact,—or suspecting it,—and hating

---

bishop of Dublin, have not been traced. The letter from John Addington Symonds (a.l.s., 19 December 1885) is in the Brotherton Collection.

[4] Robert Bridges, *Eros and Psyche: A Poem in Twelve Measures* (London: Bell, 1885).

[5] Tennyson, *Tiresias and Other Poems* (London: Macmillan, 1885).

[6] The *Pall Mall Gazette* revelations of prostitution and attendant evils in contemporary London began under the title "The Maiden Tribute of Modern Babylon— I. The Report of Our Secret Commission" (6 July 1885, pp. 1–6). Subsequent installments appeared on 7 July (pp. 1–6), 8 July (pp. 1–5), and 10 July (pp. 1–6). This concluded the series, but there was a further article on 13 July (pp. 1–3) entitled "What Changes Should be made in the Law?" The first page of the issue for 9 July reports attempts made in London to stop the sale of the Journal, and then reports "The Truth About Our Secret Commission. By the Chief Director of the Investigation" (pp. 1–2). The moving force behind the whole investigation was W. T. Stead, who actually bought a thirteen-year-old girl for £3 and took her to a house of prostitution, in order to demonstrate the nature of the crimes he was exposing; the articles contained plenty of detail, including interviews with bawds, pimps, and prostitutes, and caused an enormous sensation in London. See Frederick Whyte, *The Life of William T. Stead* (New York: Houghton Mifflin; London: Jonathan Cape, n.d.), I, 159–186.

the infliction of such a tide of filth in any case, left with a protest. This is their graceful revenge. I wish my friends to understand this.

And now farewell. Please write to me instantly if I can supply you with any data for V.P.

Ever sincerely yours

Edmund Gosse

P.S. I am afraid my "From Shakespeare to Pope" has been a great failure in America. Only one review has reached me, a very unfavourable one in the "Nation".[7] Over here it has been received extremely well.

[7] *The Nation*, XLI (12 November 1885), 409–410. The reviewer did not dispute the accuracy of the factual information, but he did question the whole theory of the literary transition and its causes. The book, of course, did not continue to be well received in England (see Introduction, pp. 20–21).

❧ 107. *Gosse to Howells* ❧

Board of Trade. [London] S.W.

10 March 1886

My dear Howells

I hope you have not thought it ungracious in me to delay thanking you for that too indulgent and most charming review in Harper's?[1] It said exactly what I wanted said, and filled me with arrogance.

H. James has been down at Cambridge, staying with me in college. I think he had a good time,—I know I did. He was anxious to hear any scrap of news of you, he always is. I wish you would put on a spurt and write him a line about anything or nothing. It would give him great pleasure. He is still at 3 Bolton St., Picadilly, W.

You will, I suppose, see Edwin Abbey presently, almost as soon as this letter. He is coming over for a month. Please tell the elder Miss H[owells] that I enjoyed her sonnet in the "Century",[2] and tell the younger Miss H. that I keep her libellous drawing on the mantel, always in sight, to inflame my undying resentment, and also to blush at the pretty profile she has given me.[3] Everybody recognises it, I am glad to say, and then says "Who's that

[1] See Letter 105, n. 4.
[2] Winifred Howells, "Past," *Century*, XXXI (April 1886), 838.
[3] See Letter 105.

repulsive old female?" "O, that's Obloquy",[4] I answer, easy like, as you might say O that's Miss Cleveland,[5] or the Queen.

Love to you all.
My dear Friend, I am ever
thine affectionately

Edmund Gosse

[4] See Letters 103 and 105.
[5] Daughter of President Grover Cleveland.

❧ 108. *Gosse to Holmes* ❧

29 Delamere Terrace / London, W.

3 April 1886

My dear Dr. Holmes

The newspapers announce this morning that you are coming over into Mesopotamia.[1] It seems almost too good to be true. But I write without delay to say how glad we are, and how proud we shall be if you will let us be of any small service to you. We do not know what ladies of your family, if any, will accompany you. Mrs. Gosse hopes that whoever they may be, whether Mrs. Holmes, or your daughter, or both, they will allow her to be their hewer of wood, if they want any wood hewn. And you will let me ask Browning to dine with you, will you not? and give me other opportunities of exhaling my pride in your friendship.

Most of all, I hope you will spend a couple of lovely May-days in college with me at Cambridge (Trinity), and sit at dinner in hall between the portraits of Dryden and Cowley, where half the English poets have sat and dined. I will take as much care of you as if you were made of porcelain, and unique,—which you are.

All this does not mean that we are conceited enough to thrust ourselves

[1] During his visit to England Holmes and his daughter called on the Gosses in London (see Letter 109), and on 12 and 13 June Gosse entertained Holmes at Trinity College, Cambridge. Holmes returned to Cambridge a few days later to receive an honorary degree, and Gosse recorded his own reaction to this second visit in a letter to Gilder (a.l.s., 18 June 1886, HU): "I have just come from the breakfast given to Dr. O. W. Holmes at St. John's College. The dear little man, in his scarlet doctor's gown, with flying pink ribbands, looked beaming, and made a delicious speech which nobody took down. He said that what he had enjoyed most in England was the sense of antiquity over all things, 'like the lichen on an old wall, or, better still, like the patina on an old coin'. He has had a triumph over here, and his heart rejoices, as one can see." See also the account in Holmes's *Our Hundred Days in Europe*, pp. 80, 108–110.

between you and the splendid welcome which awaits you in this country, but only that I should like to have some small practical opportunity of showing you my deep regard and my ever-living sense of your extraordinary kindness to me when I was in Boston.

With all affection and respect

Believe me

Dear Dr. Holmes

Yours very sincerely

Edmund Gosse

∿ 109. *Gosse to Holmes* ∿

29, Delamere Terrace, / Westbourne Square. / [London] W.

31 May 1886

Dear Dr. Holmes

Tomorrow being the evening that we are to have the delight of welcoming you here, I think you will perhaps let me tell you the names of one or two of the people whom you will meet. Among those who have accepted are Browning, Austin Dobson, Pater,[1] Andrew Lang, Sidney Colvin,[2] Henry James, W. H. Pollock,[3] Prof. Minto,[4] among literary people. Among artists, Alma Tadema, who greatly wants to see you, is the name you will know best. By rather a happy chance M. Édmond Scherer,[5] the famous French critic, is in London, and we have secured him. We shall have one or two members of parliament, one or two sculptors, and so on. But we have asked none but our own personal friends, thinking it no compliment to you or Mrs. Sargent to overcrowd our rooms with people who care nothing for us nor (really) for you.

May we hope to see you at 8.30 or thereabouts? If your coachman should

[1] Walter Horatio Pater (1839–1894), author of critical and philosophical works, notably *Studies in the History of the Renaissance* (1873) and *Marius the Epicurean* (1885).

[2] Sir Sidney Colvin (1845–1927), critic and historian of literature and of art.

[3] Walter Herries Pollock (1850–1926) was editor of the *Saturday Review* from 1883 to 1894; he wrote several works of dramatic and literary criticism, and some verse.

[4] William Minto (1845–1893), Scottish novelist and man of letters; from 1880 to 1893 he was professor of logic and literature at Aberdeen University.

[5] Edmond Henri Adolphe Scherer (1815–1889) began his career as a theologian and later devoted much of his time to politics, but it was for his critical writings, especially in such journals as the *Revue des deux mondes* and *Le Temps,* that he was best known.

not know the address, he will recognize it if you tell him "at the top of Westbourne Terrace, facing the canal". It is a drive of about 20 minutes from you.

With very kind regards and compliments to Mrs. Sargent,[6] whom I am greatly looking forward to see,

Believe me
Dear Dr. Holmes
Ever very faithfully yours

Edmund Gosse

[6] Mrs. Turner Sargent, Holmes's daughter Amelia, his second child.

❧ 110. *Gosse to Gilder* ❧

Board of Trade. [London] S.W.

14 October 1886

My dear Gilder

Don't you think it might be a good idea to get a signed article (1300 words) as an Open Letter *each month* from some well-known English writer?

I wish you would consider this. I think almost everybody would be pleased to do this. I would not ask anybody twice, and in a little while we should have had contributions from no end of interesting people. It would take up very little of your space, would amuse lots of readers, would interest gradually the whole leading literary class here in the magazine, and would be useful in advertisement.

I should propose making it really a handsome thing, say £5 a letter. Let the writer have a good deal of choice about his subjects,—everybody has something he wants to ventilate. I should especially encourage well-known specialists, in art and science as well as literature.

Here is a selection of a few of the names which have occurred to me:—
Froude,[1] Sir F. Leighton,[2] Fredk. [sic] Harrison,[3] Huxley,[4] Short-

[1] James Anthony Froude (1818–1894), churchman, historian, and close friend and biographer of Carlyle, known especially for his *History of England from the Fall of Wolsey to the Death of Elizabeth* (12 vols., 1856–1870).
[2] Sir Frederick Leighton (1830–1896), sculptor and painter; in 1878 he became president of the Royal Academy and was knighted; in 1896 he was created a baron.
[3] Frederic Harrison (1831–1923), philosopher, jurist, historian, and sociologist, also wrote several biographies, a novel, and some verse.
[4] Thomas Henry Huxley (1825–1895), the distinguished biologist and essayist, chief proponent in England of the Darwinian evolutionary hypothesis.

house,[5] Hardy, Lang, Dobson, Bryce, Symonds,[6] Alma Tadema, Thorny-croft, John Morley, Prof. Robertson Smith,[7] George Meredith,[8] Sir Henry Thompson,[9] etc.

If we made a good start, everybody would be glad to follow.

What do you say?

Ever yours

Edmund Gosse

[5] Joseph Henry Shorthouse (1834–1903), novelist, best remembered as the author of *John Inglesant* (1880); Gosse has an essay on him in *Portraits and Sketches* (London: Heinemann, 1912), pp. 151–162.

[6] John Addington Symonds (1840–1893), poet, translator, and critic. For his relationship with Gosse, see Phyllis Grosskurth, *John Addington Symonds* (London: Longmans, 1964), pp. 149–150, 230–232, 280–281, 324.

[7] William Robertson Smith (1846–1894), the Scottish Biblical scholar, philologist, orientalist, and editor of the *Encyclopædia Britannica*. At Cambridge, between 1883 and his death, he held professorships in Arabic and was for a time University librarian.

[8] George Meredith (1828–1909), the novelist and poet.

[9] Sir Henry Thompson (1820–1904), the English surgeon, famous for his work on genitourinary disease.

❧ 111. *Gilder to Gosse* ❧

Editorial Department / The Century Magazine / Union Square New York

1 November 1886

My dear Gosse:

Let me congratulate you upon the spirit and temper of your excellent reply to the brutal attack which has been made upon you.[1] I did not see the attack; in fact it has not yet reached this side I believe, but your reply certainly must be a more gentlemanly and satisfactory production than that of your ruthless antagonist. Why will literary men act in such conscienceless and indecent fashion?

With regard to your very interesting proposal about signed "Open Letters" each month: I wish to thank you for the idea, but I must tell you that the conviction is growing daily upon us that we must give place to our American writers rather than to foreign ones. Our writers are being crushed by the lack of international copyright; few of them have a proper income,

[1] Gosse replied to John Churton Collins's attack on *From Shakespeare to Pope* in the *Athenaeum*, 23 October 1886, p. 534–535. For a more detailed account of the attack and of the controversy which followed it, see Introduction, pp. 20–21. Collins (1848–1908) subsequently became professor of English at Birmingham University. See also Phyllis Grosskurth, "Churton Collins: Scourge of the Late Victorians," *University of Toronto Quarterly*, XXXIV (April 1965), 254–268.

and it seems as if it must be our duty to think first of them. "Harpers" and the "Atlantic" publish serials by English writers when they could get ones equally good, or nearly as good, by American writers; and they certainly could cultivate American writers who would do as good work if they would give them the chance. "Harpers" especially offend in this way, probably because the House desires to publish novels by Englishmen on this side of the water. Our safes are full of admirable short stories and serials which we scarcely have room for. If we should take an English serial to-day it would crowd out some American story which, in our our way of thinking, has greater claims upon us. Americans are interested in English and foreign matters and therefore we have articles on English and other foreign subjects; but we prefer as a rule to have these articles written, or else to have the illustrations made, by Americans. This is not provincialism; it is simply a matter of obvious duty. Why should American magazines let American authors starve while they go seeking after strange gods? The American policy has always been the policy of "The Century," but we feel more and more inclined to insist upon it. It is only in a very extraordinary case that we desire a foreign contribution on any subject. What applies to story writers applies also to poetry. I could tell you about a number of young poets, some of whose names you are perhaps not familiar with, who have great promise, but who have hardly any opportunity. When will we have strong literature in this country if we do not give place to it? When we have a foreign subject treated by a foreign author it is because Americans are especially interested in that subject and the foreign author is better able to tell them about it.

We telegraphed you to-day to see if you could get for us, with the right to engrave, some photographs of the recently unwrapped mummy of the great Pharaoh of Moses's time—(Rameses II.)[2] The photographs have been reproduced in this country—without authority apparently—and they have been copyrighted here. I do not know that the copyright would hold, but we do not like to touch anything that has any claim to copyright. There is a very fine profile which we would especially like to use. We have a little article by an American photographer who was at the tomb just after the discovery. I do not think the society that publishes the photographs wishes to keep any copyright on them, but we would like to be sure that we are not infringing any rights in using any photographs you can procure for us. We are in a great hurry for the photographs, and hope you will be able to send them immediately.

Sincerely
R. W. Gilder

[2] The photographs were apparently used by Edward L. Wilson in "Finding Pharaoh," illustrated by I. R. Wiles and E. J. Meeker from photographs by the author, *Century*, XXXIV (May 1887), 3–10.

112. *Howells to Gosse*[1]

302, Beacon Street, / Boston.

7 November 1886

My dear Gosse,

Thank you for sending me your defence against the Quarterly.[2] You needed none with this family, but we all thought your answer to the brutal assault which we've not yet read, admirable. I know the assault from hearsay, Perry having told me how foolish and dishonest it was. The feeling here is all one way. Aldrich says the close of your reply—the last two paragraphs—is most masterly, and I think so, too.

You will see in the December "Harper" how much I like your Raleigh,[3] but I must tell you personally that I found it only less delightful than the Gray: that remains inapproachable. Last night I met the Creightons,[4] from your Cambridge, at Norton's, and Mrs. C. tried to make me jealous by pretending that you giggled with her husband as much as you did with me. I was furious but I was too polite to show it. The (Mead's)[5] are here, and we are to give a large lunch for them on Thursday.

The Hawthorne-Lowell interview[5] has been a great sensation here; and there's no doubt but it was a most cruel betrayal. It oughtn't to be regarded in England as representative of Lowell at all.

The family joins me in love to Mrs. Gosse and yourself.

Yours ever,

W. D. Howells

[1] The text of this letter has been taken from a typed copy in the Rutgers University Library.

[2] See Letter 111, n. 1. Gosse had copies of his defense privately printed and sent out to his friends.

[3] Howells reviewed Gosse's *Raleigh* (London: Longmans, Green, 1886) in *Harper's Monthly*, LXXIV (December 1886), 158–159.

[4] Mandell Creighton (1843–1901), the English churchman and historian. He was Dixie Professor of Ecclesiastical History at Cambridge from 1884 to 1891, when he was made Bishop of Peterborough; in 1897 he became Bishop of London.

[5] Probably the Larkin G. Meads (see Letter 38, n. 5).

[6] Julian Hawthorne published the account of his interview with Lowell in the New York *World*. Lowell's quoted comments on English personalities were unfortunate, and when a controversy arose he repudiated the interview, claiming he had been taken advantage of. For a full account, see Clara and Rudolf Kirk, " 'Enchanted Guest'," Rutgers Library *Journal*, XXII (June 1959), 17–20.

113. *Gosse to Howells*

Board of Trade. [London] S.W.

19 November 1886

My dear Howells

I was exceedingly glad this morning to receive your delightful letter, and I seize a very large sheet to tell you so. The storm roused by the Quarterly continues to rumble away in quarters like the "Pall Mall Gazette", "World" and "Truth",[1] but the rest of the public is thoroughly tired of it, I think. I do not suppose that it has done me much harm: everybody has to run the gauntlet some time or other. No doubt it has been a blow,—that I would not for a moment pretend to deny, but it is a blow which has not knocked me down, and which I may even receive benefit from.

Your charming Hawaiian friends the Mott Smiths[2] are here. Nellie has seen a good deal of them, but unfortunately I have been at Cambridge almost all the time, and have hitherto seen but little of them. Very aggravatingly Dr. Mott Smith dined one day in Hall at Trinity, but as the guest of a non-resident clergyman who did not know who anybody was, and so, although I was sitting opposite to him, and although he asked who I was, he did not know me. A day or two afterwards he was calling on Nellie, and saw

---

[1] London newspapers, especially the *Pall Mall Gazette,* were for several months full of references to the Gosse-Collins affair. The most recent in the *Pall Mall Gazette* was an article two days earlier (17 November 1886, pp. 11–12), summarizing and extracting from letters received by that journal. The main theme of the article is enunciated in the opening paragraph, which declares that the quarrel of the *Quarterly Review* and "those who on this matter think with it," is not "with Mr. Gosse as such, but only with Mr. Gosse as Clark Lecturer at Trinity College, Cambridge. All that the *Quarterly* reviewer and other critics have alleged may be true, and yet Mr. Gossse will remain a very graceful writer and a contributor of good work to certain departments of literature. All that will have been proved, all that it was ever attempted to prove, is that he has not attained the same standard of accuracy and sound scholarship that is demanded at the Universities of its teachers in all other branches of study" (p. 11).

The *World* reference is presumably to a comment in the issue of 17 November 1886, p. 18. It begins: "Now that Mr. Gosse has been found out, it is to be hoped that he will try to make up for lost time, and seriously prepare himself for the due discharge of his duties as Clark Lecturer on English Literature in the University of Cambridge." In *Truth,* XX (18 November 1886), 813, the section entitled "Entre Nous" contains the following: "The amount of Gosse and Collins literature, in prose and verse, that I am receiving is enormous. My opinion of the matter is summed up in the following jingle of Dean Swift's rejingled:—

May I ask if it matters a halfpenny toss,
Whether Gosse kicked C. Collins, or Collins kicked Gosse?"

[2] Dr. Mott Smith was the Hawaiian Commissioner to the United States. Howells wrote introducing him to Gosse (a.l.s., 24 June 1886, BM) and the names of Dr., Mrs., and the Misses Mott Smith appear in the Book of Gosse for 28 November 1886.

Sargent's portrait of me[3] on the wall, and recognized it at once as the man he had been dining with at Trinity. I was very much annoyed about it.

It is very good of you to like my Raleigh. You can't think how nice a little praise is after 5 weeks' unlimited abuse! I shall look forward to December's "Harper", and your public praise will do me public good, by cheering up my friends, who feel my persecution, I think, more than I do.

I was sure you would like the Creightons. They are delightful people, and he is one of the salt of the earth. I should think he was a man whom Americans would like, he is so sincere and genial, underneath a certain brusqueness of manner. He is one of our most rising churchmen, with a bishop's mitre in his pocket.

People here were frightfully grieved at the Lowell outrage;[4] sympathy, I think, is all with him. There is one point which I should like to clear up, if possible. Thomas Hardy, our greatest novelist over here, as I think, was very much wounded by what Lowell was reported to have said about him. There are circumstances in the case which would make the sneer at Hardy's personal appearance singularly cruel: I cannot myself believe that Lowell said all that—it is quite in the Julian Hawthorne vein. Hardy, who has always been a great supporter and admirer of Lowell, is wretched at this supposed snub. I wonder if you happened to see Lowell whether you could not get from him a verbal assurance that he did not say all this? You may, of course feel it too delicate a mission. The article is decidedly a serious blow to Lowell's position here: he ought, I think, to have repudiated it all more thoroughly, much more thoroughly.

With our love
Ever yours very sincerely

Edmund Gosse

[3] John Singer Sargent (see Letter 98, n. 4) was a friend of Gosse; a reproduction of the portrait appears in Charteris, *Life and Letters of Gosse,* facing p. 182. In a letter of 1894 (BC, printed in Evan Charteris, *John Sargent,* p. 142) Sargent wrote to tell Gosse that he had refused permission for the portrait to be reproduced in the *Yellow Book.*

[4] See Letter 112, n. 6. Lowell had been quoted as making rather slighting references to Hardy's work and to his undistinguished appearance.

❧ 114. *Gosse to Stedman* ❧

29, Delamere Terrace, / Westbourne Square [London] W.

19 November 1886

My dear Stedman

I was truly delighted to get your kind and philosophic letter. I am sure you take the right view of this tiresome affair, the storm-skirts of which still go on grumbling and ⟨d⟩ropping. There has been a tremendous lot of bad blood gathering in the bosoms of journalists, and this will do them good. It will be the Letting of Envy's Imposthume in the Head-Vein, as an Elizabethan might have said. As for me, it will be my own fault if it does not do me a great deal of good,—it ought to make me more careful, more modest, more anxious to avoid offence, in short every way more human; and that I pray may be the result of it when all the sense of having stinging nettles applied to one's nerves has passed away. All the same, I am not such a Christian as to be able to overlook entirely that Mr. Churton Collins is a scoundrel. I befriended him when he was poor, I got his articles into magazines when he had no influence or connection, and his letters, which I possess, are full of eulogy of my writings. No! he is a skunk, and so guarda e passa.

I had been waiting (when this broke out) for a moment to write to you about your admirable paper on Genius.[1] I am fully with you in your argument, urged as you would naturally urge it, with every grace and every courtesy, against a foe worthy of your steel. Why should criticism ever pass out of this delightful atmosphere?

I have been enjoying your stately poem on the Bartholdi statue.[2] I am very glad your lyric vein still flows.

Believe me ever your sincere friend

Edmund Gosse

[1] Stedman, "Genius," *New Princeton Review,* II (September 1886), 145–167.

[2] Presumably an allusion to Stedman, "Liberty Enlightening the World," *Harper's Weekly,* **XXX** (30 October 1886), 702, a poem about the Statue of Liberty, the work of the French sculptor Auguste Bartholdi (1834–1904), which was unveiled in 1886.

❧ 115. *Gosse to Howells* ❧

Board of Trade. [London] S.W.

30 November 1886

My dear Howells

We are all grateful to you for the "Mouse-Trap".[1] My sister-in-law[2] read it aloud to us last night, and when she had finished we all, and she included, had laughed so much that we voted the performance incomplete, and I had to read it, as gravely as I could, right through a second time. I assure you I never read anything more laughable in my life. I congratulate you on a success of the very freshest and most sprightly kind.

Coming upon the mouse-trap was an accident, for what I really got Harper's for was to read your praise of me.[3] It is very kind, and very generous: I hope it may not lay you open to any mean attacks. The degree to which I am still made the victim here of pails of journalistic slops is really extraordinary. The attack occurred six weeks ago, and the reverberations of obloquy are going on still, in the seventh week. I am anxious to keep up my spirits so as to get the real benefit of this blow, and not be paralysed by it. It would be childish to pretend that it is not a blow. But I am tolerably young still, and I have plenty of work to do. Work must tell, even in our hurried generation. I have been too easily successful, I suppose; I have glided on, and I can see that I have been negligent and have taken for granted that everything will come right. I think that so long as one is not absolutely crushed out of competition, a blow of this kind is very useful. It makes one draw one's self together, and strengthens one's face against the world. In a hundred little ways, of course, I feel the sting of it at present; it is like being struck a blow in the face, and then tickled with nettles over the spot. But I must pray for health and vigour of brain, and live it down. And it may even turn out the best thing that ever happened to me.

Bear me in affection, as I always bear you in grateful and loving remembrance.

Yours very sincerely

Edmund Gosse

[1] Howells's farce, "The Mousetrap," *Harper's Monthly*, LXXIV (December 1886), 64–75.
[2] Probably Mrs. Lawrence Alma-Tadema.
[3] See Letter 112, n. 2.

❧ 116. *Gosse to Armour*[1] ❧

29, Delamere Terrace, / Westbourne Square [London] W.

4 December 1886

My dear Mr. Armour

I was exceedingly touched as well as gratified by your kind letter of this morning. Your gift is princely, but it is almost obscured, for the moment, by your delicate and generous sympathy shown in the manner of giving it. I am telling you the simplest truth when I say that no present could have pleased me more, nor have been more calculated to flatter and sooth my susceptibilities.

I am truly sorry that you failed to find me at Trinity and here. If I could have found you here in my library I should have shown you a lasting memorial of our earlier correspondence, for I have a letter of yours bound up in a volume of MSS. respecting the Gray Monument at Pembroke.[2]

Mrs. Gosse, who was no less charmed with your letter than I was, joins

---

[1] George Allison Armour (1856–1936) was the son of a Scottish engineer who came to the United States as a young man and enjoyed great success in Chicago both as an engineer and as a businessman; there was no relationship between this family and that of Philip D. Armour, head of the meat-packing business. For a few years after his father's death Armour was engaged in business in Chicago but he increasingly devoted his time to the things which chiefly interested him in life: travel and books. In the course of his frequent visits to England he met Gosse—they seem first to have been in correspondence in 1884, over the monument to Thomas Gray (see note below)—and the two quickly became close friends; during Armour's visits to Europe he and Gosse spent vacations together, sometimes with their families, and traveled together on the Continent. In 1895 Armour and his family moved to Princeton, where he had himself been a student and where he now endowed the classical seminary; his house has recently been given to the University by his daughter, Mrs. Walter Lowrie, and is used to entertain distinguished guests. Armour's fine library was dispersed after his death: his son, Norman Armour, recalls his expressed wish "that others might have the pleasure he had had in book collecting" (letter to Paul F. Mattheisen, 12 June 1963). Norman Armour speaks of the friendship between Gosse and his father extending to the members of both families and mentions that his youngest brother was named Edmund after Gosse, who became his godfather. Philip Gosse also spoke of this family friendship and recalled his father's saying that Armour was the best example he knew of a person who gave the impression of being simply a "born aristocrat" (conversation with Paul F. Mattheisen, December 1958). Charteris, who prints several of Gosse's letters to Armour (usually in truncated form), notes Armour's "strong distaste for correspondence," and adds: ". . . he had a more magnificent method of reply by arriving in person at unexpected seasons" (p. 203). See also Introduction, pp. 35–36.

[2] Gosse was instrumental in getting Thornycroft the commission to do a statue of Gray for Pembroke College and, subsequently, a copy for Johns Hopkins University. The volume of letters regarding the Gray Monument, which was unveiled in 1885, is in the Brotherton Collection; it contains two letters from Armour, the only letters he wrote to Gosse which seem to have survived.

with me in hoping that you will let us know beforehand of your coming in April, that she may call at once on Mrs. Armour, and in the wish that we may see you both at this house. Perhaps I might have the pleasure of going with you to Cambridge for a day or two: we must see: at all events I shall not at that time be lecturing there. In April and May the undergraduate mind is too much disturbed by examinations to get much good from lectures.

I feel that you ought not to have robbed yourself of Langbaine.[3] But you will at least know that no one in London will appreciate the book more than I. It is the very apex of the collection of Restoration drama which I have been forming for so many years. Some day I shall bore you by making you look at my books. By the way, I have been commissioned by the "Independent" of New York to write a series of fortnightly gossips on my books.[4] You will not mind, I hope, if I make Langbaine the subject of one of them?

You allude, with exquisite tact and feeling, to the worry I have been undergoing.[5] I will not pretend to you that I have not felt it. One does not stand in the pillory of the press for eight weeks, daily being pelted with rotten eggs, without beginning to be rather tired of it. It becomes monotonous, looked upon as merely as a performance. But I have had a great deal of sympathy from almost all the first literary men in the country, even from some who were previously complete strangers to me, and my own university is splendidly staunch. I hope to make the blow a matter of real advantage to me. I mean to pull myself together, and do work so sound and good that the very fools and knaves that are hooting now shall be forced to listen to me with respect. Such sympathy as yours is of inestimable service to me, and I thank you for it with all my heart. I hope you will write to me again.

Yours very sincerely

Edmund Gosse

[3] This was the gift mentioned in the first paragraph; a copy of Gerard Langbaine's *An Account of the English Dramatick Poets* (1691) is listed in E. H. M. Cox, *The Library of Edmund Gosse* (London: Dulau, 1924), p. 167, and described as "the gift of Mr. G. A. Armour."

[4] Gosse's essays in the *Independent,* later collected in *Gossip in a Library* (London: Heinemann, 1891), appeared as follows: XXXIX (1887), 1, 101, 230, 359, 518, 646, 935, 1441; XL (1888), 130, 420, 578, 964; XLI (1889), 67, 291. There was no article on Langbaine, however.

[5] The attack by John Churton Collins. See Letters 111æ115 and Introduction, pp. 20–21.

১৩ 117. *Gosse to Gilder* ১৩

Board of Trade. [London] S.W.

17 December 1886

My dear Gilder

I have allowed too long a time to go by since receiving your last letter. It is really because that letter was so kind and full, and because I did not wish to send you back a mere perfunctory word of thanks. But the fact is I have been exceptionally busy, and weary to an extent you will hardly realise. I have felt it proper and necessary to hold a brave face in public and private about this wretched business of the last two months. It would have been silly not to do so, with all the best lights on your side of the ocean, as well as here, assuring me of their confidence. But the nightly insults of the papers, (particularly of the Pall Mall Gazette, which has scarcely omitted for one single evening for eight weeks to have an insulting article or paragraph about me)[1] have at last fatigued and excited me to a very ridiculous extent. I would give a large sum of money to be sure that my name would not appear in print for three months. It is not a question, you understand, of right or wrong, it is the intense mental strain of being always in evidence. I suppose you have seen and heard little of the coarser part of the attacks. The incident will be remembered, I think, as the most resolute endeavour, by newspaper conspiracy, to murder a man of letters socially and professionally, that was ever made. I know the principal malefactors, they form a regular little gang. For many a long day to come I shall find it impossible to secure anything like justice for anything I do. On either side this belt of journalists, there is the public—here, and the recognised Olympians of literature—there, both on my side. In lecturing last week at Manchester and Leeds I got perfect ovations from popular audiences.[2] But oh! the weariness of it all, the horrible

---

[1] Gosse exaggerated slightly in saying that the *Pall Mall Gazette* had had some item about him nearly every evening for eight weeks, though that journal covered the matter fully enough. The last direct reference to Gosse seems to have been on 11 December, p. 5, in the course of a joint review of J. A. Symonds's *Sir Philip Sidney* (English Men of Letters Series) and of Gosse's article on Sidney in the *Contemporary Review*, L (November 1886), 632–648. But the *Pall Mall Gazette* had been running a series of occasional articles, entitled "English at the Universities," dealing with the Gosse-Collins affair, and Number VII of the series had appeared on 17 December, pp. 1–2. By this time, however, the debate had moved on to wider issues, and in this particular article Gosse was neither named nor directly referred to.

[2] Gosse lectured on "Hans Christian Andersen" before the Leeds Philosophical and Literary Society on 7 December; the report in the *Leeds Mercury* (9 December 1886, p. 8) notes simply the final applause. When Gosse gave the same talk in Manchester on 14 December, as the second in a series of popular lectures at the Sale Public Hall, the chairman (Mr. George Milner) made a direct reference to the "somewhat angry controversy" in which Gosse had been engaged and observed that "he (the chairman)

paragraphs about one's wife and one's servants, the anonymous insulting letters,—if people like to become notorious I am sure they pay dearly for it! They are welcome to all my notoriety for a penny.

However, we have so much to be thankful for that it is impious to pipe an eye. We have all been wonderfully well hitherto this winter. I had rather a poor account of you in the summer. I hope that your holiday set you up. We sympathised much with you and Mrs. Gilder in your troubles, of which you speak to me, and of which I had heard. These things seem to come all of a heap. I hope you will at least enjoy a calm winter, void of excitement.

I am sending you a little book printed by the Students of Edinburgh,[3] which I hope has not yet reached you. You will find in it charming things by Lang and R. L. Stevenson.

I hope that "Scribner's Magazine"[4] is not going to worry you and give you anxiety. Warne[5] has taken it here, as we supposed he would. Murray is starting a magazine too,[6] about which a young Oxford man, Mackail,[7] made a good remark, that "even if Byron did recommend them to issue it, they need not have been in such indecent haste!" No one reads the moribund existing English magazines, so I do not know how yet another is to succeed.

This comes wishing you and yours all household joys in the Xmas of 1886 and the New Year of 1887. Bear me in kindly thought, and believe me

Ever yours sincerely

Edmund Gosse

hoped they did not think he came off second best. (Applause)"—report in the Manchester *City News*, 18 December, p. 2.

[3] *The New Amphion, Being the Book of the Edinburgh University Union Fancy Fair . . .* (Edinburgh: Edinburgh University Press, 1886). "The Dog" by Andrew Lang (pp. 5–19) and "Some College Memories" by Robert Louis Stevenson (pp. 221–240).

[4] The American publishing firm of Scribner's had given up its interest in *Scribner's Monthly* in 1881, when the magazine was purchased by Roswell Smith and its name changed to the *Century* (see Letter 18, n. 1). In January 1887, however, a new journal, *Scribner's Magazine*, began to appear.

[5] Frederick Warne (1825–1901) was an assistant and subsequently a partner in the publishing firm of Routledge until in 1865 he set up his own publishing business. He was the first English publisher of the *Century* (see Letter 18, n. 5), but was soon succeeded by T. Fisher Unwin. Gosse refers here to his taking over the English publication of *Scribner's Magazine*.

[6] *Murray's Magazine* first appeared in January 1887 and ran until December 1891.

[7] John William Mackail (1859–1945), scholar and critic, best known for his classical studies and his *Life of William Morris* (1899).

✑ 118. *Gosse to Gilder* ✑

Board of Trade. [London] S.W.

22 February 1887

My dear Gilder

I sent you, about nine months ago, the article on the Fitzwilliam which you ordered.[1] I should be very much obliged if you would send me a proof, as you promised to do at once. I am constantly in horror—lest you should issue it as it is, for there are in it certain strictures of the University, which are just enough, but which it would be very undesirable to publish. In my late worries, the authorities of my own university stood by me most manfully, without exception, and it would seem the grossest abuse of their kindness if I published an article satirically animadverting on what is really no business of mine. You will see the importance of this, and send me a proof, will you not? *I depend upon you in this matter.* You wanted certain alterations made. Will you let me know what those are?

I am very sorry you have determined, as you tell me, to boycott all English contributions. It seems to me a step in the wrong direction. I cannot think that an editor has to "protect" the literature of his country.[2] If I were an editor I should try to "protect" by getting the best things wherever they came from, England and America alike. But I will not presume to criticise you.

Yours most truly

Edmund Gosse

Have you been worried by an awful woman (called Baws or Bowds or something) who wanted to write on Dukes' houses? She said she should give you a piece of her mind!

[1] The article on the Fitzwilliam Museum, Cambridge, never appeared in *Century*.

[2] Gosse voiced a similar complaint in a letter to Clinton Scollard, 25 March 1887 (a.l.s., YU): "There can be no patriotism in matters of literature. A man writes good verse or bad verse whether he is a Bostonian or a dweller in the parts of Libya about Cyrene. I am afraid this 'protection' in criticism will do a great deal of harm: I believe in free trade, myself, and letting the real poet work out his own salvation. Five-sixths of the poets lauded in the 'Century' have no more notion what *verse* is than a tom-cat. I dare to whisper this to you, because you do know the rules of your art. What with America patting everybody on the back and English writers hitting everyone in the stomach, literature has a pretty unwholesome time of it in the Anglo-Saxon world."

119. *Gosse to Gilder*

[London?]

18 March 1887

My dear Gilder

I thank you very cordially indeed for your extremely interesting long letter of the 7th.;[1] it puts things very plainly indeed, and stimulates my feeble faith to look ahead. I assure you that my belief in the "Century" is unshaken: I am quite sure that it has a future by the side of which its past successes will seem tame. Only, you must understand that alone over here, I get sometimes a little depressed and impatient. I want each number to scintillate in my own particular way, which I have no doubt is not really the best way. If I seem ever petulant about it, pray believe that it is only because the magazine has become a part of my main life-interests, and because I cannot always bear with sufficient patience to wait for the development you look for.

I shall take the liberty of showing your letter to Mr. Unwin, because we sometimes croak a little together over what we do not personally enjoy in the magazine. It is a great comfort to me to have Mr. Unwin instead of Warne.[2] There is all the difference between them that there is between butter and oleomargarine.

Once more I thank you for the great patience and fullness of your letter, and for the confidence you place in me. Regard me, please, as Penitent Peter.

Yours very sincerely

Edmund Gosse

[1] Gilder's letter of 7 March 1887 is quoted in Smith, "Editorial Influence of Gilder" (dissertation, Rutgers), pp. 377–378. See also Introduction, pp. 33–34.
[2] Thomas Fisher Unwin (1848–1935), the publisher, first established the firm of T. Fisher Unwin in 1882. At the time of this letter he had just taken over the English publication of the *Century* from Warne (see Letter 117, n. 5).

120. *Gosse to Armour*

29, Delamere Terrace, / Westbourne Square. / [London] W.

21 August 1887

My dear Armour

We expect you both to our ordinary dinner (not dress, of course, and only ourselves) on Thursday next, at 6.30, if that suits you, with bien beaucoup de plaisir.

I have just come back, much excited, from saying farewell to R[obert] L[ouis] S[tevenson].[1] I did not in the least expect to see him, but I had a summons last night. He is in a quiet family hotel (he calls it the real Todgers)[2] in Finsbury, ready to sail early tomorrow morning. I went over directly after breakfast, not expecting to see himself, except for a moment in bed. But when I got there, after waiting ½ an hour, suddenly he came in to the room, looking rather white, and a little dazzled in the eyes, but otherwise much better and less emaciated than I feared. I was allowed to be with him for a whole hour. He is in mourning for his father,[3] and he was quite stylishly dressed in a black velvet coat and waistcoat, a black silk necktie and dark trousers, so that instead of looking like a Lascar out of employment, as he generally does, he looked extremely elegant and refined, his hair over his shoulders but very tidy and burnished like brass with brushing. He prowled about the room, in his usual noiseless panther fashion, talking all the time, full of wit and feeling and sweetness, as charming as ever he was, but with a little more sadness and sense of crisis than usual. I had to be one witness to his will, the housekeeper of the hotel being summoned to be the other. No one else, except his wife was there; there was absolute Sunday peace all around; it was very interesting and very affecting.

My Tessa is so much obliged to you for your beautiful gift. She will tell you so herself. With our affectionate regards to you both

Yours sincerely

Edmund Gosse

[1] Robert Louis Stevenson (1850–1894), whom Gosse had known for many years, had sailed for New York on 17 August. In June 1888 he sailed from San Francisco, and after extensive travels in the Pacific he settled at last in Samoa, where he spent the last four years of his life.

[2] Stevenson stayed overnight at Armfield's Hotel; "Todgers" is the name of the London hotel in Dickens's *Martin Chuzzlewit*.

[3] Thomas Stevenson (1818–1887) died in Edinburgh on 8 May 1887.

❧ 121. *Gosse to Armour* ❧

Stanley Villa / Sands Rd. / Paignton

22 September 1887

My dear Armour

Your letter was very welcome this morning. And first of all, as parent of a gaggle of thankless infants, I must say how ashamed I am that they have not thanked you for the delicious and acceptable butter-scotch, which they have been nibbling ever since, and which I (alas! for manly pride) am sucking now. They are on the shore from morning to night, and cannot be led, even for a moment, and with cries and tears, to the writing-table.

We have had ten delightful days. I came down in a feverish and agitated mood, not very well in soul or body. I seem to have been blown through and through by the strong sea wind. I never enjoyed so much the society of my children, and my intercourse with my father has been entirely pleasant. I find him gentle and approachable, he is wonderfully mellowed, and I do not think that ever before I had such sincere (as opposed to conventional) pleasure in being with him. But he is certainly weaker and older, and nears his 78th. year with a new appearance of venerableness. My step-mother, who is one of the most loveable of mankind, has been our guest here all this week, —the parental abode being about 4 miles off. So you see, altogether, we have been very domestic.

It is very good of you to send us Dr. Holmes's "100 Days in Europe".[1] When those papers appeared in the "Atlantic", I glanced at them, but did not notice till now his very gracious references to my little attempts at hospitality. He is a very appreciative old thing, I am sure. The book is full of gossip that one would be sorry to lose, and yet I cannot help feeling a perverse wish that it had been kept back awhile, or not published at all in this form. It is so uniformly balmy and rose-colored, that it gives one an impression of senile superficiality. This sounds unkind, but you will know what I mean. There should be a thorn or two in such a bed of roses; and I happen to know that there were.

I am glad you were a little bit "gratified and satisfied" with my Nuremberg papers in the "Saturday".[2] I found my impressions so definite, that I was sorry I had not made similar notes at Ratisbon. I always notice that other people's descriptions of places leave one surprised when one does see the places for one's self. Now, if one can define in what the surprise consists, there is the basis for a description, which, however hackneyed the theme, will have a certain novelty. Of course I had always known what Adam Krafft's stations were, but the medium in which they existed, the modern suburb air, surprised me, and made a key-note for my paper.

Since I have been down here I have read a long Russian novel (in French of course), by Dostoievsky,—"Le Crime et le Châtiment". Do you know it? It is a masterpiece of psychological study. On the whole I think it is the most powerful, the most successfully daring, domestic novel I have ever read. The subject,—a murder and robbery by an educated man, and the conduct of his mind after the event,—is distressing enough, but most thrilling and entrancing in its carrying out. I should like you to read it.

[1] Holmes, *Our Hundred Days in Europe*, especially pp. 109–110. The chapters appeared serially in the *Atlantic Monthly*, LIX–LX (March–October 1887).
[2] Gosse, "The Fountains of Nuremberg," *Saturday Review,* LXIV (27 August 1887), 286–287; "Nuremberg," *ibid.* (17 September 1887), 385–386.

Next Monday I am to go back to town. My wife and the chicks intend to stay till about the 10th. of October. Now, how would you like me to come to you for Sunday week at Brighton? I don't know at all how far Mrs. Armour could bear a visitor, nor what your plans are. You must decline my offer as frankly as I make it.

We have been so quiet since we came that Nellie insists on one great spree. So we are all going for a 40 miles drive tomorrow up on Dartmoor. We shall pass with a mile or two of Dean Prior.[3]

I am ever,

My dear Friend

Yours sincerely

Edmund Gosse

[3] This is the village in Devon, on the edge of Dartmoor, where Robert Herrick is buried. In a letter to Armour of 13 September (a.l.s., PU), Gosse had expressed the wish that the two of them might make a trip to Dean Prior together.

∾ 122. *Gosse to Stedman* ∾

29, Delamere Terrace, / Westbourne Square. [London] W.

6 December 1887

Private and confidential

My dear Stedman

I am going to appeal to your tried and proved good-nature, by making a certain confidence to you. The matter of which I am about to speak is one which is very delicate, and which I have mentioned to no one over here but Austin Dobson, with whom I have no secrets. In America, I am particularly anxious that no one should know it but yourself.

The matter is this. For 8 years I have received a handsome salary from the "Century" people to act as their agent over here.[1] The work has dwindled, they have grown more and more exclusively American in their ways of editing, and finally (in the kindest and most considerate way possible, for they are very generous people) they have let me know that I shall not be wanted any longer. There has been no quarrel, as far as money is concerned they are letting me down as lightly and slowly as could possibly be done, and they are extremely anxious that it should not be known or supposed that we have parted, which indeed we have not done.

[1] Gosse's first regular payment from *Century* seems to have been in November 1881, for £100; each succeeding year through 1886 he got £200; in 1887 he got £232; in 1888 and each succeeding year through 1893 he got £100; in 1894 he got £8.8.0, and that year he noted in his diary that the account was closed.

But I am in this dilemma. My income has been very seriously diminished, and yet I am not permitted to go out into the market-place and ask for work. The American magazines have got to think of me as wedded to the "Century", and make me no offers.

Now, it struck me that if I might so far presume on our old friendship as to take you into my confidence, you, with your great influence in New York, might perhaps be able to secure for me something occasional, if you knew I should be glad of it. A monthly literary letter, or anything of that kind, or an invitation to contribute to some magazine, like the "Forum",[2] for instance.

I feel as though it were indecent to make this appeal. But you will not misunderstand it, and above all you will not take any trouble about it. Only if apples are falling about, here is a mouth wide open for one. You know that I work rapidly and clearly. In that connection I permit myself to quote Mr. Roswell Smith's words in reference to my 8 years' agency for the "Century": "I take this occasion to say, after diligent inquiry in all departments of the business, that the service which you have rendered us has been wholly and entirely satisfactory." I, on my side, would testify to their great generosity and delicacy. I cannot speak too highly of their treatment of me.

I have taken a great liberty in writing to you in this way, my dear Stedman, but I think you will forgive it.

Ever yours sincerely

Edmund Gosse

[2] Gosse wrote several articles for the *Forum* between 1888 and 1891, mostly on controversial topics: "Has America Produced a Poet?" VI (October 1888), 176–186; "What is a Great Poet?" VII (April 1889), 175–184; "Making a Name in Literature," VIII (October 1889), 189–198; "The Limits of Realism in Fiction," IX (June 1890), 391–400; "Is Verse in Danger?" X (January 1891), 517–526. It is interesting to note how many of these were on subjects which had been a source of contention between Gosse and Howells or between Gosse and Gilder; apparently Gosse chose this opportunity to express his side of the matters in a formal and public way.

❧ 123. *Gosse to Moulton* ❧

29, Delamere Terrace, / Westbourne Square. [London] W.

27 December 1887

My dear Mrs. Moulton

Pray accept my thanks for the gift of your beautiful little selection of Marston's poems.[1] I am struck painfully by the extract from Rossetti's letter

[1] Philip Bourke Marston, *Garden Secrets* (Boston: Roberts, 1887). With biographical sketch by Louise Chandler Moulton.

on pp. 16–17.[2] Could anything be more cruel, more wanton, than to enflame the hopes of a boy with such monstrous praise as this? I am firmly convinced that a great part of the disappointment and disillusion of poor Philip's later years came from the unwholesome atmosphere in which his intellectual being was formed. In your very tender and affectionate preface I miss nothing but a phrase or two to show—what I am sure you must feel—your disapproval of this unhealthy exaggeration. I look back, myself, to that circle of twenty years ago[3] with a mingled sense of admiration and horror,—admiration of its strenuous ideal of what literary work should be, horror at its sickly resignation of all the bonds of character, and its terrible air of personal bad-breeding.

But I am led too far, when all I meant to do was to thank you,—who will always seem to me to have been Philip's true guardian Fay or better Genius, —for your delightful and attractive selection from his poems.

Yours sincerely

Edmund Gosse

[2] The quotation from Rossetti's letter appears in Mrs. Moulton's introductory chapter (see n. 1): "Only yesterday evening I was reading your 'Garden Secrets' to William Bell Scott, who fully agreed with me that it is not too much to say of them that they are worthy of Shakespeare in his subtlest lyrical moods."

[3] For Gosse's relationships with Rossetti and the Pre-Raphaelites see Charteris, *Life and Letters of Gosse*, pp. 25, 32–38, etc.

❧ 124. *Gosse to Armour* ❧

Board of Trade. [London] S.W.

16 January 1888

My dear Armour

We were very glad indeed to hear from you this morning, for one never can learn the lesson that No news is mostly good news, and we have been in a crescendo state of anxiety. The news you do give us is rather encouraging, except that we do not at all like the idea of the instant exile to Calumet Avenue. But your whole horizon is clouded just now,[1] and all that one can say is that one rejoices to know that your own particular family—your inner holy of holies—keeps well and happy.

[1] This is conceivably a reference to the sense of crisis induced, especially in business circles, by President Cleveland's call for drastic tariff revisions, in his annual message to Congress in December 1887.

Not much has happened since you left us. The worst news is that Cotter Morison,[2] whose health has long been failing, has now completely broken down. His death, indeed, is now a question of days. I saw him, for half an hour at a time, three times last week. I am going there again this afternoon, but each time I see him he is so much altered, so visibly shrunken, that I am afraid next time to find the blinds drawn down. It is very painful to watch the eclipse of a mind so exceptionally bright and alert. He is still bright, but only in flashes, and is so overwhelmed with weakness and tiredness and nausea, that one merely wonders he can be so fairly patient and wholly affectionate as he is. He was reading Addison's Tour in Italy the other day when I went in, in the original huge quarto edition of Tickell, because of the great letters of the type. He talked about the book and the man and the age for a little in his old sage luminous way, and then the little stream of talk sunk into the sands, the sands of his symptoms and his pains. All his life he has very keenly followed Theological inquiry, and has taken, as you know, a prominent position among the Positivists. Now that he is dying, he exhibits no interest in these subjects at all, never refers to religion in any form, and shows no desire to see even the priests of his own sect. Literature and his friends, and the wish to live in this warm world, are the only things left to him apparently. But I ought not to trouble you with all this about a man who is a stranger to you. But he is on my mind all the time. I shall never cease to regret that I never brought you and him together: he was (alas! I have written *was*) a man whom you would have appreciated. In certain ways I shall never see his like again.

Since I saw you I have been going on pretty steadily with my Eighteen [sic] Century book.[3] I hope, by the way, you got and appreciated Saintsbury's vol. ?[4] There would be things in it, no doubt, to which you would demur, but I think you would approve the general air of thoroughness, the courageous critical position, and something nutty in the style—which however is far from perfect. I have got to Junius and Wilkes in my volume, so you see that I sight land, for I stop about 1780. But I have the concluding chapter to write, and this is the most difficult in the whole.

Already I am making collections for my Life of Congreve.[5] But there is so little material that I am dismayed. I find G. Montagu telling Horace Walpole that he has been looking over, in Dublin, a multitude of Congreve's

[2] James Augustus Cotter Morison (1832–1888), the English biographer and miscellaneous writer, was on the staff of the *Saturday Review*, where most of his essays appeared. He subsequently devoted his time to philosophical writing, and was a leading disciple of Comte's Positivism.

[3] Gosse, *History of Eighteenth Century Literature (1660–1780)* (London: Macmillan, 1889).

[4] George Saintsbury, *History of Elizabethan Literature* (London and New York: Macmillan, 1887). See Letter 129, n. 3.

[5] Gosse, *Life of William Congreve* (London: Walter Scott, 1888).

letters.[6] Where can these be now? For I find a plentiful lack of correspondence, and what is biography without it?

I desire to be so bold, although unknown to her, as to send my respects to Madam Armour. To Mrs. George, and to George and to Norman I must positively send nothing less than my love.

Ever my dear friend am I

Yours sincerely

Edmund Gosse

[6] See W. S. Lewis and Ralph S. Brown, Jr., eds., *Horace Walpole's Correspondence with George Montagu* (London: Oxford University Press; New Haven: Yale University Press, 1941), II, 28 and n. The "vast collection" of letters mentioned by Montagu, writing in May 1762, has apparently been lost.

∾ 125. *Gosse to Holmes* ∾

29 Delamere Terrace / London W.

1 September 1888

My dear Dr. Holmes

I have just made a discovery of no small importance and interest to myself, which I cannot help hoping you will also deign to be interested in. You have perhaps seen the notice of the death of my poor Father?[1] He was a man very much isolated from human affairs; his first wife (my Mother) died in my infancy, and my Father never happened to tell me anything whatever about her parentage. But among his papers I have found her full pedigree. By both grandfather and grandmother on the mother's side I am pure Massachusetts, and I descend directly from the Rev. John Hancock, Minister of Lexington.

My mother, Emily Bowes, was the daughter of William Bowes (baptized at Brattle St. Meeting House in 1771) and Hannah Troutbeck of Boston (born 1768). My great-grandfather, William Bowes, of Boston, (born 1734), married 1) Mary Stoddard and 2) Anne Whitney. My great-great-grandfather, Nicholas Bowes, of Boston, (b. 1706, took his M.A. at Harvard 1723) married Lucy Hancock, oldest child of John Hancock of Lexington.

My great-great-grandmother, then, was the aunt of Governor Hancock, and therefore, by marriage, of Dorothy Quincy. Is not this your Dorothy Q.?[2]

[1] Philip Henry Gosse died on 23 August 1888.
[2] Dorothy Quincy, the subject of Holmes's poem, "Dorothy Q.," was the aunt of the

I must not weary you; but I am so entirely delighted to find the true blue blood of Boston, unadulterated from colonial times, flowing in my veins, that I feel bound to tell you. I have told no one else, as yet, in America. Surely I am the most Massachusetts man-of-letters England has attempted to produce since 1775? I am prouder than if I had traced myself back to belted Earls.

Forgive my tiresome egotism, and believe me

With great respect

Affectionately yours

Edmund Gosse

American patriot Josiah Quincy; Gosse here confuses her with her niece, the Dorothy Quincy who married Governor Hancock.

ꙮ 126. *Gosse to Gilder* ꙮ

29, Delamere Terrace, / Westbourne Square. [London] W.
Confidential   11 January 1889
My dear Gilder

Of the three names you suggest for Bryce, two are absolutely impossible. You do not know Mr. Gladstone[1] if you suppose that anything on earth would induce the most autocratic of party politicians to write about the career of a man to whom he extends his finger from time to time with amiable patronage. In a lesser degree, but not less completely (even more completely) the hierarchy of party-rank makes it absolutely out of the question that John Morley should write about a man whom he would regard as a promising subaltern.

There remains Sir John Playfair,[2] whom I have asked. I have very slight hopes of his acceding. I wonder whom you would like me to ask next. I think it should be some one out of politics, a good writer and an intimate personal friend; the person who occurs to me is Sir Frederick Pollock,[3] who, I think, would probably consent. Owing to a variety of circumstances, the number of competent people willing to undertake this particular task is very

[1] William Ewart Gladstone (1809–1898), the statesman, was at this time in opposition.

[2] Gosse presumably means Sir Lyon Playfair: see Letter 47, n. 4.

[3] Sir Frederick Pollock (1845–1937), the noted English jurist, author of books on law and philosophy, including *The Principles of Contract* (1876) and *Spinoza, His Life and Philosophy* (1880).

much smaller than you would suppose.[4] Bryce,—who is one of the best of men, and a man whom I thoroughly like,—is not popular over here.

I await your reply.

Ever yours sincerely

Edmund Gosse

[4] Gosse eventually wrote the article himself (see Letter 129).

∾ 127. *Gosse to Howells* ∾

29 Delamere Terrace / London / W.

30 January 1889

My dear Friend

I take your good, gracious and kindly words in February's *Harper*[1] as a personal greeting. Oddly enough in January's *Fortnightly* I permitted myself a little friendly word about you.[2] It is sad that in the toil and bustle of life we find so little opportunity of crossing words with one another. But Nellie and I often talk of you, and always with grateful affection. How we laughed! Shall we ever laugh so loudly and so long again? I don't find very much to laugh about now.

Well! I am glad you bear me still in mind, and I am proud of your praise.

Ever affectionately yours

Edmund Gosse

[1] *Harper's Monthly*, LXXVIII (February 1889), 489; Howells's "Editor's Study" contains a bantering discussion of Gosse's *Forum* article, "Has America Produced a Poet?" (see Letter 122, n. 2).
[2] Gosse, "Ibsen's Social Dramas," *Fortnightly Review*, LI (January 1889), 107–121. He mentions Howells only once: "The critic who is bored with Tolstoi, who cannot understand what Howells is aiming at, and who sees nothing but what is 'improper' in Guy de Maupassant, will not be able to put up with Ibsen."

∾ 128. *Howells to Gosse* ∾

330 East 17th St., N[ew] Y[ork]

24 February 1889

My dear Gosse:

I was perfectly delighted to get your lovely note, and I immediately went to the expense of the February Fortnightly—pirated edition—so as to see what you had said of me. It was richly worth the money; and I am very proud and thankful. I have to take my humility in both hands in order to ⟨keep⟩ a place so far above the salt.

I'm especially obliged to you for writing about Ibsen[1] just now, and for being what Mrs. Howells calls so informatory, for we've just been reading his wonderful plays, and wanted to know all about him. Perry tells me (from Paris) that there's a regular Ibsen boom in Germany. No, black care has not left so much laugh in me as there used to be, but I don't abide your being less gay so patiently. Our poor Winny is a wreck of health and youth —sick for years yet to come, I'm afraid. John is in Harvard, a Sophomore, and Pilla is here with us studying art. She was lately at Boston, where she almost danced herself dead, and has been slowly resuscitating since she came home. She is nearly seventeen and I nearer fifty-two. Doesn't it seem absurd for a contemporary to have got past the half century in that way? I never can make it seem right. They celebrated Lowell's 70th. birthday at the Tavern Club[2] on the 22nd.

When we lived in Cambridge, an old gentleman came 80, and a lady sent him 80 English violets. These graceful acts console us for the loss of youth.

Our principle is against going out, and Mrs. Howells really doesn't, but she drives me forth, and acquires merit with her own conscience while she stores up a just contempt for my inconsistency. In this way I see a good deal of society. Every body has an evening, and as there are about 1,500,000 people in New York, you can imagine how many evenings there are in a week. For instance this is Stedman's evening, and so is it Huttons. I ought to go both, but I shall not. Which would *you* go to?

I suppose if I were not old and sore and sad I should like life here. It's very simple and irresponsible, and hell seems farther than at Boston, because people agree not to think about it.

I wonder if you'll care to read my N[ew] Y[ork] story that's coming out in Harpers Weekly soon?[3]

The family join me in love to both [of] you. Farewell. Drop a giggle now and then to the thought of

Your faithful

W. D. Howells

[1] See Letter 127, n. 2.

[2] For the Tavern Club, see Letter 76, n. 1.

[3] Howells's "New York Story" was *A Hazard of New Fortunes* (New York: Harper, 1890) published serially in *Harper's Weekly*, XXXIII (March–November, 1889).

✣ 129. *Gosse to Gilder* ✣

[London?]

7 March 1889

My dear Gilder

I am in despair about Bryce.[1] You know that Sir Frederick Pollock under-
took to write it. When Bryce came back he saw him at once, and the result
was that Pollock wrote to me to say he could not do it. I immediately saw
Bryce, and found him rather obstinate. He had refused to help Pollock in
any way, and he said to me that he would give nobody any information at
all. Well, then I had a shot at John Morley. In vain! Then at Augustine
Birrell,[2] who refused by return of post. Then Saintsbury,[3] who took it up
for a day or two, and then wrote to decline. Then Stopford Brooke,[4] who
refused at once. Then Fred Myers,[5] ditto. Then Canon Creighton, who
agreed to do it, and actually went to Oxford to see what he could pick up.
He writes this morning to say that he can make nothing of it.

I can really think of nothing now, but to propose that I should write you
about 1500 words myself, *not signed*, to accompany the picture.[6] It is evident
to me that nobody will deal with Bryce, in the way you wish. Let me hear
your wishes in the matter.

Yours very sincerely

Edmund Gosse

[1] See Letter 126.

[2] Augustine Birrell (1850–1933), the English barrister, politician, and writer. He
was a Liberal M.P. from 1889 to 1900 and from 1906 to 1918, and Chief Secretary for
Ireland from 1907 to 1916. His books include *Obiter Dicta* (1884) and *Frederick
Locker-Lampson* (1920), a biographical study of his father-in-law.

[3] George Edward Bateman Saintsbury (1845–1933), the distinguished critic and
historian of literature.

[4] Stopford Augustus Brooke (1832–1916), Irish clergyman and writer, was appointed chaplain to Queen Victoria in 1872, but in 1880 he left the Church and became a Unitarian minister. He was a brilliant preacher, and several volumes of his
sermons were published; he also wrote studies of Shakespeare, Browning, and Tennyson.

[5] Frederic William Henry Myers (1843–1901), the poet and critic; with Henry
Sidgwick and others he founded the Society for Psychical Research in 1882.

[6] [Gosse], "Professor James Bryce, M.P.," *Century*, XXXIX (January 1890),
470–472. The article was signed "X."

〜 130. *Gosse to Gilder* 〜

Board of Trade. [London] S.W.

16 April 1889

My dear Gilder

Almost as soon as this letter reaches you, you will have a visit from Mr. S. S. McClure,[1] the founder of the Associated Literary Press, whom you already know. He will tell you that about 6 weeks ago he invited me to help him editorially with the English part of his business.[2] I told him at once that for the last ten years I had served the "Century Co." in a confidential capacity, and that I had received such constant kindness from yourself and Mr. Roswell Smith, and took so much personal interest in your splendid enterprise, that I could do nothing without your sanction, nor anything that would interfere with your interests. You will see, by talking with him, that what services he demands from me will interfere in no degree with such now attenuated help as it is my privilege to render to the "Century Co.", but I want to have this put very plainly before you, and in such terms as admit of no uncertainty.

I have formed an extremely high opinion of Mr. McClure['s] genius and future, and I feel it a great privilege to throw in my lot with him. I think his ideas are of great breadth and importance, and I have no doubt that you, with your own views and experience, think so too.

Let me have a line from you on this subject and believe me

Ever sincerely Thine

Edmund Gosse

[1] Samuel S. McClure (1857–1949) emigrated to the United States from Ireland. In 1884 he founded the Associated Literary Press and in 1893 *McClure's Magazine*, of which he later became the editor. In *My Autobiography* (London: John Murray, 1914) p. 208, McClure says that it was Gosse who suggested the name of *McClure's Magazine*.

[2] Gosse at this time became London editor for McClure's Associated Literary Press, a newspaper syndicate devoted to providing the literary press in America and England with "literary contributions of high quality by the best writers, including novels and short stories, critical essays, popular sciences and records of travel and adventure." The service was announced as beginning on 14 September 1889, and in a brochure dated August 1889 the following are named: "S. S. McClure, Proprietor: Edmund Gosse, General European Editor: Robert McClure, London Manager: Frances Hodgson Burnett, editor of Youth's Department." Gosse's income from this venture increased steadily and then declined sharply: in 1889 he received £50; in 1890, £75; in 1891, £100; in 1892 he dropped to £25; in subsequent years he received nothing. In a letter of 16 April 1889 (a.l.s., PU) Gosse asked Armour to let McClure visit him in Chicago, and to write his impressions: "I want you to be kind to him while he is in Chicago, and to give him there any social help he may require. And I want you to talk freely with him, and to give me your impressions of him."

❧ 131. *Gosse to Gilder* ❧

Board of Trade. [London] S.W.

24 June 1889

Dear Gilder

I was the first person in this country to see Dr. Nansen,[1] the Greenland explorer. I thought you would like to secure him, so I cabled to you. Your reply mystifies me—you say "Century has already secured Nansen". Now Dr. Nansen himself positively denies this. He now says, what he did not tell me before, that he has had a letter from some one—he does not remember who—asking him to write for some magazine—he thinks it may be the "Century"; but declares that he has not answered it, and is certainly not secured by you.[2]

Under these circumstances, sorely tempted as I am to wire you again on the subject, it seems better, perhaps, not to do so. All I could do, and this I have done, is to beg Dr. Nansen to look up the letter, and if it is from you to answer it, if he can, in the affirmative. But he was *in my hands* when I wired you, and if you had chosen to encourage me, I could have got anything out of him which you liked to ask. Moral —?

Yours

E. G.

[1] Fridtjof Nansen (1861–1930), the famous Norwegian explorer and humanitarian. In 1888 Nansen made the first crossing of Greenland from east to west, and subsequently wrote of his experiences there, in *The First Crossing of Greenland* (1890).

[2] Nansen did not write for *Century*, but see his article, "A New Route to the North Pole," *Forum*, XI (August 1891), 693–709.

❧ 132. *Gosse to Howells* ❧

29, Delamere Terrace, / Westbourne Square. [London] W.

8 January 1890

My dear Howells

I took away with me into the country at Christmas only one book—"An Indian Summer"[1]—which it happens I never before read. I feel forced to write and tell you how much it has charmed me, what a quintessence of delicate wit and tenderness and matured wisdom I find in it. A most beautiful book, indeed, combining the freshness of youth with the strength of maturity.

[1] Howells, *Indian Summer* (Boston: Ticknor, 1886).

Henry James comes here every week, and we generally speak of you. Every one in this house is taught to love you—I hope you know that. My wife has lost her mother this winter. It has made us rather grave than actually sad, perhaps, through these gloomy iron weeks.

Affectionately yours

Edmund Gosse

✑ 133. *Gosse to Field*[1] ✑

29, Delamere Terrace, / Westbourne Square. [London] W.

21 October 1890

Dear Sir

In reply to your obliging letter, I do not like to say no to your request. At the same time, I can imagine the translating of perfunctory German odes on the bigness of America to be a burden not endurable. All I think I can say is, that if any German and Norse pieces are in due time forthcoming which seem to me to be in any sense poetry, and translatable, I will be glad to try my hand on them.

Permit me to thank you for the courtesy of your note, and to remain

Dear Sir

Yours faithfully

Edmund Gosse

[1] Eugene Field (1850–1895), the American humorist, had written to Gosse from South Kensington on 16 October 1890 (a.l.s., BC). Using Stedman's name as an introduction, Field explained that he was acting on behalf of the Chicago *Daily News*, which was seeking European tributes to the greatness of America for publication in 1892 in connection with the four-hundredth anniversary of Columbus's arrival; he wanted to know if Gosse would be willing to undertake the translation of any poems by German or Scandinavian writers which might be submitted.

✑ 134. *Holmes to Gosse* ✑

Boston,

27 November 1890

My dear Mr. Gosse,

I have waited too long before thanking you for your very kind message of congratulation on my birthday, August 29th. I wanted to send you [my]

new book[1] which is ready at last, and of which I hope you will receive a copy at the same time that you get this note.

I need not ask you to look into its pages indulgently,—I know you will. Do not think yourself bound to read it or to write a formal note of thanks for it. I will take it for granted that you had something better to do than to give your time to one of these occupations or to waste your phrases on the other.

Always faithfully and affectionately Yours,

Oliver Wendell Holmes

---

[1] Holmes, *Over the Teacups* (Boston and New York: Houghton Mifflin, 1891). Holmes inscribed the book: "Edmund Gosse With the kind regards and affectionate remembrances of Oliver Wendell Holmes November 27th 1890." See Cox, *The Library of Edmund Gosse*, p. 147.

∾ 135. *Gosse to Gilder* ∾

29 Delamere Terrace / [London] W.

24 January 1891

My dear Gilder

I am bursting a long-preparing shell upon you today. By this post I send you, done up like a book, a novel called *Benefits Forgot*,[1] the author of which is an American, now resident in London, but long resident in your West.[2] I have read this book, and I fear to exaggerate if I tell you how highly I think of it. It is extremely American, extremely racy, of the new school; it has, it seems to me, all the qualities which I should expect from the first book of a new man of real importance.

The name of the author is probably well known to you, and he has allowed me to make the first and only offer of his book to you on the express understanding that this name should not be given up to you till you have read the book. Then, it is as you will. But for the present all I am to tell you is that *Benefits Forgot* is the first long story of a new American author, who would rather see his book in the *Century* than anywhere else.

I am
Dear Gilder
Ever yours sincerely

Edmund Gosse

---

[1] Wolcott Balestier, *Benefits Forgot* (London: Heinemann, 1893; New York: Appleton, 1894). See Letter 140, n. 3.

[2] For the author, Wolcott Balestier, see Letter 138 and n. 1.

ೆ 136. *Gosse to Armour* ೆ

29, Delamere Terrace, / Westbourne Square. [London], W.

31 January 1891

My dear G[eorge] A[llison] A[rmour]

I have twice lately had signs of your goodness—first a lovely Grolier Milton[1] (a perfect gem of typography) and second a charming little volume of Sherman's verses.[2] Thank you much for them and for the goodness which thought of me.

It is just a month, I think, since I wrote to you a New Year's letter from Marley. The month has been very quiet and busy. The Rider Haggards[3] leaving, as probably you know, for Mexico, we took in their son Jock, a very intelligent boy about the size of our Philip. He brought germs of the measles with him, and he and our two youngest verily developed the disease,—Teresa, being fortunately away at the Alma Tademas, has missed it. So that has kept my wife busy, but we have got through it and all are fumigated now and out of this little state of quarantine. Have your children had the measles?

Mrs. Brightwen[4] was asking about you last week. She was genuinely sorry to miss you, but looks forward to seeing both Mrs. Armour and yourself when you are here in the spring. How nice that will be; we often speak of it.

What charming books your Grolier Club produces! I look upon them as on the whole the most satisfactory pieces of printers' work now being made in the world. What are they going to do next? I tell you what would be a very interesting thing for them to undertake,—a reprint of Sir Thomas Browne's "Urn Burial". If they added "The Garden of Cyrus" to it (as in the original edition) that would make an exquisite little book. Do you not think you might suggest this to them? A good edition of The "Urn Burial" is one of the principal disiderata of literature at this moment.

What do you think of Stevenson's "Ballads"?[5] I confess we are all dis-

---

[1] *Areopagitica: A Speech of Mr. John Milton . . .*, Intro. James Russell Lowell (New York: The Grolier Club, 1890).

[2] Frank Dempster Sherman, *Lyrics for a Lute* (Boston and New York: Houghton Mifflin, 1890); in a letter to Clinton Scollard of 6 June 1886 (a.l.s., YU) Gosse mentions having met Sherman (1860–1916) while he was in America.

[3] Sir Henry Rider Haggard (1856–1925), the English novelist, author of *King Solomon's Mines* (1886) and *She* (1887).

[4] Gosse's aunt, Mrs. Brightwen, lived at Great Stanmore, Middlesex. The Armours stayed nearby in the summer of 1887 and Gosse wrote to Armour on 24 June 1887 (a.l.s., PU) to say that he had asked his aunt to call on them. She was, he said, "a very sweet and a very intelligent woman, full of all sorts of ingenious cleverness, and with a great sense of humour. She is one of the people I have known longest and loved best in the world." At the same time, "her condition and temperament have combined to induce in her a morbid religiousness, and excess of evangelical zeal, which it is only fair that I should forewarn you of."

[5] Robert Louis Stevenson, *Ballads* (London: Chatto and Windus, 1890).

appointed here. The effort to become a Polynesian Walter Scott is a little too obvious, the inspiration a little too mechanical. And,—between you and me and Lake Michigan,—the versification is atrocious. Nor is his prose above reproach. There has been a good deal of disappointment among the few who have read the approaching "South Sea Letters".[6] The fact seems to be that it is very nice to *live* in Samoa, but not healthy to *write* there. Within a three-mile radius of Charing Cross is the literary atmosphere, I suspect.

Kipling,[7] our last much over-advertised but not I think over-appreciated genius goes on. He is a thorough artist, absorbed in his work, a little maddened but not poisoned yet by praise, and wants but health to be astoundingly great. You would be struck with him.

Our love to you all. *Do* write to me. You know there are very few people to whom I would say that.

Affectionately yours

E. G.

[6] Stevenson, *The South Seas: A Record of Three Cruises* (London: Cassell, 1890).
[7] Rudyard Kipling (1865–1936), recently returned to England from India, was already famous although only in his middle twenties.

❧ 137. *Harland*[1] *to Gosse* ❧

144, Cromwell Road, / [London] S.W.

Friday [1 May 1891][2]

Dear Mr Gosse:

I can't begin to tell you how much pleasure it gave me, the letter from you which I found here upon coming home rather late last night. That a busy literary man should sit down and *read* a poor three-volume novel,[3] let alone *write* discriminatingly of it, is more than a fellow has any right to expect.

[1] Henry Harland (1861–1905) began his literary career by writing novels about Jewish immigrants under the pseudonym "Sidney Luska." In 1890, however, he came to Europe, where he became a leader of the Aesthetic Movement and, in 1894, the editor of the *Yellow Book*. He was Stedman's godson, and there are several references to him in Stedman and Gould, *Life and Letters of Stedman* (e.g., II, 97, 320, 325, 358, 382).
[2] Harland rarely dated his letters. The date for this is taken from the postmark on an attached envelope. In this and other such cases, internal evidence suggests that the envelopes were those in which the letters were mailed, though absolute certainty is of course impossible.
[3] Henry Harland, *Mea Culpa: A Woman's Last Word* (London: Heinemann, 1891).

I am heartily glad that you were able to find some good in the performance; though I think I thank you more for pointing out the bad. That was
harder to do, and I take it as a token of friendship. Criticism coming from
you I should always especially weigh and prize; and in this case I can say
at once that your opinion seems to me entirely just. The story does degener-
ate into melodrama: and of all literary pinchbeck, melodrama is the variety
which I personally detest the most. Of course I didn't realise that my
puppets were becoming melodramatic while I was "whittling" at them; but
I realise it all too clearly now.

Alas poor Julian![4] he is indeed a pitiable shadow, though I wore away
pounds of my own flesh and blood, trying to give him *soul*. Léonticheff too
I fear is a failure—I had great hopes of him in the beginning. I'm afraid
Armidis is the only one of the lot who can in any sense be held to hang together, and even of him I'm not very certain.

Anyhow, I thank you very much for your letter; next time I'll try to do
better. Try, indeed! but succeed . . .?

Faithfully yours

H. Harland

[4] The names in this paragraph are those of characters in the novel.

ꙮ 138. *Gosse to Gilder* ꙮ

Board of Trade. [London] S.W.

4 June 1891

Private.

My dear Gilder

I am very glad you liked Balestier[1] and are struck with the value of his
work. I think it very courageous of you to be ready to publish the Kipling-
Balestier novel,[2] but I think your courage will be crowned with success.
Balestier's talent is extraordinary, but I wish, like you, that he could be

[1] Charles Wolcott Balestier (1861–1891), American author and publisher, came to
England in 1888 as the representative of an American publishing house. He was a
young man of unusual charm and soon made many friends, among them Gosse and
Henry James. His name, and the names of his sisters Caroline and Josephine, appear
many times in the Book of Gosse in 1889 and the years immediately following. Balestier became especially friendly with Rudyard Kipling and they collaborated in the
novel, *The Naulahka* (see n. 2 below); Kipling married Caroline Balestier in 1892
(see Letter 141).

[2] *The Naulahka* first appeared in serial form in the *Century*, XLIII (November
1890–April 1891); it was published in book form the following year (London and
New York: Macmillan, 1892).

taken away from business. I don't think it helps him any way, and it distracts his energies.

You will want to print my Kipling article[3] in the October No. I presume, as you begin the novel in November? I have put aside everything else for it, and mean to write you the very best study of this remarkable phenomenon that I can. But, deary me, if I might really say what I know on that subject, and "how it strikes a contemporary", the *Century Magazine* would hum around for one number, and then kind of collapse. Kipling is one of the most extraordinary beings ever created, out of Naples or Malacca. He is like an infant might be that smoked manilla cigars all day and was none the worse; or a tarn among the mountains with a volcano concealed underneath; or lots of other incongruous things. What he really and soberly is most like, I suppose, is the child of god-fearing dissenting parents who has run away and enlisted in a thoroughly blackguard cavalry regiment. Only that does not account for the Malay element and a suspicion of knives whipped into your vitals. Not a commonplace young gentleman, Mr. R. K., nor do I suppose that anyone has a sweeter or more deferential smile and a more awful use of language, both at the same time on tap.

His conversation and company fascinate me horribly, but they are in their effects, like long potations of green chartreuse. They make one's hand tremble and one's eyes see visions. All this has nothing to do with his books, which are quite ordinary by the side of himself, because he is not allowed to talk in print of the things he has seen and known and grown bold in.

Ever yours, my dear Gilder

Edmund Gosse

[3] Gosse, "Rudyard Kipling," *Century*, XLII (October 1891), 901–910.

❧ 139. *Gilder to Gosse* ❧

[New York]

7 December 1891

My dear Gosse:–

I am terribly grieved at the news that has come this morning of the death of Balestier.[1] I did not know him very well personally, as you are aware, but

[1] Wolcott Balestier died in Dresden on 6 December 1891. Gosse and James both wrote substantial obituary articles: Gosse, "Wolcott Balestier," *Century*, XLIII (April 1892), 923–926; James, "Wolcott Balestier," *Cosmopolitan*, XIII (May 1892), 43–47. Gosse also had his essay privately printed in the form of a pamphlet.

in my whole editorial life I have seldom been so profoundly interested in the beginnings of a career,—and this sudden stop of everything is overwhelmingly afflicting. What it must be to those who were nearer and dearer to him I can easily imagine.

He not only showed genius, but that patience and conscientiousness which are among the most valuable attributes of genius. His ambition was refined and noble, and seemed to grow with his capacity to express himself with satisfaction. He always wanted to do better, as the very last letters and proofs from him show. He had the artist's passion for perfection, and notwithstanding the excellence of his performance already, I anticipated for him even higher achievements. Everyone in the office is miserably sad. I cannot write any more about it today.

All this makes us tremble for Johnson,[2] though he at least is at home where the very best nursing bears him up.

Sincerely

R. W. Gilder

[2] Robert Underwood Johnson (see Letter 6, n. 7) had been seriously ill with typhoid for some time (information from Johnson's daughter, Mrs. Frank Holden).

❧ 140. *Gosse to Gilder* ❧

29, Delamere Terrace, / Westbourne Square. [London] W.

22 December 1891

My dear Gilder

I am very much obliged to you for your most kind and sympathetic letter about our poor dear Wolcott. The event has completely overwhelmed me, and has involved me, too, in an immense deal of writing and business. I know not how to get on without him,—without his sympathy, his energy, his encouragement.

His posthumous works will be brought out here by Heinemann after they have passed thro' your hands. I suppose you have his admirable latest story of "Captain, My Captain".[1] What shall you do about "Home", which he partly revised, I think, after you sent it back?

My little memoir for you[2] will be ready shortly. It is terribly hard to write it.

[1] This story was included in a posthumous collection: Wolcott Balestier, *The Average Woman: A Common Story; Reffey; Captain, My Captain!* With a biographical sketch by Henry James (London: Heinemann, 1892).

[2] See Letter 139, n. 1.

If you want a good portrait to engrave, apply to Cox[3] in your city. He took some admirable ones.

We are having a wretched Christmas. And are so anxious, too, to hear news of Johnson.

Ever yours sincerely

Edmund Gosse

[3] A portrait of Balestier, taken from a photograph by G. C. Cox, accompanies the first installment of "Benefits Forgot" in *Century*, XLV (December 1892), 192. The novel was serialized in eleven installments, from December 1892 to October 1893.

141. *Gosse to Gilder*

[London?]

18 January 1892

My Dear Gilder

Rudyard Kipling was hurried into matrimony, like a rabbit into its hole, this afternoon.[1] At 2.8 the cortège (a party of eight persons in all) entered the Church, and at 2.20 left it, the sharpest thing of modern times. Henry James gave away the bride and I supported the bridegroom. Having committed the deed, like clever criminals, they went into lodgings immediately round the corner. Rudyard appeared from the vestry to tell us that they had sent a child of fifteen (meaning the curate) to marry them, but having peeped in again, consoled us that "he looks as pretty as pie-crust now he's in his petticoats". Both bridegroom and bride are possessed by a very devil of secrecy and mystery, and hope that no one will ever know of the event. But trust the newspaper reporters.

It is Caroline of course, not pretty Josephine, who is now "Mrs. R. K."

Ever yours,

E. G.

[1] Kipling and Caroline Balestier were married on 18 January 1892 at All Soul's Langham Place. For the relationship between Kipling and the Balestier family, see C. E. Carrington, *Rudyard Kipling: His Life and Work* (London: Macmillan, 1955), Chapter IX, "Kipling and the Balestiers," pp. 175–196. In his account of the wedding (p. 193) Carrington says that the couple went to Brown's Hotel two days after the wedding, since Carrie had to look after her mother, who was suffering from influenza.

142. *Gosse to Gilder*

Board of Trade. / [London] S.W.

10 February 1892

My dear Gilder

The proofs of the March "Century" have just reached me, and I have read your poem on Paderewski's playing[1] with such extreme pleasure that I must write and tell you so. I think this is one of the most beautiful poems you have written, so sinuous and languishing in the plaintive parts, so fiery and rapturous in the vehement ones, and altogether so aptly suggestive of the whole business of the player's execution. A most exquisite tribute of one artist to another, of one art to another.

I hope you remain well. We try to keep on, in spite of Things.

With kindest regards

Yours very sincerely

Edmund Gosse

[1] Gilder, "How Paderewski Plays," *Century*, XLIII (March 1892), 727.

143. *Furness to Gosse*

222 West Washington Square [Philadelphia]

29 March 1892

By this same mail, my dear Gosse, I send you a newspaper containing the news of the departure of our old friend in Camden.[1]

Let us hope that he is now more favourably situated than erstwhile for giving a 'yawp over the roofs of the world.' I should be sorry to think that the yawp would reverberate through our cellars.

I'm not sure that the very best of Walt was not his Jovian looks. Latterly when I used to see him in his room, with that majestic avalanche of a beard flowing in snowy luxuriance over his broad chest, it was not hard to convert his blue wrapper into blue sky and the vast and innumerable newspapers piled knee deep around him in the clouds of Olympus. And, oh, the lot of funny stories about him, gossip pure and simple but nourishing, which 'twould take too long to write and must be reserved for the pleasant time

[1] Walt Whitman died on 26 March 1892.

when you and I can ha'e a crack thegither [sic]. 'When will that be? say the bells of Stepney.'

Yours, dear lad, as ever
Horace Howard Furness

ᘓ 144. *Gosse to Gilder* ᘓ

29, Delamere Terrace, / Westbourne Square. [London] W.

27 April 1892

My dear Gilder

I have received your letter about Alma Tadema. After a great deal of reflection I can think of no one to propose better than my wife. She was Tadema's pupil and assistant in the old times, and thoroughly understands his mode of work. She writes nicely, and has of late written a good deal anonymously on modern art in "The Saturday Review" and the "Academy". I would, of course, superintend and revise. I think this is really the best way of getting a good account of Tadema's methods and views, as he is very restive and difficult with strangers.

If you like to encourage Mrs. Gosse, she would write (say) 7000 words, and submit the article to you.[1] It would not be fair to expect you to take it without seeing it. I suppose you would like to secure as many original illustrations as possible? Mrs. Gosse could certainly do that better than any one, as she and Tadema are on such an intimate footing.

Please let me know.

Ever yours sincerely
Edmund Gosse

[1] Ellen Gosse, "Laurens Alma-Tadema," *Century*, XLVII (February 1894), 483–497.

ᘓ 145. *Gilder to Gosse* ᘓ

[New York]

26 December 1893

My dear Gosse:—

Your recent delightful letter was a pleasure to me. I would not have been alarmed at our friend's[1] somewhat bungling kindness were it not for his

[1] In a letter to Gosse of 30 October 1893 (carbon copy, GL), Gilder said that

official position, so to speak, which might enable him to whang the great drum in my interest in London, and to have a procession of military as well as of the citizens generally.

It looks very far off, my visit to the old town, and when I do come it will be as quiet as thought,—no dinners, or club receptions, or anything of that kind, I devoutly hope. I love my friends, but the more I love 'em the less I want to be a burden to them, as you well understand, I am sure.

I can never get over my great regret that you did not see the World's Fair.[2] I dare say if you had seen it, when you went back you would have (gained) a terrible reputation as a liar; but it would have been a comfort to us on this side, anyway, to know that we had a spokesman. You know they say that whenever an Indian comes from the plains to Washington and returns to his people, he is a lost man. No one will believe his accounts of the actual truth. I suppose you think we were all crazy about the Fair, but we were not. The world has never seen such a spectacle, and I doubt if it ever will within the outlook of the youngest inhabitant.

With all the best wishes in the world for the best season in the world, I am,

Very sincerely yours,

R. W. Gilder

P.S.—Dec. 26.—Your letter has just come. No we are not scared and our programme is Excellence!—Super excellence! Nothing but the hard times affects us, and that not nearly as much as it does some other businesses.

—I deeply appreciate all your kind expressions.

Douglas Sladen (1856–1947), the Australian writer, had written to say that when Gilder came to London he would be delighted to introduce Gilder to local literary figures and arrange an Authors' Club dinner in his honor. Gosse had given Sladen a letter of introduction to Gilder several years before (a.l.s., Gosse to Gilder, 7 October 1888, GP).

[2] Gilder's extraordinary enthusiasm for the Chicago World's Fair also appears in Letter 147 and in his letter of 30 October (see n. 1 above); see also Rosamond Gilder, *Letters of R. W. Gilder*, pp. 240–242.

ᘉ 146. *Gosse to Armour* ᘉ

29, Delamere Terrace, / Westbourne Square. [London] W.
2 December 1894

My dear George

I have received in perfect safety the exquisite copy of Lodge's "Wits' Misery", 1596, which you have so generously and so thoughtfully sent me.

It is indeed a treasure. The book is very rare in any state, and in such condition probably unique. At all events, the British Museum copy is not nearly so fine. You could not have made me a present that I should more thoroughly appreciate: I have been always longing, and without the least expectation of success, to have an original Lodge for my own.

Your budget of included papers was welcome, but I searched in vain for any scrap of your own writing. I shall appreciate "Poor Richard" when he comes. Chicago seems fast coming to the front in matters of bibliography.[1]

I suppose you know all about the changes in the *Saturday Review*. A second revolution happened about three weeks ago, when Frank Harris,[2] ex-cowboy, late of the *Fortnightly*, took over the S. R. and got rid of all the old staff. Fortunately, at that very moment, a new paper, *The Realm*,[3] was started, and to this many of us immediately repaired,—Lang, Traill, Alfred Austin and myself in particular. I am engaged to do a middle for them every week. It is a 3d paper. If it only lasts, it will be quite a boon, for I shall have a much freer hand than on the *S. R.*, which had grown crotchety and tiresome, as well as dull.

I am sending you my little biography of Pater, reprinted from this month's *Contemporary*.[4] I hope you will like it. Did my poems[5] reach you? I suppose they are out.

William Watson's new book[6] has been loudly puffed by the Bodley Head

---

[1] The Chicago edition has not been identified, but there was a fascimile of *Poor Richard's Almanack* published in New York in 1894 by the Duodecimos, with an introduction by John Bigelow.

[2] Frank Harris (1856–1931), the British-American writer and editor. He was born in Ireland, but went to New York at the age of fifteen, where he worked in a series of laboring jobs until he studied law at the University of Kansas in 1874. He later returned to England, and became a controversial editor of, successively, the *Evening News, Fortnightly Review, Saturday Review*, and in New York, *Vanity Fair*. He knew many important writers of his day, and wrote four series of provocative *Contemporary Portraits* (1915–1923). His autobiography, *My Life and Loves* (1922–1927), was banned as pornographic.

[3] *The Realm* was a short-lived periodical, running fifty-eight numbers, from 16 November 1894 to 20 December 1895 (Vols. I–III). In the first issue there is a signed poem by Alfred Austin, "A Dream of England," (p. 16) and a favorable review of Gosse's *In Russet and Silver* (p. 22). There are several "middle" articles; none of them is signed, but the one most likely to be by Gosse is entitled "Negligence in Literature" (pp. 13–14). Similarly, the second issue (23 November 1894) contains a "middle" entitled "The Responsibilities of Criticism" (pp. 55–56), which may also be by Gosse. Again, however, all articles are unsigned, and attribution to Gosse seems problematical.

[4] Gosse, "Walter Pater: A Portrait," *Contemporary Review*, LXVI (December 1894), 795–810. Gosse had the article privately reprinted.

[5] Gosse, *In Russet and Silver* (London: Heinemann, 1894).

[6] William Watson, *Odes and Other Poems* (London: John Lane, 1894). Watson (1858–1935) published several volumes of verse in the 1890's; he was knighted in 1917.

set, but is a great disappointment to his more serious admirers. Some of the odes are dignified, but there is no sign of advance, and the Tennysonian and Wordsworthian echoes are more obtrusive. John Davidson, on the other hand, has made quite a hit with his new volume of "Ballads"[7]—very unequal, but containing some superb things. We three are the only "potes" of the season as yet.

We are all quite well. I have been down in Norfolk, at the Marchioness of Lothian's house-party,[8] where pheasants were shot by day, and the fool was played at night. My aunt Brightwen has found in a forgotten portfolio, and has given to me, a collection of nearly 100 drawings by the Old Masters,—Dutch and late Italian. I should like to sell them, but I don't know who buys such things. Our girls are going to be confirmed, and are combining with that graceful exercise the toil of rehearsing Robert Bridges' play, "Achilles in Scyros",[9] which their school is going to act. I shall send you a play-bill of it! You should see Teresa, as Achilles, dancing about in a golden scaly garment which passes for a cuirass. The maidens of Scyros are to be excused if they thought her a soft female slip like themselves.

London has gone crazy about a diminutive draped woman, who asks the way at dead of night, and then stabs you in the eye![10] Servants won't take letters to the post or go a-shopping after dark. I delight at these outbreaks of multitudinous panic: they are the direct result of our ridiculous coddling civilisation.

Our love to you all.

Your affectionate

Edmund Gosse

[7] John Davidson, *Ballads and Songs* (London: John Lane; Boston: Copeland, 1894). John Davidson (1857–1909), the Scottish poet and playwright, is best remembered for his volume of poems, *Fleet Street Eclogues* (1893), and for several volumes of ballads.

[8] Shomberg Henry Kerr, tenth Marquess of Lothian (1833–1900), was Lord Rector of Edinburg University from 1887 to 1890; in 1865 he married Victoria Alexandrina Montagu-Douglas-Scott, daughter of the fifth Duke of Buccleuch. One of their residences was at Blickling Hall, near Aylsham, Norfolk. Their son, the eleventh marquess, became British ambassador to the United States, 1939–1940.

[9] Robert Bridges, *Achilles in Scyros* (London: Bell, 1892).

[10] This story may be related to the murder of a woman in Kensington, reported in the London *Times* for 27 November 1894, p. 11; according to this account, a "shoemaker's knife," about six to seven inches long, was found nearby and was presumed to be the instrument used in the murder.

꧁ 147. *Gilder to Gosse* ꧂

[New York]

24 January 1895

My dear Gosse,

Illness sometimes gives opportunity to stop and think. After finishing some of the most engrossing work of my life in the Tenement House Commission[1] I was taken—not down, but "to-house" with a suppressed Grippe.

And now I take a moment of convalescence to say—alas Stevenson![2]— and, again, I say thanks for your book;—and I add my thanks for that review[3]—which gave me a strange feeling—its kindness, its praise—from far off. Somehow I have felt that my rhymes were truly not desired by islanders;—I disapprove of the "international" note in literature— or at least in literary criticism; and it seems to me a mistake to be thinking of readers of another English-speaking, and -thinking, country in a foreign sense. But I fear it cannot be helped—and my rather confessional verse I would rather like to restrict to a home group;—i.e. to those who truly care for it—wherever in the world they may be, without any apparent reaching out for them. I have labored with my publisher and Mr. Unwin not to go through the vain form of publication abroad—but to no apparent purpose. —Such a note as you have sounded in the Review is therefore a welcome to a very shy guest.

I see no immediate chance of getting to London. But, now, when are *you* coming back: you yourself, or some of your tribe? I am longing for the old world. You might at least come over and talk about it with us. We are somewhat changed since you were here, and some things are worth looking up, perhaps: though I shall never quite get over your not seeing our incomparable group of exhibition buildings.[4] Nothing like it will ever be seen again in our lives, I fear.

Always sincerely
Yours

R. W. Gilder

[1] Gilder, always active in the cause of social reform, was chairman of a Committee of Investigation into tenement-house conditions which had been set up by the governor of New York in the spring of 1894. See Rosamond Gilder, *Letters of R. W. Gilder*, pp. 254–277.

[2] Robert Louis Stevenson had died on 3 December 1894.

[3] In an unsigned review of Gilder's *The Great Remembrance and Other Poems* (*Saturday Review*, LXXVIII [1 December 1894], 575). Gosse had praised his friend as the outstanding American poet below the age of fifty-five.

[4] See Letter 145, n. 2.

230

❧ 148. *Harland to Gosse* ❧

Paris   Sunday [5 May 1895][1]

Mon très-cher Maître:

Your letter about Rosemary[2] was very sweet to read. Thank you a thousand times for it. I am glad the story pleased you.—

It was a great disappointment for us, when we heard you couldn't join us here. It would have been such a renewal of youth, if we could all have romped in and about this town arm-in-arm again. But this spring has not been as that spring was. Do you remember the unbroken sequence of blue and golden days? This year we have had grey skies and bitter winds. Even so, though, Paris is beautiful and adorable, and we have been moderately silly. Beardsley[3] joined us a fortnight ago, and he's capital company. He says he's going back to London and work to-night. We shall follow in a fortnight. Yes, his absence from the Y[ellow] B[ook] is deplorable: but what is one to do with a capricious boy whose ruling passion is a desire to astonish the public with the unexpected? He'll be in the July number, I hope, larger than ever.

Oh, poor Oscar, indeed! We have followed the story of his ruin with the keenest pain. I suppose he *is* ruined, even though he may not be convicted. The case for the prosecution can never be stronger than it was. Yet, if a first jury disagreed, it is hardly likely that a second jury will convict.[4] It seems to us a pity that the law should take cognizance of a man's private morals, his vices, his bad tastes. If they could prove *détournement de mineur* against him, it would be different. But, dear me, if all the men of Oscar's sort in England were suddenly to be clapped into gaol, what miles of new prison-houses Her Majesty would have to build, and what gaps would be left in the ranks of artists, statesmen, and men o' letters! Do you know that on the night of Wilde's arrest 600 gentlemen crossed from Dover to Calais? The average number is 60.

It is Sunday; and I fancy Delamere Terrace; and in spite of the beauty of Paris, my heart closes in a little spasm of homesickness. Heaven bless you all in every way. Aline[5] joins me in love.

Yours always

H. Harland

---

[1] Not dated in Harland's hand: no postmark.

[2] "Rosemary for Remembrance," a story subsequently collected in Henry Harland, *Comedies and Errors* (London and New York: John Lane, 1898).

[3] Aubrey Vincent Beardsley (1872–1898), artist and illustrator, was art editor of the *Yellow Book*.

[4] Harland's prediction proved unfounded: on 25 May, Oscar Wilde was sentenced to two years' imprisonment with hard labor.

[5] Harland's wife, Aline Herminé.

ᘰ 149. Howells to Gosse ᘰ

Garden City, Long Island, [New York]

22 September 1895

Dear Gosse:

I will try to love Hall Caine[1] a little because I love you so much, though I think he loves me not at all. We get back to town (40 West 59th street) about the first of October, and I will look out for your arch-romanticist.

I wish I might see you again. I tried last year, but you know I was suddenly called home by the fatal sickness of my dear old father.[2] This year I wished to try again, but I could not leave Mrs. Howells, who wants Noah's Ark rebuilt for her to visit Europe in. We sent Pilla over, however, to be with John, and they are now about starting from Etretat, for a little sojourn in England. We have urged them to go to a Sunday of yours unbidden, if they are on one in London, and I know you will be good to them. Pil, I think, is going to be a writer; John who has been studying architecture at the Beaux Arts for three years past, can write too. But they are both very proud and shy, and perhaps they wont report themselves, after all, in spite of our ⟨Pocock-hints⟩ of your hospitable willingness to receive them.

Sha'n't you come to America again? I believe it could be made profitable to you; and I should like another dinner for a good giggle. You still giggle? I do, but more and more sadly. Death has come into the world[3] since I saw you, and it is not as merry here below as it used to be. Still there is plenty to do, and enough to eat, and I don't complain.

My wife joins me in love to Mrs. Gosse and yourself, and the children.

Yours ever

W. D. Howells

[1] On 13 September 1895 (a.l.s., HU) Gosse had written to Howells: "I do not often impose the travelling Englishman upon you, do I? But I should very much like you to see Hall Caine, who starts this week for your latitudes. You will like him, I believe, he is ardent and natural and not like other people." Thomas Henry Hall Caine (1853–1931) was the author of melodramatic and highly popular novels. He was knighted in 1918, largely for his services to British wartime propaganda in the United States.

[2] William Cooper Howells died in the summer of 1894. For Howells's brief visit to Europe earlier that summer, see Smith and Gibson, *Mark Twain-Howells Letters*, p. 659. It was on this occasion that Howells advised Jonathan Sturges to "live all you can," the remark which subsequently became the starting point of James's novel *The Ambassadors* (see F. O. Matthiessen and Kenneth B. Murdock, eds., *The Notebooks of Henry James* (New York: Oxford University Press, 1961, p. 226).

[3] Apart from his father, Howells had also lost, in 1889, his elder daughter Winifred (see Letter 101, n. 4).

ᘓ 150. *Gosse to Gilder* ᘓ

29, Delamere Terrace, / Westbourne Square. [London] W.

Xmas Eve 1895

My dear Gilder

I don't want Xmas to pass without a word of greeting to you, at this miserable hour.[1] If you were here, and could listen to what people say in clubs, in the streets, in public and private places—you would marvel at the anger of your politicians. All this week I have not heard, from high or low, any expression of passion against America—nothing but sorrow, bewilderment, unaffected surprise.

What are *you* doing for the cause of peace? You who know England so well, you who have the ear of the President,[2] what are *you* doing to check this tide of rage? It is a solemn question,—it is one which I do not doubt you can answer before God.

Nothing in all my life has seemed to me so shocking as this vast, unaccountable misunderstanding. Columns of telegrams every day tell us of the hatred of our nation by yours. What about? What have we done to injure you? Have we not welcomed you to our hearts and houses; have we not treated you to our best? Have not you always made us welcome with a large and rich hospitality? What is it all about, my dear Gilder, and do you realise what you are talking about when you lightly promise to wipe us off the face of the globe, and massacre us and yourselves in hundreds of thousands?

It is a terribly gloomy Xmas that you and your President are giving us, and we ask one another as we meet 'Why?' Stupefaction is the main sentiment here. There is no popular heat, no counter threats or defiance, but we

[1] The long-standing dispute between Britain and the United States regarding the boundary between Venezuela and British Guiana had been brought to the point of crisis by President Cleveland's "warlike" message to Congress, 17 December 1895. The dispute was resolved when Britain agreed to international arbitration of the question.

[2] Gilder was a close personal friend of the Clevelands. In a letter to Gosse of 20 July 1909 (carbon copy, GL) Gilder wrote: "You will perhaps remember that his [Cleveland's] wife was one of your Wells College admirers, and, do you know, that was one reason for our intimacy with the Clevelands, because you told me—you and one or two others, but you especially—that if I ever got an invitation to Wells College I should go, because it was such an interesting place and there was such an interesting Miss Smith there—now retired. Well, this is the reason I accepted Miss Smith's invitation—how many years ago?—and it has led to one of the richest friendships of our lives, that with the Clevelands." In Gosse's account of his visit to Wells College on 21 January 1885 (American diary), he mentions that Miss Helen Smith was at the station to meet him and that after his lecture she supplied him with whiskey.

ask 'why?' It is as though we were at dinner together, and one of us suddenly stabbed the other as he was drinking.

Very solemnly and affectionately yours

Edmund Gosse

༈ 151. *Harland to Gosse* ༈

144, Cromwell Road, / [London] S.W.

Thursday [11 June 1896][1]

Mon très-cher maître:

I don't know when I have enjoyed reading anything so much as I have just enjoyed reading your Life of your father.[2] The exquisite writing of the book apart, the charm and simplicity, the touching and beautiful filial note, —was there ever a more interesting *life,* was there ever a more interesting or more perplexing *character?* One falls in love with the man, you know, in spite of his reserve, his sternness. And one is perpetually fascinated by his supreme *humanity.* After all, wasn't it supremely human of him to be at once, as he was, a careful scientific observer and a Primitive Christian? What is more supremely human than *apparent* inconsequence? Oh, I have enjoyed the book and the Man immensely, and I can't thank you enough for giving it to me. The old ready-made phrase—more interesting than a romance—is too pale to express my pleasure in it. And I recur again and again to the exquisite tenderness and beauty of the writing.

I'm going down to Rye on Saturday to pass Sunday with our dear H[enry] J[ames].

Do you know—I am folding this letter with the Japanese ivory paper-knife you gave me at Christmas dinner—how many years ago?

Yours always

H. Harland

We did enjoy seeing you both—all, rather, for wasn't there Sylvia?—so much on Sunday.

---

[1] Date by postmark of 12 June (Friday).
[2] Gosse, *Life of Philip Henry Gosse, F.R.S.* (London: Kegan Paul, 1890).

ᘓ 152. *Gosse to James* ᘓ

29, Delamere Terrace, / Westbourne Square. [London] W.

14 June 1896

My dear James

For the last fortnight my life has been in such a whirl that I have not had time for the plainest duties, one of which certainly was to write and tell you that Philip is now definitely attached to Edw. FitzGerald's expedition.[1] We are conscious,—and we give you our affectionate thanks for it,—that your cordial words, spoken at the right moment, had a great deal to do with this happy arrangement. We have received great kindness all round. The people at the Zoological Gardens, in the most charming and surprising way, have put their best dissector at his service to teach him the whole art of preserving birds, and even Thiselton Dyer, the rebarbative and formidable Dyer,[2] who chivvies Royal Princesses off the grass, and repulses the amiable advance of Cabinet Ministers, has been amiability itself, and gives the boy the run of Kew. The naturalists are amused at what they think an atavism, the grand-papa reapparant [sic]. At all events the boy has a superb chance, and all must now depend on his own brain and character.

I am giving weekly lectures on Matt Arnold at Mrs. S. Dugdale's[3] to some of the smartest ladies in London, to whom the presence of one another evidently supplies a complete confidence in the importance of the lectures. The Duchess of Bedford[4] is convinced that dear Lady Carnarvon[5] would not come if it were a second-rate article, and the presence of Mrs. Asquith[6] gives everybody security,—"she's so clever". They are all ladies, except a bearded figure at the back, semi-recumbent on a sofa, like a water-god—

[1] Gosse's son, Philip, became a naturalist, as Gosse's father had been (see Letter 19, n. 11); the expedition on which he accompanied Edward Arthur Fitzgerald, the explorer, was to the Andes. The expedition returned in the late summer of 1897. Philip contributed a paper, "Notes on the natural history of the Aconcagua Valleys," to E. A. Fitzgerald, *The Highest Andes: A Record of the First Ascent of Aconcagua and Tupungato in Argentina, and the Exploration of the Surrounding Valleys* (London: Methuen, 1899), pp. 338–378.

[2] Sir William Turner Thistleton-Dyer (1843–1928) had become director of the Royal Botanic Gardens at Kew in 1885; he retired in 1905.

[3] Mrs. Stratford Dugdale. Gosse delivered six private lectures on Matthew Arnold at her home during May and June of 1896, for which he received £50.

[4] The wife of Herbrand Arthur Russell, eleventh Duke of Bedford (1858–1940).

[5] Lady Carnarvon's husband, George Edward Stanhope Molyneux Herbert, fifth Earl of Carnarvon (1866–1923), became famous as an Egyptologist; he died during the excavation of the tomb of Tut-ank-amen.

[6] Margaret ("Margot") Asquith (1865–1945), wife of Herbert Asquith, the future Prime Minister (see Letter 200, n. 2), was a brilliant conversationalist.

235

Sir Wilfred Lawson.[7] Unless Mrs. Dugdale muffs it fearfully, I ought to get quite a nice lot of money, but the countesses come streaming up and whether anyone takes their guineas is what is unknown to me and to Lady Audrey Buller[8] (my faithful familiar, who has really got up the whole thing.). But this, you will justly say, is vulgar without being amusing.

In an evil hour I was overpressed to write an article about Barbey d'Aurevilly,[9] and I am in the Valley of the Shadow of Boredom in consequence. Every page I read makes him seem more insignificant and more impertinent. I believe that as a person he lent himself to comic biography, but I have no details. Did you not, years and years ago, meet him at Edmond de Goncourt's[10] and did he not say to you "Je n'aime que des femmes stériles"? It seems to me that I have a vague recollection of it, which has been recalled by a fatuous passage in one of his stories, where he declares that those who deeply love always sterilise their passion. He was a poor mouldy affair, I'm afraid.

Still I don't know your address. Artful creeper into rabbit-holes, you shall, nevertheless, not escape detection.

We all send our love to you and I am ever affectionately yours

Edmund Gosse

At this moment, comes your new book of stories. I re-open the envelope, to slip in this word of thanks.

E. G.

[7] Sir Wilfred Lawson (1829–1906), Radical politician and energetic champion of the temperance movement.
[8] Wife of Sir Redvers Henry Buller (1839–1908), the British general, on whom Gosse later wrote an article (see Letter 155, n. 3).
[9] Jules Amédée Barbey d'Aurévilly (1808–1889), French novelist and critic.
[10] Edmond Louis Antoine Huot de Goncourt (1822–1896), the longer-lived of the de Goncourt brothers.

❧ 153. *James to Gosse* ❧

Point Hill, / Playden. / Sussex.

16 June [1896]

My dear Gosse.

I am delighted with your news of Philip's definite attachment; and congratulate heartily both you and his mother. Great things, I am sure, open out before him—I mean sound, sane, large, educative, not banal or second-rate things. All the omens are genial almost excessively—but let us not tremble where *he* won't. It's a good chance and a good boy—and now you must let them shake down together.

Your London news comes to me as the breath of hot rooms and the prattle—almost—of strange tongues. I don't allude either to *your* room or your tongue—but as regards the one, to Mrs. Dugdale's, and as regards the other to the *macabre* Barbey's. "Je ne peux souffrir que les vierges ou les femmes stériles": he said that (I think) to Sargent, who repeated it to me. But I dined with him once in Paris—with one other person only—and he scared and depressed me. He was *falot*—and he *was* macabre. He had probably been a rare talker—but he was grotesquely self-conscious, and invraisemblablement figged out. I pity you for having to write of him—he was a *pen* and praeteria nihil.

I would like to contend with you—had I time (àpropos of these things) over the manner—the way you I thought *took*, as it were, your last *Cosmopolis* causerie.[1] But there is too much to say—and I can't. It is more—much —of a chance for you than your preliminary remarks expressed—it is a great chance, and I wish you would see it more as one. But I am not saying what I mean—and as you wouldn't do what I mean, it doesn't matter. Only excuse this rudely imperfect beginning—and—ending. May the Countesses prove honest! But there is no class that requires more looking after. *When* will you come for a Sunday? It is really very nice—though hot, alas; and I want you with a rigour which you marked evasion of the question doesn't at all discountenance. Will the *27th* suit you? I don't want to bore or bully you—but may I have a sole wee word to say *whether* you could manage that: as I have only one spare room. Harland was here two days since—very pleasantly indeed—to me. There is a good 4.30 from Charing Cross to *Rye*: reaching Rye at 6.45. I am 10 minutes from Rye Station. Be you, on your side, not too far from

Yours ever,

Henry James

[1] Gosse, "Current French Literature," *Cosmopolis*, VI (June 1896), 637–654.

❧ 154. *Gosse to Harland* ❧

29, Delamere Terrace, / Westbourne Square. [London] W.

2 April 1898

My dear Harland

It was a very kind and happy inspiration of yours to send me your new book,[1] and it came at a very happy moment, when I really had some evenings

[1] Harland, *Comedies and Errors*. See Letter 148, n. 2.

of leisure, and was not tempted to put it aside, in this world of outrageously superfluous books. So I have read it right through, every word of it, and must now write and tell you how admirable I think it. Oh! but *admirable, my dear Harland*, this is the real thing, this is literature. All through there runs that peculiar richness which is so uncommon, that sense of deep colour and odour and freshness. Now for particulars. I have my favourites, even here; and first amongst them stands "Flower o' the Clove", a masterpiece. It could not be better: the double problem so courageously stated and so exquisitely solved. And then comes "The Confidante", so beautifully written —so peculiarly well written where all is distinguished and graceful. And then my old friend "Rosemary for Remembrance".[2] And then, in a lump, "The Friend of Man" and "Cousin Rosalys" and "Tirala-tirala". I take these six stories (not to depreciate the others) and I say that nothing of the kind more perfect, more instinct with beauty, has been written in our time. There, I have come to the right word at last,—it is *beauty* that peculiarly distinguishes this book. I give you a poor impression of my pleasure, but it is intense. This book puts you high among living makers; it appeals, with success, to the European standard. I congratulate you and I rejoice. Thank you once more for the kind thought of sending the book to me: for I would not have missed it for the world. And you may be sure I shall proselytize.

Yours very sincerely

Edmund Gosse

[2] See Letter 148.

✎ 155. *Gosse to Munro*[1] ✎

29 Delamere Terrace / London S.W.

19 May 1898

Dear Mr. Munro

Mr. Heinemann,[2] who has just returned, tells me that you and he entered into a very kind and charming conspiracy about me, when he was in New York the other day. It appears that he suggested to you that I should write

[1] David Alexander Munro was at this time editor of the *North American Review*. He was of Scottish birth and education, but spent most of his career in the United States engaged in literary and editorial work of various kinds. He died in 1910.

[2] William Heinemann (1863–1920), the publisher, brought out many of Gosse's books from 1891 onwards, and the two men became good friends, traveling together and corresponding frequently. Gosse often referred to him in letters as "Y. V." (Young Voluptuary).

for the "North American Review" more regularly, and that you were not averse to the idea. I am sure I should be charmed.

I must tell you that I have a great suspicion of the weekly or even monthly "causerie" or "letter". I have always declined to undertake it, because I think people cannot retain their freshness, feel it become a burden and then unconsciously do it badly.

But an occasional article of a popular kind, very much varied in subject and treatment, might be kept amusing. I think 6 such articles within a year the very outside of what a really conscientious essayist, who wishes always to do his best, ought to undertake.

In the meantime, Mr. Heinemann tells me that you have given him a commission for *three* such articles from me (4000 words each), and that you will use these in any case. I shall be very glad indeed to do my best for your readers, to whom I am not quite a stranger, and you will see how my work is liked. I shall be grateful for any suggestions from you, with a view to making my subjects bright and useful.

In a few days, I will send you my first article, in which I intend to speak of "Shakespeare in 1898",[3] chronicling the remarkable developments which have lately been made in Shakespeare study.

We must hope, as over here we do all hope, that your War[4] will soon end in an American triumph, and that business will resume its normal character.

Please let me hear from you. I need hardly say to you that the prospect of closer communication with the "North A. R." is extremely pleasing to me.

Believe me, very truly yours,

Edmund Gosse

[3] Gosse, "Shakespeare in 1898," *North American Review*, CLXVII (August 1898), 145–154. Gosse wrote several articles for the *North American Review* during this period: "Norway Revisited," CLXVII (November 1898), 534–542; "Literature of Action," CLXVIII (January 1899), 14–23; "Recollections of 'Orion' Horne," CLXVIII (April 1899), 490–498; "Reverses of Britomart," CLXVIII (June 1899), 720–729; "Sir Redvers Buller," CLXX (January 1900), 109–120.

[4] The Spanish-American War.

❧ 156. *Gosse to Moulton* ❧

29 Delamere Terrace / [London] W.

1 January 1899

My dear Mrs. Moulton

Accept our thanks for your most kind Xmas greeting, and accept our united best wishes for 1899. We have been disappointed not to see you in the last year—you are commonly as punctual as the precession of the equinoxes.[1] But I believe that is a motion westward, isn't it? and we want you to be moving eastward. I was very much interested by what you said to me about poor Stéphane Mallarmé.[2] I think I knew he was an old friend of yours. Such a nice creature, and so wholly and irreparably unintelligible! I think he knew it, and did it on purpose. It was very clever of him to keep it up. I used to notice that if one came upon him suddenly, or if he had to write a telegram or order something from a shop, he could write the same sort of French as other people.

We shall be particularly glad to hear that you are sailing Europewards, and depend on your letting us know. With all our most cordial greetings

Yours very sincerely

Edmund Gosse

---

[1] See Letter 5, n. 9.

[2] Stéphane Mallarmé (1842–1898), the French poet; Gosse wrote about him in the *Saturday Review*, LXXXVI (17 September 1898), 372–373, the article is collected in *French Profiles* (London: Heinemann, 1905).

❧ 157. *Furness to Gosse* ❧

Wallingford, / Delaware County, / Pennsylvania.

20 July 1899

My dear Gosse,

I'm a man of my word, I am.

I had not been on shore forty eight hours before I sent to Boston for this book of Walt Whitman[1] which goes to you by this same post.

I have looked it through and have not arisen from the reading with an increased admiration for the writer. It was no friend of Walt that instigated the printing thereof. The substance of the letters is either humdrum or revolting, and always self-centred. There can be no pretence that the tie between Walt and 'Pete' had in it a solitary fibre of intellectuality—'twas purely animal.

In one way, these Letters may do good,—albeit no good to Walt's fame. They may reveal what an out and out poseur the 'Good Grey Poet' was all his life. He posed as poor, and he died with thousands of dollars in the Bank; he posed as a writer of absolutely spontaneous lines, and his MS

---

[1] Whitman, *Calamus* [Letters to Peter Doyle, 1868–1880] (Boston: L. Maynard, 1897).

reveals the utmost fastidiousness; he posed as a child of nature indifferent to food or clothes, these Letters show that he adored buckwheat cakes and salmon.

We have his brains in alcohol at the University,[2] and when dissection has taught us more about this most subtile organ, look out for revelations of character. But don't tell this about his brains—he has friends who have so little, that if they knew it, they might make it unpleasant for us.

No, your phrase is perfect: his is poetry in solution and when to this you add that he was one of the handsomest, grandest looking men that ever strolled down from Olympus you have all I care to remember about him.

Give my kindest regards to your household, one and all, and believe me, you dear boy,

Yours affectionately

Horace Howard Furness

[2] In a letter to his sister of 21 November 1897 Furness says that Whitman's brains are in the Wistar Institute [of Anatomy and Biology] at the University of Pennsylvania (Jayne, *Letters of H. H. Furness*, I, 346). Apparently the brains no longer survive: the editors are indebted to Professor Sculley Bradley for a description of a letter (a penciled first draft) now in the University of Pennsylvania Library, in which Thomas B. Harned states that the brains were destroyed when the jar containing them was dropped by an attendant.

◈ 158. *Gosse to Furness* ◈

29, Delamere Terrace, / Westbourne Square. [London] W.
11 September 1899

My dear Furness

I returned last night from six weeks wandering in Norway, and here is your delightful letter, and the curious book of W[alt] W[hitman]'s letters.[1] It was extremely kind, and like you, to gratify immediately my whimsical wish.

Yes, the little book is a somewhat uncomfortable document. Wonderfully interesting in a way, in spite of its triviality. It settles, of course, once and for all, a certain doubt one has always had. One doubts no longer. But I cast no stone. I only do resent the horrible manner in which the book has been edited,—the sort of detestable giggle with which it is larded with scraps of the poem of "Calamus", with a sort [of] "There, now you see

[1] See previous letter.

241

what all that meant!" Yes, I see, and I weep with pity and regret. The strange old creature, in his loneliness, getting this queer gratification for his impulses. And so *innocent* with it all, so guileless. So full of genuine tenderness and solicitude, probably perfectly genuine and sincere only in these cryptic and indefinable relations. What you tell me, and told me before, of his artfulness, his partial social insincerity, is quite intelligible to me. The world is full of a number of things, as R[obert] L[ouis] S[tevenson] used to say. I wonder why we are so very anxious to have everybody cast in exactly the same mould. This astonishing old poetaster, at all events, went back centuries and centuries to the Dorian state; and when he rages at the "damned fool" that bullies his Pete, we are in presence of Harmodius and Aristogeiton.[2] Is it not so? I speak to the wise, and you are wise; but what a book! Finally, what an unseemly book! But thank you for it. I am glad to possess it. Do write to me soon again.

Ever affectionately yours

Edmund Gosse

[2] Gosse refers to the two Athenian youths who were in love with each other and achieved fame for their defiance of the tyrannical brothers Hippias and Hipparchus.

༄ 159. *Gosse to Perry*[1] ༄

29, Delamere Terrace, / Westbourne Square. [London] W.
14 December 1899

My dear Sir

Our friend Mr. Armour had very kindly carried out your commission, and prepared me for your courteous wish that I should contribute to the "Atlantic Monthly". I shall be very happy to do so. I will propose to you a subject, which Mr. Armour thinks you will be pleased with. You probably know that at Trinity College, Cambridge, we possess the original MSS. of Milton's Poems. They have been practically inaccessible until now, but there has just been printed, for a few amateurs, a volume of them in facsimile, which enables one to study them at ease. They throw singularly interesting light on his methods of composition.

If you would like me to do so, I would write you an article on the history

[1] Bliss Perry (1860–1954), critic, biographer, and novelist, was editor of the *Atlantic Monthly* from 1899 to 1909; he taught English literature at Williams, Princeton, and Harvard.

of these MSS. and give particulars of their character, and quote cancelled passages.[2] I think it would make a very popular article.

I quite understand that you do not pay the very large prices of the New York reviews which frequently offer me their hospitality. I shall be quite satisfied with your usual highest rate of payment.

Believe me to be
My dear Sir
Very faithfully yours

Edmund Gosse

[2] Gosse, "Milton Manuscripts at Trinity," *Atlantic Monthly*, LXXXV (May 1900), 586–593.

∾ 160. *Harland to Gosse* ∾

144, Cromwell Road, / [London] S.W.

Friday [2 March 1900][1]

My dear Master:

I received your letter on returning from Weymouth day before yesterday; and I'm very glad it is to be the *Roman d'un jeune homme pauvre*,[2] for that is a book with which I have a hundred pleasant associations. I shall go to work at the article at once. I think decidedly it is the best choice that can be made among O[ctave] F[euillet]'s[3] works—for English and American readers.

We made a much briefer visit to Weymouth than we had intended, because the rain rained every day, and I had a good deal of rheumatism in consequence. If the weather had been decent we had hoped that you might come down for a week's end with us. We saw a great deal of Marzials,[4] and (to our delight) we found him *saner* than we had ever known him. Those people who say that he is incoherent, off his head, and so forth, must be misled by the rapidity of change which has always characterised his talk

[1] Taken from postmark of 2 March 1900.

[2] Harland wrote a critical introduction to the translation of Octave Feuillet's *Roman d'un jeune homme pauvre* (*The Romance of a Poor Young Man* [London: Heinemann, 1912]) in the series "A Century of French Romance," of which Gosse was the general editor.

[3] Octave Feuillet (1821–1890), the French novelist and playwright.

[4] Théophile Marzials (1850–1920), author of *The Gallery of Pigeons, and Other Poems* (1873) and of the opera *Esmeralda*, first performed in 1883. Gosse had known him since the 1860's, when they were both working at the British Museum.

—the touch and go. So far from having deteriorated, we found him improved in every way. Of course, when he has had an overdose of his poison,[5] he does become incoherent: but he only took an overdose *once* during the ten days we were there. For the rest of the time he was as clear-headed as anyone. I think he must have been suffering from an overdose when Miss Newcome[6] saw him; for to us he spoke of you in the most affectionate manner, and he regretted immensely not having seen you when you were in his part of the world. He said it was due to someone meddling, and intimating to you that it would be best not to see him; and he resented that "meddling" bitterly. He is making a great success, and earning a decent income, as a teacher of singing in the country, and he is asked as a guest to the best county houses. This we know not from him merely, but from several of the county people whom we met. He is as brilliant as he ever was, he looks in better condition than I remember ever to have seen him before, and altogether I think his friends have reason to congratulate him.

In spite of the rain, we liked Weymouth very much, and we are grateful to you for having recommended it to us. We especially like so much of the country near it as the rain allowed us to visit. And we not only had comfortable lodgings, but we fell in with a specimen of that almost extinct biped: an honest landlady!

I have this day put the last touches to the last page of proof of a novel I have been trying to write. I wonder whether you will think it a terrible example of what the novel should not be?

With love from both of us to all of you,

Ever yours

H. H.

[5] The editors are indebted to Mr. John Betjeman and to Mr. Martin Secker for the information that the "poison" was "Dr. Collis Brown's Chlorodyne," which contained laudanum. Apparently Marzials was addicted, and all the shopkeepers in the town of Colyton in Devonshire (where Marzials is buried, near the farmhouse where he lived during his late years) were instructed not to supply him with it.

[6] Unidentified.

❦ 161. *Gosse to Higginson*[1] ❦

29, Delamere Terrace, / Westbourne Square. [London] W.

9 March 1900

My dear Colonel Higginson

I have received from Mr. Edwin D. Mead (whose name is entirely unknown to me) a pamphlet about yourself,[2] which I have read with very
great interest, and,—so far as it deals with your admirable work and
character,—with perfect sympathy.

But I am made aware that Mr. Mead would not have sent this pamphlet
to a stranger, had he not wished me to read certain remarks in which you
have done me the honour to mention my name, and also the remarks which
Mr. Mead has added, by way of chastising me.

The passage from your own essay I happened never to have read. It is
expressed with perfect courtesy, and contains no word which is not worthy of
so chivalrous and distinguished a writer as yourself. It is hostile—I think
regrettably hostile—to English culture. But you have a perfect right to this
opinion of Tennyson, Darwin and Arnold. A thousand times more have you
a right to any opinion upon so humble a writer as myself.

But do you think Mr. Mead fairly within the bounds of good criticism
or good manners? Does he not offend, and with a peculiar grossness, the
very law of equality which you lay down?

I am pained, and I will not deny it, by these expressions. Although you
playfully and pleasantly pillory me for one supposed act of presumption,
I think hardly any English writer deserves this particular blame less than I.
At least, my conscience tells me that I have never made the silly error of

---

[1] Thomas Wentworth Higginson (1823–1911) was a Union colonel during the
American Civil War and commanded the first regiment to be recruited from former
slaves. His later years were devoted to supporting various movements for social reform and to a wide range of literary activities. He wrote a novel, some verse, and
several works of history and biography, and it was to him that Emily Dickinson
turned, somewhat inappropriately, for advice. Gosse and Higginson met and corresponded both before and after the date of this letter.

[2] Edwin Doak Mead (1894–1937) was a cousin of Howells's wife, and Howells had
given him some encouragement as a young man; he was an energetic reformer, and
made the *New England Magazine*, of which he was editor, a platform for his views.
His pamphlet *Thomas Wentworth Higginson* was simply a reprint of the "Editor's
Table" of the *New England Magazine*, XXI (February 1900), 760–772. Mead
quotes from Higginson's essay "Unnecessary Apologies": "Had Mr. Gosse been a
New Yorker, writing in a London Magazine, would anyone on either side of the
Atlantic have seriously cared whether Mr. Gosse thought that contemporary England
had produced a poet?" Mead then adds: "Yet what enlightened man, American or
Englishman, can fail to see that Colonel Higginson's judgment upon any matter, as
compared with that of Mr. Gosse, is not simply as 'thirteen to twelve'—to echo old
John Higginson's figure—but as thirteen to one" (p. 766).

depreciating American culture or American intelligence. No one,—I may surely boast,—has made a closer study of American talent, no one has sympathised with gifted Americans, no one has striven to perceive the American standpoint, more than I. I think that I deserve less than most English writers the contemptuous hostility of such patriots as Mr. Mead.

It is, perhaps, Quixotic of me to appeal against this rather coarse attack. But the circumstances in which it has reached me, and the fact that it is combined with the praise and partisanship of a man whom I suspect so highly as I respect Colonel Higginson, move me to write you this word of expostulation.

Pray pardon me, and believe me with cordial regard and true admiration

Faithfully yours

Edmund Gosse

❦ 162. *Furness to Gosse* ❦

Wallingford, / Delaware County, / Pennsylvania.

10 March [1900]

My dear Gosse

When 'Daddy' Wordsworth beheld a rainbow in the sky his heart didn't leap up half as high as mine does when I see your handwriting on an envelope. It was too good of you to write to me from Trinity College and give me the latest news of the Vice-magisterial hand.[1] Confound it, how annoying it is to have anything the matter with your right hand—annoying is the word; because you can't sit down and cry all night. 'Tis very easy to make a pish at such ills when health is bounding through every vein, but let that health be checked ever so little and how we do fret. When Mr Emerson's house burned to the ground and he was crushed under the misfortune, some one asked him where his philosophy was; he replied 'Philosophy! I've been a humbug all my life!'[2]

[1] The vice-master of Trinity College (since 1888) was Aldis Wright (see Letter 92, n. 4). In a letter to Furness of 11 February 1900 (a.l.s., UP) Gosse wrote: "You will have known, I think, that we have been a little anxious about the V.M.'s right hand, which was suddenly crumpled up and deadened in a quite mysterious way. But altho' it has not yielded to massage, it is no worse at all, and tho' it gives him inconvenience, it gives him no pain. He is getting used to it, and is clever in balancing his pen between the 2nd and 3rd fingers."

[2] Emerson's diary for 1872 carries the entry: "Wednesday, July 25. House burned" (E. W. Emerson and W. E. Forbes, eds., *Journals of Ralph Waldo Emerson* [Boston and New York: Houghton Mifflin, 1914], X, 386.

Don't you be misled by any newspaper talk about sympathy for the Boers coupled with hostility to England. Don't you know that in a Democracy, like ours, the loudest shouts will always issue from the emptiest pates? and that these shouts will be always taken up by the sensational press. That resolution of sympathy, which you spoke of,[3] was merely proposed in the Senate,—it has not been passed and it won't be, as probably the proposer knew very well. He was merely 'playing to the gallery.'

In what I am about to say, don't think for a minute that there is anything in my heart but loyalty, admiration, and devoted love for England, and sympathy with her through thick and thin against all the world, save my own country:—an appeal for sympathy on the score that you sympathised with us in our Spanish War is hardly to the point, for two reasons: first, the majority of thoughtful men here were bitterly opposed to that wicked war. The decadence of our country, which is on the wing, will surely date from it. As a friend of mine wittily said: 'We gained Manilla with the loss of one man and of all our institutions.' The war was a mere bid for popularity by that miserable ring of low politicians, headed by that unscrupulous creature, McKinley,[4] in Washington. So that had your sympathy been withheld, I'm not sure that your position would not have been more noble.

Secondly, when we were at a death-grip with Slavery and were fighting the grandest battle for Freedom and Humanity, and pouring out blood and treasure, and there was mourning in every household—where was the sympathy then from that country that we all held so dear, our old home that we idolised? Ah, dear Gosse, *if* there is any bitterness now towards England, it has its root in those times when we stretched out our hands to

[3] In the letter of 11 February Gosse wrote: "We hear today that your Senate has passed a resolution of sympathy with the Boers. Why? We cannot conceive. When you were engaged in a not less just war with Spain, we did not pass resolutions of enmity to you through the House of Lords. On the contrary, our Government prevented the formation of a coalition which might have annoyed you. But nations have no generosity, I suppose because nations are made up nowadays of vast accretions of perfectly ignorant items." On Saturday, 10 February 1900, Mr. William V. Allen, senator from Nebraska, had presented the following resolution for consideration: "*Resolved*, That the Senate of the United States of America extends its sympathy to the people of the South African Republic in their heroic struggle for liberty and popular government, and believes it to be the duty of the Government of the United States of America to offer mediation, to the end that further bloodshed may be averted and an honorable peace may be concluded between the belligerent governments." Agreement without vote to this resolution was requested and, there being no objections, it was passed; however, one senator then protested that he had not heard the resolution and it became clear that in the confusion the resolution had been generally inaudible. Against Mr. Allen's protests the Senate agreed to reconsider the resolution, which was therefore held over. (*Congressional Record*, xxxiii, Part 2, p. 1688).

[4] William McKinley (1843–1901), President of the United States from 1897 until his assassination in 1901.

her, and not a soul to grasp them but the poor cotton-spinners of Lancashire. Just think how Thackeray turned against us, and Dickens, and Tennyson and Gladstone who proclaimed that 'Jefferson Davis had created a nation.' To this hour our merchant-marine hasn't recovered from the blow that England smote it then. But, thank God! those black days are all passed away. While they lasted, the heavens were hung with black. For 'to be wroth with one we love Doth work like madness in the brain.' The wrath has given place to the closest friendship.

I have yet to hear one word of sympathy for the Boers as a nation—a cruel, oligarchical race, an obstruction in the path of civilisation whereof its destiny is to be swept away, and by the blessing of God the besom of swift destruction is in your hand.

What did lead me into this screed? I meant to talk of pleasant things—of those 'Notes on Natural History'[5] which your boy sent to my boy and which in the latter's absence I opened and read with great interest. What Philip accomplished, starting out 'on the jump' as he did, is little less than a wonder. He reveals such in-born powers of close observation. What is he doing now? Give him my love, and admiration for his excellent work. Heigho, my boy is still away. He left me in Paris just after we were in London and had that dinner all together in the Hotel Brunswick.[6] How I did enjoy that dinner. Let's have another. Day before yesterday, I had a telegram from my boy in Mandelay saying that he [was] in capital health and spirits and had just reached there.[7] He had been many hundred miles further north among the Naga tribes—utterly unknown savages, never before visited by any but traders. He says his notebooks are bursting with religion! His next destination is Rangoon and then his face is turned homeward. Then when he comes my solitary life ends. Mrs. Wister has been at her own house in town this winter. Her little granddaughter has 'come out' —and this means balls, parties, luncheons, dinners for every day in the week. On the 7th of April I start forth with my oldest son,[8] a devoted sportsman, to go a fishing in Florida and the Gulf of Mexico—ah! what a delicious life that is! the rocking boat, the deep blue sky, the mangrove islands, and

[5] See Letter 152 and n. 1.

[6] Furness was in England in 1899 and received the honorary degree of Doctor of Letters at Cambridge on 13 June (see Jayne, *Letters of H. H. Furness*, II, 39–40). The dinner to which Furness refers must have taken place at about the same time.

[7] William Henry Furness (1866–1920), Furness's third son, was an explorer and ethonologist; in 1904 he became secretary and curator of the Free Museum of Science and Arts of the University of Pennsylvania. His publications include *Life in the Luchu Islands* (1899) and *The Island of Stone Money, Uap of the Carolines* (1910).

[8] Furness's eldest son, Walter Rogers Furness (1861–1914) was an architect; it was the second son, Horace Howard Furness, Jr., (1865–1930), who assisted his father with the editing of the Variorum Shakespeare and continued the work after his father's death.

the mighty tarpons (when you can catch 'em but I did catch one on my last visit (with a rod and reel, mind you,) which weighed a hundred and thirty five pounds. It took me three quarters of an hour, but then the thrill of rapture when he was gaffed! The day before I get back, Mrs. Wister comes out here to receive me and here she visits me till she goes in July to her own pretty cottage at North East Harbour on the coast of Maine.

Excuse these severed sheets but I had no idea of scribbling so much when I began—and I don't seem to have told you anything after all. I don't care. Tis enough if you can gather from it all that you and yours have the abiding love of

H. H. F.

༄ 163. Gosse to Walker[1] ༄

29, Delamere Terrace, / Westbourne Square. W. / London

26 March 1901

My dear Mr. Walker

I am much obliged to you for your kind letter of invitation. There is no periodical with which I should be more pleased to be identified than "The Cosmopolitan", and I recollect with great pleasure my relations with it some seven years ago.[2]

Just at present I am still extremely busy with some special work, which has for some time past been absorbing all my energies; but this is now approaching completion, and in two or three months I shall be able to consider myself free.

I should be very pleased if you would indicate to me the sort of articles which you would like me to write for "The Cosmopolitan". It would be a great help to me if you would indicate, with your experience of your vast

[1] John Brisben Walker (1847–1931), owner and editor of the *Cosmopolitan Magazine*. After a varied early career, Walker bought the *Cosmopolitan* with money earned from successful farming and land reclamation and in a few years made it one of the most popular illustrated magazines in America; he sold it to Hearst in 1905. For a short period from December 1891 to June 1892 Walker and Howells had been joint editors of the magazine: see Mildred Howells, *Life in Letters of Howells*, II, 18–20, 23–24.

[2] Gosse refers to his article entitled "Great Passions of History," *Cosmopolitan*, XVII (October 1894), 657–669. As a result of the present arrangement, he wrote an article each year until 1904: "The Isolation of the Anglo-Saxon Mind," XXXII (November 1901), 45–51; "The Influence of Victor Hugo," XXXII (April 1902), 627–634; "Ethics in Biography," XXXV (July 1903), 317–323; "Immortality and Fame," XXXVI (March 1904), 547–552.

clientele of readers, in what direction I could be most useful—subject, nature of treatment, length and so on. If I write, as I have so frequently done in the past, for American readers, I like to give them of my very best, for certainly no audience is more appreciative of it. Will you write to me freely your ideas in this respect?

I am sorry that you do not suggest the rates of payment which you think my writing worth to you, for I greatly dislike haggling about prices. But since you so distinctly ask me to say what I am in the habit of receiving, I am afraid I must say that I cannot well write for less than £5 a thousand words. If this seems much, my excuse must be that I can get it all the time, and that my leisure, and with the passage of years my strength, are so limited that if I accept less I am a loser by it.

With many thanks for the cordiality and courtesy of your letter

Pray believe me to be
Yours sincerely

Edmund Gosse

∿ 164. *Gosse to Trent*[1] ∿

17, Hanover Terrace, / Regent's Park, [London] N.W.

6 June 1902

Dear Professor Trent

I have had the pleasure of receiving and of reading the first galleys of your "American Literature".[2] At Messrs. Appletons' request, I have returned them to you through their London representative, with my comments and suggested queries marked, for your convenience, in red ink.

I must first of all express my congratulations on the character of the work, which is very thorough and careful. You will not, I hope, be annoyed with any of my suggestions, which are crudely made on the edges of the galleys, and ought to be prefaced with apologies and amenities for which there is no room. I beg you once for all to take these as intended.

I hope as the book proceeds you will contrive to find room for a little

---

[1] William Petersfield Trent (1862–1939) was professor of English at the University of the South (1888–1900), where he was a founder and editor of the *Sewanee Review*, and at Columbia University (1900–1927). He wrote many books, several of them on American history and American literature (see following note).

[2] W. P. Trent, *A History of American Literature, 1607–1865* (New York: Appleton, 1903); this was one of the series of Short Histories of the Literature of the World, edited by Gosse.

more biography and a little less positive criticism. I cannot help feeling that you take these poetasters of the 17th. and 18th. century very seriously. If you do not tell us briefly who they were and what they did, the naked bareness of their want of merit makes them rather dreary. You are not chargeable with more partiality than other critics; it seems that American amour propre demands that Wigglesworth[3] should be treated with as much gravity as Chaucer is in this country or Villon in France. This, I suppose, is the inevitable national point of view.

I entreat you to be as concise as you can, and to remember that the book should not run, at most, to more than 400 pp. I am most anxious that the various volumes of the series should bear a general and superficial resemblance to one another.

Yours very truly

Edmund Gosse

[3] Michael Wigglesworth (1631–1705) was brought from England to America as a child; he became a Congregational minister and wrote *The Day of Doom* (1662) and other verse.

ᘯ 165. *Gilder to Gosse* ᘯ

[New York]

27 February 1905

My dear Gosse,

A few nights ago I had again that dream of mine which has recurred for half a life time—It is my London dream—It is either that at last, at last, I am just sailing once more for London, or that at last I am again in London,—with all the romantic delight and passionate pilgrimage that is to me. This time I was at your house; you were well and happy—your doctor was there, but only socially. I woke with London and your household reverberating, as so often, in my remembering mind. Did I ever tell you about this dream of London and my friends there?

I think you will have to write and tell me how you all are—you and yours, and our friends there. I was lately reminded of your contributions to Browning lore.[1] It is interesting to note that, as witness Dowden[2] and the rest,

[1] Gosse, *Robert Browning: Personalia* (London: Fisher Unwin, 1890). Gilder was at this time preparing an article on the Brownings, subsequently printed as "A Romance of the XIXth. Century. Robert and Elizabeth Barrett Browning," *Century*, LXX (October 1905), 918–927. In the article Gilder quotes from several authorities, including Gosse (see Letter 167).

[2] Edward Dowden, *Robert Browning* (London: Dent; New York: Dutton, 1904).

no one can anymore write about Browning without quoting from both yourself and Mrs. Bronson,[3] my delightful sister-in-law, now gone to her friends beyond.

By the way—I am anxious to know whether there is any authority, except internal evidence (as in "Prospice") for attributing the subject of R[obert] B[rowning]'s "My Star" to Mrs. Browning. Can you give me your belief?[4]

I have had the pleasure of seeing Sir C. Purdon Clark [sic][5] several times —they wanted me to speechify at him at the Lotos[6] the other night, but I was not well enough. He makes a good impression—and his succession to poor, impossible Cesnola[7] has brought about a cordial feeling in the community toward the Museum. For a long time Cesnola has only been kept on owing to the fact that some good and liberal-handed old man was President, whom he attached to himself—though the board was against him. The growth of the Museum will be immense now that it has Morgan[8] at the head—and a capable and honest man as Director.

How do you like your present public function—and how does Dobson[9] like his present private function and how has "David"[10] gone with the Critical World; and are you sorry to lose Choate;[11] and do you still doat on the attractive Hay—and the unique Roosevelt?

I have an unsigned article in the April Century on Roosevelt[12] as a *reader* that will make your hair stand up![13] and will be the occasion of more com-

[3] Mrs. Katherine De Kay Bronson, sister of Gilder's wife, Helena, wrote two important articles on Browning: "Browning in Asolo," *Century*, LIX (April 1900), 920–931; "Browning in Venice," *Century*, LXIII (February 1902), 572–584.

[4] For Gosse's response, see Letter 167.

[5] Sir Caspar Purdon Clarke (1846–1911), English architect and art expert, had been appointed director of the Metropolitan Museum, New York, in succession to Cesnola (see n. 7 below).

[6] The Lotos was, and is, a New York literary club, now located at 5 East Sixty-sixth Street, New York City.

[7] Luigi Palma di Cesnola (1832–1904), Italian-born soldier and archaeologist, was director of the Metropolitan Museum from 1879 until his death. Gilder had played a leading part in a movement to challenge Cesnola's competence in 1882: see Rosamond Gilder, *Letters of R. W. Gilder*, pp. 108–112.

[8] John Pierpont Morgan (1837–1913) was president of the Metropolitan Museum; most of his collection of works of art was presented to the Museum after his death.

[9] Gosse had been appointed Librarian to the House of Lords in 1904; his friend Austin Dobson had retired from the Board of Trade in 1901.

[10] Unidentified.

[11] Joseph Hodges Choate (1832–1917), lawyer and diplomat, had been United States ambassador to Britain from 1899 to 1905.

[12] Theodore Roosevelt (1858–1918) was in his second term as President of the United States.

[13] "President Roosevelt as a Reader," *Century*, LXIX (April 1905), 951–954. The article is unsigned, and consists chiefly of anecdotes illustrating Roosevelt's extra-

ment than anything the (unknown) writer has ever written. It will astonish every one in England except Mr. Morley—for reasons which he can give you![14] I saw much of him here, by the way, but not enough. I *did* want an hour here at home with him; but he was absorbed by engagements and about distraught. I think he was greatly shaken up by his visit here—and he certainly was well liked—he seemed more mellow than at home—but that is perhaps because I saw less of him at home. Have you seen him since he returned?—If you see him—tell him we want him to come back and finish his visit.

And the same to you my boy!

When are you coming back to finish yours?

Faithfully
R. W. Gilder

Postscript

Feb.
no!—March 1st 1905—

My dear Gosse,

In your Kit-Kats[15] (what a pretty place that club is, by the way where our MacMillan friends took me, one happy London day) you speak of "Question and Answer" and "Inclusions" as virtually of the "Portuguese Sonnets" series. But what of "Life and Love" "A Denial," "Proof and Disproof" (then come the above two) and Insufficiency! Are not the Misses Porter and Clarke[16] (in their admirable Coxhoe edition) right in saying that "All these [6][17] poems should be regarded as supplementing the Sonnets from the Portuguese as personal lyrical expressions of the poet's soul experiences upon meeting Robert Browning." *What on earth else can they be?* Will you not deeply oblige me by glancing at them again and telling me what you think about it?—and "My Star."

---

ordinary rapid-reading ability, together with a two-page list of the President's reading during the previous two years.

[14] Morley had been much impressed by Roosevelt during his recent visit to the United States (cf. Rosamond Gilder, *Letters of R. W. Gilder*, p. 367).

[15] Gosse, *Critical Kit-Kats*, p. 13. It was this essay, "The Sonnets from the Portuguese," which led Gosse to be suspected of complicity in the forgeries of his friend T. J. Wise: see Fannie E. Ratchford, ed., *Letters of Thomas J. Wise to John Henry Wrenn* (New York: Knopf, 1944), especially pp. 31–32, 38–39, and 81–90. For a defense of Gosse, see William O. Raymond, *The Infinite Moment and Other Essays in Robert Browning* ([Toronto]: University of Toronto Press, 1950), pp. 176–192.

[16] Gilder's allusion is to *The Complete Works of Mrs. E. B. Browning,* eds. Charlotte Porter and Helen A. Clarke (New York: The Riverdale Press, 1963), III, 390–391.

[17] Gilder's brackets.

What a naughty boy you were to print that about our "civilly" but "coldly" showing the door to Stevenson, *without my footnote*![18] You know I was in Europe anyhow where you were showing me how to *enter your* door, for my happiness,—showing me the outside of your door—And—well it's all in that footnote! And so now in European literature I am to be remembered but as one who showed the beloved Stevenson the door. Oh it is damnable! and me with so many sins of stupidity to answer for which I am always trying to hide—and to be skewered forever, and by *you,* as a kicker-out of so fine a genius! so angelic a visitor.

Never-mind!—Mrs. Stevenson tells me that if I had seen Louis I *would* have turned him out! She says he looked the part; and every one *did* turn him out. Was it a dig or a compliment when she said likewise that I reminded her of him!

We see much of the Strongs—by the way—mother and son[19]—t'other night here were together Stevenson's step daughter and Kipling's sister in law[20]—so near are the great, and so far away—one in South Africa, —one on the inviolate mountain of birds—at the world's end.

If I could write like you—I would some day write out my last visit to Camden—Whitman on his death-bed—ever memorable sight that.[21]

Still referring to Kit-Kats—Did I ever tell you that in about 1872–3 the girl I married[22] in 1874 had in her possession La Farge's[23] copy of the Rubayat [sic] of Omar Khayyam and her copy in her own handwriting of the book was the litany—the tragic undertone—to our courtship: yet re-

[18] In the essay on Robert Louis Stevenson in *Critical Kit-Kats*, Gosse had written that when Stevenson first visited the *Century* office "he had been very civilly but coldly shown the door" (p. 294). For Gilder's version of what happened on this occasion, see Rosamond Gilder, *Letters of R. W. Gilder*, pp. 146–148. Apparently Stevenson arrived without letters of introduction and no one knew who he was.

[19] Isobel Stuart Strong, the wife of Joseph Dwight Strong, was the daughter of Mrs. Fanny Osbourne, whom Stevenson had married in 1880; Mrs. Strong's son was named Austin.

[20] Josephine Balestier: cf. Letter 138, n. 1, and Letter 141. She married Dr. Theodore Dunham (information supplied by Mrs. Frank Holden).

[21] Gilder, turning over the pages of Gosse's *Critical Kit-Kats*, had come upon the Whitman essay, which includes an account (pp. 100–107) of Gosse's visit to Whitman in 1885. For Gilder's relationship with Whitman, see Smith, "The Editorial Influence of Gilder" (dissertation, Rutgers), pp. 222–238.

[22] *Critical Kit-Kats* also contains (pp. 65–92) an essay on Edward FitzGerald; for further information on Helena de Kay's manuscript copy of FitzGerald's *Rubáiyát of Omar Khayyám* (first published in London in 1859, in America in 1878), see Rosamond Gilder, *Letters of R. W. Gilder*, pp. 58, 434–435.

[23] John La Farge (1835–1910), American artist and author; Helena De Kay studied with him at the Cooper Union before her marriage to Gilder.

member me as one who never imitated the metre of it by a single stanza! I tried to get a certain N[ew] Y[ork] publisher to print it—showing him our copy—but he refused.

Faithfully

R. W. Gilder

❧ 166. *Gosse to Gilder* ❧

[London?]

20 March 1905

My dear Gilder

It is always most pleasant to see your familiar handwriting, and although you do not say so, I hope that you are finding yourself completely recovered from your long and distressing illness, which gave us great concern.

Now, why do you not come to England? You would find the family, as usual, installed at 17 Hanover Terrace, and highly rejoiced to see you; and you would find me here, in what Landor would have called my "august abode", overjoyed to do the honours of the House of Lords. I should like to show you my Library, which contains more than 50,000 volumes, and is a very charming and stately retreat for the old age of an over-worked man of letters.

I am answering your various Queries about Mrs. Browning's poems by sending you a volume which has only just appeared, by M. Fernand Henry,[1] a lawyer in the South of France who has devoted himself with extraordinary energy to the elucidation of English Literature. I believe you will think his little memoir exhaustive on all the interesting points you raise.

You will believe how much anxiety and distress we feel at the bad accounts of John Hay's health.[2] I hope that when he arrives, we shall find him less radically injured than the bulletins indicate; but it is plain that he has prolonged much too far the strain of public life. His would be an overwhelming loss for England as well as for America.

We know very little now of what passes in the intellectual life of America, and I gather that you know as little of what we are doing. I deplore

[1] Fernand Henry, *Les Sonnets Portugais d'Elizabeth Barrett Browning* (Paris, 1905).

[2] Hay at this time was still in office, but he was apparently weaker than anyone thought; he sailed for Europe under doctor's orders on 17 March 1905, and died shortly after his return, on 1 July 1905.

extremely the policy of isolation ("protection"!) which you people seem obstinately to cultivate. I compare it, to its immense disadvantage, with that liberal spirit of sympathy which prevailed 25 years ago, and which I always consider that you, in person, did so very much to cultivate and encourage. All our English authors, except a few flashy novelists, have to complain now that America is no longer a field for their ideas. You have cut yourselves off entirely, in your fantastic national pride, from sympathy with us. I believe this can only be a passing phase, and the happy relations which used to exist between our provinces of literature will be resumed.

Austin Dobson will be delighted to hear that I have heard from you. He is extremely well, and I think much happier than he used to be. I see Lang seldom, because he lives now at St. Andrews, but he often writes. His health is not what one can wish. I have not seen John Morley since his return, but I dine with him in a fortnight, and shall collect your news. Whom else used you to know? George Meredith, who seemed to be dying in 1903, has had an extraordinary recovery, and although he cannot stir now, except in a bath-chair, his mind is curiously, even feverishly active. Thomas Hardy vegetates in Dorset, and writes nothing now but verse. When he appears in London, he looks, physically, dried and whitened, but he is just the same affectionate, endearing creature that he always was. Who else is there? You must come over and see for yourself, for I cannot prolong the chronicle.

By the way, I had a truncated letter from your office—unfinished and unsigned!—kindly asking me to write an article about "The Tower".[3] Will you find out who wrote it, and say, with my best thanks, that the subject is quite outside my range of subjects, and that, as my time grows short, I feel it more and more needful to keep within the ring of what I have made my own life's business? But it was extremely kind to think of me.

All my family unite in sending you and Mrs. Gilder their best regards. My three children, though so long grown up, still live at home, although Philip is now betrothed, to our great satisfaction, to a charming girl, and will marry as soon as he can afford to do so.

Ever, my dear Gilder,

Your affectionate old Friend

Edmund Gosse

[3] Presumably, from Gosse's lack of interest in the subject, he had been asked to write on the Tower of London.

∾ 167. *Gosse to Gilder* ∾

17, Hanover Terrace, / Regent's Park, [London] N.W.

17 April 1905

My dear Gilder

I cannot for a moment consent to believe that "My Star"[1] refers to E[lizabeth] B[arrett] B[rowning]. What is the analysis of the symbol? Somebody or something is like spar—an object hiding in a dark place, absolutely invisible to the ordinary gazer, but flashing (to the poet,—who stands or moves at a particular angle—) "now a dart of red, now a dart of blue". The poet has discovered this "star", and has praised it so loudly and so long that his friends cluster round and "would fain see it too".

But he cannot show it. It is invisible to any eyes but his, and they must solace themselves with the publicity of Saturn.

All this is incompatible with the idea of E.B.B., who was a famous poet, extremely before the public, herself a "Saturn" long before R[obert] B[rowning] knew her.

My own conviction has always been that R.B. did not indicate a person at all by "My Star". I think he meant a certain peculiarly individual quality of beauty in verse, or something analogous. He was sure that it flashed its red and blue at him, was a bird to him and a flower, but he despaired (this is quite an early poem) of making his contemporaries see it. They must solace themselves with Wordsworth, or with Tennyson or with the famous and popular E.B.B., or with the recognised and hieratic forms of aesthetic beauty.

Some years ago, I came across by accident a phrase of the French sculptor Préault.[2] He said: "L'art, c'est cette étoile: je la vois et vous ne la voyez pas". Was not R.B. thinking of this? Préault was by a few years his senior. I have never made use of this, but I give it to you as (I think) important. That the Star had nothing whatever to do with E.B.B. I regard as absolutely certain.

Yours sincerely ever

Edmund Gosse

[1] See Letter 165.
[2] Antoine Auguste Préault (1809–1879), French sculptor, responsible, among many other works, for the medallion of "Silence" for the Jewish cemetery at Père Lachaise (1848).

❧ 168. *Gosse to Perry* ❧

17, Hanover Terrace, / Regent's Park, / [London] N.W.

4 December 1905

My dear Mr. Perry

I have the pleasure of sending you my article on Ibsen.[1] I have taken great pains with it and I hope you will like it.

There is one point: I have spoken of his being followed to the grave by the King. I have done so because I was told that one of the things Haakon VII. had promised to do was to attend Ibsen's funeral in person, when they thought the poet was going to die the other day. You will, of course, have all the telegrams when that event does take place, and can modify the proof, if necessary.

Please send me a proof, that I may see that the proper names, etc. are all right. But if Ibsen should die in the meantime, of course you will not wait for the returned proof, but use the article at once.

This discussion of the poor great man in his lifetime would be dreadful, if he were not practically dead already! You hear different apocryphal stories about him, but the truth is that he has had softening of the brain now for more than two years, and has fallen into absolute imbecility.

Let me hear from you, please. I am very anxious that you should like the article, which is as good as I can make it.

Yours sincerely

Edmund Gosse

[1] Gosse, "Ibsen," *Atlantic Monthly,* XCVIII (July 1906), 30–44. There is no mention of King Haakon.

❧ 169. *Gosse to Perry* ❧

[London?]

3 April 1906

My dear Professor Perry

Allow me to congratulate you and Harvard University[1] in one breath. I am extremely pleased that the Professorship, which has been vacant since Lowell gave it up, has been revived, and I should look in vain for a name which could occupy it better than yours does. I am perfectly delighted.

[1] Bliss Perry was appointed professor of English at Harvard; James Russell Lowell had been Smith Professor of French and Spanish.

It is highly necessary,—I dare say in America as I am sure in England,—to fight against the growing power of the dogmatic and doctrinaire elements in the study of literature. The intolerable dryness, the obsession about unrelated details, the multiplication of dreary and unilluminating observations! We must fight in the last ditch for the aesthetic view—beauty and entertainment, we must be bold enough to insist that these come first. And that literature is an art, and not a science. You are sound, I know, on these points.

I still earnestly hope that you will manage to include London in your round. It will give Mrs. Gosse and me the greatest pleasure to see you.

Very faithfully yours
Edmund Gosse

ꙮ 170. *Gosse to Perry* ꙮ

17, Hanover Terrace, / Regent's Park, [London] N.W.

6 March 1907

My dear Mr. Bliss Perry

Let me acknowledge the very great kindness of your letter of Feb. 5, which has reached me after considerable delay,—as I think,—on your side of the Atlantic. Was it perhaps not promptly posted?

It is truly good of you to wish me to write for you about Tolstoi as I did about Ibsen. The proposal is tempting, especially as I have read Tolstoi with care for many years.

But I do not know him in the original, which must be a very great drawback. And I am less and less a believer in him. In his two great romances, of course, my faith is firmly settled. But his miscellaneous writings, especially his pseudo-theological and pseudo-political tracts fill me with a growing languor, and even some disgust. This gigantic Tartar of a Tolstoi does really settle the problems of mankind with too brutal a positivism. If his system were accepted by mankind, it would mean the adoption of the most outrageous bondage that the human spirit and body have ever languished under.

My private belief is that Tolstoi is a nodule of pure imaginative genius floating about in a quite barbarous cocoon of folly, preposterous idealism and even (not a little) insincerity. I could not speak of him in the terms one would wish to use for a great artist dead. But thank you very much all the same.[1]

[1] Gosse did, however, write on Tolstoy the following year: "Count Lyof Tolstoi," *Contemporary Review*, XCIV (September 1908), 270–285. He was also chairman of the Tolstoy Celebration, 18 June 1908.

I came across your really delightful volume on Walt Whitman,[2] and read it with such pleasure that I had to *review*[3] it also, to try and share my pleasure with others. But I don't believe in those "children"![4] For reasons, of course, precisely opposite to those put forward by the sewers of pillows to all arm-holes.[5] The real psychology of W. W. would be enormously interesting. I think the key-note to it would be found to be a staggering ignorance, a perhaps wilful non-perception, of the real physical conditions of his nature. But the truth about him (the innermost truth) escapes from almost every page for those who can read.

Very faithfully yours

Edmund Gosse

[2] Bliss Perry, *Walt Whitman* (Boston and New York: Houghton Mifflin, 1906).
[3] "Books Supplement," London *Daily Mail*, 17 November 1906, p. 1. The review is entitled "The Good Grey Bard. Walt Whitman in Camden," and is unsigned. It deals chiefly with Horace Traubel's *With Walt Whitman in Camden (March 29–July 14, 1888)*, but towards the end Gosse turns to Perry's book. In the final paragraph he says: "We are not sure that any of those who have attempted to solve the enigma of Whitman have come nearer to success than Mr. Perry." Gosse was editor of the Supplement at this time (see Charteris, *Life and Letters of Gosse*, p. 300.
[4] Perry, in his book (pp. 44–46), accepts the story that Whitman had several illegitimate children.
[5] A quotation from Ezekiel 13:18.

ꙴ 171. *Furness to Gosse* ꙴ

Wallingford, / Delaware County, / Pennsylvania.

2 February [1908]

Dearest Gosse

Your delightful letter of the 17th made my lungs crow like Chanticleer over your accusation of 'sternness' and over your Parthian arrow 'that I was such a lazy correspondent.' Lord! Lord! there's but one honest man left, and he's old and deaf in Wallingford!

Your 'Father and Son'[1] duly arrived. I dipped into it here and there before I handed it to my secretary to have the leaves cut. In an unhappy hour, I spoke, at dinner, in such glowing terms of the contents, that my eldest son at once fastened on it, and from it could not be torn until he had read the very last page and pronounced it as 'fascinating as a novel.' It was then resigned to me, and, my dear, at two sittings I read every word of it. It is a very great

[1] [Gosse], *Father and Son: A Study of Two Temperaments* (London: Heinemann, 1907).

book. The very best you have written and the most enduring; with it, you will celebrate your century. English literature cannot afford to let such a book die. Independently of its records of a rapidly vanishing faith it is told with an evident truth as unflinching as it is tender. There is not a shred of sentimentality or of a mawkish appeal for sympathy for a childhood whereof the pathos rises almost to tragedy. Your eyes must have run over when you wrote some of those pages, and how bravely you brushed them away! Possibly, your highest achievement lies in the treatment of your father. You have so depicted him that one closes the book with a thorough respect for him. Of course there are deep regrets for his lost opportunities for happiness, but you have so represented his sincerity that it commands our admiration. And how easily, without any blame you might have made it otherwise.

Indeed, as I said before, you have written a great book, which will be prized for all time. What student of psychology can ever afford to over-look it?

The only record of a childhood overshadowed by a cruel stern religion that I can recall as at all parallel to yours, is in the 'Autobiography of W. J. Stillman,'[2] which if you never read I do entreat you to do so incontinently— a remarkable book, published six or seven years ago. Stillman, a regular down-east Yankee, was the London 'Times' correspondent for many years. Note his remarkable confirmation of Milton's 'airy tongues that syllable men's names On sands and shores,[3] etc.

Do I remember when you dined with me in Philadelphia? How can I forget it? And can you remember, that just as you were leaving (the streets and pavements were a glaze of ice) you told me something a timorous old woman said to you, over which we laughed together consumedly? Can you recall it? I cannot. I remember only the laughter. This is enough for the present. When next I write I'll tell you the specific instance that made me sign my name 'friend remembered not.' But there's room enough so I'll tell it now:—Garnett, whom I had never seen, sent me his volumes of 'English Literature,' and you whom I had known and loved never sent me yours.[4] Bohoo! Bohoo! I had to go and ignominiously buy them! and I cried all night. But bless ye, pretty one, I don't mind it now and am as always fondly thine own

H. H. F.

[2] William James Stillman, *The Autobiography of a Journalist* (Boston and New York: Houghton Mifflin, 1901).

[3] *Comus*, ll. 207–208.

[4] Richard Garnett and Edmund Gosse, *English Literature: An Illustrated Record* (London: Heinemann; New York: Macmillan, 1903). Of the four volumes of this history, Garnett wrote the first, he and Gosse collaborated in the second, and Gosse wrote the third and fourth.

ᴖ 172. *Gilder to Gosse* ᴖ

[New York]

Sunday 3 May 1908

My dear Gosse,

Kept on my back to-day, my imprisonment has been brightened by "Father and Son," which I have read from cover to cover at a lying.—Besides being a masterly piece of literature that is surely one of the most useful books of our time—useful and well-nigh unique historically—and useful as a warning.

My own experience (how many must have told you that!) was somewhat similar, but without the *parental* stress. I suppose my orthodox father was not as logical as yours.

I wish to Heaven I could chat with you oftener than once in five or ten years.

Faithfully

R. W. Gilder

Gosse! the deaths here are making an ancient of me! It makes me blue when I think of those who are dropping out.—Your friend Cawein[1] was here lately—with his good head and his frappant wife. We talked of you— of course.—So you see some are dropping in!

[1] Madison Julius Cawein (1865–1914) wrote lyrics—some thirty-six volumes in all—about his native Kentucky. A selection entitled *Kentucky Poems,* with an introduction by Gosse, was published in England in 1902 (London: Grant Richards). Howells, who particularly admired Cawein's work, thought Gosse's introduction was lukewarm (see Introduction, p. 42).

ᴖ 173. *James[1] to Gosse* ᴖ

The Reform Club [London]

1 June 1909

My dear Gosse.

I thank you very kindly for your renewed inquiry, and send this poor word—so charged with dreary references—off after you into high-breasted Tuscany where it will seem to you, when it reaches you, wretchedly irrele-

[1] For Gosse's friendship and correspondence with Henry James (1843–1916), see Introduction, pp. 37–38. The first letter from James to Gosse in the Brotherton Collection is dated 2 August 1882. For published letters on both sides see Percy Lubbock, ed., *Letters of Henry James* (New York: Scribner's, 1922); Leon Edel, ed., *Selected Letters of Henry James* (London: Hart-Davis, 1956); and Charteris, *Life and Letters of Gosse.*

vant and inferior. I am better, thank you, and was able on Sunday to hobble down to some friends in Oxfordshire, whence I returned to-day, still hobbling and unable to wear a proper shoe, but with most of my torment of pain gone and only lumpishness and a slight residuum (of local anguish) remaining. The lumpishness declines but slowly and takes patience. Such are my prosy little facts. Yours, by this time, must be all romantic and delightful; and I hope you are now up to your necks in the whole wondrous matter. Give my love to every old stone and my blessing to every old woman—as that of an older one still. Go to San Gimignano—and *drive* back in the late June p.m. It has been a lovely Whitsuntide—save for desperately wanted rain to-day—during which it has bravely and beautifully poured. I was motored 30 miles of Monday—through a beauty of country and *moment* that had nothing to envy even Tuscany. Amusez-vous-bien. My bestest love to your comrades.

Always your

H. J.

℘ 174. *James to Gosse* ℘

Reform Club, / Pall Mall. [London] S.W.

4 June 1909

My dear Gosse.

I have read your 'Swinburne' in the Fortnightly[1] and find it admirable—delightfully done and very *interesting*; the best, on the whole, I think of your portraits in that kind—and with the advantage of so excellent a subject. I am sending you with this, àpropos of it, the *Times* Lit. Supp. of Thursday last for the two long Stedman letters[2] (*favoured* Edmund Clarence!) which you may have seen, but which I post on the chance. I find them quite charming—and deserving *that* particular description more than anything of C[harles] A[lgernon] S[winburne][3] that I can remember—certainly than any other morsel of his prose.

Happy fugitives from a horror of black cold and wet—fires and overcoats and rivers of mud—to which we have fallen heirs since you left. You breathe of course a golden air and perspire in pearls and diamonds. I still hobble in a grandmother shoe—but am thankful to circulate even so. The

[1] Gosse, "Swinburne: Personal Recollections," *Fortnightly Review*, XCI (June 1909), 1019–1039.

[2] Two letters from Swinburne to Stedman were published in the *Times Literary Supplement*, 27 May 1909, p. 106, and two more the following week.

[3] This inversion of Swinburne's initials is James's own.

Holbein Duchess has been saved—by a veiled lady who has bought her off for £40,000.[4] Can you lift the veil? I am afraid on second thoughts that you are not at a hotel, but wherever you are I invoke all the local graces upon you and am yours all auspiciously

Henry James

[4] In the *Times* for 4 June 1909, appears (p. 6) a letter from the honorary secretaries of the National Art-Collections Fund stating that Holbein's "Duchess of Milan" had been saved for the nation and would remain in the National Gallery: "One contributor, whose identity we are not at liberty to disclose, has given no less a sum than £40,000."

❧ 175. *Gosse to James* ❧

G[ra]nd Hotel Continental / Siena

11 June 1909

My dear James

You have given us immense pleasure by two most welcome letters. What you say about the little Swinburne portrait gratifies me very much indeed.

You are in some sense the source of the success of our present visit, for, after becoming conscious of the isolation from all other scenes of this exquisite remote Siena, we bethought us of your suggestion, and said "Motor!" to one another, with a guilty flush and rising pulse, as of those who really—this time—were going, in the most abandoned manner, to the Devil. On inquiry, it appeared that Siena possesses a motor, and that an "arrangement" was possible, an arrangement meaning that a vivid demon, like a handsome wicked gargoyle, proposed (as such a sacrifice!) terms so preposterous that we broke violently from him, and sat down contemptuously (with our backs to him) to drink "tre vermouth con selz", so that the demon had, with twitching hands spread wide, and appealing to high heaven, to invite *us* to name a sum, which, with heads still averted we did, the result being that he fled, or feigned to fly, from the hotel-lounge, as one who was offered bankruptcy to his very face by scorners; and then, we hardly knew how, a medium price—horribly exorbitant still, but no longer insane—had been agreed between us. The demon possesses a splendid car, and he drives with the skill and daring of the Father of all demons. We have been to Cortona, and to Montepulciano, and all round the Lake of Trasimeno, and to Perugia and Assisi and as far as Foligno, and have run in the demoniac car right up to the very tip-top of perfectly impossible mountain-towns, and have rioted like the levin into depths beneath. Now we are "lying up" to rest, and let a little money accumulate, and then we are going, non obstante diavolo, to do it again on the other side. There is unbridled licence for you, and how after it are we to face the decent world of London? But it was thou who willed it, Georges Dandin.[1]

The weather has been absolutely exquisite, except for rather too frequent thunder-storms. I have said nothing of Siena itself, which is a paradise. This hotel,—it must be *your* hotel,—is a delightful place, the people all so kind, our rooms high up and vast, commanding the whole trough of the city between the Duomo and S. Domenico, and an endless campagna. We stay here (d.n.o.) until Thursday the 24th. So glad you are better: but if you were only *here*, you would be quite well.

Love from us all three.

Your devoted
E. G.

[1] In Molière's comedy *George Dandin, ou le mari confondu*, the nouveau riche George Dandin realizes he has only himself to blame for the miseries which result from his determination to marry above his station: "Vous l'avez voulu; vous l'avez voulu, George Dandin, vous l'avez voulu" (Act I, scene ix).

❧ 176. *Gosse to James* ❧

The Ashfield Hotel / Settle

27 August 1909

My dear James

It will be a fortnight tomorrow since I came down to Rye, and so much (tho' in fact so little) has confusedly happened since then. I must tell you how wonderfully, for the moment, your kind cheerful hospitality quieted my nerves and banished my cares, but they crowded in again on Monday.

Nellie was extremely touched by your letter. She has, no doubt, told you so; at any rate she will. She was wonderfully brave all that week, and went with me, and with the girls, to the funeral[1] at Kensal Green, which was a hurried affair in hideous plashing rain, but "went off", as people say, very well. Poor Tadema was sustained by having a great deal to do, and by quite a shower of letters and telegrams from the King, the Queen, the Princess and Prince of Wales, Princess Louise and I know not whom, things which have strangely, in these times, their consolatory and digressive use.

[1] Funeral of Laura Alma-Tadema, Mrs. Gosse's sister.

Down here I came the next day, and met A[rthur] C[hristopher] B[enson],[2] who, I am sure you will be glad to hear, appears really and substantially better. It is a huge pleasure really to dare to say that at last. We have had extremely cold wet weather, but we have managed to motor every day, a little. Yesterday was dry and we went over to Haworth, 30 miles there and 30 back. Have you ever been to Haworth? It was a surprise to me to find it so much prettier, much more tufted with trees and gay with gardens than I expected,—but this is all introduced since the grim Brontës looked out of the stern vicarage windows across the crowds of tombstones; and to see that it lies close above, and is almost a suburb of, a large town, Keighley. But we went up above the last houses of Haworth, behind the cemetery, and there you are at once in the endless moor, in the country of "Wuthering Heights" and Wildfell Hall.

I am coming back to town next Wednesday. A. C. B. sends you his faithful love. I am

Ever yours
E. G.

[2] Arthur Christopher Benson (1862–1925), man of letters, Fellow of Magdalene College, Cambridge, from 1904, and Master of the College from 1915 until his death.

꙯ 177. James to Gosse ꙯

Lamb House, / Rye, / Sussex.

28 August 1909

My dear Gosse.

All thanks for your letter, with its note of the wretched actual surmounted and overpast—so far as such wretched actualities may be; which brings home to one that there is always an *after* to current events, however damnable *as* current, and that so long as one lives (by which I mean the longer,) this blest subsequence seems to ⟨se⟩ *faire de moins en moins attendre*. It is already with us at the acute moment, getting the moment acute behind it— though only, unfortunately, that particular one. It has, alas, itself other acute moments up its sleeve. But in short let us go on taking them one by one. Which reflection indeed is better addressed, in its very imperfect ingenuity, to you than to your wife—to whom the blackness of a couple of weeks ago may have become a relative greyness—but a greyness that won't so soon in turn change colour. A very hard grim fact that of charming Laura Tadema's unmitigated absence and extinction, surely. And you must still be under the projected shadow of that dreadful consciousness of your daughter-in-law's.

Poor Philip—who is so very *straight* under it! I quite unspeakably feel for them—and for Mrs. Nelly in this sore maternal connection too. Let her not dream of "writing" me a single syllable. What a horrible addition that to the other burdens of bereavement and anxiety!—I am extremely glad meanwhile that you were able to work through, in A[rthur] C[hristopher] B[enson]'s company, into another aspect of things; and particularly another aspect of his condition, since you can definitely report it as ameliorated, for which I definitely congratulate *you* almost more than anybody else—that is almost more than the suffering subject himself—in whom you must have done more than anybody else to bring the happier result about. Very interesting and charming your account of the classic Haworth,[1] which I have watched, in my long life, *grow* classic, and yet never seen scarce been within miles of, but which you make me want to see. I don't despair of it yet, for I don't mind travelling (by which I am afraid, however, I but sneakingly mean motoring) in these islands. On the mainland I more and more hate it. It is very tranquil here, for a wonder; in spite of motors—and very beautiful—and I am unsociably and inhospitably applying myself—in view of having to be away a part of next month. Today here has really been a ravishment. But good-night, and please speak afresh, at home, of the continued participation of

Yours ever
Henry James

[1] See Letter 176.

❧ 178. *Howells to Gosse* ❧

130 West 57th Street, [New York]

28 May 1910

My dear Gosse:

It was sweet of you to write, and of Mrs. Gosse to send me a word of pity.[1] At moments it seems as if my sorrow were more than I could bear, but I know it is sorrow that comes in some form to all, and I try to be a man.

You will forgive me if I cannot reply fitly to you.

My daughter and I are going to England in June and I shall hope to see you.

With my love to Mrs. Gosse, believe, dear friend of happy days, that I am

Yours affectionately
W. D. Howells

[1] Howells's wife, Elinor Mead Howells, died on 7 May 1910.

❧ 179. *Gosse to Howells* ❧

17, Hanover Terrace, / Regent's Park, [London] N.W.

14 July 1910

My dear Howells

"The Kentons" and "Questionable Shapes"[1] have arrived, in the wake of your most kind letter. Is it possible that I can have addressed an envelope to you as W. H.?[2] I am not less frightened than ashamed, for I find myself now too frequently the victim of these aberrations, due wholly to tiredness and old age. If there is a name engraved upon my memory it is the very dear one of Dean.

Now I want you to tell me with perfect frankness if there is any one of my recent books which you would like to receive? They are all at your feet, only I don't like to burden you with the weight of them. Would the "Life of Ibsen",[3]—which has been honoured in Norway itself as being the fullest and best,—offer you any attraction? Inside "Father and Son", which you must have now received, you will find a catalogue of my ineptitudes. Is there one therein which I might send you?

I suppose you saw Henry[4] yesterday? It was a very joyful surprise to me.

Ever affectionately yours

Edmund Gosse

I have not thanked you for anything! I will do so as adequately as I can a little later. Meanwhile, I pounce upon "The Kentons". You are good, indeed.

[1] Howells, *The Kentons* (New York and London: Harper, 1902); *Questionable Shapes* (New York and London: Harper, 1903).

[2] In a letter to Gosse dated 13 July 1910 (a.l.s., C. Waller Barrett Collection, University of Virginia), Howells had said that he would be sending Gosse two books and hoped to add *Literary Friends and Acquaintance* later; Gosse was to inscribe them "To Edmund Gosse from his affectionate W. D. (not H.) Howells, 302 Beacon St., December, 1883." Information supplied by Professor George Arms.

[3] Gosse, *Ibsen* (London: Hodder and Stoughton, 1907).

[4] Henry James. He had been on the Continent with his brother (see Letter 180, n. 1) and was not expected to return to England so soon.

❧ 180. *Howells to Gosse* ❧

18 Half Moon Street, [London]

14 July 1910

Dearest Gosse:

No, no, no! *You* never called me W. H., but Hardy did, and introduced me round as such. I told you of it, the other night, when we were each so full of himself, that he had no room for any other; and you naturally thought I was talking of you.

James has just been here, looking better than he felt, and now I am going out to find his brother and sister-in-law.[1]

I should delight to have your life of Ibsen, who has been so much in mine; and any book of yours. The "Father and Son" hasn't come yet; but it will, and welcome.

We are still in the glow of seeing you; and my daughter joins in regards to you all.

Yours affectionately

W. D. Howells

[P.S. on envelope] The beautiful little book has just come.

[1] William James and his wife Alice (see Mildred Howells, *Life in Letters of Howells*, II, 287).

❧ 181. *Howells to Gosse* ❧

18 Half Moon Street, [London]

16 July 1910

My dear Gosse:

I read slowly and faithfully, and I have got only to the point of your mother's death.[1] But what a world I have passed through! There is a universal truth to child life in it all, and the specialized truth is most wonderful and pitiful. I have fairly ached along the story. In all the autobiographic books I have read, I remember nothing equalling it. I should like to talk over every page of it with you.

Yours ever

W. D. Howells

[1] Howells was reading Gosse's *Father and Son*.

ᘓᘔ 182. *Howells to Gosse* ᘔᘓ

18 Half Moon Street, / [London]

21 July 1910

Dear Gosse:

I finished your wonderful book yesterday morning at 6.30. It clung to me like a limpet (What *is* a limpet, anyway?) I have told you about its absorbing interest; now I want to praise its diction, which seems to me exquisite in its tender precision. The pathetic tale could not be better worded if a syndicate of masters rose from their graves to do it: say Milton, Dante and Shakespeare. Truly a most beautiful book.

Yours ever

W. D. Howells

ᘓᘔ 183. *Gosse to Howells* ᘔᘓ

17, Hanover Terrace, / Regent's Park, [London] N.W.

26 July 1910

My dear Howells

I thought you left town for the drinking of rotten waters a week ago, and therefore did not write, tho' I had very much to say.

Yes, indeed, I received the Academic papers,[1] with many thanks. And I hope you saw in the Times of last Wednesday the actual constitution and launching of our Academy?[2] It has been received by the Press with less derision than might have been expected, but the body is composed of violently

---

[1] A postcard from Howells to Gosse dated 25 July 1910 (BM) reads: "Did E. G. ever get the Proceedings of the American Academy which his faithful W. D. H. sent while his Little Mary was still distended with E. G.'s meat and drink?" The card was sent in an envelope, and on the reverse side is a note in Howells's hand: "I was afraid to send this naked through the post; the English officials are so very particular." Howells was the first president of the American Academy of Arts and Letters; he was elected on 7 November 1908 and remained president until his death (Mildred Howells, *Life in Letters of Howells*, II, 259). At Christmas 1909, Howells wrote to James: "Last week I went to Washington, where our poor Academy held its first public sessions. The papers read were really fine, but I think the public did not care in the least. The President had us all to tea in the White House, and was very civil" (*ibid.*, 277).

[2] The London *Times*, 20 July 1910, p. 10, has a report on the foundation of the Academic Committee of the Royal Society of Literature, and a definition of its duties.

individualised atoms, and whether it can be drawn in any one way remains to be seen.

I have been very much in your company mentally, for not only have I studied your three admirable stories forming "Questionable Shapes",[3] but I have come across, quite by accident, a volume called "In After Days",[4] of which I must speak to you. There are nine essays in it, seven of which are quite babbling and ineffectual, but there is one of yours in the opening and one of H[enry] J[ames]'s at the close which are most remarkable. James' essay is the perfect quintessence of his laborious candour, so dense that one's mind sticks upright in it like a spoon in molasses. Through it he fights for the utterance of his thought, and his thought is so shadowy and tentative that he does not quite know how to defend it, or whether it is there at all. It is an extraordinary piece of gymnastics, and almost as bracing to read as it must have been to write.

But yours, my dear Howells, your "Counsel of Consolation", how am I to tell you with what tender glow of appreciation I read it? Every word in it is instinct with wisdom and sweetness and beauty. I cannot say how it moved me, even to tears, which were not tears of pain, but of joy and hope and immense sympathy. This is a very lovely essay of yours.

Also, since I am full of you, I must speak of your Presidential Address,[5] which is excellently adapted to its purpose. Lord Morley[6] is to be our President, but I am afraid he is too much dissipated by his political duties to be very serviceable.

If I had the happiness of seeing you more, there are many things I should like to discuss at length, and learn of you. Your stories breathe the very atmosphere of reality, and therefore one questions the causes of their action, just as one would those of veritable incidents. What puzzles me, and has always puzzled me, is the scrupulousness of your characters. Hewson, in "His Apparition",[7] is absolutely life-like, and drawn with your delicate humour. But why is he so high-strung and lady-like? Are you drawing him

[3] See Letter 179 and n. 1.

[4] *In After Days: Thoughts on the Future Life*, by W. D. Howells, Henry James, John Bigelow, Thomas Wentworth Higginson, Henry M. Alden, William Hanna Thomson, Guglielmo Ferrero, Julia Ward Howe, Elizabeth Stuart Phelps . . . (New York and London: Harper, 1910). Henry James's essay is the final one, entitled "Is there a Life after Death?" (pp. 199–233). The essay by Howells is entitled "A Counsel of Consolation" (pp. 3–16).

[5] "Opening Address of the President, William Dean Howells," *Proceedings of the American Academy*, 10 June 1910, I, 5–8. The address was given in Washington, D.C., on 14 December 1909. See n. 1 above.

[6] John Morley had been invited to become president of the new Academic Committee of the Royal Society of Literature (see n. 2 above).

[7] "His Apparition," first published in *Harper's Monthly*, CIV (March 1902), 621–648, is the first of the three stories comprising *Questionable Shapes* (see Letter 179, n. 1).

as a caricature, or are there men of this spinster type in America? All this, and much more, I should like to talk and talk and talk to you about. But you may thank your stars that the flood-gate closes. I shall come round, however, and try some day to catch you between the horns of the Half Moon.[8]

Yours affectionately

Edmund Gosse

I have no news of the poor James'es. Have you?

[8] Howells was staying at 18 Half Moon Street.

❧ 184. *Gosse to Wharton*[1] ❧

17 Hanover Terrace, Regent's Park / [London] N.W.

14 February 1911

Dear Mrs. Wharton

. . . .

In the course of last autumn I began to think seriously about the Nobel Prize for Henry James. The English Committee votes once a year, after Christmas, and this year I gave my vote to him, and induced one or two other people to do the same. That was merely to accustom the Swedes to his name. Lord Avebury,[2] who is chairman, is strongly in favour of Lord Morley, and exercises a good deal of influence in that direction. Moreover, the Swedish Committee, although it constantly appeals to us for advice, has never, on one single occasion, taken it. We were unanimous, year after year, for Swinburne, but the prize was never given to him.

[1] Edith Newbold Wharton (1862–1937) was at the height of her powers as a novelist during the years of her friendship with Gosse. In her autobiography, *A Backward Glance* (New York and London: Appleton-Century, 1934) Edith Wharton speaks of Gosse as one "who always showed me great kindness" (p. 220), and recalls that she first met him at the home of Lady Essex in the early years of the century. The Book of Gosse records visits by Mrs. Wharton on 8 December 1908 and 17 July 1913, and in a letter of 10 [July 1913] (a.l.s., BC) she wrote to accept the invitation for 17 July, adding: "It will be *such* a pleasure to see you again. . . ." Apart from the letters included here, a number of other letters from this correspondence are in the Brotherton Collection and in the American literature collection of Yale University Library; those at Yale are at present in the "restricted" category. The text of the present letter has been taken from an incomplete, typed copy in Harvard University Library; the original has not been found, but the subject matter seemed of sufficient importance to justify publication of the letter in its present form.

[2] John Lubbock, first Baron Avebury (1834–1913), banker, politician, and man of affairs, also wrote numerous books of a popular kind on science and natural history.

My idea now is that the best way to further James's interests is to press him as an *American* candidate. America has not yet received the Nobel Prize for Literature, and there will be (and I know is) a considerable feeling that it is America's turn. I may tell you—what it may be useful to you to know—that a strong effort has been (and perhaps is still being) made to secure it for Winston Churchill,[3] the American novelist.

I advise very strong American influence to be exercised. One of the three final judges this coming year is the novelist Per Hallström,[4] the Academician, who in his youth lived for a long while in America, and is open to American types of thought. The worst of such people is that, though charming writers in their own language, in ours they think Conan Doyle[5] "so strong" and Marie Corelli[6] "so passionate".

If you can do anything to produce a strong current of the best American opinion to beat upon the Nobel Committee at Stockholm, I will endeavour privately to press home your efforts. I will, in due season, write a strong letter to Per Hallström,[7] and to Baron Bildt[8] (another of the Eighteen, and one who exercises a great deal of influence). I do not think much good can be done, this year, by any public efforts on the part of the English Committee, which is foolishly pledged to Morley (who most certainly will not get it), but if America would immediately concentrate its efforts on our friend, much might be done. Is there a Nobel Prize sub-committee in America?

I would take any trouble, and fling any form of conscientious scruple or

[3] Winston Churchill (1871–1947), popular American novelist, dealt in some of his better novels, such as *Coniston* (1906) and *Mr. Crewe's Career* (1908) with contemporary political issues; he himself played some part in New Hampshire politics as a member of the legislature and as candidate for the governorship.

[4] Per August Leonard Hallström (1866–1960), Swedish novelist and writer of short stories, had been a member of the Swedish Academy since 1908.

[5] Sir Arthur Conan Doyle (1859–1930), romantic novelist and creator of Sherlock Holmes, the detective.

[6] Marie Corelli (1855–1924), the highly popular romantic novelist.

[7] For Gosse's letter to Hallström, dated 24 April 1911, see Elias Bredsdorff, ed., *Sir Edmund Gosse's Correspondence with Scandinavian Writers* (London: Heinemann, 1960), pp. 287–288. Supporting the recommendation of the American Academy that the prize be awarded to James, Gosse writes: "I suppose that all the competent critics of this age would combine in agreeing that he is the greatest living writer of America. With the sole exception of Thomas Hardy, he is doubtless the most eminent living writer of the English language" (p. 287). In an earlier letter of 22 March 1911 (p. 286) Gosse had merely sent Hallström a list of the thirty original members of the English "Academy"—the Academic Committee of the Royal Society of Literature (see Letter 183, n. 2).

[8] Karl Niels Daniel Bildt, Baron Bildt (1850–1931), Swedish diplomat and historian, had been a member of the Swedish Academy since 1901. His name appears in the Book of Gosse twice in 1903 and once in 1905.

self-respecting delicacy to the winds, if so I could give our dear friend more confidence in the future.

I am very sincerely yours

Edmund Gosse

᧡ 185. *Wharton to Gosse* ᧡

53, Rue de Varenne [Paris]

18 February 1911

Dear Mr. Gosse,

I didn't write you because I never, if I can help it, send a superfluous letter to a Man of Letters; and knowing that Mr. Lapsley[1] was a friend of many of your friends, I thought that he, or some one else, would be able to "touch you a word" on the question that interests us.

I can't regret that my considerate conduct has, after all, resulted in your writing me, for your letter shows me how right I was in thinking you would and could help us.

I know nothing definite about Mr. James's financial situation, except that there is very little money in the family, and that his "rentes" must be extremely small. As to what he makes from his books, it is safe to say that he cannot compete with any of the favourite authors of the Swedish Committee—and certainly not with Mr. Winston (U.S.A.) Churchill!

But the main thing is that he is undoubtedly worried about his future, and that this material anxiety is not helping him to get well. On this ground he is certainly a proper subject for the Nobel prize—while as to the other: his claim as our first man of letters, I suppose there can be no question of his fitness.

I am finding out through Count Gyldenstolpe,[2] the Swedish Minister here, if there is an American Committee. I am also writing to Mr. Howells, who is one of Mr. James's intimate friends, and (next to him) the *doyen* of American novelists; and I am hoping he can give a start to the movement in America, or tell us what to do to set it going.

---

[1] Gaillard Thomas Lapsley (1871–1949), the historian, was born and educated in the United States but settled in England in 1904 as tutor at Trinity College, Cambridge. He was a close friend of Henry James and, especially, of Edith Wharton: see Percy Lubbock, *Portrait of Edith Wharton* (London: Jonathan Cape, 1947), pp. 7–8 and *passim*. Lapsley had apparently called on Gosse at Mrs. Wharton's request (a.l.s., BC, Wharton to Lapsley, 7 February 1911).

[2] August Louis Fersen Gyldenstolpe, Count Gyldenstolpe (1849–1928), was Swedish ambassador to Paris from 1905 to 1918.

I may be in England toward the end of February for a week or ten days—when I say England I mean London—and if I am, I will send you a line and ask you to talk over the plan of action with me.

Thank you mean while for your letter, and for all you mean to do for our dear friend.

It would be a great pleasure to see you again.

Yours sincerely

Edith Wharton

❧ 186. *Howells to Gosse* ❧

Hamilton, Bermuda,

6 March 1911

My dear Gosse:

Mrs. Wharton has written me from Paris, enclosing your letter about the Nobel prize for James. I hate you for having thought of it first, but it is so absolutely fit, so perfectly right, that I can almost forgive you. Of course I am moving at once in the matter, and am trying to start the Academy and other literary bodies. Will you tell me where we may bring our action to bear? Can we tag onto you? There is no American point d'appui that I know of. What can you suggest? Will you kindly write me in care of Harper & Brothers, Franklin Square, N.Y.?

I sent you "Literary Friends and Acquaintance,"[1] last fall, as I promised. I am afraid it did not reach you.

My daughter is here with me; we have a pretty little white-roofed house among the cedars and red-birds; but we go home at the end of the month.

Saturday we went to see Tom Moore's[2] house; it would just suit you, and there is a calabash tree that he used to write poems in; you would like it. Say the word, and I will buy it for you. You will have Waller and Marvel[3] [sic] and me for neighbors. With best regards to Mrs. Gosse.

Yours ever

W. D. Howells

[1] Howells, *Literary Friends and Acquaintance* (New York: and London: Harper, 1900).

[2] Thomas Moore (1779–1852), the Irish poet, was appointed registrar of the admiralty prize-court in Bermuda in 1803; the following year, however, he appointed a deputy and returned to England.

[3] Alludes to two poems: "The Battle of the Summer Islands" by Edmund Waller and "Bermudas" by Andrew Marvell.

17, Hanover Terrace, / Regent's Park, [London] N.W.

22 March 1911

My dear Howells

I am very much obliged to you indeed for your charming letter from the still-vext Bermoothes (which must indeed be vexed at your going away from them). What a life of luxurious indolence you lead, while I moil and toil in the dust! Well! I will dwell first of all on the great subject, how the Nobel Prize (of 37,000 dollars) can be secured for "dear old Uncle Henry" as the children call him at Rye.[1]

First of all, it is extremely generous and like yourself that you take up the idea so warmly. You ask my counsel? Well, I should think that the best way would be to do it through the American Academy. Whatever use I can be, as a channel or a chain, I devote myself to the task with eagerness.

Now let me tell you. This enormous sum of between £7000 and £8000 has been left to be given *every year* to some "idealistic" (by which we take "imaginative" to be meant) writer. It has been given to Björnsen, Mistral, Carducci, Rudyard Kipling (!), Echegaray, Sully Prudhomme, and I know not whom else. It is given by the Nobel Committee of the Swedish Academy, and finally rests with 3 Academicians.

When I tell you that for years and years the English committee unanimously recommended Swinburne for it, and were annually and finally snubbed by seeing it given to Kipling whom nobody had recommended, you will see that it is not a very easy body to deal with. It is, indeed, an obstinate, conceited, clever and ignorant body. It is well aware of the importance its annual gift bestows upon it.

But I know several of the innermost ring. And in particular, the boss of the show for the moment, the novelist Per Hallström, who is very intelligent, reads English and has been a long time in America. I suggest that you get up, very privately (no newspaper par[agraph]s, I mean) a petition from the Academy of America, signed by you as President. Before sending it, communicate privately with Per Hallström through me. I shall rejoice to confirm the matter from my own point of view, as he (poor thing!) supposes me to be a person of assured taste.

They want dreadfully to do the right thing, but they don't know what the right thing is. They have been told that Winston Churchill is the leading living writer of U.S.A.[2] and I gather that he himself confirmed that view by word of mouth in a recent triumphal progress through Europe. It is highly

---

[1] Henry James lived at Lamb House, Rye, Sussex.
[2] See Letter 184, n. 3.

desirable that America should without delay impress upon the Swedes that this is not the official view in America.

I have now crudely put the matter before you. But here I am at your service for anything you like to set me as a task.

———————

Yes, indeed I received your beautiful autobiography,[3] and read every word of it with admiration and joy. But you have a most annoying way of disappearing, leaving no address or means of tracking you, and then blaming your friends for not writing to you. To tell the plain truth, I thought you behaved rather unkindly to us last summer, for after our doing our poor little level best to make you feel how fond we were of you, and how glad to be in close relations with you, you suddenly vanished, without saying goodbye, without a written word of farewell, and without a sign of an address. No, you are too fond of blaming your friends for the effects of your own caprice. There! I have spoken my mind quite out, and I have no thought now but gladness that the prodigal correspondent has returned.

Yours ever sincerely and affectionately

Edmund Gosse

[3] *Literary Friends and Acquaintance* (see Letter 186, n. 1).

ᖇᖇ 188. *Howells to Gosse* ᖇᖇ

130 West 57th Street, [New York]

7 April 1911

My dear Gosse:

Your very darling letter came while I was still in Bermuda, waving our flag in the artificial teeth of your decrepit lion; and I have lost no time since my return in getting together the enclosed documents. I wish I could duly stamp them, but I can only enclose some American stamps which you can send our editors for use in returning your rejected MSS.

Dearest fellow, you are truly—or untruly—it comes to the same thing—sweet to take up the cause of H[enry] J[ames] so generously. It is such a good cause I feel it *must* fail, and you may think I have done my worst to hurt it. But I haven't *tried* to hurt it in my letter to Per Gynt Hallström. (Oh, why had I never read any of his novels!) I hope you will think well of it.

H. J. is here in N[ew] Y[ork], very much recovered at last from his accursed Fletcherizing,[1] and all of us are round him, shoo-ing each other so that he may not know what we are doing for him.

I will write later in reply to your shameless and insincere reproaches. You know you were glad to have us clear out last summer without a sign. Our love to you all.

Yours ever

W. D. Howells

[1] "Fletcherism," named after its inventor, Horace Fletcher (1849–1919), involves the prolonged mastication of food until it has become a liquified mass. The practice was said to have nutritional advantages, but James's friends were convinced that it was damaging his health.

☙ 189. *Wharton to Gosse* ☙

53 Rue de Varenne [Paris]

5 May 1911

Dear Mr. Gosse,

I know that you have heard from Mr. Howells how actively the Nobel Prize propaganda is being forwarded in America in behalf of Henry James, and how much all his friends there appreciative [sic] the way in which you have preached the cause in England.

The last news of him is not good. He has been spending the greater part of the winter with my sister-in-law[1] in New York, and she writes that, in spite of occasional moments of encouragement, his general condition has not improved much, and that he has not been able to do any work at all.

I am going to America next month, and hope to have him with me in the country during the whole of July, as he does not return to England till August.

This is just a word to tell you again how grateful I am to you for all you have done and are doing, and say how sorry I am that my thanks must be written instead of spoken.

Next year I hope to be in England again, and to see you there if not here. But don't you ever come to Paris?

Ever yours sincerely

Edith Wharton

[1] Mrs. Mary Cadwalader [Rawle] Jones, living at 21 East Eleventh Street, New York City, was the wife of Edith Wharton's brother, Frederic Rhinelander Jones.

∾ 190. *Howells to Gosse* ∾

Hotel Wellington / 7th Ave. 55th Street / New York.

13 May 1911

My dear Gosse:

Per Hallström has written me a kind but forbidding letter as regards this year; it is too late, so I understand him, to do anything for James at present. But he says he will send my letter to the committee. Meantime I will write him and ask what steps we shall take for next year.

So far we have kept our plot out of the papers, and though it is the secret of many we hope to keep it from the most—including James.

I have just heard from the friend whom he was stopping with here[1] that he is low in mind and body at Cambridge. He has put off going back to England, until August, and will be with us awhile (I hope) in June at Kittery Point.

We have begun to dream, my daughter and I, of a vicarage, say from Aug. 15, to Oct. 15. Are there still Vicars in England, and do they let their ages?

It is very hideous here with the noise, dust and heat; but I love you.

Yours ever

W. D. Howells

[1] Presumably Mrs. Cadwalader Jones (see Letter 189, n. 1).

∾ 191. *Gosse to Howells* ∾

17, Hanover Terrace, / Regent's Park, [London] N.W.

24 May 1911

My dear Howells

Hallström has not answered my letter, so that I am glad to hear that he has written properly to you. I did not hope that we should conquer at the first clang of our bucklers, but we must go on clanging. It is a very great thing that America has never yet had her turn. They must feel that. Then, the thing is to make it absolutely evident to them that H[enry] J[ames] is their man. Let me say, in crudity and frankness, that I do not take the line of pushing *your* name, because of the simple fact that H. J. is mortified and

279

subdued by a poverty which makes us disregard all the civilities in other cases. I think it is most unselfish and like-yourself that you join in this, since you are so manifestly the Leader of American Literature. But I accept (if I dare to say I "accept" anything!) your sacrifice, because the necessity of doing something to give H. J. peace of mind has become imperative.

By the way, is he not well enough to answer letters? If you see him, you might indicate gently to him that even a post-card would be welcome in this house. But, as a fact, how ill or how well is he? The most conflicting accounts reach us. Mrs. Wharton tells me she is going over to take charge of him, when he leaves Mrs. Cadwallader Jones. I am very glad he will come to you for a little. You always do him good.

We shall, I hardly doubt, be still here until the end of August. Do let us know before you come, so that we may not miss you.

We all unite in very affectionate regards, and

I am always yours

Edmund Gosse

ꙮ 192. *Howells to Gosse* ꙮ

18, Half Moon Street, / Mayfair. [London] W.

2 September 1911

Dear Gosse:

I don't know whether you are in town; but I am, and I hope to see you. Could you look in some day on your way to or from the ruins of the House of Lords? It ought to be spelled Lloyds,[1] I suppose, now.

Yours ever

W. D. Howells

P.S. Pilla, who cannot speak above her breath for a sore throat, wishes to join me in love to all of you in writing.

[1] I.e., after David Lloyd George (1863–1945), then Chancellor of the Exchequer. In August 1911 the passing of the Parliament bill by the House of Lords brought to an end the long political crisis which had begun in November 1909 when the Lords threw out Lloyd George's "People's Budget."

193. *Howells to Gosse*

18 Half Moon Street, [London]

9 September 1911

My dear Gosse:

I am sorry enough to be leaving London so soon that I shall not see you here. We go to Paris on Wednesday next, and after a week there we expect to push on to Spain where we hope to do a month's travel, settling down for repose and reflection at Algeciras, and sailing home from Gibraltar late in November. The programme is a bold one, but what will a stripling of 74 not dare?

We have seen rather much of James, who is in very good case in spite of the weather he has been weathering all summer. I think he will begin work again. We spoke of you, and he may have dissembled (as people used) but there was only kindness in his tone. I do not believe your machinations or mine have come to his knowledge, but I'm afraid they have been fruitless; I've no doubt he would be properly grateful in any event.

Your daughter sweetly acknowledged my letter, and I knew of your absence. What a pity for it!—We hope to be at the Hotel Regina, 2 Place de Rivoli in Paris, but my safest address is c/o Brown Shipley & Co., 123 Pall Mall.

Pilla joins me [in] affection for you both.

Yours ever

W. D. Howells

194. *Gosse to James*

Grand Hôtel / & Hôtel d'Angleterre-Annecy. / (Hte. Savoie)

11 September 1911

My dear James

We hear from so many people of your return to England, and of your recovered health and happiness. We cannot yet any longer go by without telling you of our joy in it. I did rather hope that I should have been among those to whom you wrote on your return, and have been perhaps a little jealous! (Excuse this frailty, of which I ought to be ashamed!) You did not answer my last letter, now many months ago, but I knew how painful the

281

exercise of writing was to you: but now, even if you only rank us in the third line of your friends, you must take us up again!

We came to France about 3 weeks ago, originally on a visit to the Paul Desjardins[1] at Poligny, and since then we have been wandering in the fiery furnace of Burgundy, and at Aix-les-Bains, which was hotter still, and now for the first time we are cool in this most exquisite place, where we linger on, and may linger yet a week. But before the end of September we must be home again.

I am very sorry to miss Howells, from whom I have had some delightful letters, giving good news of you. I gather that he has been with you in Rye, but he writes from Half Moon St. They go this week, by Paris, to Spain, which in this more than torrid weather seems a little rash, but they are seasoned travellers.

If you find it in your heart to write me a line, send it to 17 Hanover Terrace, Regent's Park N.W., whence all our letters are forwarded. I quite long to see your handwriting again: I have not been so long without it for a quarter of a century. There does not seem to be any news to give you. We have had a most exciting public year, and at the House of Lords the months of July and August were almost intolerably painful:[2] however, all ended as well as the fatality of things would permit,—not well, and yet as little ill as could be hoped for by an ancient order obstinately posed against public feeling. It is the crépuscule des dieux into which we now enter.

Nellie sends you her love, and all sorts of kind and anxious wishes. You don't know how much we have talked about you and wondered about you, during this sad past year. I see a new book of yours announced:[3] that will be one of the joys of the autumn.

Ever yours

Edmund Gosse

[1] Paul Desjardins (1859–1940), the French critic and polemicist, was a founder of what is now called Moral Rearmament.

[2] See Letter 192, n. 1.

[3] James, *The Outcry* (London: Methuen, 1911).

❧ 195. *James to Gosse* ❧

Millden Lodge, / Edzell, / Forfarshire.

19 September 1911

My dear Gosse.

Your good letter reaches me in this remote and contrasted clime—so different a milieu, I mean, from sweet Savoy—and I cordially welcome it and thank you for the welcome it contains—thank you both, that is, all faithfully and impatiently. I am impatient to see you, after so strangely and woefully long, and rejoice that there appears a good near prospect of it. I came up hither on the 15th to spend a week with an old American friend (who has occupied this grouse-moor every summer for many years,) and shall be here till toward the end of this week, probably—by which time, or very shortly after it, I seem to make out that No. 17 will enclose you again. Then I shall knock at your door—making sure of the case first; on my way back to Lamb House, which I have occupied but few of these days since my return to England. I fled at the end of the first ten days from the hot glare and the parched and stricken state of the South Coast, and have had something of a troubled and restless time since—so uncanny so many of the conditions here even after the great American uncanniness—which I have but just barely outweathered; and now I strain toward my too-long forsaken hearthstone and the possible favours of an outraged and abandoned muse—whom I must use every art to appease. I stayed my hand from writing to you—indeed writing to any one during the torrid transatlantic time was out of the question; for I thought of you as too worried and even tormented (over the crash of institutions, or at least of every propriety, about you)—so that superficial signals seemed a mockery and searching ones an indiscretion—or even an anguish. The legend of my having let off epistolary squibs in other quarters, as I approached, I shall be able, I think, when I see you, very effectually to dissipate. Everything went to pieces for me during the awful weeks between May 1st and the end of July—I mean through my constitutional intolerance of 98° in the shade—and all that order of impressions, which were so far from being eased off on my arrival in England. But they have a little eased off since, and I am bearing up as I can—with a strong sense of all there is to bear up *against*. I am delighted to gather that you have all, on your sides, had a happy frisk—it all sounds most rare and romantic. I hope to be able to try for you either on the 25th or 26th p.m. —Your "before the end of the month" would seem to consort with the possibility of then finding you. But if I should fail I should look to another pretty early though not immediate chance—for I must be at home again not later than the 27th—at least for some little time. You'll have lots to tell me, of a hundred people and things—and I await it all with a yearning ear. I really come back from very far off indeed. I saw Howells in London early in the month, girding himself for Spain even like another Conquistador.[1] His capacity to knock about excites my liveliest envy—but clearly it assuages a restlessness in him that makes it a sharp need: if it were all mere elderly fire and flame it would be *too* humiliating—to one's self. But his stoutness and toughness are yet wonderful enough. Clearly yours and Mrs. Nelly's compare with it bravely—only you and Mrs. Nelly are not elderly.

I shall send this of course to 17 [Hanover Terrace]—and if it should extract from you the *beau geste* of a sign of presence please address that sign to *Reform Club Chambers*, 105 Pall Mall S.W. I scarcely even send loves —I shall like so much better delivering them in person—even in the ponderous person of

Your all-faithful old

Henry James

[1] For Howells's visit to Spain see Letter 193 and Mildred Howells, *Life in Letters of Howells,* II, 300–309.

༈ 196. *Wharton to Gosse* ༈

53 Rue de Varenne [Paris]

17 November 1911

Dear Mr. Gosse,

I am aghast and pale at the announcement that the Nobel Prize has been given to Maeterlinck.[1] In the first place I understood from you that the vote was not taken till January—in fact, on referring to your letter of last February, I see you say that the English committee vote after Christmas, and quaint as are the customs of the Nobel Institute, I can hardly suppose that their committees vote after their prize has been awarded!

I have been pressing the good cause in America with unexpectedly encouraging results, and was looking forward to reporting them to you next month, when I am hoping to go to England for a short time. Now I am entirely disconcerted, both by the discovery that this year's prize is awarded and by the fact that, apparently, only millionaires need apply. If the Nobel Institute is looking for "best sellers" and successful playwrights, it is evident that several hundred candidates will have precedence over ours, and

[1] Count Maurice Maeterlinck (1862–1949), the Belgian playwright.

that unless dear Henry James can get a few hints from Mr. Barrie[2] or the Bensons,[3] our struggle will be vain.

However I don't mean to give up, and I am sure you don't either; and if I am able to go to London next month we will hatch a fresh plot.

Every yours sincerely

Edith Wharton

Please excuse my dictating. I am laid up with conjunctivitis.

[2] Sir James Matthew Barrie (1860–1937), Scottish novelist and playwright, author
[3] A reference to the brothers, Arthur Christopher Benson (see Letter 176, n. 2),
[3] A reference to the brothers: Arthur Christopher Benson (see Letter 176, n. 2), Edward Frederick Benson (1867–1940), and Robert Hugh Benson (1871–1914). They were the sons of Edward White Benson (1829–1896), Archbishop of Canterbury, and all three made literary reputations.

✂ 197. *James to Gosse* ✂

Lamb House / Rye / Sussex

31 October 1913

My dear Gosse.

When some little time since I read in the Times your admirable letter of reply to Galsworthy's[1] portentous allocution on the Propriety of Books I was much moved to write you in lively congratulation—and if I didn't I fear it was because my poor physical consciousness has the effect of keeping all initiative, for me, all doing of anything whatever, extremely low. Here I am doing *this*—but see how long it has taken me to come to it. And I have the incentive that I have more lately read your further remarks on the Censorship matter at the Meeting[2] of the other day, and seen thereby you were at home again—I had made out before that you were still on the Continent. Thus I seem in some sense supported and uplifted toward telling you that I find your expressions on the great subject exactly in the right and happy note and tone, incisive without solemnity, and as effectually explosive, even though gently so, of the great Galsworthiness, as need have been

[1] John Galsworthy (1867–1933), novelist and playwright. Gosse's letter, given the editorial heading "Censorship of Books," appeared in the London *Times,* 7 October 1913, p. 9; it was a reply to Galsworthy's letter published in the *Times* on 3 October 1913, p. 9. The controversy concerned the action of circulating libraries in restricting the circulation of novels by such authors as Hall Caine and Compton Mackenzie.
[2] Unidentified.

desired. Your letter was a charming ironic thing. And I am somehow brought into touch with you by receiving a notice of the Dinner to dear old Brandes[3] which has my full sympathy even though I mayn't hope to be present at it—dinners being impossible to me now. It gives me pleasure none the less to see you concerned in it and to think that I may thus a little later on be perhaps able to give you a message to brave B. This will be helped by the fact that I am now arranging, so far as I can arrange anything, to get up to town, for the winter, from one week, or almost one day, to the other. (I am planning hard for the 15th.) Weren't it for this I should say to you Won't you come down for a couple of nights even yet?—and should have said it before, on learning, by inference, your return, if I hadn't been, frankly, so inapt, physically speaking, for any easy or graceful discharge of the office of host even in the very modest conditions to which it is restricted with me. I have had to live all summer and autumn with the last unsociability —the fruit of the blighted initiative. But the rigour of this here has now become very depressing and an early return to Carlyle Mansions[4] quite urgently indicated. I hope you both have come home much refreshed and reinforced. I am very eager to hear your story, and shall make a prompt overture for it as soon as I am in town. I send my best love to Mrs. Nelly and am yours and hers

all faithfully

Henry James

[3] Georg Morris Cohen Brandes (1842–1927), the Danish critic and historian of literature, best remembered for his studies of Shakespeare and Ibsen.
[4] James's London home.

ᑫᑫ 198. Gosse to James ᑫᑫ

17, Hanover Terrace, / Regent's Park, / [London] N.W.
Friday [31 October 1913][1]

My dear James

It gave me the very greatest pleasure to see your handwriting, the more as I have been excluded from company where I might have news of you, and had been wishing much to hear. We came back from Wiesbaden nearly four weeks ago, and on the very day after I was attacked by sciatica, which mended a little and occasionally let me out, and was I thought, under doctors and a masseur, really going, when last Sunday I was felled by an enteric attack, which has kept me in bed ever since. Today I am much better, and

[1] Gosse simply dated the letter "Friday." "Oct. 13, 1913" is written in another hand.

have just eaten my first tiny slice of bread and butter; and am just waiting to see whether that brings on a relapse! I don't remember that ever before in my life I have been actually *starved*, but nothing but a fade [sic] mixture of milk and barley-water (on which it appears life can be indefinitely prolonged) has passed my lips till today. It is curious how fine the nerves of gustation become. That little piece of bread and butter tasted to me like angels' food. The doctors see a gouty condition in all these ailments, which I can only hope will storm themselves out, and restore me in more or less shattered condition to society by the time that you return to Chelsea, for I long to see you.

I am very happy indeed to know that you approved of my letter. How very pompous all the clever young men are nowadays, are they not? Galsworthy is quite the type. One must be a little ironic with them, and as they don't perceive the worm-tongue in the elderly cheek, no harm is done.

You saw, I suppose, that I have been made an Officier of the Légion d'Honneur?[2] No one was ever more astonished than I, and I still think it must be a hoax or a blunder. But if ever one goes to France again (and I feel that all my travelling days are over) I am told that the rosette ensures one an easy time in the Customs.

This is such a wholly and shamelessly egotistical letter, but what can a poor wretch confined to his bed find except himself to talk about? I read books till my eyes wheel in my head, but I will not bore you by speaking of them, and that is all of the world that reaches me.

I am thankful to say that Nellie, whose health gave me grave anxiety in the summer, seems really better for her cure at Wiesbaden. She sends her best love to you and so do I. I feel that your good welcome letter has pushed me several steps nearer to convalescence.

Ever yours sincerely

Edmund Gosse

[2] Charteris quotes Gosse's comment to Austin Dobson on being awarded the Légion d'Honneur: "I do not feel at all worthy of so rare a distinction, but if we only got what we are worthy of, where would luck be?" (*Life and Letters of Gosse*, p. 335).

∾ 199. *James to Gosse* ∾

Lamb House / Rye / Sussex

1 November 1913

My dear Gosse.

This is a very sad showing, yet I am glad not to have remained longer in ignorance of your troubles. I sounded at one time—a number of years since

—the depths of sciatica; but have been pretty well ever since out of peril of it—so take to yourself the comfort that one *can,* that one does, cast it out. Sweet indeed the uses of starvation and incredible, on occasions, the bliss of barley water. But I greatly rejoice that you climb back to life and liberty even up the steep stair, or whatever it is, of enteric—and I'm not sure I know even what *that* is, in its manifestations. But you will luridly tell me, and you have meanwhile all my sympathy—over your horrid time. I think it must have been inflicted on you a little as a makeweight to the dazzling glory of your ruban rouge,[1] of which I hadn't heard, but which, lest you should go mad with these worldly lusts, a thoughtful providence has been inspired to handle a bit coolingly. It is really very interesting—how graceful is the French tradition, dear old thing! How much you will have to tell me—and how I count the days to it! How solemn indeed, also, are ces messieurs!— were *we* so solemn at their ages? Certainly they won't be so gay at ours. I am the gayer for hearing that your wife made a good cure. Do you now the same.

Yours all faithfully

Henry James

[1] See Letter 198, and n. 2.

✺ 200. *James to Gosse* ✺

21 Carlyle Mansions / Cheyne Walk / [London] S.W.

25 June 1915

My dear Gosse.

Remarkably enough, I should be writing you this evening even if I hadn't received your interesting information about Léon Daudet,[1] concerning whom nothing perversely base and publicly pernicious at all surprises me. He is the cleverest idiot and the most poisonous talent imaginable, and I wait to see if he won't somehow swing—!

But il ne s'agit pas de ça; il s'agit of the fact that there is a matter I should have liked to speak to you of the other day when you lunched here, yet hung fire about through its not having then absolutely come to a head. It has

[1] Léon Daudet (1867–1942), son of Alphonse Daudet, was an active polemicist as well as a critic and novelist; he was a leader of the Royalist party and editor of *Action Française.* James is referring to a newspaper cutting about Daudet—headlined "Le poignard dans le dos!" and beginning: "Léon Daudet est un criminel, traître au pays de son père"—which Gosse had sent him, with an accompanying note, on 24 June 1915 (HU).

within these 3 days done so, and in brief it is *this*. The force of the public situation now at last determines me to testify to my attachment to this country, my fond domicile for nearly forty years (40 *next* year), by applying for naturalization here: the throwing of my imponderable moral weight into the scale of her fortune is the *geste* that will best express my devotion—absolutely nothing *else* will. Therefore my mind is made up and you are the 1st person save my Solicitor (whom I have had to consult) to whom the fact has been imparted. Kindly respect for the moment the privacy of it. I learned with horror just lately that if I go down into Sussex (for 2 or 3 months of Rye) I have at once to register myself there as an Alien and place myself under the observation of the Police. But that is only the *occasion* of my decision—it's not in the least the cause. The disposition itself has haunted me as Wordsworth's sounding cataract haunted *him*—"like a passion"—ever since the beginning of the War. But the point, please, is this: that the process for me is really of the simplest, and *may* be very rapid, if I can obtain 4 honourable householders to testify to their knowledge of me as a respectable person, "speaking and writing English decently" etc. Will you give me the great pleasure of being one of them?—signing a paper to that effect? I should take it ever so kindly. And I should further take kindly your giving me if possible your sense on *this* delicate point. Should you say that our admirable friend the Prime Minister[2] would perhaps be approachable by me as another of the signatory 4?—to whom, you see, great historic honour, not to say immortality, as my sponsors, will accrue. I don't like to approach him without your so qualified sense of the matter first—and he has always been so beautifully kind and charming to me. I will do nothing till I hear from you—but his signature (which my solicitor's representative, if not himself, would simply wait upon him for,) would enormously accelerate the putting through of the application and the disburdening me of the Sussex "restricted area" alienship—which it distresses me to carry on my back a day longer than I need. I have in mind my other two sponsors, but if I could have from you, in addition to your own personal response, on which my hopes are so founded, your ingenious prefiguration (fed by your intimacy with him,) as to how the P.M. would "take" my appeal, you would increase the obligations of yours all faithfully

Henry James

[2] Henry Herbert Asquith, first Earl of Oxford and Asquith (1852–1928), Prime Minister from 1908 to 1916.

201. *Gosse to James*

17, Hanover Terrace, / Regent's Park, [London] N.W.

25 June 1915

My dear James

I read your letter with the liveliest emotion. It is splendid of you, and beautifully like yourself, to make this sacrifice for us. You give us the most intimate thing you possess. It is most moving, and most cheering, a grand geste indeed.

Now as regards Asquith, I am as sure as I can be about anything that he will rejoice to be your sponsor. I cannot conceive an objection, and I can think of no occasion on which he would more certainly desire to express his own natal citizenship. Don't hesitate to ask him.

How I rejoice to think of you as about to be *of* us in this anxious time, as you have been *with* us without fail ever since the troubles began! I think it even an augury of good news, which, Heaven knows! we have waited long for, and I suppose must wait long yet.

I shall keep your secret religiously, even though it is possible that I shall see Asquith tomorrow evening. But you must produce to him your own delightful tale.

Always most sincerely and "patriotically" yours

Edmund Gosse

202. *James to Gosse*

21 Carlyle Mansions / Cheyne Walk / [London] S.W.

28 June 1915

My dear Gosse.

I can't sufficiently thank you for your so generous and understanding letter. My decision has brought me a deep and abiding peace. I have written then without hesitation to the Prime Minister, and every instinct tells me that he will be more than kind. This is but a stopgap word—I will write again as soon as I shall have heard from him.

Yours all gratefully

Henry James

∾ 203. *Gosse to James* ∾

17, Hanover Terrace, / Regent's Park, [London] N.W.
Thursday [8 July 1915]

My dear James

You must have thought it very odd that you heard no word from me, but for ten days past I have been crushed (and mainly cloué au lit) by a terrible attack of lumbago. I creep about the house today for the first time. You might write me a line to say how the Great Scheme, of which I constantly think, progresses. Of course I have not seen Asquith, but a word written from Downing St. showed me that he knew I knew and that he was romantically pleased to be in *it*.

Ever yours

Edmund Gosse

∾ 204. *Gosse to James* ∾

17, Hanover Terrace, / Regent's Park, [London] N.W.
9 July 1915

My dear James

Mr. Nelson Ward[1] has been here today, with the Man of Oaths, and I have made with emotion my Statutory Declaration.

And now I want to be paid—by receiving a copy, all in your writing and signed, of the beautiful and touching and dignified sentence in which you make your declaration.

Ever yours

E. G.

[1] James's solicitor.

291

21 Carlyle Mansions / Cheyne Walk / [London] S.W.

9 July 1915

My dear Gosse.

I am distressed and dismayed to hear how you have been suffering, and all the more that I can measure with the last competence the force of your visitation. Lumbago of the fiercest temper was my perpetual company for long years—the first thirty in fact of my long life in London, and was really an awful blight to me. (I could only little by little *sweat* it out and used to take heroic measures to that end.) But the great thing is that it *goes,* that it will, and that I have been practically exempt from it for several years now. So be of good heart and take my assurance that you will outgrow and outlive it. I have lived into other troubles, but left that one (absit omen.) behind me. I would very gladly have come to see you had you but breathed into the telephone. I heartily hope that you are well on your feet now. As for the Gran' Rifiuto—to be longer a Child of the West—it is going forward, I think, with all due celerity. I have done my own part, as the law requires, and the P[rime] M[inister] has been most kind about backing me. I am expecting to hear from my Solicitor that he has already—or will have very presently, waited upon you for your kind signed attestation (of *your* knowledge of my respectability and my acquaintance with the tongue;) and after this has been accomplished with my 2 other backers—with one other, making the 4th, it was accomplished 3 or 4 days ago—the affair will be on the march.

Ah, it *is* on the march! for I just receive your note telling me that Nelson Ward has been with you: I do rejoice! At this rate we move. Bless you, I will with the greatest pleasure send you my autograph of that Declaration, but shall have 1st to see it again to get it straight—I don't absolutely remember it! Count on it as soon as I can copy it and believe me again all gratefully yours

Henry James

17, Hanover Terrace, / Regent's Park, / [London] N.W.

26 July 1915

My dear James

Thank you for your declaration of faith. I predict that it will be often quoted.

I still am rather the victim of several gouty vexations, but I think steadily, though very slowly, throwing them off.

What are your movements? We stay here till the very last day of August. If you are not leaving London, do let us meet: in this backwater of time, I so long for the company of old friends.

Confidential:

An intimate friend of mine, who spent an hour alone with Kitchener[1] on Saturday, tells me that he was far from depressed, even about Russia, and that he said "We have settled, I believe, the submarine danger". There have been many encouraging and wonderful feats at sea of which we are allowed to know nothing. And if I am informed correctly, Rumania is absolutely fixed to join us.[2]

Ever most truly yours

Edmund Gosse

[1] Horatio Herbert Kitchener, Earl Kitchener (1850–1916), Secretary for War.
[2] Rumania entered the War on the side of the Allied Powers in August 1916; her armies were defeated, however, and an armistice was arranged in December 1917.

ᘏ 207. *James to Gosse* ᘏ

21 Carlyle Mansions / Cheyne Walk / [London] S.W.

26 July 1915

My dear Gosse

Your good letter makes me feel that you will be interested to know that since 4.30 this afternoon I have been able to say Civis Britannicus sum! My Certificate of Naturalization was received by my Solicitor this a.m., and a few hours ago I took the Oath of Allegiance, in his office, before a Commissioner. The odd thing is that nothing seems to have happened and I don't feel a bit different; so that I see not at all how associated I have become, but that I was really too associated before for any nominal change to matter. The process has only shown me what I virtually *was*—so that it's rather disappointing in respect to acute sensation. I *haven't* any, I blush to confess!

I shall be in town like yourselves till the very end of next month—I have let Lamb House for 5 weeks to some friends of the American Embassy, the E. G. Lowrys[1]—I can't stand in these public conditions the solitude and se-

[1] Edward George Lowry (1876–1943), a journalist by profession, was a special agent of the Department of State attached to the American Embassy in London.

questration of the country. (E. G. L., ardent for our cause, is "Attaché to the A[merican] E[mbassy] for the German Division"—and has been quartered all winter at the German Embassy.) I thank you enormously for your Confidential passage, which is most interesting and heartening; as is also this evening's news that the Boches have sunk—torpedoed—another ship; I mean another American one. That affects me as really charming! And let me mention in exchange for your confidence that a friend told me this afternoon that he had been within a few days talking with Captain McBride one of the American naval attachés,[2] whose competence he ranks high and to whom he had put some question relative to the naval sense of the condition of these islands. To which the reply had been: "You may take it from me that England is absolutely impregnable and invincible!"—and McBride repeated over—"impregnable and invincible!" Which kind of did me good.

Let me come up and sit on your terrace some near August afternoon—I can always be rung up, you know: I *like* it—and believe me yours and your wife's all faithfully

Henry James

[2] Not further identified.

⧼ 208. Wharton to Gosse ⧽

53, Rue de Varenne [Paris]

6 August 1915

Dear Mr. Gosse,

About three weeks ago I started to lay the foundation stones of a book[1] on the "Book of France" lines, to be published in New York, in the hope of getting some money for the winter expenses of the army of refugees I have been looking after here since last autumn.[2]

I wrote to *your* Henry James[3] to beg him to attack one or two inaccessibles, (such as Mr. Hardy) and then, as I was about to send my own timid appeal to the more "adorables" (or so I hope!) an old governess and friend who lives with me fell gravely ill, and my plans were interrupted, ex-

[1] Edith Wharton, ed., *The Book of the Homeless* (London: Macmillan; New York: Scribner's, 1916).
[2] For Edith Wharton's activities in support of "Le Foyer Franco-Belge" see Percy Lubbock, *Portrait of Edith Wharton*, pp. 101–102.
[3] A reference to James's having become a naturalized British citizen.

cept in so far as the making of verbal appeals to the Parisian group on my list.

Now I am at last able to take up the quest, and I come to you first, because you are always so kind to me on my too rare visits to London that I feel you'll not only listen to me yourself but give me a helping hand with the others!

You may fancy that I don't at all yearn for the thing "de circonstance". It needn't as much as recognize or allude to the existence of a refugee. What I'd like best of all from you—I grow bolder—is a poem, if you have one somewhere that hasn't yet seen publicity. And, failing that, I shall like anything else you are willing to give me.[4]

The date originally fixed for the sending in of contributions was Aug. 10th; but the delay in my appeal has obliged me to put it off till August 25, which I hope still gives the New York publisher time for his Christmas advertising.

Our dear friend Gide[5] (who has been working with me over these same refugees for nearly a year) sends you many messages à l'appui of my appeal, and is himself editing the book with me.

Please say yes!—and believe me

Yours ever sincerely

Edith Wharton

[4] Gosse contributed an essay entitled "The Arrogance and Servility of Germany," pp. 101–104.

[5] André Gide (1869–1951), the French novelist and critic. He was a close friend of Gosse, and their correspondence has been published: Linette F. Brugmans, ed., *The Correspondence of André Gide and Edmund Gosse, 1904–1928*, (London: Peter Owen, 1960).

ᴄᴠ 209. *Wister[1] to Gosse* ᴄᴠ

Butler Place / Logan Station / Philadelphia.

28 October 1915

Dear Sir:

It is a great pleasure to receive your letter, and it was very kind in you to write it. I am able to assure you that what I have tried to say in "The

[1] Owen Wister (1860–1938) wrote poems, essays, and biographies, including one of his friend Theodore Roosevelt, but is best known for his novels, especially *The Virginian* (1902). In a later letter to Gosse, dated 22 April 1923 (a.l.s., BC), he thanks him for a generous review of his book, *Neighbors Henceforth* (New York: Macmillan, 1922).

Pentecost of Calamity"[2] expresses the feeling of many Americans beside myself. This I know from the letters which still arrive nearly four months after the first publication of the essay in The Saturday Evening Post— one of our illustrated weeklies with a circulation of about two million. The notices in our various other papers are mostly to the same effect: so you must think of my remarks as the remarks of a very large chorus of my countrymen.

You style yourself most gratifyingly as one of my "unknown" admirers; I can't reciprocate because I not only know your books but have also shaken hands with their author! There's no reason you should remember this, though; for in the first place it was in 1884; in the next, I merely made you my bow and made way for persons more important; and lastly, you couldn't have caught the names of half or a quarter of those persons, because we were streaming in upon you as you stood in the drawing-room of Mr. Howells, in Beacon Street, Boston.[3] So I'll just venture to say that through all those years your pages have given me pleasure always, and sometimes more—namely, assistance.

Yours sincerely

Owen Wister

[2] Wister, "Pentecost of Calamity," *Saturday Evening Post*, CLXXXVIII (5 July 1915), 3–5, 26–29. It was later published in book form (New York: Macmillan, 1915). The article deals with Wister's experiences in Germany and with the outbreak of the War, and is, in effect, a plea for American intervention on the side of the Allies.

[3] For the occasion here recalled by Wister, see Introduction, p. 13.

ᘒ 210. *Gosse to Chase*[1] ᘒ

17 Hanover Terrace / Regent's Park / London N.W.1.

16 May [1917]

Dear Mr. Chase

Your letter of the 14th. of April has just reached me. I need not tell you that I have read it with a great deal of pleasure and sympathy.

You do not mention in it two matters of absorbing interest. 1st. (Public) the entering of America into the War on our side. 2nd. (Private) the

[1] Gosse exchanged a number of letters with the American critic Lewis Nathaniel Chase (1873–1937), who also visited him in London (see Charteris, *Life and Letters of Gosse*, pp. 361–363).

publication of my Life of Swinburne,[2] which came out here, and I believe simultaneously in New York, early in April. It has enjoyed a very great success here, but I have no news yet of its reception in America.

Your course of lectures on the poets is a most interesting enterprise, and I cannot but be excited at learning your intention of including me [in] your series. But I feel it very difficult to supply the data which you so courteously ask for. In "Father and Son" you will find recorded the early awakening of a passionate interest in poetry, partly from hearing my Father recite Virgil, later from hearing him read Walter Scott (particularly the Lady of the Lake) to my step-mother. My own earliest verses dated from 1865, before I was sixteen. They were very poor, and founded, if I remember right, on Gray. I went on, teaching myself metrical skill, but it was not until much later that I wrote anything decent. If you look at "Madrigals, Songs and Sonnets"[3] (1870) you will see very little evidence of promise, except perhaps in one or two of the sonnets. The sonnet on "Webster" (which both Swinburne and Rossetti praised very highly) is the best. It was written, I think, late in 1869.

Very oddly, the strongest stimulus to poetical writing which I received in my early youth came from Walt Whitman.[4] I do not know that any one would guess that, because I was entirely unaffected by his form (or formlessness), but in the "On Viol and Flute" of 1873, where there is a great deal which I never reprinted after 1876, you will find many pieces which own their *ethical* movement to Walt Whitman (such as "Lying in the Grass", the prelude, "In the Bay" etc.) I was affected, of course, by coming into personal contact with the pre-Raphaelites, but particularly with D. G. Rossetti.

My drama of "King Erik" shows the influence of Swinburne, but I believe only superficially. I think this is my earliest *adult* work, and I believe, in spite of its form, which is out of date, you will find in it some qualities of independent thought and feeling.

Of my later writings you are a better judge than I can be. But I should like to commend to you my little ironic lyrical drama called "Hypolympia".[5] It mystified the public, and was never popular, though a few select readers were immensely pleased with it. I think myself that it is the least insignificant of my poetical excursions. It is still on sale: for the large first edition has never been exhausted (Heinemann).

You are kind enough to ask me for names that should be on your list.

[2] Gosse, *The Life of Algernon Charles Swinburne* (London: Macmillan, 1917).

[3] Gosse (with J. A. Blaikie), *Madrigals, Songs and Sonnets* (London: Longmans, Green, 1870).

[4] See Letter 1 and Introduction, pp. 28–30.

[5] Gosse, *Hypolympia, or The Gods in the Island: An Ironic Fantasy* (London: Heinemann, 1907). Among the personal friends who praised the book highly was Richard Burdon, Viscount Haldane (Haldane to Gosse, 29 December 1905; typed copy, RU).

Among the living you will naturally have Hardy, Dobson, Bridges.[6] You will also remember Hewlett,[7] Yeats, John Drinkwater,[8] Masefield,[9] Newbolt,[10] Abercrombie.[11] Among the very latest Ralph Hodgson,[12] Maurice Baring[13] and Siegfried Sassoon[14] have great merit.

Do let me hear from you again soon. I am very sincerely yours

Edmund Gosse

[6] Robert Bridges (1844–1930) was Poet Laureate at this time, having succeeded Alfred Austin in 1913.

[7] Maurice Hewlett (1861–1923), poet and novelist, one of Gosse's regular luncheon companions at the National Club (see Charteris, *Life and Letters of Gosse,* p. 208).

[8] John Drinkwater (1882–1937), poet and playwright; although he and Gosse were on friendly terms, Gosse seems to have had some reservations about his verse (see *ibid.,* p. 381).

[9] John Masefield (1878–   ) succeeded Bridges as Poet Laureate in 1930.

[10] Sir Henry John Newbolt (1862–1938), barrister and poet.

[11] Lascelles Abercrombie (1881–1938), poet and critic.

[12] Ralph Hodgson (1871–1962), poet.

[13] Maurice Baring (1874–1945), poet and author, was a close friend of Gosse; for Gosse's high opinion of his verse see Charteris, *Life and Letters of Gosse,* pp. 409–410.

[14] Siegfried Sassoon (1886–   ), poet and author, was another younger writer whom Gosse admired and encouraged (see *ibid.,* pp. 314, 318–319, etc.).

APPENDICES

APPENDIX A

Checklist of Letters

Since the letters printed in this volume have been collected from widely scattered libraries and collections in the United States and England, a check-list is given below in which the provenance of each letter is indicated. The following abbreviations and short names are used:

BC—Brotherton Collection, University of Leeds
BM—British Museum
Cambridge—Cambridge University Library
CU—Columbia University Library
Duke—Duke University Library
GL—Gilder Letterbooks, New York Public Library; these contain carbons of Gilder's letters to Gosse. All letters from them which are listed here bear a notation of either "autograph carbon, signature carbon" or "typed carbon, signature carbon"
GP—Gilder Papers, in possession of Miss Rosamond Gilder
HU—Harvard University, Houghton Library
LC—Library of Congress
NYP—New York Public Library
PU—Princeton University Library
RU—Rutgers University Library
UP—University of Pennsylvania, Horace Howard Furness Memorial Library
YU—Yale University Library

a.l.s.—autograph letter signed

1. Gosse to Whitman, 12 December 1873, a.l.s., private collection of Mr. Charles Feinberg
2. Stedman to Gosse, 29 November 1875, a.l.s., BC
3. Stedman to Gosse, 12 June 1876, a.l.s., BC
4. Gosse to Stedman, 6 August 1876, a.l.s., CU
5. Gosse to Stedman, 28 April 1879, a.l.s., CU
6. Stedman to Gosse, 5 May 1879, a.l.s., BC
7. Gosse to Stedman, 17 July 1879, a.l.s., CU
8. Gosse to Stedman, 12 September 1879, a.l.s., CU
9. Stedman to Gosse, 20 September 1879, a.l.s., BC
10. Stedman to Gosse, Christmas 1879, a.l.s., BC
11. Gosse to Gilder, 29 December 1879, a.l.s., GP

12. Gosse to Stedman, 11 February 1880, a.l.s., CU
13. Gosse to Stedman, 8 March 1880, a.l.s., Pennington School, New Jersey
14. Stedman to Gosse, 16 March 1880, a.l.s., BC
15. Gosse to Gilder, 18 October 1880, a.l.s., GP
16. Gosse to Stedman, 4 January 1881, a.l.s., CU
17. Gosse to Stedman, 18 June 1881, a.l.s., CU
18. Gosse to Gilder, 20 July 1881, a.l.s., GP
19. Gosse to Stedman, 14 August 1881, a.l.s., CU
20. Stedman to Gosse, 15 January 188[2], a.l.s., BC
21. Gosse to Stedman, 3 February 1882, a.l.s., CU
22. Gosse to Gilder, 20 March 1882, a.l.s., GP
23. Gosse to Howells, 26 July 1882, a.l.s., HU
24. Howells to Gosse, 1 August 1882, a.l.s., BM
25. Gosse to Howells, 2 August 1882, a.l.s., HU
26. Gosse to Stedman, 21 August 1882, a.l.s., CU
27. Howells to Gosse, 26 August 1882, a.l.s., BM
28. Gosse to Howells, 30 August 1882, a.l.s., HU
29. Howells to Gosse, 9 September 1882, BM
30. Gosse to Howells, 12 October 1882, a.l.s., HU
31. Howells to Gosse, ⟨26⟩ October 1882, a.l.s., BM
32. Gosse to Howells, 8 November 1882, a.l.s., HU
33. Gosse to Howells, 14 November 1882, a.l.s., HU
34. Howells to Gosse, 16 November 1882, a.l.s., BM
35. Howells to Gosse, 9 January 188[3], a.l.s., BM
36. Gosse to Howells, 12 January 1883, a.l.s., HU
37. Gosse to Stedman, 5 March 1883, a.l.s., Pennsylvania State University
38. Howells to Gosse, 3 April 1883, a.l.s., BM
39. Gosse to Johnson, 31 May 1883, a.l.s., HU
40. Gosse to Aldrich, 2 June 1883, a.l.s., HU
41. Gosse to Gilder, 13 June 1883, a.l.s., HU
42. Howells to Gosse, 15 June 1883, a.l.s., BC
43. Gosse to Johnson, 16 June 1883, a.l.s., HU
44. Howells to Gosse, 26 June 1883, a.l.s., BM
45. Gosse to Gilder, 4 July 1883, a.l.s., HU
46. Gosse to Osgood, 25 July 1883, a.l.s., HU
47. Gosse to Gilder, 28 July 1883, a.l.s., HU
48. Aldrich to Gosse, 2 August 1883, a.l.s., BC
49. Stedman to Gosse, 27 August 1883, a.l.s., BC
50. Howells to Gosse, 9 September 1883, a.l.s., RU
51. Gosse to Gilder, 10 September 1883, a.l.s., HU
52. Howells to Gosse, 9 December 1883, a.l.s., BM
53. Gosse to Howells, 20 December 1883, a.l.s., HU
54. Howells to Gosse, 2 January 188[4], a.l.s., RU
55. Gosse to Howells, 29 February 1884, a.l.s., HU
56. Gosse to Howells, 4 March 1884, a.l.s., HU
57. Howells to Gosse, 4 March 1884, a.l.s., BM
58. Gilder to Gosse, 8 March 1884, autograph carbon, signature carbon, GL

59. Gosse to Howells, 8 March 1884, a.l.s., HU
60. Howells to Gosse, 23 March 1884, a.l.s., BM
61. Gosse to Howells, 5 April 1884, a.l.s., HU
62. Gosse to Howells, Easter Sunday [13 April] 1884, a.l.s., HU
63. Gosse to Stedman, 20 April 1884, a.l.s., CU
64. Gilder to Gosse, 24 April 1884, dictated carbon, signature carbon, GL
65. Howells to Gosse, 27 April 1884, a.l.s., BM
66. Gosse to Howells, 7 May 1884, a.l.s., HU
67. Gosse to Howells, 8 May 1884, a.l.s., HU
68. Howells to Gosse, 20 May 1884, a.l.s., BM
69. Gosse to Howells, 6 June 1884, a.l.s., HU
70. Gosse to Howells, 8 July 1884, a.l.s., HU
71. Gosse to Stedman, 21 August 1884, a.l.s., CU
72. Lowell to Gosse, 6 September 1884, a.l.s., BC
73. Holmes to Gosse, 7 September 1884, a.l.s., BC
74. Gosse to Holmes, 18 September 1884, a.l.s., LC
75. Stedman to Gosse, 18 September 1884, a.l.s., BC
76. Howells to Gosse, 25 September 1884, a.l.s., BM
77. Gosse to Gilder, 26 September 1884, a.l.s., HU
78. Gosse to Howells, 8 October 1884, a.l.s., HU
79. Gosse to Holmes, 5 December 1884, a.l.s., HU
80. Gosse to Holmes, 12 December 1884, a.l.s., HU
81. Holmes to Gosse, 13 December 1884, a.l.s., BC
82. Gosse to Moulton, 20 December 1884, a.l.s., LC
83. Gosse to Howells, 20 December 1884, a.l.s., HU
84. Howells to Gosse, 24 December 1884, a.l.s., BC
85. Gosse to Howells, 7 January 1885, a.l.s., HU
86. Gosse to Lounsbury, 7 January 1885, a.l.s., YU
87. Howells to Gosse, 19 January 1885, a.l.s., BC
88. Howells to Gosse, 25 January 1885, a.l.s., BC
89. Gosse to Holmes, 26 January 1885, a.l.s., HU
90. Gosse to Howells, 15 February 1885, a.l.s., HU
91. Howells to Gosse, 9 March 1885, a.l.s., BM
92. Furness to Gosse, 22 March 1885, a.l.s., BC
93. Gosse to Lowell, 8 May 1885, a.l.s., HU
94. Lowell to Gosse, 10 May 1885, a.l.s., BC
95. Gosse to Lowell, 27 May 1885, a.l.s., HU
96. Bancroft to Gosse, 30 May 1885, a.l.s., BC
97. Gilder to Gosse, 30 [June] 1885, autograph carbon, signature carbon, GL
98. Gosse to Furness, 28 September 1885, a.l.s., UP
99. Gosse to Roswell Smith, 23 October 1885, a.l.s., HU
100. Furness to Gosse, 25 October 1885, a.l.s., BC
101. Howells to Gosse, 26 October 1885, a.l.s., BM
102. Gosse to Stedman, 10 December 1885, a.l.s., CU
103. Gosse to Howells, 28 December 1885, a.l.s., HU
104. Stedman to Gosse, 13 January 1886, a.l.s., BC
105. Howells to Gosse, 24 January 1886, a.l.s., BM

106. Gosse to Stedman, 25 January 1886, a.l.s., CU
107. Gosse to Howells, 10 March 1886, a.l.s., HU
108. Gosse to Holmes, 3 April 1886, a.l.s., LC
109. Gosse to Holmes, 31 May 1886, a.l.s., HU
110. Gosse to Gilder, 14 October 1886, a.l.s., HU
111. Gilder to Gosse, 1 November 1886, typed letter signed, BC
112. Howells to Gosse, 7 November 1886, typed copy, RU
113. Gosse to Howells, 19 November 1886, a.l.s., HU
114. Gosse to Stedman, 19 November 1886, a.l.s., CU
115. Gosse to Howells, 30 November 1886, a.l.s., HU
116. Gosse to Armour, 4 December 1886, a.l.s., PU
117. Gosse to Gilder, 17 December 1886, a.l.s., GP
118. Gosse to Gilder, 22 February 1887, a.l.s., HU
119. Gosse to Gilder, 18 March 1887, a.l.s., HU
120. Gosse to Armour, 21 August 1887, a.l.s., PU
121. Gosse to Armour, 22 September 1887, a.l.s., PU
122. Gosse to Stedman, 6 December 1887, a.l.s., CU
123. Gosse to Moulton, 27 December 1887, a.l.s., LC
124. Gosse to Armour, 16 January 1888, a.l.s., PU
125. Gosse to Holmes, 1 September 1888, a.l.s., LC
126. Gosse to Gilder, 11 January 1889, a.l.s., HU
127. Gosse to Howells, 30 January 1889, a.l.s., HU
128. Howells to Gosse, 24 February 1889, a.l.s., BM
129. Gosse to Gilder, 7 March 1889, a.l.s., HU
130. Gosse to Gilder, 16 April 1889, a.l.s., GP
131. Gosse to Gilder, 24 June 1889, a.l.s., HU
132. Gosse to Howells, 8 January 1890, a.l.s., HU
133. Gosse to Field, 21 October 1890, a.l.s., University of Texas Library
134. Holmes to Gosse, 27 November 1890, a.l.s., BC
135. Gosse to Gilder, 24 January 1891, a.l.s., HU
136. Gosse to Armour, 31 January 1891, a.l.s., PU
137. Harland to Gosse, [1 May 1891], a.l.s., RU
138. Gosse to Gilder, 4 June 1891, a.l.s., GP
139. Gilder to Gosse, 7 December 1891, typed carbon, signature carbon, GL
140. Gosse to Gilder, 22 December 1891, a.l.s., HU
141. Gosse to Gilder, 18 January 1892, a.l.s., HU
142. Gosse to Gilder, 10 February 1892, a.l.s., HU
143. Furness to Gosse, 29 March 1892, a.l.s., Alderman Library, University of Virginia
144. Gosse to Gilder, 27 April 1892, a.l.s., HU
145. Gilder to Gosse, 26 December 1893, typed carbon, signature carbon, GL
146. Gosse to Armour, 2 December 1894, a.l.s., PU
147. Gilder to Gosse, 24 January 1895, autograph carbon, signature carbon, GL
148. Harland to Gosse, [5 May 1895], a.l.s., RU
149. Howells to Gosse, 22 September 1895, a.l.s., BM
150. Gosse to Gilder, Christmas Eve 1895, a.l.s., GP

151. Harland to Gosse, [11 June 1896], a.l.s., RU
152. Gosse to James, 14 June 1896, a.l.s., Cambridge
153. James to Gosse, 16 June [1896], a.l.s., Duke
154. Gosse to Harland, 2 April 1898, a.l.s., Cambridge
155. Gosse to Munro, 19 May 1898, a.l.s., HU
156. Gosse to Moulton, 1 January 1899, a.l.s., LC
157. Furness to Gosse, 20 July 1899, a.l.s., BC
158. Gosse to Furness, 11 September 1899, a.l.s., PU
159. Gosse to Perry, 14 December 1899, a.l.s., HU
160. Harland to Gosse, [2 March 1900], a.l.s., RU
161. Gosse to Higginson, 9 March 1900, a.l.s., HU
162. Furness to Gosse, 10 March [1900], a.l.s., BC
163. Gosse to Walker, 26 March 1901, a.l.s., University of Kentucky Library
164. Gosse to Trent, 6 June 1902, a.l.s., CU
165. Gilder to Gosse, 27 February 1905, autograph carbon, signature carbon, GL
166. Gosse to Gilder, 20 March 1905, a.l.s., HU
167. Gosse to Gilder, 17 April 1905, a.l.s., GP
168. Gosse to Perry, 4 December 1905, a.l.s., HU
169. Gosse to Perry, 3 April 1906, a.l.s., HU
170. Gosse to Perry, 6 March 1907, a.l.s., HU
171. Furness to Gosse, 2 February [1908], a.l.s., UP
172. Gilder to Gosse, 3 May 1908, autograph carbon, signature carbon, GL
173. James to Gosse, 1 June 1909, a.l.s., BC
174. James to Gosse, 4 June 1909, a.l.s., LC
175. Gosse to James, 11 June 1909, a.l.s., HU
176. Gosse to James, 27 August 1909, a.l.s., HU
177. James to Gosse, 28 August 1909, a.l.s., LC
178. Howells to Gosse, 28 May 1910, a.l.s., BM
179. Gosse to Howells, 14 July 1910, a.l.s., HU
180. Howells to Gosse, 14 July 1910, a.l.s., BM
181. Howells to Gosse, 16 July 1910, a.l.s., BM
182. Howells to Gosse, 21 July 1910, a.l.s., BM
183. Gosse to Howells, 26 July 1910, a.l.s., HU
184. Gosse to Wharton, 14 February 1911, typed carbon, signature carbon, HU
185. Wharton to Gosse, 18 February 1911, a.l.s., BC
186. Howells to Gosse, 6 March 1911, a.l.s., BM
187. Gosse to Howells, 22 March 1911, a.l.s., HU
188. Howells to Gosse, 7 April 1911, a.l.s., BM
189. Wharton to Gosse, 5 May 1911, a.l.s., BC
190. Howells to Gosse, 13 May 1911, a.l.s., BM
191. Gosse to Howells, 24 May 1911, a.l.s., HU
192. Howells to Gosse, 2 September 1911, a.l.s., BM
193. Howells to Gosse, 9 September 1911, a.l.s., BM
194. Gosse to James, 11 September 1911, a.l.s., HU
195. James to Gosse, 19 September 1911, a.l.s., Duke
196. Wharton to Gosse, 17 November 1911, dictated letter, signed, BC

197. James to Gosse, 31 October 1913, a.l.s., BC
198. Gosse to James, [31 October 1913], a.l.s., HU
199. James to Gosse, 1 November 1913, a.l.s., BC
200. James to Gosse, 25 June 1915, a.l.s., LC
201. Gosse to James, 25 June 1915, a.l.s., HU
202. James to Gosse, 28 June 1915, a.l.s., BC
203. Gosse to James, [8 July 1915], a.l.s., HU
204. Gosse to James, 9 July 1915, a.l.s., HU
205. James to Gosse, 9 July 1915, a.l.s., BC
206. Gosse to James, 26 July 1915, a.l.s., HU
207. James to Gosse, 26 July 1915, a.l.s., LC
208. Wharton to Gosse, 6 August 1915, a.l.s., BC
209. Wister to Gosse, 28 October 1915, a.l.s., BC
210. Gosse to Chase, 16 May [1917], a.l.s., LC

APPENDIX B
"Algernon in London"

"Algernon in London," a parody of Algernon Charles Swinburne's *Atalanta in Calydon,* published anonymously in the Portland [Maine] *Press* on 16 May 1876, page 1 (see Letter 3), was the work of Elisabeth Jones Pullen (1849–1926), wife of the proprietor and editor of the *Press.* It was republished in the London satirical magazine, the *Hornet,* on 14 June 1876, page 430 (see Letter 4). Mrs. Pullen's inspiration was the following item, which had appeared in the Portland *Press* a few days earlier (13 May 1876):

The poet Swinburne was expelled from the art club in London on account of his intemperate habits. The members have bore long with his infirmity, but one night, unable to find his hat, the frenzied poet seized the hats of all the members, hurled them upon the floor, and executed an Indian war dance upon them, all the while yelling and shouting frantically. Then it was deemed time to stop his drunken performances, and he was expelled.

Such an incident, as Gosse says in Letter 4, had its basis in fact, but it took place not in 1867, as Gosse says, but in 1870, a year before Gosse's first meeting with Swinburne, and six years before the appearance of the parody. In his *Life of Algernon Charles Swinburne* (1917), Gosse mentioned Swinburne's resignation from the Arts Club in 1870, but gave no further details; these he recorded, though without indicating the sources of his information, in an essay on Swinburne which he left unpublished at the time of his death but which Cecil Y. Lang has recently included as an appendix to the final volume of *The Swinburne Letters.* According to Gosse, Swinburne was entertaining Charles Duncan Cameron at the Arts Club in the spring of 1870; they got drunk, and when on leaving Swinburne could not find his hat—"which, on account of the great size of his head, was of excessive capacity"—he danced in anger upon the hats of other Club members and their guests. This incident followed upon several other disagreements which Swinburne had had with the Club and he was forced to resign.[1] The appearance of the parody in the *Hornet* may not be unconnected with the expressions of hostility to this and other "satirical journals" which recur in Swinburne's letters in the early months of 1877.[2]

[1] Cecil Y. Lang, ed., *The Swinburne Letters* (New Haven: Yale University Press, 1960), VI, 242; see also *ibid.,* I, 161, n. 2.
[2] Ibid., III, 266, 278, 281.

The authoress, Elisabeth Jones Pullen, began her career as a writer of sketches and reviews for the Portland *Press,* but in 1885 she married Nino Cavazza and lived for a number of years in Modena, Italy. On her husband's death seven years later she returned to the United States, where she married Stanley T. Pullen, the proprietor and editor of the Portland *Press.* In 1892, as Elisabeth Cavazza, she published *Don Finimondone: Calabrian Sketches,* and in 1902, as Elisabeth Pullen, *Mr. Whitman: A Story of the Brigands.* According to the *Portland City Guide,*[3] the source of most of the preceding information about Mrs. Pullen, the Swinburne parody "brought acclaim from members of the Century Club of New York, who sent her a card of admission, believing her literary effort was the work of a man." Stedman, it may be noted, was a leading member of the Century Club at this time.

The text given below is based on the first publication in the Portland *Press* but incorporates a number of corrections and emendations from the version printed in the *Hornet.*

[3]Portland, Maine: Forest City Printing Company, 1940.

[Written for the Portland Press]

ALGERNON IN LONDON

———

A TRAGEDY

———

The Persons

Algernon Charles Swinburne, a Poet.
Chorus of Members of the Arts Club.

———

The Argument

Mr. Algernon C. Swinburne, having heavily drunken
of strong wine, would fain set his face homeward;
but not finding the hat of him, was wroth because
of it; and danced upon the hats of other men in
such mad wise that he became banished for this cause
from the Arts Club. (*Vide contemporary history.*)

The Drama

CHORUS OF   When the steeds of Spring have broken the traces,
CLUB MEN   The weather reports for mountain and plain
Fill the newspaper columns' spaces
    With caution-signals and areas of rain;

308

And the medical men are unanimous
That this sort of weather is bad for us;
It takes a man in all sorts of places,
  With colds in the head and rheumatic pain.
What worth is Spring, and what would we take for
    her?
  Shivering, we sit by the fire and sing,
O that our feet were as fire and could make for her,
  Fire—or anything warm for Spring!
For the evening and morning are dismaller
Than the tunes of an amateur harp-player.
To cheer the time that we shiver and shake for her
  Wine and cigars are the only thing!

ALGERNON   Since young Apollo in Admetus' field
Set on his head a thick-leaved myrtle wreath;
Since on the windy battle plains of Troy
The helmet of Hector was a light for men;
Since Arthur's plume tossed in the tourney's front—
Lo! what a whirling fashion and voluble
Hath man in careful covering of his head!
Look ye, I hang my hat upon the peg—
Apollo's wreath, the sunstruck steel of war,
The blown white plume were crown no worthier!

CHORUS   Before the beginning of years,
    There went to the making of man
  Nine tailors with their shears,
    A coupé and a tiger and span,
  Umbrellas and neckties and canes,
    An ulster, a coat, and all that—
  But the crowning glory remains,
    His last, best gift was his hat.
  And the mad hatters took in hand
    Skins of the beaver, and felt
  And straw from the isthmus land,
    And silk and black bears' pelt;
  And wrought with prophetic passion,
    Designed on the newest plan,
  They made in the height of fashion,
    The hat for the wearing of man.

ALGERNON   Not happier Narcissus at the pool
Mirrored the beauty of him—crowned with pale buds

That grow beside the marge of water brooks,
Than British youth, wearing his new silk hat,
Who sees in mirrors of maids' liquid eyes
In passing, admiration of his style.

CHORUS We have seen thee, young man, thou art fair and
thy hat is a love;
Thy side whiskers wave in the air as the wings of a
dove;
And twain go forth beside thee, umbrella and dog—
Through Pall Mall, through the way that is wide, and
made dim of the fog.
We have seen them, we know them too well, both the
terrier and man;
And the name of thee is the Swell, and his name Black-
and-Tan!

ALGERNON Bring matches, bring cigars! There is a weed
Grown in gray earth, that knew the South wind's
song
Of tropical forests, where the palms grow tall,
And passionate lianas are a vail
For lairs of tigers; where the red sun flames,
Where night's dark dog follows the white doe day,
And storm and lightning and the earthquake's terror
Are as the tiger to slay—and dead, brown leaves,
Ye hold a fire unburned, the dream of day
That sleep hath not, nor night, remembering them.

SEMI-CHORUS He bit off the end of his weed,
As the frost in the field a flower;
He threw the small end away—
His face is lit redder than day,
His face is made glorious indeed,
With the light of the match, and its power!
He lit his cigar with fire,
He kindled a flame with his breath.
As the mouth of a flute-player
So did his mouth appear;
The smoke rises higher and higher—
He is crownéd with smoke for a wreath!

ALGERNON So is my fame, a wind-blown changeful smoke,
Lit at a sudden fire, that fails with breath.

Bring hither wine, boy—bring the sinuous steel
To draw the cork forth from the bottle's mouth
Glassy and green as mouth of water-snake.
Then leave me. I would fain forget the cold
Of hands and feet, of heart and mouth of me.
Fire that I drink, burn in the songs I sing!
O that I were on some sweet sunlit hill
To see the glad vines crowding aslant its slopes,
Straining strong arms about it in the sun;
And through the light and shadow of the leaves
See Bacchus' self dancing among the grapes;
And drink my fill, until my blood grew warm
As juice of madness in the veins of vines,
Until my song grew sweet, fulfilled of fire
And joy of wine, and rich, luxuriant words
Clustered as purple grapes upon my lips!
So would I follow all the day the dance
Of Bacchanals, and wearied in the way
Lay me asleep in shadow of the vines.
Or would that I in midst of silver seas
Had felt the ship staid suddenly on her course,
And seen the masts made green with vine-leaves, when
Bacchus was crowned, and rode triumphant, borne
By lithe and spotted leopards out of the sea.
Dead dreams, alas, and past! I will away,
Leaving the club of clods for mine own house.
Where is my hat? I thought I had seen two—
This is a mocking fantasy of wine!
Where is it? Fret, and irony of chance,
Shall I be hatless, shall I walk uncrowned
In shadow of no brim among the bards,
While they have, for the shade of laurel boughs
Bound on their brows, broad rims of beaver hats?
Shall I to common laugh of unwashed lips
Expose my parted length of uncut hair?
Shall I, an uncrowned crown, discrowned of Fate,
Bare to the breath of winds blown every way,
And chill the burning brain it bears beneath?
See all these hats—Morris' hat, Rossetti's!
I trample them beneath my feet—I dance
Upon them! Ah, would I could trample out
The bitter hardness of the fate of me!

The impelling mad delirium of delight,
The agony of joy, are in my brain—
Hats, take your last farewell of foolish earth—
And thus, and thus, I crush ye!

SEMI-CHORUS   As forests with tempests that wrestle
      From the hat-rack our hats are torn down.

ALGERNON   Ye are my foes, silk hats! Ye mock at me,
Black cylinders, as engines of the pit,
Cry ye and crackle underneath my feet!

SEMI-CHORUS   The Englishman's house is his castle,
      The Englishman's hat is his crown.

ALGERNON   Impertinent broadbrim, let me dance on thee,
      Wide-awake hat, I hate thee unto death.
Soft hat, my heart is hard, and hard my feet!

SEMI-CHORUS   His heart has grown hot as the South—
      Shall we reason with him, or complain?

ALGERNON   Straw hat, prepare to die the craven's death;
Slouched hat, droop lower underneath my feet;
Look how I dance above thee, silken tile!

SEMI-CHORUS   The enemy set in his mouth
      Has stolen, has stolen his brain.

ALGERNON   Flatter and duller underneath my feet
Ye are not than the brains once under ye!
Alas, I am spent with anger—and thus—I fall!

SEMI-CHORUS   He has finished his devastation;
      He is fallen—he cannot stand.

ALGERNON   Alas, my force has failed, and fury of me—
They are crushed as grass, they are shattered as
    shattered helms
Upon lost fields of war—I am as dead.

SEMI-CHORUS   Lament with a long lamentation;
      Is not a policeman at hand?

ALGERNON   Let your hands meet
      Round the weight of my head;
Lift ye my feet
      As the feet of the dead.

For the force of my feet is forgotten, the limbs of
me heavy as lead.

CHORUS   O thy fatuous face,
    Thy delirious eyes!
He is fallen without grace;
    On the carpet he lies!
    Whose hats are these, broken and bent, with
        tears and compression of size?

ALGERNON   Is this treatment fair,
    When a man feels weak?
There you stand and stare,
    With unlimited cheek,
    At me and the hats I demolished, and my name
        not in blessing you speak!

CHORUS   Thou wert easily chief
    In poetical powers;
This is past all belief—
    Thou has trampled—as flowers
    Are trampled of horses in battle, these hats which
        were not yours, but ours.

ALGERNON   I would that with feet
    Too heavily shod,
Over bold, over fleet,
    I had danced not, nor trod
    On the hats that lie scattered about me, as
        autumn leaves crushed on the sod.

CHORUS   Ah! remember your praise,
    How the Club cheered you on,
In those happier days
    When our dear Algernon
Had just published his classical drama,
    Atalanta in Calydon.

ALGERNON   Would ye had found me
    At home in my house!
Would ye had found me
    Hard to arouse,
    With the sleep of the just in mine eyes, and the
        nightcap of peace on my brows!

313

CHORUS   We must call the police
        That he be held fast;
    The court will release
        Him with fines at the last,
        But who shall restore us our hats—our hats
           over which he has passed!

ALGERNON   They may not have again
        The good form they had erst;
    Yet they may not remain
        Of all bad hats the worst—
        For the hatter perhaps can re-block them, in the
           shape they were made in at first.

CHORUS   What thing wilt thou leave us
        Now these hats are flat;
    New hats wilt thou give us,
        A hat for a hat,
        For the wide-awake hat thou hast danced on,
           for the beaver on which thou hast sat?

ALGERNON   Might a 'bus bear me back?
        Could a cab take me home?
    From decorum's dull track
        It was wine made me roam;
        Please send for some brandy and soda, cool
           mixture of spirit and foam!

CHORUS   The club are hungry
        At this time of day;
    The club are angry,
        And this we say:
        You are hereby expelled from the Arts Club,
           so make the best of it you may!

ALGERNON   Hail ye: but I with heavy face and feet
    Turn homeward and am gone out of your eyes.

CHORUS   Who on our silk hats shall stand,
        Dance on them, or do them wrong?
    Who shall burst binding or band?
        Who then shall kick them along?
    The Englishman's hat is as sacred
        As English traditions are strong.

314

INDEX

Titles not otherwise identified are works of Edmund Gosse.

Abbey, Edwin Austin: identified, 176 and n. 3; mentioned, 8, 27, 187

Abercrombie, Lascelles: identified, 298 and n. 11

Academy: review of Stedman's *Lyrics and Idylls* in, 7, 72 and n. 1 (L. 10), 72–73, 77; mentioned, 74

Adams, Henry: 16

Aldrich, Thomas Bailey: identified, 68 and n. 11, 112 and n. 1 (L. 40); attitude of, toward Oscar Wilde, 89 n. 1; mentioned, 8, 13, 98, 109, 111 and n. 5, 144, 156, 193. SEE ALSO Gosse, Edmund, letters of, to Aldrich; Gosse, Edmund, letters of, from Aldrich

"Algernon in London. A Tragedy": 63 and n. 7, 63–64, 66, Appendix B

Alma-Tadema, Laura: identified, 76 and n. 1; death of, 265 and n. 1 (L. 176), 266–267; mentioned, 84, 93 and n. 1 (L. 25), 111, 128, 197 and n. 2

Alma-Tadema, Lawrence (Laurens): identified, 76 and n. 1; proposed *Century* article on, 226 and n. 1; mentioned, 8, 93 and n. 1 (L. 25), 98, 109, 110, 128, 135, 142, 165, 189, 191

America. SEE Anglo-American relations; Gosse, Edmund, American tour of

American Academy of Arts and Letters: 270 and n. 1

Anderson, Mary: identified, 132 and n. 2

Anglo-American relations: Gosse's special position in, 10, 27–28, 51–52; America's attempt to establish artistic and cultural superiority in, 10, 44–45; sensitivity of, 10, 45; bias of, in reviews of *Gossip in a Library*, 21; debate on realism-romanticism in, 22, 42–44; democracy-monarchy controversy in, 45–47, 103–104; America's interference in Patrick O'Donnell case, 127 and n. 3; Bancroft on founda-

tions of, 172–173; Venezuela-British Guiana boundary dispute in, 233 and n. 1, 233–234, during Boer War, 247 and n. 3, 247–248; during Spanish-American War, 247; on Civil War, 247–248. SEE ALSO democracy-monarchy debate; Dickens-Thackeray controversy; Howells, William Dean; realism-romanticism debate

Anthology of American Poetry (Stedman): Gosse's review of, 44

Armour, George Allison: relationship of, with Gosse, 27, 35–36, 198 and n. 1; identified, 198 and n. 1; mentioned, 48, 203, 242. SEE ALSO Gosse, Edmund, letters of, to Armour

Arnold, Matthew: American visit of, 8, 10, 125 and n. 3, 125–126, 133; Gosse's lecture series on, 235 and n. 3, 235–236; mentioned, 149, 150, 177–178, 186

Arthur, Chester Alan: Gosses meet, 17 and n. 39

Aspects and Impressions: American reception of, 25

Asquith, Henry Herbert: identified, 289 and n. 2; mentioned, 290

Asquith, Margaret ("Margot"): identified, 235 and n. 6

Atalanta in Calydon (Swinburne): parody on, 63 and n. 7, 63–64, 66, Appendix B

Athenaeum: review of Stedman's *Lyrics and Idylls* in, 74 and n. 3 (L. 12), 75, 77; review of *Firdausi in Exile* in, 185 and n. 2; mentioned, 40–41, 183

Atlantic Monthly: reviews *On Viol and Flute*, 9, 111 and n. 5, 112; editorial policy of, 192; Gosse contributes to, 242–243 and n. 2 (L. 159); mentioned, 19, 38, 45, 66, 120, 205

Austin, Alfred: identified, 65 and n. 7; mentioned, 228

Autobiography of a Journalist, The: (Stillman): 261 and n. 2

Balestier, Caroline: marriage of, to Kipling, 27, 221 n. 1, 224 and n. 1
Balestier, Josephine: identified, 254 and n. 20; mentioned, 27, 221 n. 1, 224
Balestier, Charles Wolcott: desire of, to publish in *Century*, 218 and nn. 1, 2; identified, 221 and n. 1; collaboration of, with Kipling, 221 and n. 1; readiness of *Century* to publish, 221 and n. 2, 221–222; death of, 222 and n. 1, 222–223, 224 and n. 3; posthumous works of, 223 and n. 1; mentioned, 27
Baltimore, Maryland: Gosses in, 16, 17
Bancroft, George: meets Gosse in America, 16–17, 172 n. 2; identified, 172 and n. 1; mentioned, 163 and n. 2. SEE ALSO Gosse, Edmund, letters of, from Bancroft
Barbey d'Aurevilly, Jules Amédée: identified, 236 and n. 9; Gosse on, 236; James on, 237
Baring, Maurice: identified, 298 and n. 13
Barrett, Lawrence: entertains Gosses in New York, 14, 157 and n. 1; in Philadelphia, 15; in *A Blot on the 'Scutcheon*, 15; relationship of, with Boker, 15 and n. 32; in *Julius Caesar*, 18–19; identified, 132 and n. 3 (L. 57); in *Yorick's Love*, 132 and n. 3, 137; mentioned, 8, 139, 141, 142, 167, 178–179
Barrie, Sir James Matthew: identified, 285 and n. 2
Bartholdi, Auguste: identified, 196 and n. 2
Beardsley, Aubrey Vincent: identified, 231 and n. 3
Bedford, eleventh Duke of: 235 and n. 4
Bedford, Duchess of: 235
Beers, Henry Augustin: Gosse recommended to, for Yale professorship, 34, 138, 139; identified, 138 and n. 1 (L. 64), 138–139; mentioned, 160
Benefits Forgot (Balestier): efforts of Gosse to publish, 218 and n. 1
Benson, Arthur Christopher: identified, 266 and n. 2, 285 n. 3; mentioned, 267
Benson, Edward Frederick: identified, 285 and n. 3
Benson, Edward White: identified, 285 and n. 3

Benson, Robert Hugh: identified, 285 and n. 3
Bertini (Domenico or Pietro): identified, 123 and n. 3
Beswick, Samuel: Gosse on, 117 and n. 4
Bigelow, John: identified, 14 and n. 27
Bildt, Karl Niels Daniel: identified, 273 and n. 8
Birdseye, Miss (*The Bostonians*): controversy over, 164 and n. 3, 164–165, 167–168
Birrell, Augustine: identified, 214 and n. 2
Blaine, James: meets with Gosse in America, 16 and n. 37, 17
Blind, Mathilda: identified, 114 and n. 2
Board of Trade: Gosse on, 3; grants Gosse leave of absence, 130 and n. 1; Gosse on retirement from, 166
Boer War: American attitude toward, 247 and n. 3, 247–248
Boker, George Henry: at dinner in Gosse's honor, 15; relationship of, with Barrett, 15 and n. 32; Gosse's description of, 15, 159; identified, 159 and n. 2
"Book of Gosse": 34 and n. 86, 38, *et passim*
Book of the Homeless (Wharton): 294 and n. 1
Booth, Edwin: at reception for Gosses, 13; in *Merchant of Venice*, 13; identified, 98 and n. 7; mentioned, 18
Boston, Massachusetts: Gosses in, 11–14 *passim*; mentioned, 156, 158, 160
Botta, Mrs. Anne Charlotte Lynch: identified, 18 and n. 42
Bourne, Randolph: review of *Three French Moralists* by, 25; mentioned, 27
Bowen, John Eliot: 21
Bowker, Richard Rogers: identified, 88 n. 3; mentioned, 89
Boyesen, Hjalmar Hjorth: identified, 18 and n. 45
Brandes, Georg Morris Cohen: identified, 286 and n. 3
Bridges, Robert: *Eros and Psyche* of, 186; *Achilles in Scyros* of, 229; identified, 298 and n. 6
Bright, John: identified, 119 and n. 1; proposed article on, 119, 124
Britain, relations of, with America. SEE Anglo-American relations
Bronson, Katharine De Kay: identified, 252 and n. 3

Brooke, Stopford Augustus: identified, 214 and n. 4

Brooks, Van Wyck: reviews *Leaves and Fruit*, 26; on Gosse as a critic, 26; mentioned, 27

Brown, Ford Madox: 6

Browne, Sir Thomas: Gosse quotes from, 150 and n. 4; mentioned, 219

Brownell, William Crary: identified, 115 and n. 1

Browning, Elizabeth Barrett: in Stedman's *Victorian Poets*, 183; mentioned, 252, 253, 255, 257

Browning, Robert: Gosse dedicates *King Erik* to, 7, 67 n. 5; style of, discussed, 9; attack on Alfred Austin in *Pacchiarotto and How He Worked in Distemper*, 65; publishes *Dramatic Idyls*, 68; Gosse's research on, 251–252; inspiration of, for "My Star," 252, 257; mentioned, 15, 176, 186, 189

Brunetta, Eugenio: identified, 125 and n. 2

Bryce, James: identified, 119 and n. 3; article on, 211–212, 214 and n. 6; mentioned, 124, 126, 191

Buchanan, Robert Williams: identified, 151 and n. 7; in Stedman's *Victorian Poets*, 180–181, 183

Buller, Lady Audrey: identified, 236 and n. 8

Buller, Sir Redvers Henry: 236 n. 8

Bunner, Henry Cuyler: identified, 81 and n. 20; mentioned, 18, 124

Burne-Jones, Sir Edward: identified, 128 and n. 5

Burroughs, John: identified, 110 and n. 2

Cable, George Washington: identified, 14 and n. 29; mentioned, 33

Caine, Thomas Henry Hall: identified, 232 and n. 1; mentioned, 89–90

Calamus (Whitman): revelation of Whitman's character in, 240–242

Cambridge University: Gosse as Clark Lecturer at, 9, 31, 140–141, 142, 146; gives honorary degree to Holmes, 31

"Captain, My Captain!" (Balestier): 223 and n. 1

Carnegie, Andrew: 13

Carnovon, fifth Earl of: 235 n. 5

Carnovon, Countess of: 235

Carte, Richard D'Oyley: identified, 88 and n. 5

Cawein, Madison Julius: identified, 262 and n. 1 (L. 172); mentioned, 42, 49

Cecil Lawson: A Memoir: review mentioned, 111; mentioned, 102 and n. 3

Century Illustrated Monthly Magazine: Gilder as editor of, 7, 32, 84 n. 1; Gosse as London agent for, 7–8, 32–34, 206 and n. 1, 206–207, 215; Gosse's usefulness to, 8, 10; editorial policies of, 32–34, 173–175, 191–192, 202, 203; Civil War Series in, 33, 173 and n. 3, 173–175; treatment of Stevenson by, 254 and n. 18; mentioned, 13, 38, 40, 45, 92, 101, 104, 124, 136, 225. SEE ALSO *Scribner's Monthly*

Cesnola, Luigi Palma di: identified, 252 and n. 7

"Charcoal Burner, The": inspiration for, 79 and n. 9

Charteris, Sir Evan: 6, 9–10, 20

Chase, Lewis Nathaniel: identified, 296 and n. 1; mentioned, 36, 37. SEE ALSO Gosse, Edmund, letters of, to Chase

Child, Francis James: identified, 151 and n. 6

Choate, Joseph Hodges: identified, 252 and n. 11

Churchill, Winston (American novelist): identified, 273 and n. 3; mentioned, 274, 276–277

Civil War (American): series on, in *Century*, 33, 173 and n. 3; 173–175; English attitude during, 247–248

Clarke, Helen A.: 253 and n. 16

Clark, Sir Caspar Purdon: identified, 252 and n. 5

Cleveland, Grover: identified, 172 and n. 5

Collected Essays: review of, in *Nation*, 23

Collins, John Churton. SEE Gosse, Edmund, and Gosse-Collins affair

Colvin, Sir Sidney: identified, 189 and n. 2

Comedies and Errors (Harland): 237 and n. 1

Congreve, William: Gosse's biography of, 4, 209

Corals and Coral Islands (Dana): 101 and n. 1

Corelli, Marie: identified, 273 and n. 6

Cornell University: Gosse's visit to, 18; declines Gosse's request to lecture at, 131 and n. 3, 140, 145, 150

Cornhill Magazine: 87 and n. 10

317

Corson, Hiram: identified, 145 and n. 2; mentioned, 150
Cosmopolitan Magazine: Gosse's association with, 249 and n. 2, 249–250
Counterfeit Presentment, A (Howells): and n. 4, 133, 142
Craddock, Charles Egbert. SEE Murfree, Mary Noailles
Creighton, Mandell: identified, 193 and n. 4; mentioned, 195, 214
Crime and Punishment (Dostoevsky): Gosse on, 205
Critic: interview of Gosse in, 19; review of *Gray* in, 19; on Gosse-Collins affair, 20–21; Holmes honored by, 30, 147–148; 150; mentioned, 44
Critical Essay on the Life and Works of George Tinworth, A: 102 and n. 3, 133 and n. 1
Critical Kit-Kats: "Walt Whitman" essay in, 16, 28; Gilder on Gosse's reviews in, 253 and n. 15
Criticism and Fiction (Howells): 43, 46
Cross, John W.: biography of George Eliot by, 114 and n. 1, 114–115; opposes publication of George Eliot portrait, 115 and n. 3 (L. 43)
culture. SEE Anglo-American relations; democracy-monarchy debate; realism-romanticism debate
Curtin, Andrew Gregg: identified, 160 and n. 6

Daily News (Philadelphia): 15
Dana, James Dwight: 101 and n. 1
Daudet, Léon: identified, 288 and n. 1 (L. 200)
Davenant, Sir William: 137
Davidson, John: identified, 229 and n. 7; Gosse on success of, 229
de Goncourt, Edmond Louis Antoine Huot: identified, 236 and n. 10
De Kay, Charles: identified, 78 and n. 3; Gosse on, 78–79
De Kay, Helena (Mrs. R. W. Gilder): 78 n. 3, 254 and n. 23
democracy-monarchy debate: literary products of, 45–47; Gosse on, 103–104; Howells on, 104–105; mentioned 50, 51. SEE ALSO Anglo-American relations; Dickens-Thackeray controversy
Deschamps, Pierre Charles Ernest: identified, 109 and n. 3

Desjardins, Paul: identified, 282 and n. 1
Dickens, Charles: 8, 248. SEE ALSO Dickens-Thackeray controversy
Dickens-Thackeray controversy: Howells's slight to Dickens and Thackeray, 40–41; Gosse's reaction to, 40–41, 50, 102; Howells's surprise at, 45, 104–105; Gosse on Howells's dislike of Dickens and Thackeray, 45–46, 103–104; democracy-monarchy issue in, 45–46, 103–104; 104–105; Howells's on, 104–105
Discourses of Sir Joshua Reynolds, The: Gosse on, 145; Stedman on, 150 and n. 4
Dobson, Henry Austin: identified, 60 and n. 2; in Stedman's *Victorian Poets*, 61, 181, 183; Stedman on, 64, 77; Gosse on, 75, 80, 82, 83, 186, 256; dedication of *Firdausi in Exile* to, 182 and n. 2, 182–183; mentioned, 34, 68, 71, 78, 84, 87, 108, 120, 121, 133, 145, 189, 191, 252, 298
Dostoevsky, Fëdor Mikhailovich: Gosse on *Crime and Punishment* of, 205
Doyle, Sir Arthur Conan: identified, 273 and n. 5
Drake, Joseph Rodman: Gosse on, 86; identified, 86 and n. 3
Dramatic Idyls (Browning): 68
Drinkwater, John: identified, 298 and n. 8
Dugdale, Mrs. Stratford: identified, 235 and n. 3; mentioned, 236
Du Maurier, George: identified, 115 and n. 2
Dyer, Louis: identified, 166 and n. 2

Edgar Allan Poe (Stedman): first published as article, 76 and n. 5; later published as book, 81 and n. 2
Edgett, E. F.: review of *Aspects and Impressions* by, 25
Eggleston, George Cary: identified, 18 and n. 45
Eggleston, Edward: identified, 14 and n. 29
Eliot, Charles William: identified, 162 and n. 3; mentioned, 12
Eliot, George: controversy over portrait of, 111, 115 and n. 3 (L. 43); Gosse on biography of, 114 and n. 1, 114–115
Emerson, Ralph Waldo: Gosse compared to, 9; Gosse visits grave of, 13; Gosse on, 90–91 and n. 2; 108 and n. 6; Arnold's lecture on, 125 and n. 3; philoso-

phy of, 246 and n. 2; mentioned, 12, 44, 45, 150

English Literature: An Illustrated Record: American reception of, 22; mentioned, 261

English Odes: 83

"Epistle to Dr. Oliver Wendell Holmes on his Seventy-fifth Birthday, An": 30, 145, 147–148

Escott, Thomas Hay Sweet: identified 124 and n. 1

Estebanez, Joaquin: identified, 132 n. 3; mentioned, 139, 142

Father and Son: American reception of, 22; Howells's admiration of, 48, 269 and n. 1 (L. 181), 269–270; Furness on, 260–261; Gilder on, 262; mentioned, 49, 297

Fearful Responsibility, A (Howells): 41

Fernandez, James: identified, 137 and n. 2

Feuillet, Octave: identified, 243 and n. 3

Field, Eugene: identified, 217 and n. 1. SEE ALSO Gosse, Edmund, letters of, to Field

Fields, Annie Adams: identified, 134 and n. 2

Firdausi in Exile and Other Poems: critical reception of, 20, 31, 185 and n. 1, 185–186; Stedman on, 182–183

Fitzgerald, Edward Arthur: identified, 235 and n. 1

Foregone Conclusion, A (Howells): Gosse on, 165 and n. 6

Fortnightly Review: Bancroft on, 172 and n. 3; mentioned, 212, 228

Frazer, William Lewis: identified, 177 and n. 3

Frederick Warne & Company: 85 and n. 5. SEE ALSO Warne, Frederick

French Dramatists of the 19th Century (Matthews): 80 and n. 16

"From Shakespeare to Pope": Gosse's lecture series on, 16, 134 and n. 1 (L. 59), 137–138

From Shakespeare to Pope: critical reception of, 20, 187 and n. 7; attacked by John Churton Collins, 20; mentioned, 178, 180

Froude, James Anthony: identified, 190 and n. 1

Furness, Horace Howard: relationship of, with Gosse, 16, 21, 27, 36; identified,

159 and n. 3; mentioned, 151 and n. 6. SEE ALSO Gosse, Edmund, letters of, to Furness; Gosse, Edmund, letters of, from Furness

Furness, Walter Rogers: identified, 248 and n. 8; mentioned, 176 and n. 5

Furness, William Henry: identified, 248 and n. 7

Galsworthy, John: identified, 285 and n. 1; mentioned, 287

Garfield, James Abram: identified, 17 and n. 39

Garland, Hamlin: friendship of, with Gosse, 27, 36, 37; mentioned, 50

Garrison, Wendell Phillips: identified, 14 and n. 27

Gaugengigl, Ignaz Marcel: 152 n. 1

Gide, André: identified, 295 and n. 5

Gilder, Richard Watson: and Gosse's American tour, 8, 9, 10–11, 140; relationship of, with Gosse, 7, 8, 32–35, 51; identified, 73 n. 1; health of, 77; mentioned, 12, 18, 36, 38, 52, 61, 63, 75, 136, 140. SEE ALSO *Century Illustrated Monthly Magazine*; Gosse, Edmund, letters of, to Gilder; Gosse, Edmund, letters of, from Gilder

Gilman, Daniel Coit: offers Gosse post at Johns Hopkins, 17–18; identified, 116 and n. 2; mentioned, 34, 134, 143

Gladstone, William Ewart: identified, 211 and n. 1; mentioned, 248

Godkin, E. L.: identified, 14 and n. 29

Godwin, Mrs. Bryant: identified, 158 and n. 1

Gosse, Edmund: preparation of, for career, 3, 5; education of, 3, 5, 50; success of, during lifetime, 3; failures of, in scholarship, 3–4; work of, in Jacobean and Restoration literature, 4, 6; as biographer, 4; works of, in Scandinavian studies, 4, 5; tendency of, to become literary "institution," 4–5, 24, 25, 26, 27, 50; interest of, in American writers, 6; desire of, to establish American reputation, 6–7, 51; relation of, with Pre-Raphaelites, 6, 27, 29–30, 42; offered professorship at Yale, 8–9; early success of, in England, 9; appointed Clark Lecturer at Cambridge, 9; realization of early ambitions, 27; literary outlook of, in early period of career, 28; knowledge of American literature, 28; attitude of, toward American life and literature, 29, 49–50; reaction of, to morality of father, 29–30; attitude of, toward art and life, 29–30, 50; discovers American ancestry, 31; associated with American magazines, 32–34; American friends of younger generation, 36; death of American friends, 36; decline of American correspondence, 36; views of, on realism, 42–43; article of, on American poets, 44; on patriotism in literary criticism, 44, 52; on "patriotic fallacy" in literature, 44; on democracy's influence on literature, 45; meets with Stark Young, 49–50; attempts to maintain critical proportion, 50; lacks understanding of American society, 50; interest of, in American personalities, 51; position of, in Anglo-American literary relations, 51–52

— American trip of: success of, 3, 9–10, 14, 19; purposes of 8, 9; efforts to secure Lowell Institute Lectures for, 9, 122 and n. 1, 122–123, 125, 127, 129, 130–131, 131–132, 135; attitude toward American audiences on, 10, 138, 145; social activities during, 10–19 passim, 152, 156, 159–160; lecture tour of, 11, 12, 14, 16, 17, 18, 145, 150, 155, 160–161; financial arrangements for, 131, 134 and n. 1 (L. 60), 134–136, 136 and n. 1, 138, 140, 141, 165; subjects of lectures given during, 132, 134 and n. 1 (L. 59), 136, 137–138; mentioned, 149, 150, 153–154, 157, 158, 159, 163

— and Century Illustrated Monthly Magazine: Gosse as London agent for, 7–8, 32–34, 206–207, 215; Gosse's usefulness to, 8, 10; Gosse and Gilder conflict on editorial policy, 33 173–175

—, as critic: handicaps of, 5; selects fields of study, 5–6; aims of, 5, 27; range of authority of, 5, 27; reception of, 20–22, 22–27; dislike of patriotic criteria in evaluating literature, 34, 44, 46. SEE ALSO Gosse, Edmund, literary reputation of

—, friendships of: range of, 4–5, 8; deliberate initiation of, 4–5, 50–51; cultivation of Americans, 8, 10–18 passim, 27–38 passim, 50–51; facility in establishing, 50–51. SEE ALSO Armour,

George Allison; Furness, Horace Howard; Gilder, Richard Watson; Holmes, Dr. Oliver Wendell; Howells, William Dean; James, Henry; Stedman, Edmund Clarence; Whitman, Walt

—, and Gosse-Collins affair: effect of, on Gosse's reputation, 4, 20–21; Collins's attack in Quarterly Review, 20; Gosse's reply to, 20, 191 and n. 1, 193; public opinion on, 20–21; Gosse on, 194, 196, 197, 199, 200–201

—, literary reputation of: in America, 4, 6, 7, 10, 19–27, 51–52; as scholar, 4, 19, 20–21, 22, 23; effect of Gosse-Collins affair on, 4, 20–21; quick rise of, 4, 27; eclipse of, after death, 4, 27. SEE ALSO Gosse, Edmund, as critic; Gosse, Edmund, style of

—, style of: compared to Emerson, 9; compared to Browning, 9; as seen by younger critics, 22, 27; criticism of, by Pound, 23–24; American criticism of, 24; American defenders of, 25; identified with Victorianism, 25; influences on, 27, 42–43, 297

—, works of, SEE Aspects and Impressions; Cecil Lawson: A Memoir; Collected Essays; Critical Essays on the Life and Works of George Tinworth, A; Critical Kit-Kats; Discourses of Sir Joshua Reynolds, The; English Literature: An Illustrated Record; English Odes; Father and Son; Firdausi in Exile and Other Poems; From Shakespeare to Pope; Gossip in a Library; History of Eighteenth Century Literature; Ibsen; In Russet and Silver; Hypolympia, or the Gods in the Island: An Ironic Fantasy; Jacobean Poets; King Erik; Leaves and Fruit; Life and Letters of John Donne; Life of Algernon Charles Swinburne; Life of Philip Henry Gosse, F.R.S.; Life of Sir Thomas Browne; Life of Thomas Gray; Life of William Congreve; Madrigals, Songs and Sonnets; New Poems; On Viol and Flute; Portraits and Sketches; Questions at Issue; Raleigh; Robert Browning: Personalia; Seventeenth Century Studies; Short History of Modern English Literature; Some Diversions of a Man of Letters; Studies in the Literature of Northern Europe; Three French Moralists; Two Visits to Denmark; Un-

known Lover, The; Works of Thomas Gray
—, letter of, to Aldrich: on review of *On Viol and Flute*, 112. SEE ALSO Aldrich, Thomas Bailey
—, letters of, from Aldrich: on review of *On Viol and Flute*, 120; on "Unheard Music," 120 and n. 1. SEE ALSO Aldrich, Thomas Bailey
—, letters of, to Armour: on Armour's gifts, 198, 199 and n. 3, 219, 227–228; on attack by Collins, 199 and n. 5; on Robert Louis Stevenson, 204 and n. 1, 219–220; on Gosse's health, 205; on Holmes's *Our Hundred Days in Europe*, 205 and n. 1; on Gosse's Nuremberg papers, 205; on Dostoevsky's *Crime and Punishment*, 205; on illness of Cotter Morison, 209; on *History of Eighteenth Century Literature*, 209; on *Life of William Congreve*, 209–210; on Gosse's children, 219; on the Grolier Club, 219; on Kipling, 220 and n. 7; on *Saturday Review*, 228; on Watson's *Odes and Other Poems*, 228–229; on Davidson's *Ballads and Songs*, 229. SEE ALSO Armour, George Allison
—, letters of, from Bancroft: on *Fortnightly Review*, 172; on Grover Cleveland, 172; on Anglo-American relations, 172–173. SEE ALSO Bancroft, George
—, letters of, to Chase: on *Life of Swinburne*, 297; on Chase's lecture series, 297, 298; on Gosse's early works, 297; on influences on Gosse's works, 297; on Gosse's later works, 297; on *Hypolympia*, 297. SEE ALSO Chase, Lewis Nathaniel
—, letters of, to Field: on translating poetry, 217 and n. 1. SEE ALSO Field, Eugene
—, letters of, to Furness: on Halliwell-Phillips's priory, 175–176; on photography by Furness's son, 176 and n. 5; on Browning, 176; on *Calamus*, 241–242. SEE ALSO Furness, Horace Howard
—, letters of, from Furness: on *Gray*, 168, 169 and n. 5; on Gosse's visit to him, 169; on Aldis Wright, 169, 246; on *From Shakespeare to Pope*, 178; on Halliwell-Phillips's priory, 178; on Whitman, 178–179, 225–226, 240–241; on the Boer War, 247 and n. 3, 248; on

Spanish-American War, 247; on England during the Civil War, 247–248; on Philip Gosse's work, 248; on Furness's sons, 248; on vacationing in Florida, 248–249; on *Father and Son*, 260–261; on *English Literature: An Illustrated Record*, 261 and n. 4. SEE ALSO Furness, Horace Howard
—, letters of, to Gilder: Gosse's invitation to visit, 73 and n. 2, 73–74; on Gilder's *New Day*, 74 and n. 3; on Gosse's American acquaintances, 78; on Lowell, 78; on poems of De Kay, 78–79; on Swinburne, 79; on *New Poems*, 79 and n. 8; on Thornycroft's work, 79 and n. 10, 79–80; on St. Gaudens, 80; on Dobson, 80, 256; on Lang, 80, 91, 256; on Brander Matthews, 80; on Gilder's *Poet and His Master*, 80; on professorship at Oxford, 80 and n. 18; on Roswell Smith, 84 and nn. 1, 2, 84–85, 113; on Century Company, 84 and n. 4, 84–85 and n. 5; on Stanley article, 85 and n. 6; on Emerson, 90–91 and nn. 2, 3; on extracts from Carlyle's diaries, 91 and n. 4, 91–92; on sculpture articles, 112–113, 120; on the Lazarus sisters, 113 and nn. 2, 3; on American visitors, 113, 116 and n. 3; on *Seventeenth Century Studies*, 113, 119 and n. 7, 119–120; on *Century*, 117, 124, 190–191, 216; on John Bright article, 119, 124; on Howells's *A Woman's Reason*, 124; on Watt's "Love and Life," 152; on Gosse-Collins affair, 200 and n. 1, 200–201; on English magazines, 201; on Fitzwilliam Museum article, 202; on Gilder's editorial policies, 202, 203; on John Bryce article, 211–212 and n. 4, 214; on becoming associated with S. S. McClure, 215 and n. 2; on Balestier, 218 and n. 1, 221–222, 223–224; on Kipling, 221, 222, 224; on Gilder's poem on Paderewski, 225; on article on Alma-Tadema, 226; on Venezuela-British Guiana boundary dispute, 233 and n. 1, 233–234; on Gilder's friendship with Cleveland, 233 and n. 2; on Elizabeth Barrett Browning, 255; on health of John Hay, 255 and n. 2; on American literary isolationism, 256; on Morley, 256; on Meredith, 256; on Hardy, 256; on Browning's "My Star,"

321

257. SEE ALSO Gilder, Richard Watson; *Century Illustrated Monthly Magazine*
—, letters of, from Gilder: on Gosse's book on Tinworth, 133; on Matthew Arnold, 133; on offer of Yale chair to Gosse, 138–139; on English editions of Gilder's works, 173 and n. 2, 230; on *Century*, 173 and n. 3, 173–174, 175, 191–192, 254 and n. 18; on Gosse's interest in art and literature, 174–175; on Collins's attack, 191 and n. 1; on desire to cultivate American authors, 192; on death of Balestier, 222 and n. 1, 222–223; on proposed London visit, 226 n. 1, 227, 230; on World's Fair, 227 and n. 2, 230; on death of Stevenson, 230 and n. 2; on Gosse's contribution to Browning studies, 251–252; on Browning's "My Star," 252, 253; on Metropolitan Museum, 252; on Dobson, 252; on Hay, 252; on Roosevelt, 252–253; on Morley, 253; on Browning's *Sonnets from the Portuguese*, 253; on *Father and Son*, 262; on Madison Cawein, 262 and n. 1. SEE ALSO Gilder, Richard Watson; *Century Illustrated Monthly Magazine*
—, letters of, to Harland: on Harland's *Comedies and Errors*, 237–238. SEE ALSO Harland, Henry
—, letters of, from Harland: on Gosse's criticism of Harland's *Mea Culpa*, 220–221; on Beardsley, 231; on Oscar Wilde, 231 and n. 4; on *Life of Philip Henry Gosse, F.R.S.*, 234; on Octave Feuillet, 243; on Marzials, 243–244; on visit to Weymouth, 243, 244. SEE ALSO Harland, Henry
—, letters of, to Higginson: on Mead's pamphlet *Thomas Wentworth Higginson*, 245–246. SEE ALSO Higginson, Thomas Wentworth (Col.)
—, letters of, to Holmes: on desire to meet Holmes, 148–149 and n. 1; on Holmes's *Ralph Waldo Emerson*, 154–155, 163; on Holmes's attendance at lectures, 155, 163; on *On Viol and Flute*, 155 and n. 1; on American visit, 163; on Holmes's visit to England, 188 and n. 1, 188–189; on reception for Holmes, 189–190; on Gosse's American ancestry, 210–211. SEE ALSO Holmes, Dr. Oliver Wendell

—, letters of, from Holmes: on Gosse's poem in his honor, 147–148; on *On Viol and Flute*, 156; on Holmes's *Over the Teacups*, 218 and n. 1. SEE ALSO Holmes, Dr. Oliver Wendell
—, letters of, to Howells: extends Howells invitation to visit, 92, 93 and n. 1 (L. 25), 93–94; on Howells's *A Modern Instance*, 97; on Howells's visit to England, 99; on Howells's *The Parlour Car*, 99; on Howells's *The Lady of the Aroostook*, 99; on Howells's *Their Wedding Journey*, 99–100; on bluebooks on Hong-Kong, 100; on desire for Howells's portrait, 102, 107 on Harriet Preston, 102 and n. 1, 104, 127; on Howells's article on Dickens and Thackeray, 102 and n. 2, 103–104; on Howells's "Lexington," 103 and n. 4; on Howells's gift, 106; on society, 107; on James, 107 and n. 1, 127, 164–165, 187, 217, 280; on Lowell Lectures, 127, 128 and n. 4, 130, 131–132; on review of Mildred Howells's book, 127 and n. 1; on *Seventeenth Century Studies*, 127 and n. 2; on the O'Donnell case, 127 and n. 3; on arrangements for lecture tour, 131, 132, 134, 135–136, 141, 143, 144; on arrangements for American visit, 136, 142, 153–154; on performance of *Yorick's Love*, 137; on appointment to Cambridge, 140–141; on Howells's *Three Villages*, 144 and n. 1; on arrival in New York, 157; on stay with the Barretts, 157 and n. 1; on General Sherman, 159; on Boker, 159; on Furness, 159; on visit to Walt Whitman, 159; on Lowell, 164; on James's "Miss Birdseye," 164 and n. 3, 164–165; on Howells's *Rise of Silas Lapham*, 165; on financial success of American tour, 165–166; on criticism of Gosse's works, 181–182; on review in *Harper's*, 187; on Howells's daughter's drawing, 187–188; on Collins attack, 194 and n. 1, 197; on the Mott Smiths' visit, 194 and n. 2, 194–195; on *Raleigh*, 195; on the Creightons, 195; on Lowell-Hawthorne interview, 195; on Howells's "The Mousetrap," 197; on "Has America Produced a Poet?" 212; on Howells's *Indian Summer*, 216; on Howells's *The Kentons*, 268; on Howell's *Questionable*

Shapes, 268, 271–272; on Academic Committee of the Royal Society of Literature, 270–271; on *In After Days,* 271; on Howells's speech at the American Academy of Arts and Letters, 271; on effort to secure Nobel Prize for James, 276–277, 279–280; on Howells's *Literary Friends and Acquaintance,* 277. SEE ALSO Howells, William Dean

—, letters of, from Howells: on Gosse's invitation to visit, 93; on Howells's *A Modern Instance,* 96; on visit with Gosse, 96; on not writing, 97–98; on Howells's *A Woman's Reason,* 98, 100–101; on Gosse's *Gray,* 98–99, 101, 193; on Howells's vacation, 101; on Dickens and Thackeray, 104–105; on James, 104–105, 167–168, 269, 278, 279, 281; on Harriet Preston, 105, 126; on stay in Florence, 105–106, 108–109; on Howells's *Tuscan Cities,* 109 and n. 1, 168; on Italy, 109; on Alma-Tadema, 109; on difficulties in finding lodgings, 114 and n. 2 (L. 42), 123; on Gosse's dinner party, 115–116; on Lowell Lectures, 122 and n. 1, 122–123, 125, 129; on Augustus Lowell, 125; on Matthew Arnold's American visit, 125–126; on Howells's *Indian Summer,* 126 and n. 5, 130 and n. 6; on play written with Twain, 126; on Howells's daughter's book, 128–129 and n. 2; on the O'Donnell case, 129; on opera written with Henschel, 130 and n. 5, 142–143; introduces Gosse to Lawrence Barrett, 132–133; on financial arrangements for Gosse's lecture tour, 134 and n. 1, 134–135, 140; on Gosse's subject for lectures, 135; on Howells's *Yorick's Love,* 139–140; on Gosse's appointment to Clark Lectureship, 142; on *Seventeenth Century Studies,* 142; on Gosse's American visit, 152–153; on *The Rise of Silas Lapham,* 158, 162, 179; on success of Gosse's tour, 158; on Gosse's parlor lectures, 161 and n. 1; on possibility of Harvard chair for Gosse, 162; on Gosse's departure from America, 162–163; on Charles Craddock (Murfree), 167; on association with *Harper's,* 180 and n. 5, 184; on *From Shakespeare to Pope,* 180; on Howells's *The Minister's Charge,* 184 and n. 5; on *Firdausi in Exile,* 185; on Collins's attack on Gosse, 193; on *Raleigh,* 193; on meeting the Creightons, 193; on Hawthorne-Lowell interview, 193 and n. 6; on Gosse on Ibsen, 213, 269; on Howells's children, 213, 232; on New York society, 213; on Hall Caine, 232 and n. 1; on death of Howells's father, 232 and n. 2; on death of Howells's wife, 267 and n. 1 (L. 178); on *Father and Son,* 269, 270; on effort to secure Nobel Prize for James, 275, 277, 279; on desire to see Gosse, 280. SEE ALSO Howells, William Dean

—, letters of, to James: on Philip Gosse's attachment to Fitzgerald expedition, 235 and n. 1; on Gosse's lectures on Matthew Arnold, 235 and n. 3, 235–236; on Barbey d'Aurevilly, 236; on vacation in Siena, 264–265; on death of Laura Alma-Tadema, 265; on Haworth, 266; on James's return to England, 281–282; on vacation in France, 282; on Howells, 282; on Gosse's health, 286–287, 291, 293; on letter to Galsworthy, 287; on award of the Légion d'Honneur, 287 and n. 2; on James's desire to become an English citizen, 290, 291; on Kitchener's views on World War I, 293. SEE ALSO James, Henry

—, letters of, from James: on Philip Gosse's attachment to the Fitzgerald expedition, 236–237; on Barbey d'Aurevilly, 237; on Gosse's lectures, 237; on James's health, 263, 283, 286, 292; on Gosse's article on Swinburne, 263; on Holbein's "Duchess of Milan," 264 and n. 3; on death of Laura Alma-Tadema, 266–267; on desire to see Gosse, 283, 284; on Howells, 284; on Gosse's reply to Galsworthy's letter, 285 and n. 1, 285–286; on Gosse's health, 288, 292; on Léon Daudet, 288 and n. 1 (L. 200); on desire to become English citizen, 289, 290, 292, 293; on World War I, 294. SEE ALSO James, Henry

—, letters of, to Johnson: on John Burroughs, 110; on the *Century,* 110–111; on Zimmern article on Queen of Roumania, 111; on *On Viol and Flute,* 111; on drawing of George Eliot, 111; on recall of Laffan, 111; on Cross's biography of George Eliot, 114–115. SEE ALSO Johnson, Robert Underwood

—, letters of, to Lounsbury: on desire to lecture at Yale, 160–161 and nn. 2, 3. SEE ALSO Lounsbury, Thomas Raynesford

—, letters of, to Lowell: on unveiling of Gray Memorial, 170, 171 and n.1; on Lowell's address on Coleridge, 170 and n.2; on admiration for Lowell, 171. SEE ALSO Lowell, James Russell.

—, letters of, from Lowell: on Gosse's poem to Dr. Holmes, 147 and n.3 (L. 72); on Lowell's poem to Dr. Holmes, 147; on unveiling of Gray Memorial, 170; on address on Coleridge, 171. SEE ALSO Lowell, James Russell

—, letters of, to Moulton: on enjoyment of American visit, 156–157; on Moulton's *Poems of Philip Bourke Marston*, 207–208; on Stéphane Mallarmé, 240 and n. 2. SEE ALSO Moulton, Louise Chandler

—, letters of, to Munro: on *North American Review*, 238–239. SEE ALSO Munro, David Alexander

—, letters of, to Osgood: on American edition of *Seventeenth Century Studies*, 118. SEE ALSO Osgood, James Ripley

—, letters of, to Perry: on *Atlantic Monthly*, 242–243; on Gosse's article on Ibsen, 258 and n.1; on Perry's appointment to Harvard, 258 and n. 1, 258–259; on Tolstoy, 259 and n.1; on Perry's *Walt Whitman*, 260. SEE ALSO Perry, Bliss

—, letters of, to Roswell Smith: on book on pilgrim places of English literature, 177 and n. 2, 177–178. SEE ALSO Smith, Roswell

—, letters of, to Stedman: on Stedman's collected poems, 64–65, 70; on Stedman's future works, 65; on Browning, 65, 68; on Swinburne, 65–66, 68; on Stedman's poem on Hawthorne, 66; on Lathrop's *Masque of Poets*, 66–67 and n. 4; on review of *On Viol and Flute* and *King Erik*, 66, 67 and n. 5; on Louise Chandler Moulton, 67–68; on Aldrich, 68; on James, 68; on Bret Harte, 68; on Dobson, 68, 75, 83; on visit of Stedman, 70–71 and n. 1; on Stedman's *Lyrics and Idylls*, 74 and n. 3; on Gosse's autobiographical sketch, 74–75, 87 and n. 11; on the Gilders, 75; on Stedman's review of *New Poems*, 75; on Stedman's study of Poe, 76, 81; on

Swinburne, 76; on American edition of *On Viol and Flute*, 82 and n.3, 108; on [Henry] Holt, 82 and n. 3, 108; on misunderstanding between Gosse and Stedman, 82–84; on O'Shaughnessy's death, 83 and nn. 1,2; on Stedman's "Poetry in America," 86; on American critics, 86; on Stedman's "Corda Concordia," 86; on Oscar Wilde, 86–87, 89–90; on Christina Rossetti, 87; on O'Shaughnessy's posthumous works, 87; on Lang's poetry, 87; on Gosse's review of Whittier, 90 and n. 4; on Stedman's proposed London visit, 90; on meeting John Hay, 94, 95; on reception of *Gray*, 94–95; on Howells, 95; on Stedman's sudden return to America, 95 and n. 6; on gift of Haynes's *Poems*, 107; on Stedman's article on Emerson, 108; on Emerson's poetry, 108; on Lowell lectures, 137–138, 145; on seeing Stedman, 138; on supplementary lectures, 138, 145; on Gosse's *Discourses of Sir Joshua Reynolds*, 145; on Gosse's poem in honor of Holmes, 145; on visit of Mrs. Sherwood, 146; on offer of Yale chair, 146; on Stedman's *Poets of America*, 180; on revision of Stedman's *Victorian Poets*, 180–181, 186; on reception of *Firdausi in Exile*, 185–186; on Gosse's lack of success, 186; on success of Robert Bridges, 186; on Tennyson, 186; on Browning, 186; on Arnold and Morris, 186; on Swinburne, 186; on *Pall Mall Gazette* abuse, 186–187; on *From Shakespeare to Pope*, 187; on Churton Collins's attack, 196; on Stedman's article on genius, 196; on Gosse's relationship with the *Century*, 206–207; on Gosse's desire to work with American magazines, 206–207. SEE ALSO Stedman, Edmund Clarence

—, letters of, from Stedman: on Gosse's omission from Stedman's *Victorian Poets*, 60–61; on Gosse's poetry, 60–61, 62; on review of *King Erik* and *On Viol and Flute*, 61–62; on Stedman's financial problems, 62–63; on Stedman's collected poems, 63; on "Algernon in London," 63–64; on *Studies in the Literature of Northern Europe*, 69–70; on Gosse's future, 69; on death of Bayard Taylor, 69–70; on visit with Gosse, 71–72; on de-

sire for portraits of the Gosses, 72; on Gosse's review of Stedman's *Lyrics and Idylls*, 72–73, 77; on Gosse's autobiographical sketch, 76; on Alma-Tadema's portrait of Gosse, 76–77; on Dobson, 61, 77; on *New Poems*, 77; on Gilder's breakdown, 77; on Alfred Trench, 77–78; on Oscar Wilde's American visit, 88 and n. 6; on Stedman's bankruptcy, 121 and n. 1, 121–122; on Swinburne, 122 and n. 2; on taste in Americans, 149–150; on Gosse's proposed American visit, 150; on Stedman's paper on Holmes, 150; on Gosse's poem to Holmes, 150; on *Discourses of Sir Joshua Reynolds*, 150; on Gosse's Yale offer, 150–151; on duties of a professor, 151; on gift of *Firdausi in Exile*, 182; on review of *Firdausi in Exile*, 182–183; on revision of Stedman's *Victorian Poets*, 183. SEE ALSO Stedman, Edmund Clarence
—, letters of, to Trent: on Trent's *History of American Literature*, 250. SEE ALSO Trent, William Petersfield
—, letters of, to Walker: on invitation to contribute to *Cosmopolitan*, 249–250. SEE ALSO Walker, John Brisben
—, letters of, to Wharton: on nominating James for Nobel Prize, 272–274. SEE ALSO Wharton, Edith Newbold
—, letters of, from Wharton: on nominating James for Nobel Prize, 274–275, 278, 284–285; on James, 278; on Nobel Prize for Maeterlinck, 284; on her refugee activities, 294–295. SEE ALSO Wharton, Edith Newbold
—, letters of, to Whitman: on Whitman's *Leaves of Grass*, 59–60; on Whitman's influence on Gosse, 59–60. SEE ALSO Whitman, Walt
—, letters of, from Wister: on Wister's "Pentecost of Calamity," 295–296; on meeting with Gosse, 296. SEE ALSO Wister, Owen
Gosse, Ellen (Mrs. Edmund): on Gosse's reaction to Stark Young, 49; health of, 128, 287; article of, on Alma-Tadema, 226; mentioned, 93, 101, 103, 162
Gosse, Philip: identified, 96 n. 3; Gosse on expedition of, 235 and n. 1; James on career of, 236–237; Furness on ability of, 248; mentioned, 256
Gosse, Philip Henry: identified, 87 and n.

11; death of, 210; mentioned, 3, 101 and n. 1
Gosse, Sylvia: identified, 96 n. 3
Gosse, Theresa: identified, 96 n. 3; mentioned, 101
Gossip in a Library: reviews of, 21–22; effect of, on Gosse's literary reputation, 21–22; mentioned, 199 and n. 4
Grant, Ulysses S.: 174 and n. 5
Gray. SEE Life of Thomas Gray
Gray Memorial: 170, 171, and n. 1, 198 and n. 2
Guiney, Louise Imogen: identified, 156 and n. 2
Gyldenstolpe, August Louis Fersen: identified, 274 and n. 2

Haggard, Sir Henry Rider: identified, 219 and n. 3
Hale, Edward Everett: identified, 154 and n. 2; mentioned, 13, 14
Halliwell-Phillips, James Orchard: identified, 175 and n. 1; mentioned, 178
Hallström, Per August Leonard: identified, 273 and n. 4; mentioned, 276, 277, 279
Hancock, John: Gosse's relationship to, 31, 210–211
Hancock, Lucy: 31, 210
Hardy, Thomas: first meeting of, with Howells, 115 and n. 3 (L. 44); and Hawthorne-Lowell interview, 195; Gosse on, 256; mentioned, 109, 191, 269, 294, 298
Harland, Henry: relationship of, with Gosse, 27, 36, 51; Sidney Luska as pseudonym of, 36; identified, 220 and n. 1. SEE ALSO Gosse, Edmund, letters of, to Harland; Gosse, Edmund, letters of, from Harland
Harper, Joseph L.: 13
Harper's Cyclopaedia of British and American Poetry: Gosse on, 86 and n. 4
Harper's Monthly: Howells as editor of, 180 and n. 5, 184, 187; editorial policy of, 192; reviews "Has America Produced a Poet?" 212 and n. 1; mentioned, 19, 45, 77, 87 and n. 10, 89, 193
Harper's Weekly: and Cross's *Life of George Eliot*, 114 and n. 1; mentioned, 117, 213 and n. 3
Harris, Frank: identified, 228 and n. 2; takes over *Saturday Review*, 228
Harrison, Frederic: identified, 190 and n. 3

Harte, Bret: identified, 68 and n. 14; mentioned, 98
Harvard University: Gosse lectures at, 12, 161; mentioned, 30, 139, 258
"Has America Produced a Poet?": controversy over, 44; review of, in *Harper's*, 212 and n. 1
Hawthorne, Julian. SEE Hawthorne-Lowell interview
Hawthorne, Nathaniel: 12, 43, 66, 97, 120
Hawthorne-Lowell interview: American reaction to, 193 and n. 6; English reaction to, 195 and n. 4; Hardy's reaction to, 195
Hay, John (Col.): identified, 94 and n. 1; health of, 255 and n. 2; mentioned, 8, 95, 109, 252
Hayne, Paul Hamilton: identified, 107 and n. 1 (L. 37)
Hazard of New Fortunes, A (Howells): 213 and n. 3
Heinemann, William: identified, 238 and n. 2 (L. 155); mentioned, 223
Henry, Fernand: 255
Henschel, Georg[e]: identified, 130 and n. 5; collaboration of, with Howells, 130 n. 5, 135, 142–143
Herald (New York): 10
Herald Tribune (New York): reviews *Leaves and Fruit*, 26
Herbert, George Edward Stanhope Molyneux. SEE Carnovon, fifth Earl of
Herbert, Henry. SEE Asquith, Henry Herbert
Hewlett, Maurice: identified, 298 and n. 7
Higginson, Thomas Wentworth (Col.): identified, 245 and n. 1; mentioned, 13, 42. SEE ALSO Gosse, Edmund, letters of, to Higginson
Hill, Lucile Eaton: identified, 163 and n.4; mentioned, 12, 179
History of American Literature, A (Trent): Gosse on, 250–251
History of Eighteenth Century Literature: 209
History of Elizabethan Literature (Saintsbury): 209
Hodgson, Ralph: identified, 298 and n. 12
Holmes, Dr. Oliver Wendell: relationship of, with Gosse, 12, 14, 27, 30–32; on his *Our Hundred Days in Europe*, 31, 205; Stedman on, 150; mentioned, 156, 158, 160 and n. 7, 181, 185. SEE ALSO

Gosse, Edmund, letters of, to Holmes; Gosse, Edmund, letters of, from Holmes
Holt, Henry: and "parlor" lectures for Gosse, 17; Gosse desires as publisher 82; identified, 82 and n. 3; mentioned, 13, 18, 108, 118
Houghton, Lord (Richard Monckton Milnes): identified, 170 and n. 1
House of Lords: 3, 48, 280
Howells, Elinor Mead (Mrs. W. D.): death of, 48, 267 and n. 1; health of, 126, 128; mentioned, 93, 97, 98, 99, 110, 159
Howells, John Mead: identified, 101 and n. 3; mentioned, 213
Howells, Mildred: identified, 101 and n. 4; Gosse on book of, 127, 128–129; drawing of Gosse by, 184, 187–188; mentioned, 47, 152, 165, 213
Howells, William Cooper: identified, 167 and n. 5; death of, 232 and n. 2
Howells, William Dean: relationship of, with Gosse, 8, 9, 12, 13, 14, 36, 37–49; identified, 92 n. 1; Gosse on, to Stedman, 95; James on, 284; mentioned, 16, 19, 51, 52, 274. SEE ALSO Gosse, Edmund, letters of, to Howells; Gosse, Edmund, letters of, from Howells
Howells, Winifred: identified, 97 and n. 1 (L. 28); health of, 110, 179 and n. 4, 213; death of, 232 and n. 3; mentioned, 187
"How Paderewski Plays" (Gilder): Gosse on, 225
Hutton, Lawrence: breakfast of, for Gosse, 18; identified, 116 and n. 1; mentioned, 118, 213
Huxley, Thomas Henry: identified, 190 and n. 4
Hypolympia, or The Gods in the Island: An Ironic Fantasy: Gosse on importance of, 297 and n. 5

Ibsen: critical reception of, 23, 268
Ibsen, Henrik: Gosse's article on, 212 and n. 2, 213, 258
Il Pastor Fido (Guarini): 164 and n. 1, 166
In After Days: Thoughts on the Future Life (Howells et al.): Gosse on, 271
Independent (New York): Gosse's essays in, 21, 199; mentioned, 26
Indian Summer (Howells): Howells on,

126 and n. 5, 130 and n. 6, 135 and n. 4; Gosse on, 216

"Influence of Democracy on Literature, The": 46–47

In Russet and Silver: critical reception of, 22; mentioned, 228

Irving, Sir Henry: identified, 126 and n. 4

isolationism, American: Gosse on, 255–256

Italy: 69, 109, 128

Jacobean period: 6

Jacobean Poets: 22

James, Henry: relationship of, with Gosse, 8, 36, 37–38, 49–50, 51, 68; attempts to secure Nobel Prize for, 48, 272–280, 284–285; Gosse on, to Howells, 93 and n. 1 (L. 25), 107 and n. 1 (L. 36), 127, 164 and n. 3, 187, 217, 268 and n. 4, 271; basis for "Miss Birdseye," 164 and n. 3, 164–165, 167–168; mentioned, 189, 234, 269. SEE ALSO Gosse, Edmund, letters of, to Howells; Gosse, Edmund, letters of, to James; Gosse, Edmund, letters of, from James

James, William: identified, 269 and n. 1 (L. 180)

Johns Hopkins University: Gosse to lecture at, 9, 131, 134, 140, 143–144, 145; mentioned, 8, 34, 139

Johnson, Robert Underwood: relationship of, with Gosse, 18, 32–33; identified, 70 and n. 7; mentioned 223 and n. 2 (L. 139). SEE ALSO Gosse, Edmund, letters of, to Johnson

Jones, Mary Cadwalader: identified, 278 and n. 1 (L. 189)

Kerr, Shomberg Henry. SEE Lothian, tenth Marquess of

Kentons, The (Howells): 268

King, Clarence: identified, 98 and n. 5; mentioned, 95 n. 6, 116

King Erik: A Tragedy: dedication to Browning in, 7, 67 and n. 5; review of, 7, 67 and n. 5; influence of Swinburne on, 297; mentioned, 61, 62

Kipling, Rudyard: attempts to secure Nobel Prize for James, 48; identified, 220 and n. 7; Gosse on, 220, 222; marriage of, 224 and n. 1; mentioned, 27, 276

Kitchener, Horatio Herbert, Earl Kitchener: identified, 293 and n. 1

Lady of the Aroostook, The (Howells): 99 and n. 1, 99–100

La Farge, John: identified, 254 and n. 23; mentioned, 14, 18 n. 43

Laffan, William Mackay: identified, 98 and n. 8; mentioned, 111

La Gallienne, Richard: 25

Lang, Andrew: identified, 80 and n. 13; Gosse on poetry of, 80, 87; 186; popularity of, mentioned, 81 n. 19, 91, 134 and n. 1 (L. 59), 189, 191, 201, 228, 256

Lapsley, Gaillard Thomas: identified, 274 and n. 1

Lathrop, George Parsons: review of *On Viol and Flute* by, 9; identified, 120 and n. 3; mentioned, 18

"Laurens Alma-Tadema" (Ellen Gosse): 226

Lawson, Sir Wilfred: identified, 236 and n. 7

Lazarus, Annie: Gosse on, 117; mentioned, 113, 116

Lazarus, Emma: identified, 113 and n. 2; Gosse on, 113, 117; mentioned, 8, 10, 116

Leaves and Fruit: American reception of, 25–26

Leaves of Grass (Whitman): Gosse on, 29, 59–60; mentioned, 6

Leighton, Sir Frederick: identified, 190 and n.2

Leland, Charles Godfrey: identified, 68 and n. 13

Lewis, Estelle (or Sarah) Anna: identified, 64 and n. 3

Lewisohn, Ludwig: criticism of Gosse by, 23, 24

"Lexington" (Howells): Gosse on, 103, 144 and n. 1

Life and Letters of John Donne: critical reception of, 22

Life and Letters of Sir Edmund Gosse (Charteris): 6, 9–10, 20, *et passim*

Life of Algernon Charles Swinburne: Pound on, 23–24

Life of Philip Henry Gosse, F.R.S.: Harland on, 234

Life of Sir Thomas Browne: critical reception of, 22

Life of Thomas Gray: Critical reception of, 9, 94 and n. 2, 94–95; Howells on, 98–99, 101, 193

Life of William Congreve: 209 n. 5, 209–210

"Limits of Realism in Fiction, The": on reaction to realism, 42

Linton, William James: identified, 59 and n. 2

Literary Friends and Acquaintance (Howells): 275, 277 and n. 3

literary nationalism. SEE nationalism, literary

literature, American: Gosse's interest in, 6, 28, 50–52 *passim*; nationalist tendencies in, 10, 44–45, 52

Little Girl Among Old Masters, A (Mildred Howells): Gosse reviews, 127, 128–129

"Living English Sculptors": 111 and n. 3, 112–113

"Living English Sculptors, II": 120

Locher-Lampson, Frederick: identified, 148 and n. 5

Lodge, Henry Cabot: identified, 13 and n. 25; mentioned, 27

Longman's Magazine: 103

Lothian, tenth Marquess of: identified, 229 and n. 8

Lounsbury, Thomas Raynesford: identified, 160 and n. 1. SEE ALSO Gosse, Edmund, letters of, to Lounsbury

Lovett, Robert Morss: on Gosse, 25

Lowell, Augustus: Howells on, 125; mentioned, 122 and n. 1, 123, 130, 131–132

Lowell, James Russell: identified, 78 and n. 2, 147 and n. 1 (L. 72); Gosse on, to Gilder, 78; Gosse on, to Howells, 164; mentioned, 150, 180, 213, 258 and n. 1 (L. 169). SEE ALSO Gosse, Edmund, letters of, to Lowell; Gosse, Edmund, letters of, from Lowell; Hawthorne-Lowell interview

Lowell, Maria White: illness of, 164 and n. 2

Lowell (Institute) Lectures: efforts to secure invitation for Gosse, 9, 122–123, 125, 127, 129; demand for tickets for, 11–12; Gosse receives invitation to, 130–131, 131–132; financial arrangements for, 131, 134, 140, 141; Gosse's subject for, 132, 137–138; mentioned, 10, 20, 134, 145. See Gosse, Edmund, American trip of

Lowry, Edward George: identified, 293 and n. 1 (L. 207)

Lubbock, John, first Baron Avebury: identified, 272 and n. 2

Luska, Sidney. SEE Harland, Henry

Lyrics and Idylls, with Other Poems (Stedman): Gosse's review of, 72 and n. 1, 72–73, 74 and n. 3

MacColl, Norman: identified, 74 and n. 2

Mackail, John William: identified, 201 and n. 7

Madrigals, Songs and Sonnets: 297

Maeterlinck, Maurice: wins Nobel Prize, 48; identified, 284 and n. 1 (L. 196)

Mallarmé, Stéphane: identified, 240 and n. 2

Marston, Philip Bourke: identified, 77 and n. 5; Grosse on disillusionment of, 207–208

Marzials, Théophile: identified, 243 and n. 4; Harland on, 243–244 and n. 5

Masefield, John: identified, 298 and n. 9

Mason, Frank Holcomb: identified, 72 and n. 1 (L. 9)

Mason, William: identified, 169 and n. 5; Furness on, 169

Masque of Poets, A (Lathrop): Grosse on, 66–67 and n. 4

Matthews, James Brander: identified, 78 and n. 1; mentioned, 8, 13, 18, 80, 85, 116

McClure, Samuel S.: identified, 215 and n. 1

McClure's Associated Literary Press: founding of, 215 nn. 1, 2; Gosse's association with, 215 and n. 2

McKinley, William: identified, 247 and n. 4

Mea Culpa: A Woman's Last Word (Harland): Gosse on, 220–221

Mead, Edwin Doak: identified, 245 and n. 2; on Gosse, 245 and n. 2

Mead, Larkin Goldsmith: identified, 110 and n. 5; mentioned, 193

Meredith, George: identified, 191 and n. 8; Gosse on, 256

Metropolitan Museum: 252

Middlemore, Samuel George Chetwynd: identified, 110 and n. 4

Millet, Francis Davis: identified, 176 and n. 2; mentioned, 8, 27

Milnes, Richard Monckton (Lord Houghton): identified, 170 and n. 1

Minto, William: identified, 189 and n. 4

328

Modern Instance, A (Howells): Gosse on, 38–39, 97; Howells sends to Gosse, 96
monarchy. SEE democracy-monarchy debate
Monkhouse, William Cosmo: identified, 108 and n. 4
Montague, G.: 209–210 and n. 6
Moore, Julia A.: identified, 72 n. 2
Moore, Thomas: identified, 275 and n. 2
More, Paul Elmer: 23
Morgan, John Pierpont: identified, 252 and n. 8
Morison, James Augustus Cotter: identified, 209 and n. 2; illness of, 209
Morley, John: identified, 119 and n. 5; Gosse on, 211, 272, 273; Gilder on, 253; mentioned, 191, 214, 256, 271 and n. 6
Morris, William: 66, 81 n. 19, 186
Moulton, Louise Chandler: identified, 67 n. 9, 156 n. 1 (L. 82); London visit of, 67–68; mentioned, 8. SEE ALSO Gosse, Edmund, letters of, to Moulton
"Mousetrap, The" (Howells): Gosse on, 197
Munro, David Alexander: identified, 238 and n. 1. SEE ALSO Gosse, Edmund, letters of, to Munro
Munzig, George Chickering: 152 n. 1
Murfree, Mary Noailles ("Charles Egbert Craddock"): identified, 167 and n. 3; Howells on, 167
Murray's Magazine: Gosse on, 201 and n. 6
Myers, Frederic William Henry: identified, 214 and n. 5
"My Star" (Browning): Gilder on, 252, 253; Gosse on, 157

Nansen, Fridtjof: identified, 216 n. 1 (L. 131); and the *Century*, 216
Nation: reviews of Gosse's work in, 19, 21, 23, 187 and n. 7
nationalism, literary: in American literature and culture, 10, 44–45, 52; in reviews of *Gossip in a Library*, 21–22; in editorial policy of the *Century*, 32–34; Gosse's dislike of, 33–34, 41, 44, 52, 103–104, 202 and n. 2; as source of friction between Howells and Gosse, 43–47, 48; as source of sensitivity in Anglo-American relations, 45, 255–256. SEE ALSO Anglo-American relations; *Century Illustrated Monthly Magazine*; democracy-monarchy debate; Dickens-Thacker-

eray controversy; Gilder, Richard Watson; Howells, William Dean; realism-romanticism debate
Newbolt, Sir Henry John: identified, 298 and n. 10
New Day, A Poem in Songs and Sonnets, The (Gilder): 74 and n. 3
New Poems: review of, in *Scribner's*, 7, 77; Gosse on, 67, 79
New Republic: review of *Leaves and Fruit* in, 26; Young's article on Gosse in, 37, 49–50
New York: the Gosses in, 10–14 *passim*, 17, 18, 156, 157, 163
Nobel Prize for Literature: efforts to secure for Henry James, 48, 272–280, 284–285
North American Review: Gosse writes for, 238–239 and n. 3
Norton, Charles Eliot: identified, 154 and n. 3; mentioned, 14

Odes and Other Poems (Watson): Gosse on, 228–229
O'Donnell, Patrick: 127 and n. 3, 129
"Oliver Wendell Holmes" (Stedman): 150
On Viol and Flute: review of, in *Scribner's Monthly*, 7, 67 and n. 5; American edition of, 9, 82 and n. 3; critical reception of, 9, 111 and n. 6; Stedman on, 60–61, 62; Gosse on, 108, 155; influence of Whitman on, 297
Osgood, James Ripley: relationship of, with Gosse, 8, 12, 18; and *Seventeenth Century Studies*, 118, 119–120, 129; mentioned, 109, 116, 129, 152 n. 1. SEE ALSO Gosse, Edmund, letters of, to Osgood
O'Shaughnessy, Arthur William Edgar: identified, 83 and n. 2; Gosse on, 83, 87
Our Hundred Days in Europe (Holmes): 31, 205
Over the Teacups (Holmes): Holmes on, 218 and n. 1 (L. 134)
Oxford University: honorary degrees by, 31, 48; mentioned, 80

Pacchiarotto and How He Worked in Distemper; With Other Poems (Browning): Gosse on, 65
Pall Mall Gazette: Gosse's impressions of America in, 51; review of Holmes' *Ralph*

Waldo Emerson in, 160 and n. 7; review of Howells's *Rise of Silas Lapham* in, 179 and n. 1; review of *Firdausi in Exile* in, 182 and n. 2, 182–183, 185 and n. 1; London exposés in, 186 and n. 6, 186–187; Gosse's association with, 186–187; Gosse-Collins affair in, 194 and n. 1, 200 and n. 1; mentioned, 11, 127
Parkman, Francis: identified, 13 and n. 25; mentioned, 14, 17
"parlor" lectures: Gosse gives, in America, 17 and n. 40, 18; idea for, 161 and n. 1; income from, 165–166
Parlour Car, The (Howells): Gosse on, 99–100 and n. 1
Parsons, Alfred: 8, 27
"Passing of William Dean Howells, The": 39, 47
Pater, Walter Horatio: identified, 189 and n. 1
Patmore, Coventry: in Stedman's *Victorian Poets*, 181, 183; mentioned, 29
patriotism. SEE nationalism, literary
Paul, Kegan: and British edition of Stedman's *Lyrics and Idylls*, 69 and n. 4, 70; mentioned 7, 118
Peabody, Elizabeth, Miss: meets Gosse, 12–13; identified, 164 and n. 3, 164–165; as possible basis for James's "Miss Birdseye," 164–165 and n. 4, 167–168
Peabody Institute: 16
Pennell, Elizabeth Robins: identified, 125 and n. 9; mentioned, 27
Pennell, Joseph: identified, 125 and n. 9; mentioned, 27, 144
"Pentecost of Calamity, The" (Wister): 296 and n. 2
Perry, Bliss: identified, 242 and n. 1. SEE ALSO Gosse, Edmund, letters of, to Perry
Perry, Thomas Sergeant: identified, 158 and n. 4; and Gosse-Collins affair, 21, 193; mentioned, 13
Philadelphia: the Gosses in, 15–16, 159
Playfair, Sir Lyon: identified, 119 and n. 4; mentioned, 211
Poe, Edgar Allan: Stedman's book on, 76, 77; mentioned, 150
Poetical Works of Edmund Clarence Stedman, The: Stedman on, 63; Gosse on, 64–65
"Poetry in America: Part I" (Stedman): Gosse on, 86

Poets of America (Stedman): Gosse on, 95, 180 and n. 1
"Point of View, The" (James): Gosse on, 107
Pollock, Sir Frederick: identified, 211 and n. 3; and John Bryce article, 211, 214
Pollock, Walter Herries: identified, 189 and n. 3
Porter, Benjamin Curtis: 152 n. 1
Porter, Charlotte: 253 and n. 16
Portraits and Sketches: 12, 23
Pound, Ezra: on Gosse, 23–24
Préault, Antoine Auguste: identified, 257 and n. 2
Pre-Raphaelites: influence of, on Gosse's style, 6, 27, 42–43, 297; outlook of, on literature, 28–29; admiration of, for Walt Whitman, 28–29; mentioned, 61
Preston, Harriet Waters: identified, 102 and n. 1; mentioned, 104, 105, 126, 127
provincialism, literary. SEE nationalism, literary

Quarterly Review: review of *From Shakespeare to Pope* in, 20; Gosse-Collins affair in, 194 and n. 1
Questionable Shapes (Howells): Gosse on, 48, 268, 271
Questions at Issue: reception of, 22; realism-romanticism debate in, 22; on influence of democracy on literature, 46; mentioned, 44
Quincy, Dorothy: identified, 210 and n. 2

Rajon, Paul-Adolphe: identified, 85 and n. 7
Raleigh: American review of, 21; Howells's review of, 193, 195, 197
Ralph Waldo Emerson (Holmes): Gosse on, 154–155, 160 and n. 7
Ranke, Leopold Von: identified, 17 and n. 38
realism. SEE realism-romanticism debate
realism-romanticism debate: reflected in reception of Gosse's works, 22; in Gosse-Howells relationship, 42–43; Gosse on reaction to realism in, 42; relation of, to search for native American literature, 43–44. SEE ALSO Anglo-American relations; Howells, William Dean
Realm, The: Gosse on staff of, 228 and n. 3
Richardson, H. H.: 18 and n. 43
Rise of Silas Lapham, The (Howells):

Gosse reads, 13–14; Howells on, 158 and n. 6, 162, 168; Gosse on, 165; Gosse's review of, 179 and n. 1

Robert Browning: Personalia: 251 and n. 1

Robinson, Agnes Mary Frances: identified, 79 and n. 6; mentioned, 113

Robinson, Edward Arlington: 36 and n. 94

romanticism. SEE realism-romanticism debate

Roosevelt, Theodore: identified, 252 and n. 12; Gilder on, 252 and n. 13, 252–253

"Rosemary for Remembrance" (Harland): 231, 238

Rossetti, Christina: in *Victorian Poets*, 87, 183; mentioned, 181

Rossetti, Dante Gabriel: influence of, on Gosse, 29–30, 297; mentioned, 7, 66, 81 n. 19

Russell, Herbrand Arthur. SEE Bedford, eleventh Duke of

Saint-Gaudens, Augustus: Gosse's desire to meet, 11, 149 n. 1; identified, 80 and n. 12; mentioned, 14, 18 and n. 43

Saintsbury, George Edward Bateman: identified, 214 and n. 3; mentioned, 209

Sand, George: Gosse on, 144

Sargent, Epes: identified, 86 and n. 4; encyclopedia of poetry by, 86

Sargent, John Singer: identified, 176 and n. 4; portrait of Gosse by, 195 and n. 3; mentioned, 8, 27

Sargent, Mrs. Turner: identified, 190 and n. 6; mentioned, 31, 189

Sassoon, Siegfried: identified, 298 and n. 14

Saturday Review: reviews *Gossip in a Library*, 21; Gosse on editorial policies of, 228; mentioned, 77

Scandinavia: Gosse's work in literature of, 4, 5; mentioned, 8

Scherer, Edmond Henri Adolphe: identified, 189 and n. 5

Scribner's Magazine: organization of, 201 and n. 4. SEE ALSO *Scribner's Monthly*

Scribner's Monthly: reviews Gosse's works, 7, 67 and n. 5, 75; history of, 84 n. 1; mentioned, 61, 77, 79, 86, 173. SEE ALSO *Century Illustrated Monthly Magazine*; *Scribner's Magazine*

Scudder, Horace Elisha: identified, 13 and n. 25; mentioned, 27

Sea-Change, A (Howells): 165 and n. 7, 167

Secret of Narcisse, The: critical reception of, 22; romanticism in, 22, 42

Selected Poems (Emerson): Gosse on, 90 and n. 1, 90–91

Seventeenth Century Studies: Gosse finishes, 113; American edition of, 118, 119 n. 7, 119–120, 127, 129; Howells on, 142

Sheridan, Philip Henry (Gen.): Gosse meets in America, 16, 33

Sherman, Frank Dempster: identified, 219 and n. 2

Sherman, Stuart P.: on Grosse, 25; reviews *Aspects and Impressions*, 25; mentioned, 27

Sherman, William Tecumseh (Gen.): Gosse on, 15, 159; identified, 159 and n. 1; mentioned, 33, 51

Sherwood, Mary Elizabeth Wilson: identified, 146 and n. 6; mentioned, 152

Short History of Modern English Literature: critical reception of, 22

Shorthouse, Joseph Henry: identified, 191 and n. 5

Sinclair, Upton: 23

Sir Thomas Browne. SEE *Life of Sir Thomas Browne*

Sladen, Douglas: identified, 226 and n. 1 (L. 145)

Smalley, George Washburn: identified, 119 and n. 2

Smith, Dr. Mott: identified, 194 and n. 2

Smith, Roswell: relationship of, with Gosse, 8, 10, 13, 18, 32; Gosse on, to Gilder, 84–85, 113, 117; mentioned, 140, 168. SEE ALSO Gosse, Edmund, letters of, to Roswell Smith

Smith, William Robertson: identified, 191 and n. 7

Some Diversions of a Man of Letters: review of, 24

Songs of a Worker (O'Shaughnessy): Gosse on, 87

South Seas: A Record of Three Cruises, The (Stevenson): Gosse on, 220

Spanish-American War: 239, 247

Stanley, Arthur Penrhyn: identified, 85 and n. 6

Stedman, Edmund Clarence: relationship of, with Gosse, 6–7, 8, 9, 14–15, 18; identified, 60 n. 1; mentioned, 44, 51,

97, 213, 263. SEE ALSO Gosse, Edmund, letters of, to Stedman; Gosse, Edmund, letters of, from Stedman
Stedman, Edmund Burke (Maj.): identified, 69 n. 3
Stephen, Leslie: identified, 140 and n. 2 (L. 66); mentioned, 3, 9
Stevenson, Robert Louis: Gosse on, 204; identified, 204 and n. 1; Gosse's criticism of *Ballads* of, 219–220; Gilder on death of, 230 and n. 2; first visit of to *Century,* 254 and n. 18; mentioned, 3, 4–5, 28, 37, 201
Stevenson, Thomas: identified, 204 and n. 3
Stillman, William James: identified, 129 n. 4, 129–130; mentioned, 261
Stockton, Frank R.: identified, 13 and n. 26; mentioned, 18, 27
Stoddard, Richard Henry: identified, 81 and n. 19; relationship of, with Gosse, 81 n. 19; mentioned, 18, 108
Story, William Wetmore: identified, 98 and n. 4
Strong, Isobel Stuart: identified, 254 and n. 19
Studies in the Literature of Northern Europe: review of, in *Scribner's,* 7; Stedman on, 69; mentioned, 67, 70
Sunday Times (London): 4, 25
Swinburne, Algernon Charles: influence of on Gosse, 29–30, 297; parody on, 63–64, 65–66, Appendix B; illness of, 68; Gosse on, 76, 186; mentioned, 4, 6, 79, 81 n. 19, 122 and n. 2, 272, 276
Switzerland: Howells in, 98, 101; mentioned, 93, 98, 128
Symonds, John Addington: identified, 191 and n. 6; mentioned, 28, 185

Tadema. SEE Alma-Tadema, Lawrence (Laurens)
Tavern Club: gives dinner for Gosse, 13, 158; Howells as president of, 152; history of, 152 n. 1; mentioned, 180, 213
Taylor, Bayard: death of, 69–70; identified, 70 n. 5
Tennyson, Alfred: *Tiresias and Other Poems* of, 186; mentioned, 248, 257
Thackeray, William: 3, 8, 43, 248. SEE ALSO Dickens-Thackeray controversy
Thistleton-Dyer, Sir William Turner: identified, 235 and n. 2

Thompson, Sir Henry: identified, 191 and n. 9
Thornycroft, Hamo: friendship of, with Gosse, 11, 14; identified, 79 and n. 10; Gosse on sculpture of, 79–80; mentioned, 80, 106, 109, 115, 128, 191
Three French Moralists: review of, 25
Three Villages (Howells): Gosse on, 144 and n. 1
Times (New York): on Gosse's American tour, 20; review of Gosse's work in, 9, 19, 20, 22, 23, 94 and n. 3, 94–95; mentioned, 25, 121
"To E. W. G. in England" (Gilder): Gosse on, 90 and n. 1, 90–91
Tolstoy, Leo: Gosse on, 259; mentioned, 33
Tourguénief, Ivan: 108, 124 and n. 8
transatlantic relations. SEE Anglo-American relations
Tree, Herbert Beerbohm: identified, 165 and n. 6
Trench, Alfred Chevenix: identified, 77 and n. 8; mentioned, 90
Trench, Richard Chevenix: 185
Trent, William Petersfield: identified, 250 and n. 1. SEE ALSO Gosse, Edmund, letters of, to Trent
Twain, Mark: Howells writes play with, 126, 128; mentioned, 98 n. 3, 109, 139, 141
Two Visits to Denmark: critical reception of, 22–23
XXII Ballades in Blue China (Lang): Gosse on, 80
XXII and X, XXXII Ballades in Blue China (Lang): 87
Tyler, Moses Coit: identified, 18 and n. 44

Unknown Lover, The: 7, 67
Unwin, Thomas Fisher: identified, 203 and n. 2

Victorianism: Gosse identified with, 25
Victorian Poets (Stedman): Gosse's absence from, 60–61; Gosse on, 87, 180–181; second edition of, 180–181, 183, 186; mentioned, 63
Victorian Studies (White): 28
Villari, Pasquale: identified, 106 and n. 2
Vinton, Frederic Porter: Tavern Club meets at studio of, 13, 152 n. 1
"Visit to Whittier, A": 12

Walker, John Brisben: identified, 249 and n.1. SEE ALSO Gosse, Edmund, letters of, to Walker
"Walter Pater: A Portrait": 228
Ward, Thomas Humphrey: identified, 79 and n. 7
Warne, Frederick: identified, 201 and n. 5; mentioned, 85 and n. 5, 203
Warner, Charles Dudley: identified, 98 and n. 6; mentioned, 40
Washington, D.C.: Gosse in, 16–17, 160; Howells in 184–185
Watson, Francis Sedgwick: 152 n. 1
Watson, Robert Spence: identified, 119 and n. 6
Watson, William: identified, 228 and n.6; *Odes and Other Poems of,* 228 and n. 6, 228–229
Watts, George Frederic: identified, 153 and n. 1
Watts [-Dunton] Walter Theodore: identified,122 and n. 3
Wellesley College, 12, 155, 163, 179
Wells College, Gosse lectures at, 18, 163 and n. 3
Wharton, Edith Newbold: relationship of, with Gosse, 27, 36–37, 48; identified, 272 and n. 1. SEE ALSO Gosse, Edmund, letters of, to Wharton: Gosse, Edmund, letters of, from Wharton
Whistler, James McNeill: 6
White, Andrew Dickson: identified, 145 and n.1; mentioned, 18, 150
White, Stanford: 18 n. 43
Whitman, Walt: Gosse's early admiration for, 6, 28–30; Gosse visits in America, 15–16, 28, 159; Gosse on reputation of, 28–29, 241–242; financial condition of, 178 and n. 3, 178–179; Furness on, 225–226, 240–241; Gosse on psychology of, 260; influence of, on Gosse, 297; mentioned, 51, 150, 176, 254 and n. 21. SEE ALSO Gosse, Edmund, letters of, to Whitman

Whittier, John Greenleaf: identified, 155 and n. 5; mentioned, 12, 51, 90 and n. 4
Wigglesworth, Michael: identified, 251 and n. 3
Wilde, Oscar: American tour of, 10, 88 and n. 6; Gosse on, 86–87, 89–90; Harland on, 231 and n. 4
Wilson, Edmund: on Gosse as a critic, 26; mentioned, 27
Wise, T. J.: 4
Wister, Dr. Casper: identified, 160 and n. 5
Wister, Owen: identified, 295 and n. 1; mentioned, 13, 36. SEE ALSO Gosse, Edmund, letters of, from Wister
Wister, Mrs. Annis Lee: identified, 160 and n. 5; mentioned, 248, 249
Woman's Reason, A (Howells): 39, 98
Woolner, Thomas: identified, 116 and n. 4
Works of Thomas Gray: critical reception of, 19; mentioned, 95, 101
World: attack on Gosse in, 185 and n. 1, 194 and n. 1
World War I: Gosse on, 293; James on, 293–294; mentioned, 36, 296
World's Fair (Chicago): Gilder's enthusiasm for, 227 and n. 2, 230
Wright, William Aldis: identified, 169 and n. 4; Furness on, 169; Gosse on, 246 and n. 1; mentioned, 176

Yale University: Gosse lectures at, 18, 140, 160–161, 161 n. 2; offers Gosse professorship, 139, 146; mentioned, 34, 139, 150
Yorick's Love (Howells): Gosse on, 137, 142; Howells on, 132 n. 3, 132–133, 139–140
Young, Stark: friendship of, with Gosse, 27, 36, 37, 49–50

Zimmern, Helen: identified, 111 and n. 4